THE ART OF LIVING

*The Stoics on the Nature
and Function of
Philosophy*

John Sellars

D1552467

Bristol Classical Press

This edition published in 2009 by
Bristol Classical Press
an imprint of
Gerald Duckworth & Co. Ltd.
90-93 Cowcross Street, London EC1M 6BF
Tel: 020 7490 7300
Fax: 020 7490 0080
info@duckworth-publishers.co.uk
www.ducknet.co.uk

© 2003, 2009 by John Sellars

First published by Ashgate Publishing Limited

A catalogue record for this book is available
from the British Library

ISBN 978 1 85399 724 2

Typeset by John Sellars

Contents

PART II: λόγος and ἄσκησις

Preface to the Second Edition

I am delighted that Duckworth is publishing this paperback edition of *The Art of Living*, first published in hardback by Ashgate in 2003. I am especially pleased that it will take its place alongside the many respected volumes already published in the Bristol Classical Paperbacks series. My hope, of course, is that it will now reach a much wider audience than it has thus far.

The first edition received a number of careful and thorough reviews that brought to light both issues about which I might have said more and places where I might have been clearer. This new preface gives me the welcome opportunity to address some of the comments that have been made.

As a number of reviewers have noted, this book can be taken on two levels.[1] On the one hand it is simply an attempt to explicate how the ancient Stoics conceived philosophy. I argue that they conceived it as an art or craft and the principal consequence of this is that, like other arts and crafts, mastery of philosophy will require not only a grasp of theoretical principles but also an element of practical training designed to digest those principles. As such it may be read as a contribution to the scholarly history of ancient philosophy. On the other hand it hopes to show how thinking about ancient conceptions of philosophy might contribute to much wider debates about the nature and function of philosophy. The remarks in the Introduction and Conclusion hopefully indicate how this might be so, where I draw a contrast between a purely theoretical understanding of philosophy and philosophy conceived as an art or craft, which I call the technical conception of philosophy. There are many dangers with trying to do two things at once in a single piece of work. There is the risk that one might fail to reach either target audience or, if one does reach them, to alienate them both. I certainly hope that this has not been the case. One reviewer did seem uncomfortable with this two-fold agenda.[2] He suggested that my foray into metaphilosophy 'seems to depend more closely on the lingering tensions between continental and analytical traditions in contemporary philosophy than it does on the evidence from the ancient philosophical tradition which has been so sadly drafted into a foreign war'. This is indeed an unfortunate impression as I had deliberately tried to undercut just this sort of reading. In the Introduction I draw a contrast between the conceptions of philosophy held by Hegel and Nietzsche (both 'continental' philosophers) and try to illustrate the same contrast in a debate between Richard Sorabji and Bernard Williams (both trained in the analytic tradition). These pairings were chosen precisely to show that the distinction between the two conceptions of philosophy outlined in the Introduction *does not* correspond to a distinction between

---

[1] See e.g. Trevor Curnow in *Practical Philosophy* 8/1 (2006), 61-2; Michael FitzGerald in *Colloquy* 11 (2006), 268-70.

[2] See Brad Inwood, writing for the online journal *Notre Dame Philosophical Reviews* (http://ndpr.nd.edu/).

continental and analytic philosophy and, moreover, that both conceptions of philosophy can be found *within both* of these two supposed traditions.[3]

This attempt to undercut the assumption that the distinction I draw maps onto the analytic-continental division not only failed in its task for one reviewer but also created a problem for another. This reviewer accused me of setting up Bernard Williams as a straw man.[4] This criticism is not without grounds. In the Introduction I focus on two short occasional pieces by Williams and do not seriously engage with his more substantial work, such as *Ethics and the Limits of Philosophy*, despite having read it. Indeed, in many ways Williams is much more of a philosophical ally than my passing remarks on him imply and I am happy to acknowledge this here. I would particularly like to note his essay 'Philosophy as a Humanistic Discipline', in which he rejects the attempt to assimilate philosophy to science and situates philosophy within a wider humanistic enterprise of trying to make sense of our lives, an enterprise concerned with reflecting on our ideas and acting on the basis of those ideas.[5] The occasional remarks by Williams that I cite in the Introduction certainly do not do justice to the full range of his reflections on the nature and role of philosophy.

Another philosopher who turned away from the scientistic image of philosophy towards a humanistic one was Isaiah Berlin.[6] A central theme in Berlin's work that echoes one of the guiding metaphilosophical ideas in this book is a concern with what Berlin called the power of ideas. Philosophical ideas are not merely objects of abstract and idle amusement but rather vital forces that can transform an individual's life and, in some cases, impact upon the lives of millions. Berlin's principal concern was with the impact of ideas at the social and political level, but the same point may be made at the level of the individual. I would want to argue, although I do not have the space to do it here, that this concern with the practical impact of philosophical ideas stands

---

[3] This is not the place to venture into the murky waters of the analytic-continental divide but I will note two recent books written from very different perspectives which in their own ways highlight the limitations of both labels: Simon Glendinning, *The Idea of Continental Philosophy* (Edinburgh: Edinburgh University Press, 2006) and Hans-Johann Glock, *What is Analytic Philosophy?* (Cambridge: Cambridge University Press, 2008). I should add that when claiming that both conceptions of philosophy may be found within the analytic tradition, I understand the term 'analytic' broadly, so as to include figures such as Bernard Williams and Isaiah Berlin, both of whom explicitly rejected the label conceived in a much narrower sense as an exclusive focus on linguistic analysis.

[4] See A. A. Long in *Classical Review* 56/1 (2006), 81-82.

[5] See Bernard Williams, 'Philosophy as a Humanistic Discipline', *Philosophy* 75 (2000), 477-96, and repr. in his *Philosophy as a Humanistic Discipline* (Princeton: Princeton University Press, 2006), 180-99. I am not suggesting that Williams holds onto any notion of philosophical exercise though.

[6] See in particular Berlin's essay 'The Purpose of Philosophy', in *The Power of Ideas* (London: Chatto & Windus, 2000), 24-35, and 'Two Concepts of Liberty', in *The Proper Study of Mankind* (London: Chatto & Windus, 1997), 191-242, at 192: 'the German poet Heine warned the French not to underestimate the power of ideas: philosophical concepts nurtured in the stillness of a professor's study could destroy a civilisation'.

within the same broad tradition containing the Stoics (and others), the origins of which may be traced back to Socrates.[7]

It has been suggested that although I claim to remain impartial with regard to the two different conceptions of philosophy I outline (see p. 175 below) this may be slightly disingenuous, given my clear focus on philosophy conceived as an art of living.[8] While I am clearly attracted to the idea that philosophy be conceived as an art of living, I would like to restate that I do not hold that this is the correct, proper, true, or only way in which philosophy might be conceived. I do not hold that other conceptions of philosophy are inevitably misguided, confused, or false. Instead I should like to propose what I shall call metaphilosophical pluralism. Drawing an analogy with Isaiah Berlin's value pluralism, which holds that there exist a number of equally objective but ultimately incommensurable values, I advocate a metaphilosophical pluralism in which there may exist a number of equally justifiable but incompatible conceptions of what philosophy is, and there are no definitive grounds for ruling that any one of these conceptions deserves to be given priority. My account of philosophy as an art of living is offered as a contribution to this metaphilosophical pluralism rather than an attempt to legislate dogmatically on what philosophy is or should be.

I should also like to stress that the idea that philosophy is concerned with one's way of life should not be assumed to imply that practical concerns outweigh a commitment to truth. Instead it combines a commitment to truth with the claim that that commitment is not merely theoretical but will also have real-world consequences. A contrast is sometimes drawn between analytic philosophy committed to 'truth and knowledge' and populist forms of philosophy serving up 'moral or spiritual improvement' or 'chicken soup for the soul'.[9] Yet, as Glock rightly notes, 'the case of ancient philosophers like Socrates demonstrates that one can seek moral or spiritual improvement, yet do so through the reasoned pursuit of truth and knowledge'.[10] This is clearly related to the famous Socratic thesis that virtue is knowledge, though it is

---

[7] By claiming this, I am not suggesting any wider affinity between Berlin and either Socrates or ancient Stoicism. On the contrary, Berlin seems to me to be one of the most incisive philosophical critics of Stoicism, even though his explicit references to the Stoa are few. I note in particular his comments in 'Two Concepts of Liberty' (n. 6 above), 210-11, and his essay 'The Pursuit of the Ideal', also in *The Proper Study of Mankind* (London: Chatto & Windus, 1997), 1-16, and 'The Birth of Greek Individualism', in *Liberty* (Oxford: Oxford University Press, 2002), 287-321, esp. 306-10. Berlin may share something at the metaphilosophical level regarding the power of philosophical ideas while at the same time rejecting any notion of moral perfectionism.

[8] See Curnow (n. 1 above), 62.

[9] The first two phrases come from Scott Soames, *Philosophical Analysis in the Twentieth Century: Volume 1. The Dawn of Analysis* (Princeton: Princeton University Press, 2003), xiv, and cited in Glock (n. 3 above), 200. The phrase 'chicken soup for the soul' is borrowed from Simon Blackburn, *Being Good* (Oxford: Oxford University Press, 2001), 38. Soames goes on to note that 'there is very little in the way of practical or inspirational guides in the art of living to be found' in twentieth century analytic philosophy.

[10] Glock (n. 3 above), 200.

not identical to it. One might reject that thesis while remaining committed to the view that a philosophical pursuit of truth and knowledge will have an impact upon and express itself in one's way of life.

Having dealt with some of the issues arising out of the metaphilosophical side of the book it is now time to turn to its historical side. This is the more substantial side and I suspect that the majority of readers will be more interested in ancient Stoicism than abstract metaphilosophy. Yet it is worth stressing the metaphilosophy in order to keep in focus the nature of the claims I make about Stoicism. One reviewer has greeted the volume as a contribution to the literature on Stoic practical ethics, while another has lamented that it fails as a contribution to the literature on Stoic moral theory.[11] The book claims to do neither. It is explicitly not about that narrow part of philosophy commonly called practical ethics but rather about a wider conception of philosophy as such, embracing logic, physics, and ethics, both practical and theoretical. I argue that for the Stoics the traditional view of a tripartite conception of philosophy ('logic, physics, ethics') may need to be complicated. In particular I suggest we think of six elements within Stoic philosophy: logical, physical, and ethical discourse, along with corresponding logical, physical, and ethical exercises.[12] This book does not attempt to add to the ever-expanding body of work on Stoic moral theory either, which is just one of these six parts, but rather to reconstruct the metaphilosophical architecture within which such moral theory finds its home.

One of the central figures in my account of the nature of Stoic philosophy is Epictetus. It has been suggested that my account of Epictetus' understanding of philosophy does not do full justice to some passages in which he seems to hold an intellectualist conception of virtue.[13] In these passages, Epictetus seems to suggest that knowledge (of, say, virtue) is on its own enough to impact on a person's life, making any sort of philosophical exercise superfluous. Although Epictetus does elsewhere emphasize the need for exercises, the presence of these intellectualist passages makes it seem as if Epictetus' position is more complex than I acknowledge. Beyond the textual details of the *Discourses*, one might argue more generally that if the Stoics truly are follows of Socratic intellectualism then surely philosophical exercises will serve little purpose. This objection clearly goes right to the heart of the issues that I discuss in this book (it was first raised by Aristo; see below pp. 76-8). Yet it also presupposes a conception of knowledge that is precisely what I attempt to challenge with my central claim that, for the Stoics, knowledge should be conceived as knowledge of an art or craft. The objection that, as Socratic intellectualists, the Stoics should have no need for exercises because knowledge should be sufficient on

---

[11] See Christopher Gill in *Phronesis* 50/2 (2005), 173, and Inwood (n. 2 above), respectively.

[12] See pp. 78-81 below. I have elaborated on this point in an article that draws upon material from this book: 'Stoic Practical Philosophy in the Imperial Period', in Richard Sorabji and Robert W. Sharples, eds, *Greek and Roman Philosophy 100 BC – 200 AD: Volume 1*, Bulletin of the Institute of Classical Studies Suppl. 94 (2007), 115-40, esp. at 126.

[13] See John Mouracade in *Ancient Philosophy* 26 (2006), 216-20. Mouracade cites as examples Epictetus *Diss.* 3.9.2, 4.6.23, 4.11.8. On this question I have also benefitted from discussions with M. M. McCabe. I have attempted to respond to this issue elsewhere, in John Sellars, *Stoicism* (Chesham: Acumen & Berkeley: University of California Press, 2006), esp. 47-9.

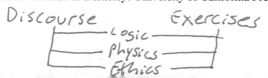

its own assumes that the theoretical principles underpinning an art or craft will on their own constitute knowledge. In other words, it assumes that philosophical knowledge should be identified with mastery of philosophical doctrines. But in what I take to be a key passage (*Diss.* 1.15.2; key because it is the only explicit definition of philosophy he offers us) Epictetus does not conceive philosophical knowledge in this way. Because he conceives philosophy as an art or craft, philosophical knowledge will require *both* mastery of philosophical doctrines *and* a subsequent period of training or exercise designed to digest those doctrines, just as mastery of other arts and crafts do. However, Epictetus can remain a Socratic intellectualist while holding this conception of philosophical knowledge for – like Socrates – he can then argue that once one does have philosophical knowledge (conceived in this way as knowledge of a craft) then it will necessarily transform one's behaviour. In those passages where Epictetus suggests that correct beliefs or judgements (ὀρθὰ δόγματα) are enough, I would argue that we understand these as instances of craft-type knowledge.

In order to bring the central issues into focus my analysis may at times appear too blunt, especially with regard to the division between theoretical arguments and practical exercises.[14] This, I think, is more a matter of presentation than conceptualization. I do not intend to present these as 'distinct and competing' forces; on the contrary, the whole thrust of the argument throughout the book is that these are complementary and both necessary components of a technical conception of philosophy such as the one articulated by the Stoics. Analysis, by its very nature, involves breaking a thing down into its constituent parts, sometimes at the cost of artificially isolating those parts. This process of analysis also inevitably involves neglect of the rhetorical aspects of the texts under discussion.[15] Although I explicitly hope that the account in this book will have implications for the literary study of ancient philosophical texts (see e.g. pp. 126-8 below), I do not pretend to engage in a literary study here. While the rhetorical force of philosophical texts may well be significant for their potential impact upon readers or listeners, and so their transformative effect,[16] that rhetoric is of far less relevance to the conceptual analysis of the nature of philosophy of the sort that I am engaged in here.

Another reviewer locates a central issue in the book as the attempt to respond to the competing characterizations of ancient philosophy by Pierre Hadot and Michel Foucault (see esp. pp. 115-18).[17] While Hadot presents ancient philosophy as a 'spiritual exercise', Foucault characterizes it as a 'technique', and I suggest that the latter is closer to the mark, if we understand 'technique' etymologically, deriving from τέχνη. Hadot's identification of philosophy with exercise is based upon two brief doxographical texts, which I suggest are of limited significance and, in any case, don't quite say what Hadot implies they do (see p. 116, n. 43). This reviewer

---

[14] See Inwood (n. 2 above).

[15] This is a concern raised by Long (n. 4 above).

[16] See Long (n. 4 above), 82.

[17] Jean-Baptiste Gourinat in *Philosophie antique* 6 (2006), 223-26.

suggests that I dismiss these texts too quickly.[18] I remain sceptical about their significance, but even if one were to accept them as important sources, it would still leave open the question of what they actually say, for they also connect philosophy with the notion of an art or craft, and not just with exercise. The same reviewer suggests that elsewhere Hadot fully acknowledges the significance of philosophical discourse alongside spiritual exercises, the implication being that Hadot's considered position is closer to mine than my account suggests.[19] If this is the case then I am happy to acknowledge it.

* * *

Beyond this new Preface, the rest of the book remains unchanged (though the original Preface has been omitted). One reviewer found the proliferation of both words in Greek and footnotes distracting.[20] I certainly hope they are not too distracting, though the reviewer is no doubt correct to note that both could be reduced in quantity without affecting the central argument to any great extent. Yet on balance it seems more helpful to readers to avoid such changes and so preserve the identity of pagination between the two editions. A couple of reviewers speculated whether my choice of title is a deliberate reference to Alexander Nehamas' book of the same name (cited in the Bibliography).[21] It is not. Given that my aim is to articulate a conception of philosophy conceived as an art concerned with transforming one's way of life, *The Art of Living* seemed the most natural title and it was chosen before I encountered Nehamas' book (which is wonderful, but not about the art of living in the very specific sense that I use the phrase in this book). My discussion of the philosopher's beard (pp. 15-19) is intended as a light-hearted and 'entertaining' (p. 20) opening into proceedings and should not be taken too seriously.[22]

Finally, I must express my thanks to Deborah Blake at Duckworth for welcoming the book into Duckworth's rich and important list of works on ancient philosophy. The cover image for this new edition, showing Marcus Aurelius writing his *Meditations*, reproduces the frontispiece of an early edition of the *Meditations* in my possession.[23]

---

[18] See Gourinat (n. 15 above), 225.

[19] See Gourinat (n. 15 above), 226.

[20] See Curnow (n. 1 above), 62.

[21] See FitzGerald (n. 1 above), 268, and Anna Ntinti in *Rhizai* 2/1 (2005), 123-9, at 125.

[22] With apologies to Inwood (n. 2 above) and Ntinti (n. 21 above) for not making this more explicit.

[23] *Marci Antonini Imperatoris Eorum quae ad seipsum Libri XII* (Oxoniae, E Theatro Sheldoniano. MDCCIV).

Socrates' thesis may be seen as the foundation for a more general claim that philosophy – conceived as a matter of λόγος,[13] an activity primarily concerned with giving a rational account of the world – will not have any direct impact upon an individual's actions (ἔργα). Williams, in his remarks concerning Chrysippus, can also be seen to define philosophy in terms of λόγος when he characterizes it as a subject primarily understood as 'rigorous argument'.[14]

Moreover, the idea of an ancient–modern dichotomy is further challenged by the fact that there have been a number of modern philosophers who have affirmed the idea that philosophy might be primarily expressed in an individual's behaviour.[15] This is a recurrent theme in the works of Nietzsche and is particularly prominent in his essay *Schopenhauer as Educator*:

> I attach importance to a philosopher only to the extent that he is capable of setting an example. [...] The philosopher must supply this example in his visible life, and not merely in his books; that is, it must be presented in the way the philosophers of Greece taught, through facial expressions, demeanor, clothing, food, and custom more than through what they said, let alone what they wrote.[16]

For Nietzsche, the true philosopher must offer an image of a complete way of life rather than focus upon the abstract notion of attaining 'pure knowledge' (*reine Wissenschaft*).[17] The philosopher is an artist and his life is his work of art.[18] As is well known, Nietzsche was intimately familiar with ancient philosophy and in particular

---

Alexander of Aphrodisias *In Metaph.* 5.16-20, 15.22-30). For further discussion of Aristotle's conception of philosophy see Chapter 2 § 1.

[13] By λόγος in this context I mean a rational account, explanation, or definition expressed in discourse (see the substantial entry in LSJ). By using this word I want to capture the twin ideas of rational explanation and verbal expression (λόγος is a verbal noun of λέγω and literally means 'something said'). I shall use 'philosophy conceived as λόγος' as shorthand for philosophy conceived as an activity concerned with developing a rational understanding of the world that is expressed in discourse or argument (as opposed to a philosophy expressed in actions (ἔργα) or way of life (βίος)).

[14] Williams, 'Do Not Disturb', p. 26.

[15] For a preliminary discussion of the significance of the idea of the philosophical life in modern philosophy see Miller, 'From Socrates to Foucault'.

[16] Nietzsche, *Schopenhauer as Educator* § 3 (*KGW* III 1, 346; Complete Works 2, 183-84). Note also § 8 (*KGW* III 1, 413; *Complete Works* 2, 246): 'The only possible criticism of any philosophy, and the only one that proves anything, is trying to see if one can live by this philosophy'.

[17] See Nietzsche, *Schopenhauer as Educator* § 3 (*KGW* III 1, 347; Complete Works 2, 184).

[18] See in particular the following from Nietzsche's Nachlaß: 'The philosopher's product is his *life* (first, before his *works*). It is his work of art [*Kunstwerk*]' (*KGW* III 4, 29 [205]; Complete Works 11, 274-75); 'One should have a philosophy only to the extent that one is capable of living according to this philosophy' (*KGW* III 4, 30 [17]; Complete Works 11, 299); 'As long as philosophers do not muster the courage to advocate a lifestyle [*Lebensordnung*] structured in an entirely different way and demonstrate it by their own example, they will come to nothing' (*KGW* III 4, 31 [10]; Complete Works 11, 311).

with the anecdotal history of the lives of the philosophers by Diogenes Laertius.[19] More recently, two philosophers greatly influenced by Nietzsche, and also each drawn to the ancient image of the philosopher, have considered the relationship between philosophy and biography. The first of these, Michel Foucault, has suggested that philosophy might be conceived as an activity directed towards turning one's life into a work of art:

> What strikes me is the fact that, in our society, art has become something which is related only to objects and not to individuals or to life. [...] But couldn't everyone's life become a work of art? Why should the lamp or the house be an art object but not our life?[20]

The second, Gilles Deleuze, in a reading of Spinoza influenced by his own work on Nietzsche, has developed the concept of 'practical philosophy' conceived as a mode of living or way of life in which philosophy and life are united.[21] Elsewhere, in a discussion concerning the image of the philosopher drawing upon Diogenes Laertius, Deleuze has suggested that,

> we should not be satisfied with either biography or bibliography; we must reach a secret point where the anecdote of life and the aphorism of thought amount to one and the same thing.[22]

There is, then, an ongoing debate concerning the relationship between philosophy and biography. In this study my concern is to consider the nature of this relationship and to examine the conceptions of philosophy involved in the various assessments of this relationship. Hegel, for example, is quite open concerning the nature of his own conception of philosophy and it is relatively straightforward to see how this has shaped his assessment of Socrates. In other cases, the presuppositions concerning the nature and function of philosophy remain implicit. The aim of this study is to outline a conception of philosophy that is able to deal adequately with the idea that philosophy is something that is *primarily* expressed in one's way of life. Of course one may say that none of the major figures in the history of philosophy – Aristotle and Hegel included – would deny that the study of philosophy would have *some*

---

[19] Nietzsche's early philological work focused on Diogenes Laertius: 'De Laertii Diogenis fontibus' (1868-69), 'Analecta Laertiana' (1870), and *Beiträge zur Quellenkunde und Kritik des Laertius Diogenes* (1870), all in *KGW* II 1. For a detailed analysis of their philological merit see Barnes, 'Nietzsche and Diogenes Laertius'.

[20] Foucault, 'On the Genealogy of Ethics', in *Dits et écrits*, vol. 4, pp. 392, 617; *Essential Works*, vol. 1, p. 261 (for this and other references to shorter works by Foucault I supply references to these two collections rather than their original places of publication; note that some of these shorter works were first published in English). When in this interview Foucault was questioned about this idea, he explicitly acknowledged Nietzsche's influence. Foucault's account will be discussed further in Chapter 5 § 2.

[21] See Deleuze, *Spinoza: Practical Philosophy*, pp. 3, 122, 130 (*Spinoza: Philosophie pratique*, pp. 9-10, 164-65, 175).

[22] Deleuze, *The Logic of Sense*, p. 128 (*Logique du sens*, p. 153).

impact upon the behaviour of the individual concerned. However, in many cases this is merely an incidental consequence of what is conceived to be primarily a matter of developing theoretical understanding. The aim here, then, is to explore the possibility of a conception of philosophy in which philosophical ideas are *primarily* expressed in behaviour, a conception in which understanding is developed not for its own sake but rather in order to transform one's way of life, a conception of philosophy that would make biography not merely incidentally relevant but rather of central importance to philosophy.[23]

Those modern philosophers who have been sympathetic to this idea have often turned to antiquity for inspiration. It is of course a commonplace to proclaim that in antiquity philosophy was conceived as a way of life. To be a philosopher in antiquity – a Platonist, a Stoic, an Epicurean, a Cynic, a Neoplatonist, even an Aristotelian – meant that one would live in a specifically philosophical manner.[24] However, on its own, this claim tells us little concerning how one might understand the *relationship* between an individual's philosophy and his or her way of life. Of those who have attempted to explore this question, Foucault has been the most explicit, suggesting that in antiquity philosophy was often conceived as an art of living, a *'technē tou biou'*.[25] As a matter of fact this phrase does not appear in this precise form in the ancient literature.[26] However there are references to a τέχνη περὶ τὸν βίον, an art concerned with one's way of life. Almost all of the ancient occurrences of this phrase derive from sources with Stoic connections and it is with the Stoics that this conception of philosophy as the art of living came to be developed.[27] Insofar as they

---

[23] Thus my concern here is with the idea that biography may be of philosophical relevance insofar as it expresses philosophical ideas (i.e. the impact of philosophy on one's biography); I am not concerned with the idea that certain biographical information may contribute to understanding the formation of a philosophical position (i.e. *not* the impact of biography on one's philosophy).

[24] For general studies of different conceptions of philosophy in antiquity see Hadot, *Qu'est-ce que la philosophie antique?*; Jordan, *Ancient Concepts of Philosophy*; Domański, *La philosophie, théorie ou manière de vivre?*; Gauss, *Plato's Conception of Philosophy*; Chroust, 'Late Hellenistic "Textbook Definitions" of Philosophy'.

[25] See e.g. Foucault, *The Care of the Self*, pp. 43-45 (*Le souci de soi*, pp. 60-63). Note also Nehamas, *The Art of Living*, p. 96, who also uses this phrase.

[26] This and all of the following data concerning the frequency of phrases derive from the *Thesaurus Linguae Graecae* database and the Packard Humanities Institute Latin database.

[27] The formulation τέχνη περὶ τὸν βίον occurs 4 times, all in Sextus Empiricus (*Pyrr. Hyp.* 3.272, 273, *Adv. Math.* 11.180, 209). Variations on this occur a total of 41 times, of which 34 occur in Sextus (many in his preferred form ἡ περὶ τὸν βίον τέχνη) during his series of arguments against the idea of an art of living (which will be discussed in Chapter 4 § 2). The remaining seven occurrences are: Epictetus *Diss.* 1.15.2, Chrysippus *apud* Galen *Plac. Hipp. Plat.* 3.8.16 (5.352 Kühn = 226.25-29 De Lacy = *SVF* 2.909, 911), Arius Didymus 2.7.5b10 (2.66.14-67.4 WH = *SVF* 3.560), Strabo 1.1.1 (= Posidonius test. 75 EK), Philo *Leg. Alleg.* 1.57 (= *SVF* 3.202), Plutarch *Quaest. Conv.* 613b, and Clement of Alexandria *Paed.* 2.2 (*PG* 8.420a), the most important of which will be discussed in Chapter 3 § 1. Latin equivalents would be *ars vitae* and *ars vivendi*; these occur in Cicero *Fin.* 1.42, 1.72, 3.4, 4.19, 5.16, 5.18,

appear to have been the principal ancient philosophical school to explore the nature of this relationship between philosophy and biography in any detail, it is with them that this study will be primarily concerned. The Stoic Epictetus describes philosophy thus:

> Philosophy does not promise to secure anything external for man, otherwise it would be admitting something that lies beyond its proper subject matter (ὕλης). For just as wood is the material (ὕλη) of the carpenter, bronze that of the statuary, so each individual's own life (ὁ βίος αὐτοῦ ἑκάστου) is the material (ὕλη) of the art of living (τῆς περὶ βίον τέχνης).[28]

Here Epictetus presents his philosophy conceived as an art of living as an activity directed towards the transformation of one's way of life (βίος). In contrast to the conception of philosophy as λόγος, this conception is explicitly concerned with the way in which one lives. The function of philosophy, for Epictetus, is to transform one's behaviour, and any development in genuine philosophical understanding will, for him, always be expressed in one's actions (ἔργα). This idea of an art (τέχνη) concerned with transforming one's behaviour clearly shares something with the Socrates of the *Apology* and the early Platonic dialogues where knowledge of human excellence (ἀρετή) is repeatedly compared to knowledge of an art or craft (τέχνη).[29]

A provisional generalization would be to say that for philosophers such as Aristotle, Hegel, and Williams, philosophy is conceived as primarily a matter of λόγος; for Socrates, the Stoics, Nietzsche, and Foucault, philosophy is conceived as a τέχνη, and in particular a τέχνη primarily concerned with transforming one's βίος.[30] Insofar as philosophers who conceive philosophy in terms of λόγος appear to be unable to deal adequately with the philosophical significance of biography and the more general relationship between philosophy and biography, the aim of this study is to draw upon primarily Stoic ancient philosophical resources in order to outline a conception of philosophy that can deal with this relationship.

A common objection to the characterization of philosophy as an art of living is the claim that, insofar as it downplays the role of λόγος, it makes a philosophical way of life indistinguishable from other, say, religious ways of life also common in antiquity.[31] Yet what distinguishes a philosophical way of life from these religious

---

Tusc. Disp. 2.12, *Acad.* 2.23, Seneca *Epist.* 95.7, 95.8, 95.9. Note also Seneca fr. 17 Haase *apud* Lactantius *Div. Inst.* 3.15.1 (*PL* 6.390-91).

[28] Epictetus *Diss.* 1.15.2.

[29] In general I translate τέχνη as 'art' but occasionally use 'craft', 'skill', or a combination of these. Another alternative sometimes used is 'expertise' (e.g. Annas & Barnes, *Sextus Empiricus, Outlines of Scepticism*). I often use 'expert' for τεχνίτης rather than 'artist' or 'craftsman'. Socrates' apparent use of an analogy between τέχνη and ἀρετή will be discussed in Chapter 2 § 4.

[30] Of course this is merely a generalization in order to contrast two general conceptions of philosophy. I do not mean to make any substantive claims concerning any of these philosophers at this stage.

[31] See e.g. Nussbaum, *The Therapy of Desire*, pp. 353-54, who criticizes Foucault and 'affiliated writers' (by which she appears to mean Pierre Hadot). She suggests that their accounts place too much emphasis upon 'habits and *techniques du soi*' (i.e. ἄσκησις) and do

ways of life is the fact that it is grounded upon, and expresses a desire for, rational understanding as opposed to, say, mystical insight or unquestioned faith in a system of beliefs. What makes the concept of an art of living specifically *philosophical* is the essential role that rational understanding, analysis, or argument (λόγος) plays within it. What distinguishes this conception of philosophy from that held by Aristotle, Hegel, or Williams is that this rational understanding is not constitutive but rather simply a necessary condition. It is the philosopher's distinctively rational way of life (βίος) that is constitutive, his actions and behaviour, which are of course an expression of his rational understanding.

The central task of this study will be to outline a conception of philosophy in which λόγος is a necessary component but is not the only constitutive element. In order to accomplish this task I shall draw upon those ancient philosophers who explicitly conceived philosophy in these terms, namely the Stoics, but also Socrates insofar as he can be seen to lay the foundations for their conception of an art of living, a τέχνη περὶ τὸν βίον. Central to this conception of philosophy will be the significance of philosophical exercise or training (ἄσκησις) and the role that this plays alongside rational discourse (λόγος) in the concept of an art (τέχνη).[32] The reconstruction of this conception of philosophy will allow two things. Firstly, it will make it possible to approach those ancient philosophers who conceived philosophy in these terms with a proper understanding of their implicit presuppositions concerning what it was that they thought they were engaged in. This is essential in order to avoid anachronistic judgements.[33] Closely related to this is the re-assessment of certain authors who have often been dismissed as non-philosophical without pausing to consider the assumptions implicit within such a judgement. Secondly, reconstructing this conception of philosophy will, it is hoped, form a contribution to the more general debate concerning the nature of the relationship between philosophy and biography and the nature and function of philosophy as such.

2. The Structure

The first chapter of this study is devoted to developing an understanding of the relationship between philosophy and biography as conceived in antiquity. Beginning with a series of anecdotal stories concerning the status of 'the philosopher's beard' in the Graeco-Roman world, it will move on to consider the way in which philosophy

---

not acknowledge the importance of rational argument (i.e. λόγος). I shall discuss this further in Chapter 5 § 2.

[32] It should be noted that this concern with the constitutive elements of τέχνη is quite different to the debate between the rationalist and empiricist medical schools concerning the foundation of the art of medicine. That debate – concerning the relationship between reason and experience – was primarily concerned with the acquisition of technical expertise in medicine and, in particular, how one might come to know the λόγοι underpinning a τέχνη. For further discussion see Walzer & Frede, *Galen, Three Treatises on the Nature of Science*, pp. ix-xxxiv.

[33] See Frede in Brunschwig & Lloyd, eds, *Greek Thought*, p. 4.

was often presented as a matter of actions rather than words (ἔργα οὐ λόγοι). Central here will be the *philosophical* significance attached to biographical and anecdotal literature concerning the lives of ancient philosophers. This first chapter will set the scene for the subsequent discussion.

In the second chapter I shall begin to develop an understanding of the concept of an art of living by turning to Socrates as he is portrayed by Plato in the *Apology*. In this text Socrates can be seen to outline an embryonic conception of an art (τέχνη) concerned with one's way of life (βίος). I shall also consider a number of the early Platonic dialogues in which this idea is developed, in particular *Alcibiades I* and the *Gorgias*. However my focus will be upon the historical Socrates rather than the character in Plato's dialogues.[34] Consequently I am less concerned with what these dialogues may tell us about Plato's own philosophical position and I shall also draw upon other Socratic sources, in particular Xenophon.[35] I shall also consider what I take to be a problem with one aspect of Aristotle's portrait of Socrates insofar as this will help to bring into focus the issues at hand.[36] The main reason for this focus upon the historical rather than the Platonic Socrates is the fact that the Stoics (and before them the Cynics) claimed to be followers of Socrates,[37] yet, at the same time, clearly distanced themselves from Plato.[38] The Socrates with which I am concerned, then, is

---

[34] For my approach to the 'problem of Socrates' see Additional Note 1.

[35] As with the Platonic dialogues, I shall make use of Xenophon's works (primarily the *Memorabilia*) only to the extent that they present or elaborate ideas that can be found in Plato's *Apology* (see Additional Note 1). For further discussion of Xenophon as a source for Socrates see Chroust, *Socrates Man and Myth*; Cooper, 'Notes on Xenophon's Socrates'.

[36] Beyond Plato, Xenophon, and Aristotle, there are also the portrayal of Socrates by Aristophanes in the *Clouds* (for which see Dover, 'Socrates in the *Clouds*'; Vander Waerdt, 'Socrates in the Clouds'; Montuori, 'Socrates Between the First and Second Clouds', in *Socrates: An Approach*, pp. 85-145) and numerous later *testimonia* now collected in Giannantoni's *Socratis et Socraticorum Reliquiae* (many of which are translated in Ferguson, *Socrates: A Source Book*). An exemplary example of the sort of work that still needs to be done can be found in Glucker, 'Socrates in the Academic Books and Other Ciceronian Works'. For further discussion see the works referred to in Additional Note 1.

[37] See e.g. the judgement of Grote, *Plato, and the Other Companions of Sokrates*, vol. 3, p. 505: 'Antisthenes, and his disciple Diogenes, were in many respects closer approximations to Sokrates than either Plato or any other of the Sokratic companions'; also Hicks, *Stoic and Epicurean*, p. 4. For the Cynic appropriation of Socrates see Long, 'The Socratic Tradition: Diogenes, Crates, and Hellenistic Ethics', pp. 28-46. For the Stoic appropriation see Long, 'Socrates in Hellenistic Philosophy'; Striker, 'Plato's Socrates and the Stoics'. This Cynic-Stoic appropriation of Socrates is particularly clear in the Arabic tradition where he becomes 'Socrates of the Barrel'; see Alon, *Socrates in Mediaeval Arabic Literature*, pp. 30-31, 49.

[38] On a range of philosophical topics the Stoics can be seen to respond to Platonic positions and to oppose them. For ancient awareness of this opposition see Numenius *apud* Eusebius 14.6.11 (732d = *SVF* 1.12). For their disagreement over ontology see Brunschwig, 'The Stoic Theory of the Supreme Genus and Platonic Ontology', p. 125. For politics see Plutarch *Stoic. Rep.* 1034e (= *SVF* 1.260). For ethics see Striker, 'Plato's Socrates and the Stoics', p. 242. For psychology see Sedley, 'Chrysippus on Psychophysical Causality', p. 313. In the last two cases these

the Socrates who inspired Zeno to study philosophy and eventually to begin his teaching in the Painted Stoa (Στοά Ποικίλη),³⁹ and the Socrates who appears throughout the works of later Stoics such as Epictetus as the ultimate role model for the Stoic sage.⁴⁰ It is clearly beyond the scope of this study (or perhaps any) to reconstruct fully either the Stoic image of Socrates or the historical Socrates. My remarks concerning the Socratic conception of an art (τέχνη) concerned with one's way of life (βίος) are thus to a certain extent provisional and are intended simply to function as a foundation for an understanding of the Stoic conception of an art of living.

In the third chapter I shall turn to the Stoics themselves and examine how they took up Socrates' scattered remarks concerning the nature of philosophy and used them to construct a fully-fledged concept of an art of living. Of particular importance will be the way in which the Stoics developed the Socratic idea of an art (τέχνη) concerned with the health of the soul (ψυχή), their more formal attempts to define an art (τέχνη), and their discussion of the relationship between philosophical theory (λόγος) and exercise (ἄσκησις). In order to do this I shall draw upon a wide range of Stoic sources and shall use the term 'Stoic' in a fairly broad way.⁴¹ However throughout this study I shall often return to the works of Epictetus. There are a number of reasons for this. The first is that the texts that have come down to us under the name of Epictetus constitute the largest collection of documents relating to Stoicism written in Greek.⁴² Secondly, these texts derive from a Stoic philosopher rather than an intellectual with an interest in Stoicism (such as Cicero) or a hostile member of a different philosophical tradition (such as Plutarch or Philodemus).

---

responses have been characterized as explicit attempts to rescue Socratic positions from Platonic criticisms.

³⁹ See Diogenes Laertius 7.2 (= *SVF* 1.1) who reports that Zeno was inspired to study philosophy after reading Book 2 of Xenophon's *Memorabilia*. For discussion of the Xenophonic character of the Stoic image of Socrates see Long, 'Socrates in Hellenistic Philosophy', pp. 152-54, 160-64.

⁴⁰ The sources for Socrates used by Epictetus are difficult to determine. He clearly knew the works of Plato and often cites him (for which see Jagu, *Épictète et Platon*). A passage at *Diss.* 2.17.35-36 implies that Epictetus also knew the works of Xenophon and Antisthenes, and at *Diss.* 4.6.20 he quotes from Antisthenes (although probably from his *Cyrus* rather than one of his Socratic works; see fr. 20a DC = *SSR* V A 86). However, Antisthenes' Socratic dialogues appear to have been readily available to Dio Chrysostom – Epictetus' fellow pupil under Musonius Rufus – and thus were still in circulation in the late first century AD (on which see Brancacci, 'Dio, Socrates, and Cynicism', pp. 241-54). In the light of this, it would perhaps be premature to reject certain features of Epictetus' portrait of Socrates as 'idealizations' or 'distortions' simply because they do not agree with the other sources that survive. Antisthenes was older than both Plato and Xenophon and may well have been considerably closer to Socrates than either of them. If Epictetus drew upon Antisthenes' now lost portraits then his presentation of Socrates may well be based, in part, on one of the most important ancient sources for Socrates.

⁴¹ See Additional Note 2.

⁴² For the authorship and transmission of these texts see Additional Note 3.

Thirdly, in antiquity Epictetus gained a considerable reputation as an important Stoic philosopher and as a faithful follower of the early Stoa.[43] Fourthly, the material in Epictetus is directly relevant to my concerns here, namely the relationship between philosophical discourse and one's way of life. Another important source, especially for the Stoic concept of an art of living, is Sextus Empiricus, to whom Chapter Four is devoted. While Epictetus (*c.* 55-135) was probably at his most active *c.* 100 (his *Discourses* have been dated to *c.* 108),[44] Sextus has been given a *floruit* of *c.* 150-170.[45] It is likely that the 'Stoics' to whom his polemic is addressed would have been those influenced by Epictetus and active during a period in which Epictetus' fame was at its greatest.[46] Thus, if any qualification should be placed on my use of the term 'Stoic' it should perhaps be to note this focus upon the Stoicism of the second century AD. Indeed, a number of the other authors that I shall draw upon – Marcus Aurelius (121-180), Plutarch (*c.* 50-120), Galen (*c.* 129-210), and Aulus Gellius (*c.* 130-180) – all belong to this period.

In Chapter 4 I shall consider a series of objections to the idea of an art of living raised by Sextus Empiricus. By considering each of these objections in turn I shall attempt to clarify and perhaps refine the Stoic concept. I shall also consider to what extent Sextus' scepticism, despite these objections, nevertheless still maintains the idea that philosophy is something primarily expressed in one's way of life (βίος).

These four chapters constitute Part I, all focusing on the relationship between βίος and τέχνη, and the concept of a τέχνη concerned with one's βίος. In these chapters I shall suggest that philosophy conceived as τέχνη is able to impact upon one's βίος because it involves not just λόγος but also ἄσκησις.

---

[43] For ancient testimonies see Aulus Gellius 1.2.6 (= test. 8 Schenkl), who calls Epictetus the greatest of the Stoics (*Stoicorum maximus*), Celsus *apud* Origen *Cont. Cels.* 6.2 (*PG* 11.1289 = test. 26 Schenkl) who comments upon his popularity, Fronto *Epist.* (2.52 Haines) who calls him a sage (*sapiens*), Galen *Lib. Prop.* 11 (19.44 Kühn = test. 20 Schenkl) who devoted a work to him, and Augustine *Civ. Dei* 9.4.2 (*PL* 41.259, following Aulus Gellius 19.1.14 = fr. 9 Schenkl), who says that the doctrines of Epictetus were in harmony with those of Zeno and Chrysippus. For modern assessments of his orthodoxy see Bonhöffer, *Die Ethik des Stoikers Epictet*, pp. iii-iv (= *The Ethics of the Stoic Epictetus*, pp. 3-4); Bréhier, *The Hellenistic and Roman Age*, p. 154; Hadot, *The Inner Citadel*, p. 82.

[44] See Millar, 'Epictetus and the Imperial Court', p. 142, and Additional Note 3.

[45] See Bett, *Sextus Empiricus, Against the Ethicists*, p. ix n. 3.

[46] Bett, *Sextus Empiricus, Against the Ethicists*, p. ix, suggests that Sextus' polemic was directed towards philosophers who 'lived centuries before his own time'. However it has been argued (with regard to Plotinus' polemic against the Gnostics in *Enn.* 2.9 and Simplicius' polemic against the Manichaeans in *In Ench.* 35) that such polemics were usually a response to direct contact with adherents of the position under attack (see Tardieu, 'Sabiens coraniques et "Sabiens" de Harran', pp. 24-25 n. 105; Hadot, 'The Life and Work of Simplicius', p. 287). It makes more sense to suppose that Sextus' polemic was inspired by direct contact with contemporary followers of Epictetus (who no doubt would have laid great stress on the idea of an art of living) than with written texts that would have been centuries old. As Hadot notes (*Philosophy as a Way of Life*, p. 191), it is likely that in the second century Epictetus would have been the greatest authority for questions concerning Stoic philosophy. Thus, *pace* Bett, I suggest that Sextus' target was probably Epictetus rather than the early Stoa.

In Part II I shall move on to explore the relationship between these two components of τέχνη further. Chapter 5 will focus upon the notion of a philosophical or spiritual exercise (ἄσκησις), considering its function, mechanism, and form. Particular attention will be paid to the way in which ancient philosophical exercises were often expressed in very specific forms of literature. Just as philosophical theory may be seen to have its own literary genre in the form of the treatise, so philosophical exercises may be seen to have their own genre; a form of writing that, to a modern audience, may often appear to be of limited philosophical significance.

Chapters 6 and 7 will explore the relationship between λόγος and ἄσκησις further by examining two examples of literary genres specific to philosophical ἄσκησις. These are the *Handbook* of Epictetus and the *Meditations* of Marcus Aurelius. Central here will be the way in which such philosophical exercises are closely connected to certain literary forms and the significance this may have for an assessment of a text as 'philosophical'. In particular I shall attempt to show in these chapters that, when placed within the context of philosophy conceived as a τέχνη involving both λόγος and ἄσκησις, texts such as the *Handbook* and the *Meditations* can be seen to be profoundly philosophical.

In the Conclusion I shall draw upon the ancient philosophical positions I have discussed in order to sketch the outline of a conception of philosophy that can deal adequately with the idea that philosophy might be primarily expressed in an individual's way of life (βίος). In particular I shall draw attention to a number of later thinkers who can be seen to develop the idea that philosophy is a τέχνη concerned with one's βίος in order to emphasize again that the two competing conceptions of philosophy that I have outlined so far do not form an ancient–modern dichotomy. This is important in order to show that the Socratic and Stoic conception of philosophy is not merely an interesting episode in the history of ideas but rather the foundation of a tradition concerning how one might conceive the nature and function of philosophy which has existed throughout the history of Western philosophy. What I am about to present, then, is not only a historical excursion but hopefully also a contribution to the contemporary debate concerning the nature and function of philosophy as such.

PART I
βίος and τέχνη

Chapter 1

Philosophy and Biography

1. The Philosopher's Beard

In AD 176 the Roman Emperor and Stoic philosopher Marcus Aurelius created four chairs of philosophy in Athens, one for each of the major schools.[1] When, a few years later, the holder of the Peripatetic Chair died, two equally well qualified candidates applied for the post.[2] One of the candidates, Diocles, was already very old so it seemed that his rival, Bagoas, would be sure to get the job. However, one of the selection committee objected to Bagoas on the grounds that he did not have beard saying that, above all else, a philosopher should always have a long beard in order to inspire confidence in his students.[3] Bagoas responded by saying that if philosophers are to be judged only by the length of their beards then perhaps the chair of Peripatetic philosophy should be given to a billy-goat.[4] The matter was considered to be of such grave importance that it was referred to the highest authorities in Rome, presumably to the Emperor himself.[5]

From this no doubt apocryphal story one can see that in Graeco-Roman antiquity the beard came to be seen as *the* defining characteristic of the philosopher; philosophers had to have beards, and anyone with a beard was assumed to be a philosopher.[6] Why was it that the beard became so closely associated in the popular imagination with the figure of the philosopher? What does it say about the nature of philosophy as it was conceived in antiquity? Before answering these questions, it might be helpful to consider in a little detail the origin and status of the phenomenon that came to be know as 'the philosopher's beard'.

The cultural phenomenon of 'the philosopher's beard' has a somewhat complex history. Although when thinking of bearded ancient philosophers one might first turn to the examples of Socrates and Plato, their beards were not 'philosophers' beards'. In fifth- and fourth-century Athens shaving was not a widespread practice and, as a rule,

---

[1] See Dio Cassius 72.31.3, Philostratus *Vit. Soph.* 2.2 (566), Lucian *Eunuchus* 3, with Birley, *Marcus Aurelius*, p. 195.

[2] The following story derives from Lucian's *Eunuchus* and is generally agreed to be fictional.

[3] See Lucian *Eunuchus* 8: 'One [of the judges] said that presence and a fine physical endowment should be among the attributes of a philosopher, and that above all else he should have a long beard that would inspire confidence in those who visited him and sought to become his pupils' (trans. Harmon).

[4] See *Eunuchus* 9.

[5] See *Eunuchus* 12.

[6] See e.g. Lucian *Demonax* 13, *Cynicus* 1.

every adult Greek male wore a beard. The introduction of shaving is generally credited to Alexander the Great towards the end of the fourth century BC and it seems to have become very popular. Yet in the period immediately after Alexander philosophers tended to continue to sport beards in contrast to, the newly emerging fashion. Yet these beards – the beards of Zeno and Epicurus – were still not fully fledged 'philosophers' beards'.

In the third century BC the focus of philosophical activity began to shift from Athens to Rome. According to tradition, the earliest Romans grew their beards long.[7] However, barbers were first introduced to Rome from Sicily around 300 BC, bringing with them the custom of shaving.[8] One of the first to take up the practice of daily shaving was Scipio Africanus towards the end of the third century BC.[9] If shaving was common in Hellenistic Greece, it became almost compulsory in Rome. All respectable Roman citizens were, from that point on, clean-shaven.

Having set the scene it is now possible to turn to the question concerning the origin of 'the philosopher's beard'. In 155 BC an embassy of three Greek philosophers visited Rome on a diplomatic mission. The three philosophers were representatives from the three most important philosophical schools of the day: Carneades, the current head of Plato's Academy; Critolaus, from Aristotle's Lyceum; and Diogenes of Babylon, the current head of the Stoics.[10] In contrast to their beautifully clean-shaven Italian audience, these three intellectuals all sported magnificent beards. In the mind of the Romans, there seemed to be some form of inherent connection between the fact that Carneades, Critolaus, and Diogenes were philosophers and the fact that they all had beards. At this moment, then, the specifically Roman concept of 'the philosopher's beard' was formed. After the Roman conquest of Athens in 87 BC, Rome usurped Athens as the centre of philosophical activity in the ancient world.[11] It was within the urbs of clean-shaven Rome, then, that the beard first became connected with the figure of the philosopher.

In order to examine the philosophical significance of this cultural phenomenon, it will be necessary to consider two very different attitudes towards beards. Cicero, the Roman orator and statesman of the first century BC, was also a keen philosopher and produced a number of philosophical works. As a respectable Roman citizen, Cicero was clean-shaven. It appears that he deliberately chose not to sport a 'philosopher's beard' and it is not too difficult to understand why. If Cicero had grown a beard, he would have appeared to his contemporaries as a typical Greek philosopher and would have looked just like the three philosophers who visited Rome a century before. Yet the only Greek philosophers present in Rome at that time would have been either

---

[7] See Cicero *Pro Caelio* 33.
[8] See Varro *De Re Rustica* 2.11.10.
[9] See Pliny *Nat. Hist.* 7.211.
[10] For ancient reports of the trip see Aulus Gellius 6.14.8-10 (= *SVF* 3 Diog. 8), Cicero *Tusc. Disp.* 4.5 (= *SVF* 3. Diog. 10), and others collected in *SVF* 3 Diog. 6-10. For this embassy and the introduction of Greek philosophy into Rome see Griffin, 'Philosophy, Politics, and Politicians at Rome', pp. 2-5.
[11] See Frede in *CHHP*, p. 790.

slaves and servants working in the household staff of the aristocracy as librarians and tutors, or unwashed Cynics begging on the street corner and shouting abuse at passers by.[12] Either way, the figure of the bearded philosopher was not one to which the politically ambitious Cicero would want to aspire. This suggests that Cicero was more concerned with his social standing and his political career than he was with his pursuit of philosophy. His concern was more with what he could learn from the philosophers and put to work in his oratory and his political career than with devoting his entire life to philosophy itself.[13] Consequently Cicero never adopted a philosopher's beard.

In sharp contrast to Cicero, the Stoic philosopher Epictetus affirmed the philosopher's beard as something almost sacred. This may be seen to express the idea that philosophy is no mere intellectual hobby but rather a way of life that, by definition, transforms every aspect of one's behaviour, including one's shaving habits. If someone continues to shave in order to look the part of a respectable Roman citizen, it is clear that they have not yet embraced philosophy conceived as a way of life and have not yet escaped the social customs of the majority. In the language of the Sophists, to shave is κατὰ νόμον while to sport a beard is κατὰ φύσιν.[14] For Epictetus, the true philosopher will only act according to reason or according to nature, rejecting the arbitrary conventions that guide the behaviour of everyone else. Cicero – despite the value and importance of his written philosophical works – was not a philosopher according to this very specific definition of the term.

In the light of this, Epictetus was intensely proud of his own beard, describing it as noble, dignified, and 'more majestic than a lion's mane'.[15] Indeed, the following hypothetical discussion indicates the value he placed upon it:

'Come now, Epictetus, shave off your beard'.
    If I am a philosopher, I answer, I will not shave it off.

---

[12] See Zanker, *The Mask of Socrates*, pp. 198-200.

[13] See e.g. the assessment of Clarke, *The Roman Mind*, p. 54: 'For most of his life philosophy was not in the forefront of Cicero's interests. He believed in a union of rhetoric with philosophy and of statesmanship with philosophy, and liked to think of himself as a philosophic orator and philosophic statesman, but oratory and statesmanship came first'. See also Zanker, *The Mask of Socrates*, p. 199.

[14] The distinction between what is according to custom or convention (κατὰ νόμον) and what is according to nature (κατὰ φύσιν) originated in the Sophistic enlightenment of the fifth century BC and was taken up later by both Cynics and Stoics. For a Sophist such as Antiphon, the distinction is between what is arbitrarily agreed and what is necessary (see Antiphon *De Veritate* (*POxy* 1364 = fr. 44 DK) ll. 23-34). For the Cynics, to live according to nature meant to remove everything unnecessary and was thus, to a certain extent, understood negatively (see Dudley, *A History of Cynicism*, pp. 31-32; Hicks, *Stoic and Epicurean*, p. 10), although as with Antiphon φύσις was in effect understood in terms of what is necessary. For the Stoics φύσις has a more positive content and living in accordance with nature becomes identified with living in accordance with reason (see e.g. Epictetus *Diss.* 3.1.25). For further discussion of the Sophistic use of this distinction see Kerferd, *The Sophistic Movement*, pp. 111-30; Guthrie, *History*, vol. 3, pp. 55-134.

[15] Epictetus *Diss.* 1.16.13.

'Then I will have you beheaded'.
    If it will do you any good, behead me.[16]

For Epictetus, to shave would be to compromise his philosophical ideal of living in accordance with nature and it would be to submit to the unjustified authority of another. Faced with that prospect he would – like Socrates – rather die. If this sounds extreme we should bear in mind that this was a real political issue at that time: Philostratus reports that the Emperor Domitian ordered that the philosopher Apollonius have his hair and beard forcibly removed as punishment for anti-State activities.[17] Short of killing him – which would have made him a martyr like Socrates – this was the most severe punishment the Emperor could inflict upon the philosopher. This terrible possibility must have been constantly on Epictetus' mind, for he was in Rome at the time that Domitian banished all philosophers from Italy, and Epictetus literally fled for his life.[18]

    One can now begin to see how the beard came to be associated with philosophy, or to be more precise, how it came to represent a certain conception of philosophy. According to a number of ancient sources, the philosopher's beard came in a variety of shapes and sizes. Writing in the second century AD, Alciphron describes a group of philosophers from different schools attending a birthday party:

> There was present, among the foremost, our friend Eteocles the Stoic, the oldster, with a beard that needed trimming, the dirty fellow, with head unkempt, the aged sire, his brow more wrinkled than his leather purse. Present also was Themistagoras of the Peripatetic school, a man whose appearance did not lack charm and who prided himself upon his curly whiskers.[19]

What this passage suggests is that philosophers from different schools each wore their beards in different ways. Moreover, these different beards were thought to reflect the different philosophical doctrines of the various schools.[20] For example, the Cynics, who preached strict indifference to all external goods and social customs, sported the longest and dirtiest beards. The Stoics, who argued that it is acceptable to prefer certain external goods so long as they are never valued above virtue, also sported long beards, but engaged in occasional washing and trimming for purely practical considerations.[21] The Peripatetics, who following Aristotle believed that external

---

[16] Epictetus *Diss.* 1.2.29 (trans. Hard).

[17] See Philostratus *Vita Apollonii* 7.34; Zanker, *The Mask of Socrates*, p. 260.

[18] For Domitian's banishment of the philosophers including Epictetus (*c.* AD 88-89) see Aulus Gellius 15.11.3-5 with Starr, 'Epictetus and the Tyrant'.

[19] Alciphron *Epist.* 3.19.2-3 (trans. Benner & Fobes) with comment in Anderson, 'Alciphron's Miniatures', p. 2194; Zanker, *The Mask of Socrates*, p. 110.

[20] See Zanker, *The Mask of Socrates*, p. 111.

[21] See Musonius Rufus fr. 21 (115.4-8 Hense = 128.10-13 Lutz = *SVF* 1.243): 'The remark of Zeno was well made that it is quite as natural to cut the hair as it is to let it grow long, in order not to be burdened by too much of it nor hampered for any activity' (trans. Lutz). See also Frede, 'Euphrates of Tyre', p. 10: 'There was the Stoic insistence of the naturalness of hair, yet

goods and social status were necessary for the good life together with virtue,[22] took great care of their beards, carefully trimming them as was appropriate for a member of the traditional Greek aristocracy.

From these few examples one can begin to see how different types of beard might not merely indicate visually to which school an individual belonged, but actually *express* the philosophical positions held by that school.[23] It is not that one needs a beard in order to be a philosopher; nor is it that a beard in itself is of any philosophical importance. Rather, what is of philosophical importance is what a beard can express, whether it be a certain conception of philosophy as such (as in the different attitudes of Cicero and Epictetus), or a specific philosophical doctrine (as in Alciphron's account of the birthday party). If, like Epictetus, one conceives philosophy as not merely an intellectual hobby but rather a way of life, then one's philosophy will be expressed in the way one acts, and not simply in what one might say. As such, the act of shaving or the act of growing a beard can be as philosophical as any other act. As Michael Frede has noted, 'Human life is a matter of banal things [...]. If there is something non-banal about it, it is the wisdom with which these banal things are done, the understanding and the spirit from which they are done'.[24] What makes a beard a 'philosopher's beard', then, will be the philosophical way of life that it expresses. Of course, there will be plenty of non-philosophical beards, and plenty of beardless philosophers. Yet, in Graeco-Roman antiquity at least, the serious philosopher always had a beard and he appears to have valued it more highly than his life.

Perhaps one can now begin to understand why in Lucian's tale the Athenians refused to appoint the beardless Bagoas to the chair of Peripatetic philosophy. For them, a philosopher's beard was no mere ornament or accessory. Rather it was an expression of a truly philosophical way of life and, as such, essential.

---

also the need to maintain it in a functional state. And it would be in the spirit of Stoicism to discuss such seemingly banal details of ordinary life'. Lucian refers to the close cropped functional haircuts of many Stoics and names Chrysippus in particular (see Lucian *Hermotimus* 18, *Vitarium Auctio* 20-21; note also Juvenal *Saturae* 2.15). This practice may well go back to Diogenes the Cynic (see Diogenes Laertius 6.31). For further discussion see Geytenbeek, *Musonius Rufus and Greek Diatribe*, pp. 119-23.

[22] Aulus Gellius 18.1.1-14 (part in *SVF* 3.56) records a typical debate between a Peripatetic and Stoic on this issue.

[23] The idea that an individual's philosophical position or character can be discerned from external attributes such as a beard might appear to share something in common with physiognomy (φυσιογνωμονία). Ancient physiognomy has been defined as the attempt to uncover an individual's character by means of bodily movements or physical characteristics (see esp. Ps-Aristotle *Physiognomonica* 806a22-b3). However it tends to focus upon physical attributes beyond the control of the individual concerned (e.g. ibid. 811a28: 'a nose thick at the tip means laziness') whereas the primary concern here is with behaviour. For ancient sources for physiognomy see R. Förster *Scriptores Physiognomici*, 2 vols (BT) and for modern discussion see Barton, *Power and Knowledge*, pp. 95-131.

[24] Frede, 'Euphrates of Tyre', p. 6.

2. ἔργα and λόγοι

What this entertaining yet seemingly trivial discussion concerning beards illustrates is that, for certain philosophers in antiquity, philosophy was conceived as something much more than merely the development of a theoretical understanding of the world. Instead philosophy appears to have been conceived as something that would impact upon every aspect of one's life, right down to something as apparently banal as one's shaving habits. Moreover, it suggests that philosophy was conceived as primarily a matter of actions rather than words and that a philosopher's actions might well be a more accurate indication of his philosophical position than anything he might say. This idea of an individual's beliefs being a matter of 'deeds not words' (ἔργα οὐ λόγοι) became prominent in fifth- and fourth-century Athens and, in particular, came to be associated with Socrates, forming part of his rejection of Sophistry as mere amusement with words.[25] What became especially important was the idea of harmony between deeds and words (ἔργα καὶ λόγοι) in one's way of life.[26] These ideas persisted in a number of later philosophical schools and became particularly common with the Stoics. In his epitome of Stoic ethics the doxographer Arius Didymus writes:

> It is not the person who eagerly listens to and makes notes of what is spoken by the philosophers who is ready for philosophizing, but the person who is ready to transfer the prescriptions of philosophy to his deeds (ἔργα) and to live in accord with them.[27]

Of particular relevance here is a passage in the *Discourses* of Epictetus where he suggests that his students engaged in their Stoic studies should observe themselves in their daily actions in order to find out to which school of philosophy they really belong.[28] He predicts that most will find themselves to be Epicureans while a few will be Peripatetics, but pretty feeble ones at that. However, Epictetus is doubtful that he will find any real Stoics among his students. To be sure, there will be many that will recite the arguments of the Stoics, but for Epictetus a real Stoic is one 'who is sick,

---

[25] See a number of fragments attributed to Democritus, including fr. 55 DK *apud* Stobaeus 2.15.36 (2.191.9 WH): 'One should emulate the deeds and actions of virtue, not the words' (ἔργα καὶ πρήξιας ἀρετῆς, οὐ λόγους, ζηλοῦν χρειών); also fr. 82 DK, fr. 145 DK. Further examples in Sophocles, Euripides, Thucydides, and Plato are mentioned in O'Brien, *The Socratic Paradoxes*, p. 114.

[26] See e.g. Plato *Laches* 188c-d & 193d-e, with discussion in O'Brien, *The Socratic Paradoxes*, pp. 114-17. In Xenophon, Socrates affirms actions over words as the true indicators of an individual's beliefs (e.g. Xenophon *Mem.* 4.4.10, *Apol.* 3); in the *Laches* the interlocutor Laches proposes what he calls a 'Dorian harmony' between actions and words. Socrates responds by saying that although both of them might be judged courageous by their actions, their inability to give a definition or account (λόγος) of courage means that they would be judged failures according to this criterion (193d-e). Note also Socrates *apud* Stobaeus 2.15.37 (2.191.11-12 WH = *SSR* I C 187).

[27] Arius Didymus 2.7.11k (2.104.17-22 WH = *SVF* 3.682; trans. Pomeroy).

[28] See Epictetus *Diss.* 2.19.20-25; note also 3.2.10-12. A similar idea is expressed in Bion fr. 49 Kindstrand *apud* Diogenes Laertius 4.51.

and yet happy (εὐτυχοῦντα); in danger, and yet happy; dying, and yet happy; exiled, and yet happy; disgraced, and yet happy'.[29] Such individuals are not surprisingly few and far between. His students may be able to recite Stoic λόγοι but they will not be genuine Stoics until they can produce Stoic ἔργα.[30]

On the basis of this, Epictetus warns his students against trying too hard to explain the complex writings of a Stoic such as Chrysippus to others. He suggests that, insofar as these writings are primarily concerned with offering advice on how to live, his students may find themselves humiliated if they make public displays of their mastery of these doctrines but are unable to act in accordance with them.[31] They will, he suggests, become philosophers of the kind that are 'without deeds, limited to words' (ἄνευ τοῦ πράττειν, μέχρι τοῦ λέγειν).[32] Of course, this is by no means a rejection of philosophical theory as such.[33] Instead it is the claim that a genuine philosopher will display his beliefs in both his actions and his words (ἔργα καὶ λόγοι), both being essential components of philosophy as conceived by Epictetus. His warning is that a verbal display of the manipulation of complex philosophical doctrines will be worthless unless those doctrines are also expressed in every aspect of one's life. As we have seen, one very visible expression of a philosopher's doctrines would have been the presence or the absence of a beard.[34]

3. The Philosopher's βίος

If in antiquity philosophy was conceived as something primarily expressed in actions rather than words, then the assessment of what does and does not count as 'philosophical' would have been very different from certain contemporary attitudes. One very noticeable feature of ancient philosophical traditions is the significance that was often assigned to biographical and anecdotal literature.[35] In antiquity the word βίος or 'life' referred to an individual's way of life or manner of living and was

---

[29] Epictetus *Diss.* 2.19.24 (trans. Hard).

[30] Note also Arius Didymus 2.7.11k (2.105.4-6 WH = *SVF* 3.682) where it is said that the foolish do not support the rational account (λόγος) of virtue (ἀρετή) with corresponding deeds (ἔργα).

[31] See in particular Epictetus *Ench.* 49 where he explicitly refers to the need for harmony between ἔργα and λόγοι; note also *Diss.* 1.17.13-19.

[32] Epictetus fr. 10 Schenkl *apud* Aulus Gellius 17.19.1.

[33] It has been suggested that Epictetus' warning was necessary only because his teaching would have concentrated upon the exposition of passages from earlier Stoics such as Chrysippus (see e.g. Epictetus *Diss.* 2.21.11). In this sense, Epictetus is not rejecting scholarship as such but rather emphasizing its position within a broader conception of philosophy as a way of life. See Long, 'Epictetus, Marcus Aurelius', p. 993.

[34] Of course, Epictetus knows and warns that a beard alone does not make a philosopher (e.g. *Diss.* 4.8.12). It is interesting to note that the fact that he felt this warning to be necessary indicates how strongly the connection was held to be in the popular imagination.

[35] For a survey of the use of biographical material in ancient philosophy (focusing on Hellenistic philosophy) see Mansfeld in *CHHP*, pp. 16-26.

distinct from the merely biological connotations of being a 'living being', for which the Greeks used ζῷον.[36] It also came to be used as a literary title for what may loosely be called a 'biography'.[37] However ancient biographies (βίοι) were quite different from modern biographies, being concerned less with dates of birth, death, and memorable events, and more with uncovering an individual's character and – as the very title suggests – presenting the *way* in which an individual lived. In the opening remarks to his biography of Alexander, for example, Plutarch states that he will not list all of his subject's memorable actions, the reason being that his intention is not to write histories but rather to write biographies or 'lives' (οὔτε γὰρ ἱστορίας γράφομεν, ἀλλὰ βίους).[38] As such, his primary objective is to reveal the character (ἦθος) of his subject, to paint a likeness of him in which his character can be seen, rather than merely to recount the dates of important events in his life. His intention, he says, is to focus upon the signs of the soul (τὰ τῆς ψυχῆς σημεῖα) in order to reveal the soul of his subject and, in particular, whether it is good or bad (ἀρετῆς ἢ κακίας). With this aim in mind Plutarch affirms the importance of anecdotal material:

> A slight thing like a phrase or a jest often makes a greater revelation of character than battles where thousands fell.[39]

Although Plutarch was not primarily concerned with writing biographies of philosophers,[40] his general account of the nature of ancient biography and its use of anecdotal material sets the scene for an understanding of ancient philosophical biographies. Insofar as philosophy was conceived as something expressed in actions

---

[36] In general ζῷον was used to refer to animal life or, more generally, any living being. This, along with the distinction between βίος and ζῷον is nicely illustrated by a line in Aristotle *Pol.* 1256a20-21: βίοι πολλοὶ καὶ τῶν ζῴων καὶ τῶν ἀνθρώπων εἰσίν, 'there are many ways of life both of animals and of humans'. It is worth noting that here (and elsewhere; see the examples listed in LSJ) βίος is used to refer to an animal's *way of life*. Note also that ζῷον was sometimes used to refer to humans. The distinction, then, is not between human and animal life but rather between *manner of living* and *biological life* (however ζωή was occasionally used to refer to a way of life; see e.g. Simplicius *In Ench.* 71.34-35 Hadot).

[37] The word βιογραφία is not recorded until the ninth century AD when it was used twice by Photius in his discussion of Damascius' *Life of Isidore the Philosopher* (see Damascius *Hist. Phil.* test. 3 & fr. 6a *apud* Photius *Bibl.* cod. 181 (126a5) & cod. 242 (335b14) respectively). Photius' use may date back to Damascius himself (late fifth, early sixth centuries AD). Either way, the word is both late and rare. Moreover, although βιογραφία is used to describe Damascius' account of Isidore, the title of his work (as recorded) remains Τὸν Ἰσιδώρου τοῦ φιλοσόφου βίον.

[38] See Plutarch *Alexander* 1.1-3. On the difference between history and biography in antiquity see Cox, *Biography in Late Antiquity*, pp. 4-5.

[39] Plutarch *Alexander* 1.2 (trans. Perrin): πρᾶγμα βραχὺ πολλάκις καὶ ῥῆμα καὶ παιδιά τις ἔμφασιν ἤθους ἐποίησε μᾶλλον ἢ μάχαι μυριόνεκροι.

[40] A number of Plutarch's surviving biographies deal with primarily historical figures who also had philosophical interests (e.g. Cato, Cicero). However Plutarch did write biographies of philosophers; note his lost biography of the Cynic Crates (Lamprias cat. 37; see Plutarch fr. 10 Sandbach *apud* Julian *Orationes* 6.200b = *SSR* V H 84).

rather than words (ἔργα οὐ λόγοι), biographical and anecdotal material was held to be of philosophical importance in a way in which it is not today.[41] Indeed, the development of biography as a literary genre appears to have been closely connected with philosophy throughout antiquity.[42] In the light of Plutarch's comments it is not difficult to see why: biography was conceived as an account of the character and the state of the soul of an individual, precisely the objects of a philosopher's concern.[43] In antiquity the focus was more upon the 'philosopher' as an individual who expressed his character in his behaviour rather than upon 'philosophy' conceived as an abstract discipline or activity that could be separated from the lives of the individuals who practised it. To become a student of philosophy in antiquity did not mean merely to learn a series of complex arguments or engage in intellectual debate. Rather, it involved engaging in a process of transforming one's character (ἦθος) and soul (ψυχή), a transformation that would itself transform one's way of life (βίος). Lucian, in his biography of the philosopher Demonax, makes it clear that his reason for writing this account is to provide such students with an example of a philosopher's life that they can use as a pattern or model (παράδειγμα) for their own lives.[44] In the light of this, ancient philosophy should perhaps be approached as a series of biographies of *philosophers* or examples of ideal philosophical lives rather than as a collection of theoretical systems or *philosophies*.[45] Although this may sound strange to a modern philosophical audience, it nevertheless explains the importance attached

---

[41] Unlike Momigliano, I do not intend to draw any distinction between anecdote and biography (see his *The Development of Greek Biography*, e.g. p. 76). On the contrary, I want to emphasize the anecdotal element within ancient philosophical biography. His aim in distinguishing between the two is in order to help him chart the development towards modern biography, whereas mine is to make clear the contrast between ancient and modern biography. The difference, then, does not so much reflect any dispute but simply a difference in objectives.

[42] The first great flourishing of biography in antiquity appears to have been, in part, inspired by Socrates. The Cynics had a particular taste for collections of anecdotes. Later, Aristotle became an important influence, collecting accounts of different ways of life alongside his collections of scientific and political material (this Peripatetic interest is reflected in the *Characteres* of Theophrastus). The Neoplatonists also produced a number of biographies. This relationship between philosophy and the literary genre of biography is discussed throughout Momigliano's *The Development of Greek Biography*.

[43] These were also objects of religious concern and the resemblance between biographies of philosophical sages and religious holy men has often been commented upon; see e.g. Cox, *Biography in Late Antiquity*, pp. 17-44; Anderson, *Sage, Saint, and Sophist*, pp. 5-6. The distinction became increasingly blurred in Neoplatonism.

[44] See Lucian *Demonax* 2. Demonax was a pupil of Epictetus with Cynic tendencies. For Demonax see Goulet-Cazé, 'Catalogue of Known Cynic Philosophers', pp. 393-94. For further discussion see Clay, 'Lucian of Samosata: Four Philosophical Lives', pp. 3412-13 & 3425-29.

[45] This is precisely the approach employed by Diogenes Laertius. Less well known is Porphyry's *Historia Philosophiae* (Φιλόσοφος ἱστορία) in four books (of which only the *Vita Pythagorae* survives *in extenso*); see *Porphyrii Philosophi Fragmenta*, ed. Smith (BT), fr. 193-224, and the CUF edition of *Vita Pythagorae* by des Places which includes an appendix on the *Historia Philosophiae* by Segonds, pp. 163-97. Some of the fragments derive from Arabic and Syriac sources, on which see Gutas, 'Pre-Plotinian Philosophy in Arabic', p. 4956.

to anecdotal and biographical material in ancient philosophy. In order to consider this ancient philosophical interest in biography further it may be helpful to consider some examples.

(a) Xenophon's Memorabilia

It has been suggested that the origins of biography in general can be traced back to the impact made by Socrates.[46] His life and death, it is claimed, were considered so extraordinary that the desire to record them in effect created biography as a literary genre. Whether this is true or not, it is probably less contentious to suggest that the various accounts of the life and death of Socrates at least formed the foundation for ancient *philosophical* interest in biography.[47] Beyond Plato, a considerable number of people are said to have written Socratic dialogues, including Antisthenes, Euclides, Phaedo, Crito, Aeschines, and Aristippus,[48] while the creation of this genre is credited to an otherwise unknown associate of Socrates called Simon the Shoemaker.[49] Unfortunately none of the works of these authors survive *in extenso*.[50]

---

[46] This was the suggestion of Dihle in his *Studien zur Griechischen Biographie*, pp. 13-34, and discussed in Momigliano, *The Development of Greek Biography*, p. 17.

[47] For Momigliano none of these constitute a proper biography of Socrates (ibid.). They certainly do not conform to a biography in the modern sense of the word. Yet they are clearly concerned with providing an account of the character of their subject. For further discussion of the Socratic biographical genre (and its tendency to idealize its subject) see Momigliano, *The Development of Greek Biography*, pp. 46-49.

[48] For accounts of this genre (famously mentioned by Aristotle in *Poet.* 1447b9-13 = *SSR* I B 2) see Clay, 'The Origins of the Socratic Dialogue', pp. 23-47; Kahn, *Plato and the Socratic Dialogue*, pp. 1-35. Momigliano also draws attention to the later attempts to write 'biographies' of Socrates by Aristoxenus and Demetrius (*The Development of Greek Biography*, pp. 75, 77). The fragments of these are in *SSR* I B 41-51 & 52-56 respectively.

[49] See Diogenes Laertius 2.123 (= *SSR* VI B 87). For further information see Hock, 'Simon the Shoemaker as an Ideal Cynic', pp. 41-53. Kahn doubts the historical reality of Simon (*Plato and the Socratic Dialogue*, p. 10) and suggests an otherwise unknown Alexamenos of Teos as the creator of the Socratic dialogue (p. 1), citing a fragment from Aristotle's *De Poetis* (fr. 72 Rose³ *apud* Athenaeus 505c = *SSR* I B 1; note also Diogenes Laertius 3.48). However this passage does *not* say that Alexamenos invented the *Socratic* dialogue but simply that he wrote *imitative* dialogues before the Socratic dialogues and before Plato. Evidence in favour of Simon's historical reality – although not confirmation – may be found in the discovery of a shop on the edge of the Athenian Agora, the floor scattered with hobnails, containing the base of a pot with 'Simon's' inscribed upon it (see Camp, *The Athenian Agora*, pp. 145-47).

[50] The most notable fragments to survive come from the dialogues of Aeschines, of which some were only discovered in the twentieth century in the papyri from Oxyrhynchus and published as recently as 1972 (see *POxy* 1608, 2889, 2890). These can be found in *SSR* VI A 41-100 (see also *CPF* I 1, 8). A selection of earlier discoveries are translated in Field, *Plato and his Contemporaries*, pp. 146-52.

One source for Socrates beyond Plato that does survive is Xenophon's *Memorabilia* (Ἀπομνημόνευμα).[51] This text is a fairly unstructured collection of anecdotes, reported conversations, and apologetics which has often been judged second rate on historical, literary, and philosophical grounds.[52] Nevertheless it deserves our attention because it helps to explain the philosophical significance of the anecdote. A cursory reading soon shows that Xenophon is just as concerned with recording Socrates' habits and personality as he is with any particular thing he may have said or any philosophical argument he may have made. The reason for this is simple: Xenophon repeatedly says that Socrates taught those whom he met not merely with his words but also with his actions:

In my opinion he [Socrates] actually benefited his associates, partly by the example of his actions (ἔργῳ δεικνύων ἑαυτὸν) and partly by his conversation (διαλεγόμενος). I shall record as many instances [of both] as I can recall.[53]

As such, one might say that an account of Socrates' actions – his habits and his way of life (βίος) preserved in anecdotes – will be of just as much philosophical importance as a record of his verbal arguments. Indeed, in the *Memorabilia* Socrates himself is reported to have argued that acts (ἔργα) are always more important than words (λόγοι) when it comes to debates concerning justice or virtue.[54]

Although it has been common to dismiss Xenophon as philosophically naïve compared to Plato and consequently to devalue his account of Socrates,[55] such a judgement presupposes a certain conception of philosophy which Xenophon – and more importantly, Socrates – may well have rejected. If Xenophon's primary concern is with Socrates as a philosopher who followed a certain way of life then it should not be surprising to find him focusing upon the anecdotal and the biographical. He offers a justification for doing so by saying that he thinks that nothing could be more profitable than spending time in the company of Socrates and learning from his example; now that Socrates is dead, Xenophon suggests that the next most profitable

---

[51] The Latin title *Memorabilia* was first supplied by Johannes Leonclavius in his 1569 edition of Xenophon. A better Latin equivalent might be *Commentarii*; indeed, this is how Aulus Gellius refers to it (14.3.5).

[52] See the surveys of such judgements in Zeller, *Socrates and the Socratic Schools*, pp. 82-86, and Cooper, 'Notes on Xenophon's Socrates', pp. 3-4. In the eighteenth century Xenophon enjoyed a higher reputation and his devaluation appears to have begun with Schleiermacher (see e.g. 'On the Worth of Socrates as a Philosopher', p. 138).

[53] Xenophon *Mem.* 1.3.1 (trans. Tredennick modified). See also 4.3.18: 'By enunciating such principles as these and by putting them into practice himself, he made his associates more devout and responsible'; 4.4.1: 'As for his views about what is right, so far from concealing them, he demonstrated them by his actions (ἔργῳ)'.

[54] See Xenophon *Mem.* 4.4.10; note also Xenophon *Apol.* 3, Plato *Apol.* 32d. However in Plato *Laches* 193d-e Socrates suggests that deeds (ἔργα) without words (λόγοι) will not do either. One must not simply act courageously but also be able to offer an account (λόγος) of courage in order to be truly courageous. This will be discussed further in Chapter 2 § 3.

[55] See e.g. Schleiermacher, 'On the Worth of Socrates as a Philosopher', p. 138.

thing one could do is spend time in his company indirectly by reading accounts of his life.[56] Despite his more recent detractors, Xenophon clearly sees the *Memorabilia* as in some sense a profoundly philosophical text.

Indeed, one could perhaps go further and suggest that, insofar as Socrates is reported to have defined philosophy as a matter of actions rather than words (ἔργα οὐ λόγοι),[57] then *only* a text like the *Memorabilia* will be adequate to capture his philosophy as it is expressed in his actions. However, such a claim would be an oversimplification for, as we have already seen, Socrates demands that one's philosophy must be expressed in both actions and words (ἔργα καὶ λόγοι). This may help to explain Plato's decision to use the dialogue form for his Socratic works, a form that lends itself to the inclusion of anecdotal material alongside theoretical argument, thereby offering the perfect medium in which to record both Socrates' actions and his words.[58]

(b) Diogenes Laertius' Life of Diogenes the Cynic

The recorded title of Xenophon's account of Socrates is Ἀπομνημόνευματα, 'memoirs'. Closely related to this type of biographical account are χρεῖαι, 'anecdotes'. Quintilian describes a χρεία as a biographical anecdote used in order to illustrate some moral or philosophical point.[59] The origin of the idea of a χρεία in this specific sense seems to have been the product of the Socratic schools and, in particular, the Cynics.[60] This probably reflected the fact that many of these philosophers, following the example set by Socrates himself, chose not to write themselves in the belief that philosophy was a matter of deeds rather than words (ἔργα οὐ λόγοι). As these Socratic schools developed, later members were forced to rely upon anecdotal accounts of the lives of their philosophical predecessors as a source of material for their philosophies. For these schools, the anecdote became an important form of philosophical text.

In his account of the life of Diogenes the Cynic, Diogenes Laertius preserves a number of χρεῖαι of which at least one dates back to a collection made in the third

---

[56] Xenophon *Mem.* 4.1.1.
[57] Xenophon *Mem.* 4.4.10.
[58] Roochnik, *Of Art and Wisdom*, p. 106, suggests that Plato chose to write dialogues because they are 'a logos inseparable from deeds'. However, I would not want to follow him in characterizing this as 'nontechnical knowledge'. For more on this see Chapter 2 § 7.
[59] See Quintilian *Inst. Orat.* 1.9.3-5. For the relationship between ἀπομνημόνευματα and χρεῖαι see Kindstrand, 'Diogenes Laertius and the *Chreia* Tradition', pp. 221-24. Note that Diogenes Laertius uses these terms apparently interchangeably to refer to Zeno's collection of anecdotes about his teacher Crates (6.91 = *SVF* 1.272, 7.4 = *SVF* 1.41), of which only one fragment survives, preserved in Stobaeus 4.32.21 (5.786.1-10 WH = *SVF* 1.273 = *SSR* V H 42).
[60] See Kindstrand, 'Diogenes Laertius and the *Chreia* Tradition', pp. 223-24. Collections of χρεῖαι are credited to a number of Socratics by Diogenes Laertius, including Aristippus (see 2.84 = *SSR* IV A 144), Diogenes (see 5.18 = *SSR* V B 68), Metrocles (see 6.33 = *SSR* V B 412), Zeno (see 6.91 = *SVF* 1.272), and Antisthenes (see 7.19 = *SSR* V A 137; not in DC).

century BC by the Cynic philosopher Metrocles.[61] In these anecdotes one can see Cynic philosophy 'in action'. Two examples will suffice to illustrate this. First, there is the account of Diogenes hugging statues in the middle of winter.[62] This act expresses the Cynic philosophical doctrine that all external circumstances are irrelevant to the good life and that one should engage in practical training in order to make oneself indifferent to such circumstances. The extreme nature of the act also serves to highlight exactly what is involved if one were to take the Cynic ethical ideal seriously. Second, there are the accounts of Diogenes' indecent acts in the marketplace which graphically illustrate his rejection of social customs and his adherence to a strict analysis of what is and is not appropriate behaviour in terms of what is and is not in accordance with nature (κατὰ φύσιν).[63] In both of these cases Cynic philosophy is communicated in a dramatic and powerful way. One can immediately see exactly what following the Cynic way of life (κυνικὸς βίος) might entail. Of course, one should remember that Diogenes is reported to have said that, like a chorus trainer, he deliberately 'set his note a little high' in order to ensure that everyone else should 'hit the right note'.[64]

By recording these anecdotes Diogenes Laertius preserves something of great importance, namely Cynic philosophy as it was expressed in actions rather than words (ἔργα οὐ λόγοι).[65] Of all the ancient schools of philosophy, this is especially vital for an understanding of the Cynics insofar as they held that philosophy was primarily a matter of deeds.[66] This is nicely illustrated in the following anecdote:

> Hegesias having asked him to lend him one of his writings, he [Diogenes] said, 'You are a simpleton, Hegesias; you do not choose painted figs, but real ones; and yet you pass over the true training (ἄσκησιν τὴν ἀληθινὴν) and would apply yourself to written rules'.[67]

For Diogenes, philosophy is something that is primarily expressed in one's actions (ἔργα). Any written philosophical doctrines will function merely as tools to be used in the transformation of one's way of life (βίος). If philosophical theories are studied for their own sake and not put into practice then their primary function has not been understood.

---

[61] See Diogenes Laertius 6.33 (= *SSR* V B 412). For Metrocles see *SSR* V L 1-6 and Goulet-Cazé, 'Catalogue of Known Cynic Philosophers', p. 398.

[62] Diogenes Laertius 6.23 (= *SSR* V B 174).

[63] Diogenes Laertius 6.69 (= *SSR* V B 147), *pace* Mansfeld, *CR* 38 (1988), p. 163, who dismisses this as mere exhibitionism.

[64] Diogenes Laertius 6.35 (= *SSR* V B 266). For discussion of Cynic training (ἄσκησις) see Goulet-Cazé, *L'ascèse cynique*, pp. 204-27.

[65] See Mejer, *Diogenes Laertius and his Hellenistic Background*, pp. 2-4, who notes that Diogenes conceived his history very much in terms of living 'philosophers' rather than abstract 'philosophies'.

[66] See e.g. Antisthenes fr. 70 DC *apud* Diogenes Laertius 6.11 (= *SSR* V A 134).

[67] Diogenes Laertius 6.48 (= *SSR* V B 118; trans. Hicks).

As with Xenophon, it has been common to dismiss Diogenes Laertius as a superficial and unphilosophical author.[68] Likewise, the Cynics themselves have often been dismissed as proponents of a lifestyle rather than a philosophy proper.[69] Yet such responses presuppose a conception of philosophy that the Cynics would have completely rejected. In the case of Diogenes the Cynic, one might even say that it is *only* in an anecdotal history such as that of Diogenes Laertius that one can begin to approach his philosophy conceived as a way of life.[70] Within this context, Diogenes Laertius' compendium of amusing χρεῖαι far from being philosophically trivial is, with regard to the Cynics at least, the most philosophical form of writing there can be.[71]

(c) Porphyry's Life of Plotinus

Although one might concede the importance of the anecdote for an understanding of someone like Diogenes the Cynic, it does not, at first glance, appear to be particularly important for ancient philosophy as such, especially as it developed in later antiquity. During a substantial portion of its history, ancient philosophy functioned as something much closer to the modern academic discipline. Philosophical study tended to focus upon the close study of texts, particularly those of Plato and Aristotle, and the commentary became a standard form of philosophical text.[72] Yet even in this period it

[68] See e.g. the recent judgement in Hankinson, *The Sceptics*, p. 4.

[69] Varro *apud* Augustine *Civ. Dei* 19.1.3 (*PL* 41.624) describes Cynicism as a collection of manners and customs (*habitu et consuetudine*) that may or may not be combined with a 'proper' philosophy. More recently, similar judgements have been made by Hegel (*Lectures*, vol. 1, p. 479; cited in the Introduction) and Schleiermacher, who characterized Cynicism as 'a peculiar mode of life, not a doctrine, much less a science' ('On the Worth of Socrates as a Philosopher', p. 132). For further discussion on the status of Cynicism as a 'proper philosophy' see Goulet-Cazé, *L'ascèse cynique*, pp. 28-31.

[70] See Long, 'The Socratic Tradition', p. 31: 'Diogenes Laertius's anecdotal style is generally an impediment to philosophical informativeness. In the case of the Cynic Diogenes, however, anecdote and aphorism should be construed as the essential vehicles of his thought'. Similarly, Frede, *Essays in Ancient Philosophy*, p. xxvii: 'There is no doubt that the *Lives and Views of the Philosophers* of a Diogenes Laertius are bad history of philosophy, but perhaps they do capture an aspect of ancient philosophy that the scholarly history of philosophy, given its aims, passes over, but that, nonetheless, is real and of interest'. Also Nietzsche, *Schopenhauer as Educator* § 8 (*KGW* III 1, 413; Complete Works 2, 246): 'I for one would rather read Diogenes Laertius than Zeller, because at least the spirit of ancient philosophy is alive in the former, whereas in the latter neither this spirit nor any other spirit is alive'.

[71] If this sounds like an extreme claim then I might say that, like Diogenes, I am 'setting my note a little too high' in order to counterbalance the common dismissal of biographical and anecdotal material as 'completely unphilosophical'. For a positive account of the philosophical significance of χρεῖαι see Kindstrand, 'Diogenes Laertius and the *Chreia* Tradition', esp. pp. 232-33, 242-43.

[72] For a general introduction to philosophical practice in later antiquity (*c.* AD 200-600) see Sorabji, *Aristotle Transformed*, pp. 1-30. A substantial collection of such texts may be found in *CAG*.

seems to have been standard practice to preface the study of any philosophical text with a biographical account of its author.[73]

One example of this practice that survives is Porphyry's *Life of Plotinus*.[74] This text, containing a biography and an account of the ordering of Plotinus' texts, was written by Porphyry as an introduction to his edition of Plotinus' *Enneads*. As such it belonged to a whole genre of ancient texts which often had titles of the form 'What Comes Before the Study of (Πρὸ τῆς ἀναγνώσεως) ...'.[75] One of the things that was considered to be essential 'before the study of' a philosophical text was an account of its author's life. Porphyry's text opens with an appropriate anecdote in which he recounts how Plotinus often appeared to be ashamed of being in his body and consistently refused to sit for a painter or a sculptor, exclaiming that it was already enough that nature had encased him in an image and he did not need an image of that image.[76] An anecdote such as this would have illustrated to a prospective student of Plotinus the sort of transformation of attitude that might follow from a thorough understanding of his philosophy. In effect, it shows 'in action' the Plotinian ideal of transcending the body to become more like God.[77]

Another example of this sort of prefatory biography is mentioned by the Neoplatonist Simplicius in the preface to his commentary on Epictetus:

> If the reader be curious to know Epictetus' character, he may find it at large in an account of his life and death, from which one can learn what sort of man he was in his life, written by Arrian, who also compiled the *Discourses* of Epictetus, and digested them into several distinct tracts.[78]

The account of the life of Epictetus by Arrian is unfortunately lost. It has been noted that Porphyry's account has often been thought to be unique; however this lost 'Life' by Arrian suggests that this type of text may have been quite common, a development

---

[73] See Mansfeld, *Prolegomena*, pp. 30, 97-98, 108-10. One such example of this approach can be found in the anonymous *Proleg. Phil. Plat.* 1.10-11 which opens with the line, 'Our admiration for his [Plato's] philosophy will become even greater when we follow up his life-history (ἱστορίαν) and the character of his philosophy' (trans. Westerink).

[74] The full title is *On the Life of Plotinus and the Order of his Books* (Περὶ τοῦ Πλωτίνου βίου καὶ τῆς τάξεως τῶν βιβλίων αὐτοῦ). For a general discussion see Cox, *Biography in Late Antiquity*, pp. 102-33.

[75] See Mansfeld, *Prolegomena*, p. 109. Mansfeld also discusses two examples of this genre by Thrasyllus dealing with 'what comes before the study of Plato' and 'what comes before the study of Democritus' (see pp. 58-107). This use of biography as part of a general interpretative strategy dates back at least to Cicero *Inv.* 2.117: 'one ought to estimate what the writer meant from the rest of his writings and from his acts, words, character, and life (*ex factis, dictis, animo atque vita eius*)'.

[76] See Porphyry *Vit. Plot.* 1.

[77] This ideal is outlined in Plotinus *Enn.* 1.2 (Περὶ ἀρετῶν) and 1.4 (Περὶ εὐδαιμονίας).

[78] Simplicius *In Ench.* Praef. 1-4 Hadot (trans. Stanhope modified).

from or sub-group of the 'What Comes Before the Study of ...' genre.[79] The important point to note here is that in later antiquity students of philosophy were taught, or at least expected to know, the philosophy of their subject as expressed in his life *before* they moved on to read his texts. The concrete example of the philosopher's life was considered to be essential for placing his doctrines in the appropriate context and for offering a paradigmatic example of their application. In other words, students of philosophy were shown the practical application of the philosophical ideas they were about to learn in order to remind them that real philosophical progress was a matter of deeds rather than words (ἔργα οὐ λόγοι). Even in the supposedly scholastic atmosphere of late antiquity, philosophy continued to be conceived as something directed towards the transformation of one's way of life (βίος).[80]

* * *

In the light of these examples one can see that biographical information can in some sense be just as important as theoretical discourse, offering a concrete example of how to put philosophical doctrines into practice. Furthermore, such information can illustrate the harmony between a philosopher's doctrines and his way of life. For Seneca, this is fundamental:

> Philosophy teaches us to act, not to speak (*facere docet philosophia, non dicere*); it exacts of every man that he should live according to his own standards, that his life should not be out of harmony with his words (*ne orationi vita dissentiat*), and that, further, his inner life should be of one hue and not out of harmony with all his activities. This, I say, is the highest duty and the highest proof of wisdom – that deed and word should be in accord (*ut verbis opera concordent*), that a man should be equal to himself under all conditions, and always the same.[81]

---

[79] See Mansfeld, *Prolegomena*, p. 110. He also notes that because both Porphyry and Arrian knew their biographical subjects personally, their accounts would have commanded considerable authority. However, note that Souilhé, p. i (following Asmus), has doubted the existence of a biography of Epictetus distinct from the *Dissertationes*. But its existence has been defended in I. Hadot, *Simplicius, Commentaire*, pp. 156-57.

[80] This can be seen in the way in which later Neoplatonists (e.g. Iamblichus, Proclus) combined the writing of learned commentaries on the works of Plato and Aristotle with religious ideas often deriving from Neopythagoreanism.

[81] Seneca *Epist.* 20.2 (trans. Gummere); note also *Epist.* 16.3, 75.4, 108.36. Seneca has been criticized himself from antiquity onwards for the apparent discord between his own words and actions; see e.g. Suillius *apud* Tacitus *Annales* 13.42. For other ancient attacks on philosophers for *not* displaying such a harmony see Plutarch *Stoic. Rep.* 1033a-b, Lactantius *Div. Inst.* 3.15 & 3.16 (*PL* 6.390-397). Note also that both Zeno and Cato were specifically praised for the harmony between their words and deeds (see Diogenes Laertius 7.10-11 (= *SVF* 1.7-8) & Cicero *Pro Murena* 62 respectively). This appears to have been central to their reputations for wisdom.

Moreover, such biographical information will often be able to capture something of a philosophical attitude that cannot be transmitted in written doctrines alone. However, a collection of anecdotes will always only be second best in comparison with direct personal contact. Again, Seneca takes this to be vital:

> Cleanthes could not have been the express image of Zeno if he had merely heard his lectures; he shared in his life (*vitae eius interfuit*), saw into his hidden purposes, and watched him to see whether he lived according to his own rules (*an ex formula sua viveret*). Plato, Aristotle, and the whole throng of sages who were destined to go each his different way, derived more benefit from the character than from the words (*plus ex moribus quam ex verbis*) of Socrates. It was not the classroom of Epicurus, but living together under the same roof (*sed contubernium fecit*), that made great men of Metrodorus, Hermarchus, and Polyaenus.[82]

The philosopher's life, whether experienced at first hand or via a written account, functioned as a concrete example of his written doctrines in action.[83] Indeed, Seneca himself is reported to have said at his death that the single and most noble possession that he could pass on to his friends was the example of his own life (*imaginem vitae suae*).[84] Moreover, in many instances where there were no written doctrines, the philosopher's life preserved in anecdotes and records of conversations form the *only* account of their philosophy.[85] What some of these accounts suggest is that, rather than being merely an entertaining background to the serious written doctrines, an account of a philosopher's life may be equally important. If anything, it is the written doctrines that are of secondary status, only coming to life when they are put into practice. The key to understanding exactly how a philosophical doctrine might be put to work in this way may often be an example of it 'in action' preserved in an anecdote.

---

[82] Seneca *Epist.* 6.6 (trans. Gummere); note also *Epist.* 38.1. See the discussion of *exempla* in Seneca by Newman, '*Cotidie meditare*', pp. 1491-93, and in Epictetus by Hijmans, Ἄσκησις, pp. 72-77. This theme can be found throughout ancient philosophy; see e.g. Aristotle *Eth. Nic.* 1170a11-13, Galen *Aff. Dign.* 5 (5.24-25 Kühn = 17.11-22 de Boer), Marcus Aurelius 6.48, Simplicius *In Ench.* 49.4-6 Hadot.

[83] In between first-hand experience and a written account there would have also existed oral traditions concerning the lives of philosophers (and oral traditions concerning their conversations or lectures). The relationship between oral and written transmission (with regard to the texts of Aristotle but with wider relevance) is discussed in Sandbach, *Aristotle and the Stoics*, pp. 1-3. See also Kenyon, *Books and Readers in Ancient Greece and Rome*, pp. 21-25.

[84] See Tacitus *Annales* 15.62.

[85] The most obvious examples here are Socrates, Pyrrho, and Epictetus. Note also Euphrates (expertly discussed in Frede, 'Euphrates of Tyre').

4. Summary

In this chapter I have tried to show that in antiquity philosophy was often conceived as something primarily expressed in an individual's actions (ἔργα) and way of life (βίος) rather than something restricted to written doctrines and arguments (λόγοι). In order to do this I have considered a number of anecdotes recording the behaviour of certain philosophers and have considered the philosophical significance often attached to the biographies of philosophers in antiquity. From a modern perspective much of this material may appear to be philosophically irrelevant. Yet that is precisely the point. What this anecdotal and biographical material highlights is the fact that, for this material to have been considered philosophically important in antiquity, the nature and function of philosophy itself must have been understood quite differently to the way in which it is often conceived today. Of course it would be a mistake to suggest that all ancient philosophers emphasized the philosophical importance of biography and that all modern philosophers dismiss such material as irrelevant. Nevertheless, one can see that, in general, more significance was attached to such material in antiquity than is today.

The task for the remainder of this study is to attempt to reconstruct a conception of philosophy from ancient philosophical resources that can deal adequately with the relationship between philosophy and biography. As we have already seen in the Introduction, in antiquity philosophy was conceived by some as an art (τέχνη) concerned with one's way of life (βίος), a conception whose earliest origins can be traced back to Socrates. Moreover, in this chapter we have seen that the idea that philosophy is primarily expressed in actions rather than words (ἔργα οὐ λόγοι) can also be traced back to Socrates. As such it may be appropriate to begin with Socrates in order to see what he may be able to contribute to the reconstruction of a conception of philosophy that can deal with the relationship between an individual's philosophical doctrines and their way of life.

Chapter 2

The Socratic Origins of the Art of Living

1. Philosophy and βίος

In the previous chapter I suggested that in antiquity philosophy was often conceived as something that would transform an individual's way of life (βίος), such that even one's shaving habits might gain a philosophical significance. This conception often characterized philosophy as a matter of 'deeds not words' (ἔργα οὐ λόγοι), a phrase that appears in Xenophon's *Memorabilia*.[1] Although Xenophon's account is valuable for an understanding of Socrates' philosophy as it was expressed in his way of life, unfortunately on its own it gives us little information concerning the conception of philosophy held by Socrates.

Of all the surviving texts that purport to offer evidence for the philosophy of Socrates, probably the single most important document is Plato's *Apology of Socrates*. Unlike Xenophon's later recollections or Plato's early dialogues that supposedly dramatize private conversations, it has been suggested that the *Apology* is the only document that describes a public event.[2] Consequently it would have been produced under a number of external constraints if it were to appear convincing to a contemporary audience, some of whom may have attended Socrates' trial themselves or have heard first-hand accounts of it. As such it is perhaps the most appropriate place to begin.[3]

Throughout the *Apology* it is repeatedly made clear that Socrates' principal concern is not with argument or definition or rational understanding, but rather with life (βίος).[4] Three passages in particular are relevant here. The first of these occurs

---

[1] See e.g. Xenophon *Mem.* 4.4.10.

[2] See e.g. Kahn, *Plato and the Socratic Dialogue*, pp. 88-95; Burnet, *Plato's Euthyphro, Apology of Socrates, and Crito*, pp. 63-64. Note that, in theory, the same argument also applies to Xenophon's *Apology*. However, whereas Plato is generally agreed to have been present at the trial, Xenophon's *Apology* is based upon a second-hand account from Hermogenes (although Hackforth, *The Composition of Plato's Apology*, pp. 8-46, suggests that in fact Xenophon's may have been written first). For further discussion and references see Additional Note 1.

[3] For some doubts about this approach see Morrison, 'On the Alleged Historical Reliability of Plato's *Apology*'. He argues against treating the *Apology* as a straightforward historical report of the trial. Although he is no doubt correct to be cautious here, nevertheless the *Apology* remains the best point of departure for a reconstruction of the historical Socrates (see Additional Note 1).

[4] This point is emphasized by Brickhouse & Smith, *Plato's Socrates*, pp. 12-14. Other ancient sources which make this point include Cicero *Tusc. Disp.* 3.8 (not in *SSR*), 5.10

when Socrates introduces his philosophical mission, to which he believes he has been appointed by God. He characterizes this mission as the duty to live as a philosopher (φιλοσοφοῦντά με δεῖν ζῆν), examining himself and others.[5] The second appears when Socrates expands upon what examining himself and others might involve. There he is explicit that he wants to examine lives rather than, say, beliefs or arguments:

> You have brought about my death in the belief that through it you will be delivered from submitting the conduct of your lives (τοῦ βίου) to criticism.[6]

This notion of a project concerned with examining lives is reiterated in a third passage where Socrates suggests that the best thing that anyone can do is to examine oneself and others. In contrast to this he adds that a life (βίος) without this sort of examination is not worth living.[7]

In the *Apology*, then, Socrates' philosophical concerns are clearly directed towards βίος; his concern is to examine his own life, to transform it into a philosophical way of life, and to exhort others to examine and transform their lives. Despite this, Socrates is often presented as being primarily concerned with the search for definitions and preoccupied with questions of the form 'what is *x*?'. This portrait owes much to the testimony of Aristotle who, in his brief history of philosophy in Book One the *Metaphysics*, presents Socrates as one of the first to turn away from the study of nature towards ethics, and who in his ethical studies is primarily concerned with universals and definitions.[8] Aristotle's testimony is important insofar as it attributes the search for definitions to Socrates but goes on to attribute the theory of Forms to Plato, laying the foundation for the division of the Platonic dialogues into earlier and later periods.[9] However it also forms the basis for the image of what has come to be known as 'Socratic intellectualism', namely the idea that Socrates placed total emphasis upon intellectual knowledge in his ethics.[10] Aristotle tends to present

---

(= *SSR* I C 458), *Acad.* 1.15 (= *SSR* I C 448), Seneca *Epist.* 71.7 (= *SSR* I C 537). Of course, Socrates *is* interested in argument, definition, and rational understanding, but only insofar as they contribute to his understanding of how to live.

[5] See Plato *Apol.* 28e.

[6] Plato *Apol.* 39c (trans. Tredennick).

[7] See Plato *Apol.* 38a.

[8] See Aristotle *Metaph.* 987b1-4 (= *SSR* I B 24).

[9] See Aristotle *Metaph.* 1078b17 (= *SSR* I B 26), 1086a37 (= *SSR* I B 25). Aristotle's Socratic *testimonia* are collected in *SSR* I B 1-40 and, with commentary, in Deman, *Le témoignage d'Aristote sur Socrate*. For discussions of Aristotle as a source for Socrates see Gulley, *The Philosophy of Socrates*, pp. 1-8; Guthrie, *History*, vol. 3, pp. 355-59; Kahn, *Plato and the Socratic Dialogue*, pp. 79-87; Lacey, 'Our Knowledge of Socrates', pp. 44-48; Vlastos, *Socrates: Ironist and Moral Philosopher*, pp. 91-98. It has been suggested that when Aristotle prefixes the article to the name 'Socrates' (i.e. ὁ Σωκράτης) he refers to Plato's literary character but when he does not he is referring to the historical Socrates (see e.g. Grant, *The Ethics of Aristotle*, vol. 2, p. 188; Ross, *Aristotle's Metaphysics*, vol. 1, pp. xxxix-xli; with some doubts in Taylor, *Varia Socratica*, pp. 40-90).

[10] For discussion see Nehamas, 'Socratic Intellectualism'.

Socrates as primarily concerned with definition (ὁρισμός) and knowledge (ἐπιστήμη), both being instances of rational discourse (λόγος).[11] This no doubt reflects Aristotle's own philosophical concerns and in particular his interest in logic. Yet it is made explicit throughout the *Apology* that Socrates' search for knowledge (ἐπιστήμη) and his cross-examination of those who claim to have knowledge remains subordinate to his primary concern, namely βίος.[12] His search for a definition (ὁρισμός) or rational account (λόγος) of what is good remains subordinate to the desire to become good, to transform his way of life. The philosophical question that drives his search is the personal question of how he himself should live and the more general question of how one should live. The centrality of this theme is made explicit elsewhere:

> For you see the subject of our discussion – and on what subject should even a man of slight intelligence be more serious? – is nothing less that how a man should live (ὄντινα χρὴ τρόπον ζῆν).[13]

This is clearly very different from Aristotle's presentation of the nature and function of philosophy in the *Metaphysics*, where philosophical or theoretical knowledge is contrasted with practical disciplines and presented as the search for knowledge of principles and causes.[14] In certain respects this is a definition of what today would be called science.[15] Although Aristotle would no doubt acknowledge that the possession of such knowledge would impact upon the way in which the individual concerned lived, there is a clear difference in priorities. For Aristotle, philosophers search for this knowledge and this happens to impact upon their way of life; for Socrates, philosophers search for knowledge *in order* to transform their way of life.[16] For Socrates the primary function of philosophy is this transformation of one's βίος, and

---

[11] See e.g. Aristotle *Metaph.* 987b1-6 (= *SSR* I B 24), *Eth. Nic.* 1144b28-30 (= *SSR* I B 30).

[12] See e.g. Plato *Apol.* 21c-22e, with Gulley, *The Philosophy of Socrates*, pp. 12-13.

[13] Plato *Gorg.* 500c (trans. Woodhead, in Hamilton & Cairns, modified).

[14] See Aristotle *Metaph.* 1.1, esp. 981a30-981b6 & 982a1-3. Note also 993b19-21: 'philosophy should be called knowledge of the truth, for the end of theoretical knowledge is truth (ἀλήθεια), and not action (ἔργον)'.

[15] See e.g. the anecdote concerning Thales' business success based upon a prediction of a forthcoming harvest, in *Pol.* 1259a5-18. This, Aristotle suggests, shows that *philosophers* can be wealthy if they choose. But the sort of knowledge displayed in the anecdote would today be called scientific.

[16] Of course, Aristotle does address 'practical' issues in his ethical and political works, and his division of knowledge into the practical (πρακτική), productive (ποιητική), and theoretical (θεωρητική) at *Metaph.* 1025b24-28 does not appear to prioritize one form of knowledge over any other. However, under the heading of 'theoretical knowledge' falls first philosophy (πρώτη φιλοσοφία) or theology (θεολογική), which is accorded a priority over all other branches of enquiry because it deals with that which is unmoving and eternal. Knowledge of this sort forms the paradigm for Aristotle's conception of philosophy. Indeed, he says further on that the theoretical sciences are superior to the other sciences, and that 'first philosophy' is superior to the other theoretical sciences (*Metaph.* 1026a22-23). See Guthrie, *History*, vol. 6, pp. 130-34.

the search for knowledge (ἐπιστήμη) in the form of definitions (ὅρισμοι) and rational accounts (λόγοι) remains subordinate to this practical goal. As such one might hope that a Socratic account of the nature of philosophy would offer a framework within which it would be possible to deal adequately with questions concerning the relationship between philosophy and biography. Although no explicit account survives (if one ever existed), it may be possible to reconstruct an outline of such an account from those Socratic sources which have survived. In the next three sections I shall attempt to do just this. Then, in the light of this, I shall return to Aristotle's presentation of Socrates in order to bring the Socratic conception of philosophy into sharper focus.

2. Care of Oneself in the *Apology* and *Alcibiades I*

Our first step towards understanding the concept of an art of living (τέχνη περὶ τὸν βίον) is to consider how Socrates conceived his philosophical project which, as we have just seen, is primarily concerned with life (βίος). In the *Apology* Socrates develops what he means by a philosophical project concerned with examining his life and the lives of others:

> Are you not ashamed that you give your attention (ἐπιμελούμενος) to acquiring as much money as possible, and similarly with reputation and honour, and give no attention (οὐκ ἐπιμελῇ) or thought to truth and understanding and the perfection of your soul (ψυχῆς)?[17]

He continues by saying that he will examine and interrogate everyone he meets with these words, reproving anyone who gives all of his attention to trivialities and neglects what is of the uppermost importance. He again summarizes his exhortation to all he meets:

> For I spend all my time going about trying to persuade you, young and old, to make your first and chief concern (ἐπιμελεῖσθαι) not for your bodies or for your possessions, but for the highest welfare of your souls (ψυχῆς).[18]

Socrates' project of examining himself and others may be characterized as a project that is concerned with taking care of one's soul (ἐπιμελεῖσθαι τῆς ψυχῆς).[19] Unfortunately this idea is not developed in any great detail in the *Apology*. However,

---

[17] Plato *Apol.* 29d-e (trans. Tredennick).

[18] Plato *Apol.* 30a-b (trans. Tredennick).

[19] In his commentary on the *Apology*, Burnet characterizes this as the fundamental doctrine of Socrates (pp. 123, 124, 171). Similarly, Strycker calls it a 'quintessentially Socratic expression' (*Plato's Apology of Socrates*, p. 333) and Hackforth suggests that it 'sums up the whole of Socrates' activity' ('Socrates', p. 5). This phrase also appears in Socratic *testimonia* beyond Plato, including Xenophon *Mem.* 1.2.4 and Stobaeus 2.31.79 (2.215.8-10 WH = *SSR* I C 193), and it is also used by Isocrates in *Antidosis* 304, *Ad Demonicum* 6, and *In Sophistas* 8.

it is developed elsewhere and its presence in the *Apology*, in albeit embryonic form, gives some ground for approaching these other accounts as, broadly speaking, Socratic.

In *Alcibiades I* Socrates uses a similar phrase, 'to take care of oneself' (ἐπιμελεῖσθαι ἑαυτοῦ),[20] and expands upon exactly what this might involve.[21] He begins his explanation of what it might mean to take care of oneself by drawing a distinction between taking care of oneself and taking care of what belongs to oneself. In order to illustrate this distinction he contrasts taking care of one's shoes and taking care of one's feet. The art (τέχνη) of taking care of one's shoes is clearly shoemaking he suggests.[22] However, no matter how important shoes might be for one's feet, one can hardly say that shoemaking is itself the art (τέχνη) of taking care of one's feet. Socrates and Alcibiades identify gymnastics (γυμναστική) as the appropriate art for taking care of feet, gymnastics understood in the broadest sense of taking care of the body as a whole. Thus, they conclude that the art of taking care of those things

---

[20] See Plato *Alc. I* 127e. In the course of the dialogue (130a-c) Socrates identifies the individual (ἄνθρωπος) with the soul (ψυχή). Thus it seems reasonable, following Burnet (pp. 123, 154), to equate these two phrases. Despite its presence in the *Apology*, Kahn (*Plato and the Socratic Dialogue*, p. 90) suggests that ἐπιμελεῖσθαι τῆς ψυχῆς is Plato's preferred formulation, citing the presence of ἐπιμελεῖσθαι ἑαυτοῦ in a fragment from Aeschines' *Alcibiades* (fr. 8 Dittmar *apud* Aristides *De Quattuor* 348 (412.17 Lenz & Behr) = *SSR* VI A 50), presumably with the intention of implying that this formulation is more likely to have been Socrates' own. A third phrase – ἐπιμελεῖσθαι ἀρετῆς – also appears in the *Apology* (31b, 41e); Burnet (pp. 127, 171) and Strycker (pp. 331-32) take it to be synonymous with the other two.

[21] See in particular Plato *Alc. I* 128a-129a. Following Schleiermacher, *Introductions to the Dialogues of Plato*, pp. 328-36, a number of mainly German scholars have disputed the authorship of *Alcibiades I*. However it does not appear to have been doubted in antiquity (see e.g. Diogenes Laertius 3.51) and recently a number of mainly French scholars have argued for its authenticity (see e.g. Croiset (CUF), vol. 1, pp. 49-53). Those who doubt its authenticity tend, in general, to attribute it to a member of the Academy and date its composition to *c.* 340 BC (see e.g. Bluck, 'The Origin of the *Greater Alcibiades*'). However, recent statistical analysis appears to confirm its authenticity (see Young, 'Plato and Computer Dating', p. 238). Its authenticity is not essential to my argument (although a relatively early date of composition may be) and I draw upon it as a source for Socrates insofar as it repeats and develops ideas present in the *Apology*. Indeed, Burnet described it as 'a sort of introduction to Socratic philosophy for beginners' (cited in Guthrie, *History*, vol. 3, p. 470). If not by Plato, it may conceivably be by one of the other Socratic authors to whom an *Alcibiades* is credited, including Antisthenes, Euclides, and Phaedo (see Diogenes Laertius 6.18 (= fr. 1 DC = *SSR* V A 41), 2.108 (= *SSR* II A 10), and *Suidae Lexicon s.v.* Φαίδων (Φ 154 = *SSR* III A 8) respectively). For further discussion see Denyer, *Plato, Alcibiades*, pp. 14-26.

[22] Of the various examples of τέχναι used by Socrates, shoemaking is particularly common. See e.g. Plato *Prot.* 319d, *Gorg.* 447d, *Resp.* 333a, 397e, 443c, *Theaet.* 146d, Xenophon *Mem.* 4.2.22. That Socrates constantly used the example of a shoemaker is stated explicitly by Callicles in *Gorg.* 491a and Alcibiades in *Symp.* 221e. This may owe something to the somewhat shadowy figure of Simon the Shoemaker, an associate of Socrates with whom Socrates is said to have spent considerable time conversing and who is credited with being the first to make written records of Socrates' conversations.

important for one's feet – one's shoes – is clearly distinct from the art of taking care of one's feet themselves.

Socrates takes this argument and applies it to an individual as a whole. Just as there are two distinct arts (τέχναι) in the cases of taking care of one's feet and what is important for one's feet, so there are two distinct arts in the case of oneself and what is important for oneself. In other words, the arts that take care of the sorts of things usually held to be important for an individual – possessions, wealth, reputation – are in fact distinct from, and irrelevant to, the art of taking care of oneself. Although both Socrates and Alcibiades say that they do not know what this art might be, they both agree that before one can begin to care for oneself one must first know oneself; for just as the art of shoemaking requires knowledge about shoes and the art of moneymaking requires knowledge about money, so the art of taking care of oneself requires self-knowledge. Socrates concludes by suggesting that the first step towards taking care of oneself must be to follow the famous inscription at Delphi that proclaims 'know thyself' (γνῶθι σαυτόν).[23]

There are two points in this passage from *Alcibiades I* that deserve further comment. The first is the characterization of taking care of oneself in very general terms as an art or craft (τέχνη).[24] Although in the following passage from the *Apology* the word τέχνη is not used, nevertheless one can see the same theme being developed:

> Take the case of horses; do you believe that those who improve them make up the whole of mankind, and that there is only one person who has a bad effect on them? Or is the truth just the opposite, that the ability to improve them belongs to one person or to very few persons, who are horse trainers [...]?[25]

The reason why horse trainers have the ability to improve horses is that they possess the art (τέχνη) of horse training. Just as one would not entrust the welfare of one's horse to just anyone, so Socrates suggests that one should not entrust the welfare of one's soul (ψυχή) to just anyone.[26] Yet it is of course far from clear who in fact possesses the art (τέχνη) of caring for souls. This general characterization of caring for oneself as an art or craft (τέχνη) suggests that – like other arts or crafts – it is an activity guided by knowledge (ἐπιστήμη) of its subject matter, that it is something that can be taught and learned, that an expert will be able to give an explanation or rational account (λόγος) of what he is doing, and that proficiency will require a

---

[23] See Plato *Alc. I* 124a, 129a. Note also Aristotle fr. 1 Rose³ *apud* Plutarch *Adv. Colot.* 1118c (= *SSR* I B 11, I C 502): according to Aristotle this Delphic inscription formed the inspiration for Socrates' philosophizing.

[24] See Plato *Alc. I* 128d.

[25] Plato *Apol.* 25a-b (trans. Tredennick); see also Xenophon *Apol.* 20.

[26] See e.g. Plato *Crito* 47a-d, *Laches* 184e-185a, Xenophon *Apol.* 20, *Mem.* 3.9.10-11.

certain amount of training and practice (ἄσκησις).[27] However, exactly how Socrates understands the relationship between these components is not yet clear and is something to which we shall return.

The second point worthy of note in the *Alcibiades I* passage is that, within the context of this general characterization of taking care of oneself as an art (τέχνη), Socrates draws a parallel between the art of taking care of oneself – one's soul (ψυχή) – and the art that takes care of one's body which, as we have seen, he calls gymnastics (γυμναστική).[28] Socrates suggests that the art of taking care of oneself benefits the soul (ψυχή) in a manner analogous to the way in which gymnastics benefits the body. In particular, he wants to suggest that the care of the soul is at least as important, if not more so, than care of the body, despite the fact that the former is rarely practised.[29]

So far we have seen that for Socrates philosophy is something concerned with one's way of life (βίος), that it does this by examining and taking care of one's soul (ψυχή) in a manner analogous to the way in which one might take care of one's body, and that this process can be characterized as an art, craft, or skill (τέχνη). We have also seen that knowledge (ἐπιστήμη) of this art or craft will involve being able to give an account of the rational principles (λόγοι) which underpin it. However, it is not yet clear exactly how this notion of an art (τέχνη) concerned with the soul is to be understood.

3. The Analysis of τέχνη in the *Gorgias*

The most detailed analysis of the concept of τέχνη made by Plato's Socrates can be found in a passage from the *Gorgias*.[30] The intention in this passage is to show that

---

[27] For further discussion see Brickhouse & Smith, *Plato's Socrates*, pp. 5-7; Reeve, *Socrates in the Apology*, pp. 37-45. For a survey of the various meanings of τέχνη before Socrates and Plato see Roochnik, *Of Art and Wisdom*, pp. 17-88.

[28] Elsewhere, Plato's Socrates draws a similar parallel between γυμναστική as that which is concerned with the body and μουσική as that which is concerned with the soul (see Plato *Resp.* 376e). One might understand μουσική as a specific type of τέχνη, in particular one presided over by the Muses, an example of which would be poetry (see LSJ). In the *Phaedo* Socrates is made to say that he had a dream in which he was told to practise μουσική (see Plato *Phaedo* 60e) and he continues by describing philosophy as the greatest of such arts (see 61a: ὡς φιλοσοφίας μὲν οὔσης μεγίστης μουσικῆς).

[29] See e.g. Plato *Crito* 47c-48a, *Prot.* 313a-c, *Gorg.* 512a.

[30] For the *Gorgias* I have used the edition by Dodds alongside Burnet (OCT), plus the translation with commentary by Irwin. I have also used the commentary by Olympiodorus and Galen's *Thrasybulus* (5.806-898 Kühn) which comments directly on the *Gorgias* and deals with a number of similar issues. Other Platonic dialogues that use what has come to be known as 'the τέχνη analogy' include the *Laches*, *Charmides*, *Euthyphro*, *Euthydemus*, and *Protagoras*. Roochnik supplies a complete list of occurrences of τέχνη in the early dialogues; see his *Of Art and Wisdom*, pp. 253-64.

rhetoric is not a proper art.[31] The extent to which this analysis is Socratic or Platonic may be open to dispute.[32] Nevertheless it deserves our attention here insofar as it develops a theme already present in the *Apology*. However, it is important to remember that our concern here is not with Plato's objectives in the dialogue as a whole but simply with his analysis of this Socratic concept.

In the *Gorgias* Socrates draws a distinction between the body and the soul and suggests that there is a good condition (εὐεξία) for each of them.[33] He goes on to suggest that there are two arts (τέχναι) relating to each of these. The arts which deal with the soul Socrates calls 'politics' (πολιτική).[34] Although he cannot think of an appropriate unifying term, the two arts dealing with the body are gymnastics (γυμναστική) and medicine (ἰατρική).[35] Socrates suggests that politics may be divided into two arts corresponding to these two physical arts, namely legislation (νομοθετική) and justice (δικαιοσύνη). There are, then, a total of four arts 'taking care of either body or soul, aiming at the best (ἀεὶ πρὸς τὸ βέλτιστον)'.[36]

To these four genuine arts Socrates contrasts four pseudo arts – cookery, rhetoric, cosmetics, and sophistry – his intention being to show that rhetoric is not a genuine art but merely a knack or routine (ἐμπειρία καὶ τριβή).[37] Although the credit for this detailed and highly structured analysis of the four arts and their spurious counterparts

---

[31] As Roochnik notes ('Socrates' Use of the Techne-Analogy', pp. 194-95), the τέχνη analogy is primarily used by Plato in the early dialogues as a method of refutation against claims to knowledge rather than as the basis for a positive moral theory.

[32] See in particular the discussion in Cooper, 'Socrates and Plato in Plato's *Gorgias*', pp. 31-32, who argues that the 'Socrates' of this dialogue cannot straightforwardly be taken as merely Plato's mouthpiece.

[33] See Plato *Gorg.* 463a-466a, esp. 464a; also Olympiodorus *In Gorg.* 13.1-2; Santas, *Socrates*, pp. 286-303. For an etymological gloss on εὐεξία (εὐ prefix plus ἕξις) see Galen *Thras.* 12 (5.826 Kühn).

[34] In their translation of Olympiodorus *In Gorg.* 13.2, Jackson, Lycos, & Tarrant suggest 'constitutional'.

[35] Galen offers 'therapeutic art' (θεραπευτική τέχνη) as a unifying term for these two arts concerned with the body; see Galen *Thras.* 35 (5.873 Kühn).

[36] Plato *Gorg.* 464c. This may be illustrated by means of a table (with Dodds, p. 226):

		gymnastics (γυμναστική)	–	preservation
	of the body (θεραπευτική)			
		medicine (ἰατρική)	–	restoration
arts (τέχναι)				
		legislation (νομοθετική)	–	preservation
	of the soul (πολιτική)			
		justice (δικαιοσύνη)	–	restoration

[37] Plato *Gorg.* 463b. In his commentary, Dodds suggests 'an empirical knack' (p. 225). At 463d Socrates also characterizes rhetoric as an image (εἴδωλον) of the corresponding part of politics.

should probably go to Plato,[38] the basic distinction between arts of the soul and arts of the body remains in the spirit of Socrates' definition of his philosophical project in the *Apology*, namely taking care of one's soul (ἐπιμελεῖσθαι τῆς ψυχῆς).

The distinction that Socrates draws between the four genuine arts and their spurious counterparts adds much to his conception of the arts concerned with the soul. While the pseudo-arts tend to aim at pleasure, Socrates says that the genuine arts aim at what is best (τὸ βέλτιστον).[39] This is important insofar as the best condition may not always be the most pleasant. Moreover, the pseudo-arts are presented as the product of 'trial and error' empiricism rather than the expression of a real understanding of the task at hand. A genuine art, on the other hand, will always involve and proceed according to a rational account (λόγος).[40] An individual skilled in a particular art will always be able to offer an explanation of what it is that they are doing and why it is effective. This is what makes an art something that can be taught and learned.

Within the four genuine arts, Socrates says that as gymnastics (γυμναστική) is to the body so legislation (νομοθετική) is to the soul, and as medicine (ἰατρική) is to the body so justice (δικαιοσύνη) is to the soul. While gymnastics aims at the *preservation* of the good of the body, medicine aims at the *restoration* of the good of the body. Likewise, legislation *preserves* the good of the soul, while justice *restores* the good of the soul.[41] The analogy between gymnastics and the art of caring for the soul has already been mentioned. This new analogy with medicine helps to develop Socrates' project further.[42] It suggests that the art of taking care of the soul will benefit the soul in a manner similar to the way in which medicine benefits the body. Both are directed towards the cultivation or restoration of health, that is, a good state (εὐεξία) appropriate to each.[43] As examples of τέχναι, both will proceed according to a rational account (λόγος) and will be practised by experts who are able to explain and teach their art to others. Just like a doctor, someone who is skilled in the art of

---

[38] See Dodds' commentary, p. 226: This 'is an early example of that interest in systematic classification which is so prominent in *Sophist* and *Politicus* [...] which is certainly, however, a Platonic and not a Socratic invention'.

[39] For discussion of the ambiguity of 'best' (τὸ βέλτιστον) see Irwin's commentary, p. 134.

[40] See Plato *Gorg.* 465a: 'And I say it is not a craft (τέχνην), but a knack (ἐμπειρίαν), because it has no rational account (λόγον) by which it applies the things it applies'. However, as Aristotle notes in *Metaph.* 981a1-3, a τέχνη can often be the product of ἐμπειρία, that is, learned by trial and error. Thus the key characteristic of a τέχνη is the presence of a rational account (λόγος). For further discussion see Dodds, pp. 228-29. See also Olympiodorus *In Gorg.* 12.1-2, for the importance of a rational account, and 3.2, for the role of experience in learning a craft.

[41] See Olympiodorus *In Gorg.* 13.1-2.

[42] That this analogy may also be attributed to Socrates is given weight by its presence throughout Xenophon; see e.g. *Mem.* 1.2.51, 1.2.54, 2.4.3, 2.10.2, 3.1.4. Note also Democritus fr. 31 DK, with comment in Pigeaud, *La maladie de l'âme*, pp. 17-19.

[43] Note that Galen suggests that it is necessary to draw a distinction between 'health' (ὑγιεία) and a 'good state' (εὐεξία), defining 'health' as a certain state and a 'good state' as excellence within that state; see Galen *Thras.* 12 (5.825 Kühn). However nothing much hangs on this here.

taking care of the soul will focus upon what will bring genuine good rather than short-term pleasure. More importantly, both of these arts are practical; as with the advice of a doctor, the words of someone skilled in the art of taking care of the soul will be of little value unless they are put into practice.[44] Finally, unlike many of the other examples of τέχναι, medicine involves a substantial body of theoretical knowledge and the use of this example serves to emphasize the essential role of λόγος. Although this medical analogy is only made explicit in the *Gorgias*, it is already hinted at in *Alcibiades I* where Socrates moves between the words ἐπιμέλεια and θεραπεία.[45] One might say that just as medicine cures the body, so the art of taking care of the soul functions as a form of therapy for the soul and is directed towards what one might call mental health, analogous to physical health.

This analogy with medicine, supplementing the analogy with gymnastics, fits into the scheme laid out in the *Gorgias* only because the art of taking care of oneself is divided into two distinct arts under the common heading of politics (πολιτική). Although, as we have seen, both of these analogies can be found in *Alcibiades I*, it seems reasonable to suggest that the systematic account in the *Gorgias* should be credited to Plato rather than Socrates. In both the *Apology* and *Alcibiades I* the art of taking care of oneself is presented as a unified activity that is primarily a personal affair, a task that each individual must undertake for themselves. Thus, although the account in the *Gorgias* is a useful supplement to the *Apology* and *Alcibiades I*, its use of terminology such as legislation (νομοθετική), justice (δικαιοσύνη), and politics (πολιτική), may be seen to suggest the beginning of something quite different from Socrates' essentially private and personal philosophical project.[46]

4. Different Types of τέχνη

So far we have encountered a number of different examples of arts or crafts (τέχναι) used in connection with the idea of an art (τέχνη) concerned with taking care of one's soul (ψυχή). Before continuing with the *Gorgias* it may be appropriate to consider the precise nature of these different τέχναι and to see what, if anything, this may contribute to our understanding of Socrates' project.

As we have seen, in *Alcibiades I* the analogy was made between the art that takes care of one's soul and the art that takes care of one's feet. This latter art was specified

---

[44] Aristotle makes a similar point in *Eth. Nic.* 1105b12-18. For discussion see Jaeger, 'Aristotle's Use of Medicine as Model of Method in his Ethics', pp. 54-61.

[45] See Plato *Alc. I* 131b. Note also *Laches* 185e: 'What we have to consider is whether one of us is skilled in the therapy of the soul (τεχνικὸς περὶ ψυχῆς θεραπείαν)'.

[46] In the *Apology* Socrates is of course concerned with provoking others to take care of themselves and thus there is some sort of social dimension to his project. However, once provoked, it is a task that they must undertake for themselves. It is unclear how public legislation could play a part in what he has in mind (see e.g. Reeve, *Socrates in the Apology*, pp. 155-60). His repeated use of the τέχνη analogy in discussions of political leadership (in both Plato and Xenophon) serves primarily to refute the claims of others to expertise in politics rather than forming the basis for any positive theory of a political τέχνη (see the next note).

as gymnastics. In the *Gorgias* both gymnastics and medicine were used. Elsewhere in the Platonic dialogues a whole range of examples of τέχναι are used – building, weaving, shoemaking, flute playing, fishing, hunting, mathematics, navigation – although, in general, these are used to test claims to expert knowledge made by others rather than as direct analogies with the art that takes care of one's soul.[47] Nevertheless it may be instructive to consider briefly the nature of these various τέχναι and the ways in which they can be seen to differ from one another.

The first and most obvious type of τέχνη that can be distinguished may be called *productive* (ποιητική).[48] This type of τέχνη has a product that can clearly be distinguished from its practice. Thus the art of shoemaking has a product – shoes – distinct from the activity of practising the art itself. Moreover, success in the art of shoemaking can easily be assessed with reference to that product; the excellent shoemaker is one who makes excellent shoes. It has been suggested that this type of τέχνη captures the original meaning of the word.[49] Moreover it has sometimes been assumed that this is in some sense the primary or fundamental meaning of τέχνη and consequently it has been argued that any τέχνη must ultimately conform to this model and thus must have a product distinct from its practice.[50] It is this essentially productive conception of τέχνη that Aristotle holds.[51]

---

[47] Roochnik, 'Socrates' Use of the Techne-Analogy', p. 194, draws attention to the primary uses of the τέχνη analogy in the early dialogues, namely for refutation or exhortation, but not for the construction of a positive technical conception of ἀρετή, *contra* Irwin, *Plato's Moral Theory*, p. 7. Roochnik's argument that Plato rejected the τέχνη analogy is developed at length in his *Of Art and Wisdom*. He suggests that the fact that a number of the early dialogues fail to produce adequate definitions of the virtues that they consider indicates that τέχνη is not a good model for such knowledge (p. 89). But this could simply be due to the fact that none of the characters – Socrates included – possess the expertise necessary for one of them to be able to supply such a definition. It does not mean that a definition could never be supplied. These failures could simply be read as indications of the rarity of such knowledge. However, the debate concerning Plato's use of the τέχνη analogy is not directly relevant here as our primary concern is with Socrates rather than Plato.

[48] For examples of this sort of τέχνη see e.g. Plato *Charm.* 165d. For the phrase ποιητική τέχνη see Galen *Thras.* 12 (5.826 Kühn), 27 (5.854 Kühn), 30 (5.861 Kühn), Simplicius *In Phys.* 303.10-11.

[49] See Roochnik, *Of Art and Wisdom*, pp. 18-26, who reports that the original pre-Homeric meaning would have been the production of something specifically from wood, but notes that already in Homer the range of meanings had expanded to include non-productive activities such as singing and medicine.

[50] See e.g. Irwin, *Plato's Moral Theory*, pp. 73-74, with criticism in Nussbaum, *The Fragility of Goodness*, p. 97; Roochnik, *Of Art and Wisdom*, p. 5. This leads Irwin into his 'instrumentalist' interpretation of Plato, in which happiness (εὐδαιμονία) is specified as the product of the art (τέχνη) of human excellence (ἀρετή) which becomes merely a means to this end.

[51] See Aristotle *Eth. Nic.* 1140a1-23 and in particular 1140a17: 'art (τέχνην) must be a matter of making (ποιήσεως), not of acting (οὐ πράξεως)'. On the basis of this he claims at 1140b1-2 that practical wisdom (φρόνησις) cannot be an art.

A second type of τέχνη can be seen in the case of fishing and this type may be called *acquisitive* (κτητική).[52] Although this sort of art does not construct anything in the way that a productive art does, nevertheless in some sense it has a 'product' distinct from its practice by which mastery of the art may be assessed. Thus the excellent fisherman is one who returns home with a basket full of fish and consequently his mastery of the art can be seen by all.

A third type of τέχνη is exemplified by dancing and may be called *performative* (πρακτική).[53] For arts such as these there is no material product distinct from the practice of the art itself.[54] Success in this sort of art must therefore be judged with reference to a correct performance. Plato refers to this sort of art when he distinguishes between the arts of making harps and playing harps, the latter being an art of 'use'.[55] In one ancient source, examples of arts such as flute playing and harp playing are used to characterize what Aristotle calls practical knowledge (ἐπιστήμη πρακτική), which he will say has as its goal action (ἔργον).[56] Note that the way in which the word ἔργον can refer to both products and actions may undercut any attempt to impose a rigid division between productive and performative arts.

A fourth type of τέχνη can be seen in the examples of mathematics and geometry. These arts may be called *theoretical* (θεωρητική).[57] Their precise nature is more difficult to discern. They could possibly be classified as productive (producing results), acquisitive (uncovering results),[58] or performative (primarily characterized by the correct application of procedures). However, Plato often distinguishes these sorts of arts from all of the others mentioned so far.[59] An alternative way to characterize them might be as *contemplative*. Indeed, this type of art is often understood as a correlate to Aristotle's conception of theoretical knowledge (ἐπιστήμη θεωρητική) which he distinguishes from the practical (πρακτική) and the productive (ποιητική).[60] However, these Aristotle calls types of ἐπιστήμη, and not types of τέχνη, a term which, as we have already noted, he limits to the productive τέχναι.

---

[52] For examples see e.g. Plato *Euthyd.* 290b-c. For the phrase κτητική τέχνη see e.g. Plato *Soph.* 223c, Galen *Thras.* 30 (5.861 Kühn).
[53] Alternatively, *active*. For examples see e.g. Plato *Meno* 90d-e, *Laches* 194e. For the phrase πρακτική τέχνη see e.g. Galen *Thras.* 27 (5.856 Kühn), 30 (5.861 Kühn), Eustratius *In Eth. Nic.* 58.24, 59.2.
[54] Irwin, *Plato's Moral Theory*, pp. 73-74, insists that even these arts must have a distinct 'product' (ἔργον); dancing produces movements, flute playing produces music, etc. These are of course actions rather than distinct material products, highlighting the range of the word ἔργον.
[55] See Plato *Euthyd.* 289b-c.
[56] See Diogenes Laertius 3.84 (but note also 3.100) and Aristotle *Metaph.* 993b20-21 respectively.
[57] For examples see e.g. Plato *Charm.* 165e-166a, *Gorg.* 450d. For the phrase θεωρητική τέχνη see e.g. Alexander of Aphrodisias *In Metaph.* 142.7-8, Sextus Empiricus *Adv. Math.* 2.5, 8.291.
[58] See e.g. Plato *Euthyd.* 290b-c, *Soph.* 219c.
[59] See e.g. Plato *Charm.* 165e, *Gorg.* 450d-e.
[60] See Aristotle *Metaph.* 1025b3-1026a32, Roochnik, *Of Art and Wisdom*, p. 271. Note also Diogenes Laertius 3.84 where Aristotle's threefold division of ἐπιστήμη is attributed to Plato,

A fifth type of τέχνη can be seen in medicine and navigation. These are arts that aim (στοχάζομαι) at a distinct goal (τέλος) – in the case of medicine, health – but in which the excellent practitioner does not always achieve that goal. These may be called *stochastic* (στοχαστική) arts.[61] One might say that the 'product' (ἔργον) of the art of medicine is health but that – unlike the excellent shoemaker – the excellent doctor does not always manage to produce this product.[62] In other words, excellent practice does not guarantee that one will always achieve the goal. This is due to the role played by external factors outside of the control of the practitioner.[63] In these sorts of arts a problem can be seen to arise when it comes to assessing an individual's expertise. One response to this would be to suggest that if a practitioner of a stochastic art 'omits none of the available means' (ἐὰν τῶν ἐνδεχομένων μηδὲν παραλίπῃ) then one can reasonably claim that he has an adequate grasp of the art in question.[64] So, for example, an expert doctor might be defined as one who does everything in his power to save his patient. However, this implies that only other practitioners of the art in question will be able to make such an assessment, for only they will be familiar with all of the means available.

As we can see, it is possible to distinguish between a number of different types of τέχνη and, in order to understand Socrates' concept of an art concerned with taking care of one's soul, it will be necessary to consider which type of art he may have had in mind. However, we must remember that the examples mentioned above derive from the Platonic dialogues where in a number of different passages Plato distinguishes between two or three of these types of τέχνη for his own philosophical ends.[65] It would be rash to assume that this analysis can straightforwardly be applied to Socrates' understanding of the term τέχνη.

---

but using examples of arts, including shipbuilding for the productive, flute playing for the practical, and geometry for the theoretical.

[61] See e.g. Aristotle *Top.* 101b5-10, *Rhet.* 1355b12-14. In these passages Aristotle does not use the phrase στοχαστική τέχνη but his commentator Alexander of Aphrodisias does; see e.g. *In Top.* 32.12-34.5, *In An. Pr.* 39.30-40.5, 165.8-15, *Quaest.* 61.1-28. See also Ps.-Galen *Opt. Sect.* 4 (1.112-115 Kühn). Alexander's account of stochastic arts will be discussed in Chapter 3 § 4.

[62] In *Charm.* 165c-d Plato characterizes health as the 'product' (ἔργον) of medicine alongside houses as the product of building without noting any difference in nature between the two arts. The precise relationship between goal (τέλος) and product or function (ἔργον) in stochastic arts will be discussed further in Chapter 3 § 4.

[63] See the discussion of such factors in an argument defending medicine's status as a τέχνη in Hippocrates *De Arte* 8. It is the role that these external factors play, and not any lack of precision with regard to its subject matter, that defines a stochastic art and leads to the distinction between goal (τέλος) and function (ἔργον). Roochnik is occasionally unclear about this; compare *Of Art and Wisdom*, pp. 52 & 55.

[64] See Aristotle *Top.* 101b9-10.

[65] All of the appropriate passages are outlined in Roochnik, *Of Art and Wisdom*, pp. 271-82. As he notes, Plato's primary division is between the productive and the theoretical, but these are often subdivided.

In the *Apology* Socrates holds up craftsmen in general as the only examples he can find of individuals possessing secure knowledge.[66] He does not appear to distinguish between different types of craftsmen. Yet as we have seen in *Alcibiades I* and the *Gorgias*, the arts that are explicitly used in relation to the idea of an art of taking care of one's soul are gymnastics (γυμναστική) and medicine (ἰατρική). Both of these arts are presented as being concerned with the health of the body, with preserving or restoring a good state (εὐεξία) for the body. As such, they can both be seen as examples of stochastic arts; they aim at a goal which mastery of the art in question does not necessarily guarantee. To this category one might add the only example of a τέχνη in the *Apology* – horse training – which also aims at a good state (εὐεξία) and in which mastery of the art may not be enough to guarantee success; no matter how good the horse trainer, some horses simply cannot be trained. Another characteristic that these three arts share in common and which does not apply to all stochastic arts (e.g. navigation) is that they focus upon the transformation of the condition or state of the object with which they are concerned. Although one might characterize the health or good state that each of these arts aims at as a 'product', a more appropriate way to consider them might be as an alteration of the condition of an object. As such we might characterize these as not only stochastic but also as *transformative* arts.

Should one understand the art of taking care of one's soul as a *stochastic-transformative* art? This appears to be what is implied by the examples of gymnastics, medicine, and horse training. Yet one will recall that, for Socrates, his conception of an art that takes care of one's soul in some sense guarantees success and happiness (εὐδαιμονία). Just as the master shoemaker knows that he is sure to make good shoes, so Socrates conceives of an art the possession of which will guarantee success in living well. This is clearly very different from the stochastic art of medicine in which the expert doctor, no matter how good he is, will nevertheless occasionally lose a patient due to external factors outside his control. Thus it is tempting to suggest that the key characteristic of the three examples that Socrates would want to extract is not their stochastic nature but rather their transformative function. Indeed, the self-referential nature of the art with which Socrates is concerned appears to rule out interference from external factors.[67] The art of taking care of one's soul is an art directed towards the transformation of the state of the soul into a good state (εὐεξία), developing its excellence (ἀρετή), just as medicine transforms the state of the body into one of health.[68] This, broadly speaking, may be called its 'product'. Yet it is important to note here that this art is not itself human excellence (ἀρετή) but rather an

---

[66] See Plato *Apol.* 22c-d.

[67] This will become a key characteristic later in the hands of Epictetus who will suggest that the only thing with which we should be concerned is that which is totally within our own power and independent of external factors (see e.g. *Ench.* 1.1-3).

[68] By ἀρετή should be understood not merely moral virtue but virtue in the sense of 'that by virtue of which' a thing is good, and thus excellence or goodness in general. An athlete who wins at the Olympics, for instance, is ἀρετή yet this clearly does not mean 'virtuous'. For further comment see Urmson, *The Greek Philosophical Vocabulary*, pp. 30-31; also Nehamas, *The Art of Living*, p. 77, who suggests 'success'.

art that cultivates and takes care of such excellence,[69] just as medicine and gymnastics are not themselves health but rather the arts that cultivate and preserve health. Thus ἀρετή is the *product* of the art for which Socrates searches and not the art itself.[70] For Socrates, then, it appears that human excellence (ἀρετή) is not a technique (τέχνη) but rather a certain excellent state (εὐεξία) of the soul (ψυχή).

As I have already noted, this brief detour from the *Gorgias* has focused upon the different types of τέχνη that appear in Plato's dialogues. It is difficult to know how much, if any, of this can be attributed to Socrates. The analyses of different types of τέχνη that appear in a number of the early dialogues is probably the work of Plato himself and may not owe much at all to Socrates.[71] The central theme that one finds in the *Apology* and elsewhere is Socrates' search for a secure form of knowledge concerned with how one should live. The only examples of any form of secure knowledge that he could find were associated with artisans and craftsmen, and consequently Socrates appears to have taken their model of knowledge as the paradigm in his search without necessarily considering the subtle but important differences between the various examples of such knowledge. This is a topic to which we shall return when we discuss the Stoics in the next chapter. Our primary concern here is to consider the way in which Socrates understood the nature of such τέχναι in general and the way in which he thought such knowledge could be developed.

5. The Role of ἄσκησις

As we saw earlier in the *Gorgias*, central to Socrates' distinction between an art or craft (τέχνη) and a mere knack or routine (ἐμπειρία καὶ τριβή) is the claim that one who is an expert in an art will be able to give a rational account (λόγος) of what he or she is doing.[72] It is this ability that makes an art something that can be taught and learned. Yet what exactly is involved in learning an art? Is it merely a question of

---

[69] Note again the use of ἐπιμελεῖσθαι ἀρετῆς in the *Apology* (31b, 41e) as a synonym for ἐπιμελεῖσθαι ἑαυτοῦ and ἐπιμελεῖσθαι τῆς ψυχῆς (see Burnet, pp. 127, 171, and Strycker, pp. 331-32). The τέχνη for which Socrates searches will take care of his excellence; it is not itself that excellence. In *Euthyd.* 275a it is philosophy (φιλοσοφία) that is identified as that which takes care of excellence (ἀρετῆς ἐπιμελεῖσθαι). Socrates' τέχνη analogy, then, is with philosophy, not with excellence (ἀρετή).

[70] This is based upon my earlier reading of the *Apology* and, in particular, *Alcibiades I*, which develops material in the *Apology*. It is not a claim about the early Platonic dialogues in general. But it is interesting to note that this answers one of the objections made by Vlastos and others to Irwin's instrumentalist reading of Plato (see the summary in Vlastos, *Socrates: Ironist and Moral Philosopher*, pp. 6-10). Rather than ἀρετή being reduced to a means for attaining the 'product' εὐδαιμονία, ἀρετή itself becomes the 'product', identified with εὐδαιμονία (as Vlastos suggests it must be), retaining its status as an end in itself.

[71] This is the line taken by Roochnik in *Of Art and Wisdom*, although he does not directly address questions concerning the historical Socrates.

[72] It is Socrates' own inability to give such an account (λόγος) that forms the basis for his profession of ignorance despite his reputation for wisdom in his actions (ἔργα).

gaining a theoretical understanding of the rational principles (λόγοι) behind the art? In a number of passages in the *Gorgias* Socrates suggests that he thinks that, alongside an understanding of the relevant rational principles, something else will also be required if someone is to become proficient in an art. Before considering these passages it might be helpful to consider further the nature of a τέχνη.

For any art or craft (τέχνη) it is possible to draw a threefold distinction between someone who has no knowledge of the craft in question, an apprentice in that craft, and an expert (τεχνίτης). It is the status of the apprentice that is relevant here. An apprentice might be described as someone who has studied the basic principles of the craft but has not yet mastered the practice of that craft. Although he might understand the rational principles (λόγοι) underpinning the craft (τέχνη), nevertheless he is not yet a craftsman (τεχνίτης). The student of medicine, for example, will require considerable practical experience after his education in medical theory before he can claim to be a fully qualified doctor. In other words, an understanding of the λόγοι relevant to a τέχνη is not on its own sufficient for mastery of that τέχνη.

In the light of this, let us now return to the *Gorgias*. In three separate passages Socrates hints at the role that training or exercise (ἄσκησις) might play in the acquisition of an art or craft (τέχνη).[73] After a discussion concerning the beneficial qualities of self-discipline or temperance (σωφροσύνη), Socrates sums up by saying that anyone who wants to be happy must attain this:

> If it is true then the man who wishes to be happy (εὐδαίμονια) must pursue and practice (διωκτέον καὶ ἀσκητέον) temperance.[74]

Self-discipline or temperance (σωφροσύνη) is, of course, one of the traditional human excellences or virtues (ἀρεταί). Here Socrates hints at the idea that the acquisition of this excellence will require one not merely to be able to say what it is (i.e. supply its λόγος) but also to engage in some form of practice (ἄσκησις) if one wants to acquire it fully. Later in the dialogue, where Socrates returns explicitly to the question of τέχνη, he suggests to his interlocutor Callicles that it would be foolish for either of them to stand up in public and profess themselves to be an expert (τεχνίτης) in an art or craft before they had first served a long apprentice of trial and error, followed by a period of successful practice in private.[75] Only then would either of them be ready to proclaim their ability. Here the idea that an apprentice in a craft must undergo some form of training after his initial education in the principles of that craft is made more

---

[73] As well as ἄσκησις other words used include μελέτη and γυμάζειν. These terms are often used interchangeably and in the present context I shall take them to be broadly synonymous. These terms will reappear in Chapter 5. For philosophical references to ἄσκησις before Socrates see e.g. Protagoras fr. 3 DK and Democritus fr. 242 DK, with comment in Hijmans, *Ἄσκησις*, pp. 55-57; for references to μελέτη see e.g. Protagoras fr. 10 DK *apud* Stobaeus 3.29.80 (3.652.22-23 WH): 'art without practice, and practice without art, are nothing' (ἔλεγε μηδὲν εἶναι μήτε τέχνην ἄνευ μελέτης μήτε μελέτην ἄνευ τέχνης).
[74] Plato *Gorg.* 507c.
[75] See Plato *Gorg.* 514e.

explicit (although the word ἄσκησις is not used). Later, at the very end of the dialogue, Socrates again says to Callicles that neither of them should engage in the art of politics until they have gained sufficient expertise in it:

> After such training in common (κοινῇ ἀσκήσαντες) together, then at last, if we think fit, we may enter public life.[76]

Here Socrates is explicit: before one can become an expert in an art or craft (in this case, politics) one must first engage in training or exercise (ἄσκησις). What these passages hint at is the idea that, alongside an understanding of the principles (λόγοι) involved in an art (τέχνη), one must also engage in a period of practical training or exercise (ἄσκησις) in order to master that art. This is what the apprentice must undergo in the period between leaving the classroom and publicly proclaiming expertise in his or her chosen profession.

Xenophon, in a passage defending the reputation and activities of Socrates, also draws attention to the importance of ἄσκησις and, in particular ἄσκησις concerned with the soul (ψυχή):

> I notice that as those who do not train the body (τὰ σώματα ἀσκοῦντας) cannot perform the functions proper to the body (τὰ τοῦ σώματος ἔργα), so those who do not train the soul (τὴν ψυχὴν ἀσκοῦντας) cannot perform the functions of the soul (τὰ τῆς ψυχῆς ἔργα).[77]

Although Xenophon does not explicitly attribute this remark to Socrates himself, it is clear that Xenophon takes this notion of training the soul (ψυχή) to be implicit in Socrates' philosophy and considers it necessary to make it explicit as part of his defence of Socrates.

From these remarks one can see that for Socrates learning an art or craft (τέχνη) will involve two components, λόγος and ἄσκησις.[78] In order to become a master of any given τέχνη, both components will be necessary.[79] It is not enough merely to understand the principles behind an art, one must also undertake a series of exercises in order to translate those principles into one's behaviour. It is this training (ἄσκησις) that transforms the apprentice into an expert whose mastery of the art in question is

---

[76] Plato *Gorg.* 527d.

[77] Xenophon *Mem.* 1.2.19 (trans. Marchant).

[78] A third contributory factor (but perhaps not a necessary component) would be natural ability. These three – learning, practice, natural ability – are often listed together in discussions of τέχνη and ἀρετή (e.g. Plato *Meno* 70a, *Prot.* 323d-e, *Phaedrus* 269d, Xenophon *Mem.* 3.9.1-3; note that in the last two of these μελέτη is used in place of ἄσκησις). For further discussion see O'Brien, *The Socratic Paradoxes*, pp. 144-46 n. 27, and, for further ancient examples, see Shorey, 'Φύσις, μελέτη, ἐπιστήμη'.

[79] This is rarely acknowledged in discussions of either Socrates or the early Platonic dialogues. However note Guthrie, *History*, vol. 3, p. 456: 'It must also be remembered that Socrates's constant analogy for virtue was not theoretical science but art or craft (*technē*), mastery of which calls for both knowledge and practice'; and also more recently Nehamas, 'Socratic Intellectualism', p. 46.

displayed in his or her actions (ἔργα). Unfortunately the role of training in the concept of τέχνη is rarely brought out in this context because Socrates has often been presented as being primarily concerned with the search for definitions, that is, for an account of the rational principles (λόγοι) which stand behind knowledge of an art or craft. As I have already suggested, this may well be due to the influence of Aristotle's testimony.[80] However, although such definitions may be a *necessary* condition for knowledge of an art or craft, the passages that we have just considered suggest that Socrates did not consider them to be, by themselves, a *sufficient* condition.[81]

6. Aristotle's Interpretation of Socrates

It is clear, then, that Socrates outlines the idea of an art (τέχνη) concerned with taking care of one's soul (ψυχή) or one's excellence (ἀρετή), analogous to gymnastics and medicine, and requiring two components, a rational principle (λόγος) and practical training (ἄσκησις).

In addition to this there is another important point that needs to be noted. Socrates suggests that possession of a τέχνη will necessarily impact upon the behaviour of its possessor.[82] So, when making shoes, the skilled shoemaker cannot help but make good shoes (excepting any deliberate intention or external interference). Similarly a musician, by virtue of the fact that they have mastered the art concerned with their instrument, will always play well. In short, Socrates suggests that the art (τέχνη) that takes care of one's soul (ψυχή) – also characterized as the art that takes care of one's ἀρετή – will automatically impact upon one's behaviour. To be more precise, he claims that knowledge (ἐπιστήμη) of this art (τέχνη) will necessarily impact upon an

---

[80] See § 1 above.

[81] I say '*may* be a necessary condition' rather than '*are* a necessary condition' because of the following: in both Plato *Laches* 193d-e and Xenophon *Mem.* 4.4.10 Socrates is presented as possessing the art of human excellence (ἀρετή) even though it is explicitly acknowledged in both passages that he cannot give a rational account of it. One might say that in some sense Socrates possesses ἀρετή itself, but does not possess knowledge (ἐπιστήμη) of ἀρετή. He is, for instance, courageous but has no knowledge of courage (and therefore can neither define it nor teach it to others). This is obviously closely related to the status of Socrates' profession of ignorance, an issue which goes beyond our concerns here. The important point in the present context is not whether definition (λόγος) is a necessary condition or not (at present I remain undecided) but, rather, the claim that it is *not* a sufficient condition.

[82] See e.g. Plato *Gorg.* 460b-c: 'Now is not the man who has learned (μεμαθηκὼς) the art of carpentry a carpenter? [...] And he who has learned the art of music a musician? [...] And he who has learned medicine a physician? And so too on the same principle, the man who has learned (μεμαθηκὼς) anything becomes in each case such as his knowledge (ἐπιστήμη) makes him?' This is based upon his more general claim that people only do what they think is best; see e.g. Plato *Prot.* 352c, Xenophon *Mem.* 3.9.5, 4.6.6, Aristotle *Eth. Eud.* 1216b6-9 (= *SSR* I B 28). If they do not know what is best then their mistake will be a product of ignorance; but if they do know what is best they will necessarily do it.

individual's actions (ἔργα).[83] Just as the skilled shoemaker will, by definition, always make good shoes, so one who knows the art of taking care of one's excellence (ἀρετή) will necessarily act excellently.

This idea that philosophical knowledge (ἐπιστήμη) will *automatically* impact upon one's behaviour (βίος) has often been criticized, probably most famously by Aristotle. This criticism is, of course, based upon Aristotle's own understanding of what he takes to be Socrates' position. The Aristotelian claims concerning Socrates relevant here are the following:

> He [Socrates] thought all the excellences (ἀρετάς) to be kinds of knowledge (ἐπιστήμας), so that to know justice (εἰδέναι τε τὴν δικαιοσύνην) and to be just (εἶναι δίκαιον) came simultaneously (ἅμα συμβαίνειν); for the moment that we have learned geometry or building we are builders and geometers.[84]

> Socrates thought the excellences (ἀρετὰς) were rational principles (λόγους) (for he thought they were all forms of knowledge (ἐπιστήμας)).[85]

These two passages form the core of Aristotle's presentation of what has come to be known as Socrates' 'virtue is knowledge' thesis – the theory that to know what is good will necessarily make one good.[86] The first of these passages is, in the light of what we have already seen, fairly uncontroversial. For Socrates, ἀρετή is the knowledge (ἐπιστήμη) developed by the art (τέχνη) that takes care of one's soul, and to possess that knowledge will automatically impact upon one's behaviour.[87] Just as knowing the art of shoemaking makes one a good shoemaker, so knowing the art that cultivates human excellence (ἀρετή) will make one an excellent individual. However, the second of these passages is somewhat problematic. Here, human excellence (ἀρετή) is identified with rational principles (λόγοι).[88] Aristotle in effect suggests that Socrates held that possession of these principles (λόγοι) would on its own be sufficient to guarantee knowledge (ἐπιστήμη); 'to know the principles (λόγοι) underpinning human excellence (ἀρετή) is enough to possess that excellence' says Socrates according to Aristotle.

Aristotle's implicit identification of ἐπιστήμη with λόγος in his presentation of Socrates' position leads Aristotle to attribute to Socrates the claim that an understanding of philosophical principles or theory (λόγος) will on its own

---

[83] See e.g. Xenophon *Mem.* 3.9.5.

[84] Aristotle *Eth. Eud.* 1216b6-9 (= *SSR* I B 28).

[85] Aristotle *Eth. Nic.* 1144b28-30 (= *SSR* I B 30).

[86] For further discussion see Guthrie, *History*, vol. 3, pp. 450-59. For Aristotle's presentation of this thesis see Deman, *Le témoignage d'Aristote sur Socrate*, pp. 82-98.

[87] For ἀρετή as a form of ἐπιστήμη see Plato *Meno* 87c, *Prot.* 349e-350a, 360d.

[88] See also Aristotle *Mag. Mor.* 1198a10-13 (= *SSR* I B 33) where the identification between ἀρετή and λόγος is made explicit (with comment in Deman, *Le témoignage d'Aristote sur Socrate*, p. 92). For discussion of the authenticity of this work – often dismissed as spurious – see Cooper, 'The *Magna Moralia* and Aristotle's Moral Philosophy'.

automatically impact upon one's behaviour (βίος). It is this thesis that Aristotle then criticizes for being too simplistic. Indeed, the passage in question continues with the clause ἡμεῖς δὲ μετὰ λόγου. Thus the full passage reads:

> Socrates thought the excellences (ἀρετὰς) were rational principles (λόγους) (for he thought they were all forms of knowledge (ἐπιστήμας)), while we think they involve a rational principle (μετὰ λόγου).[89]

Yet as we have already seen, Socrates does not identify ἐπιστήμη with λόγος and does not think that such principles will be enough on their own to transform one's behaviour. Instead, he identifies ἐπιστήμη with τέχνη,[90] arguing that it is *this* that will automatically impact upon one's behaviour, and not merely the possession of the λόγοι underpinning that τέχνη.[91] As Aristotle confirms in the first passage above, Socrates held ἀρετή to be a form of knowledge (ἐπιστήμη). However, in contrast to Aristotle's claim in the second passage, Socrates identifies knowledge (ἐπιστήμη) not with an understanding of the principles (λόγοι) underpinning an art but rather with the possession of the art (τέχνη) itself. As we have already seen, Socrates does not think that an understanding of the theory or principles (λόγοι) behind an art (τέχνη) is on its own enough to make one an expert in that art. Rather he suggests that one will also require training, exercise, or practice (ἄσκησις).

By identifying ἐπιστήμη with λόγος Aristotle, in effect, makes Socrates say that the apprentice craftsman who has finished his course of lectures on theory (λόγος) but has not yet undergone any practical training (ἄσκησις) will immediately be able to translate what he has learned in the classroom into practical ability. Yet what Socrates actually says is that in order for the apprentice to become a master craftsman (τεχνίτης) he must engage in practical training (ἄσκησις) in order to learn how to translate what he has learned in the classroom (λόγος) into actions (ἔργα). However, once the apprentice has finished his practical training, then his skill or expertise (τέχνη) will *automatically* impact upon the way in which he practises his craft. In other words, by identifying ἐπιστήμη with λόγος rather than τέχνη in his account of Socrates' position, Aristotle fails to take into account the importance that Socrates

---

[89] Aristotle *Eth. Nic.* 1144b28-30 (= *SSR* I B 30).

[90] See e.g. Plato *Prot.* 357b.

[91] This distinction may be used to form the basis for a Socratic response to Aristotle's criticism of Socrates' rejection of 'weakness of will' in *Eth. Nic.* (see e.g. 1145b21-27 = *SSR* I B 39). The individual who appears to know *x* but does not do *x* has an understanding of the principles concerning *x* but does not possess the art concerning *x*. On his reading of Socrates, Aristotle's identification of knowledge (ἐπιστήμη) with an understanding of the principles (λόγοι) leads to the paradox of possessing knowledge but not acting upon it. However Socrates' identification of knowledge with possession of an art (τέχνη) – as opposed to the principles underpinning that art – enables him to say that the 'weak-willed' individual does not have ἐπιστήμη even though he might possess the relevant λόγοι. The extra element required will of course be ἄσκησις.

places upon ἄσκησις for the acquisition of knowledge of an art or craft, including the art that cultivates human excellence (ἀρετή).[92]

7. Summary

The aim of this chapter has been to consider the Socratic origins of the conception of philosophy as an art (τέχνη) concerned with one's way of life (βίος). I have tried to offer an outline of Socrates' account of a τέχνη directed towards taking care of one's soul (ψυχή), a τέχνη directed at the cultivation of ἀρετή that will be expressed in an individual's actions (ἔργα).[93] I have also attempted to show that knowledge (ἐπιστήμη) of this τέχνη cannot be identified simply with the principles (λόγοι) underpinning that τέχνη but will instead involve both λόγος and ἄσκησις.[94] I have suggested that this is something often obscured by an 'intellectualist' image of Socrates, an image that owes much to Aristotle's testimony.

We can now begin to see how this Socratic conception of philosophy might enable us to understand better the relationship between philosophy and biography. By identifying ἐπιστήμη with τέχνη rather than λόγος, Socrates implicitly presents philosophy as something that will *necessarily* be expressed in an individual's actions (ἔργα), just as the craftsman's expertise will be expressed in his actions and the works (ἔργα) that he produces.[95] Yet there will be plenty of philosophical apprentices who, although they may have mastered philosophical λόγοι, are not yet philosophers in the

---

[92] However, in his own ethics Aristotle *does* take into account the role of ἄσκησις in the acquisition of ἀρετή (see e.g. *Eth. Nic.* 1099b9-18; also 1105b12-18). The major difference between Aristotle's own position and that of Socrates (and later the Stoics) is his distinction between σοφία and φρόνησις. This introduces into his philosophy the possibility of a dichotomy between knowing goodness and being good (see e.g. *Eth. Nic.* 1103b26-28) that is impossible for Socrates. This, in turn, leads to his confusion concerning Socrates' position. As we have seen, in fact Aristotle and Socrates would agree with regard to the point that ἀρετή is not merely a matter of λόγος but nevertheless *involves* λόγος. The difference between their positions lies in Socrates' emphasis upon τέχνη as a model for ἐπιστήμη and σοφία (see esp. Plato *Apol.* 21c-22e) in contrast to Aristotle's more theoretical model. For Aristotle τέχνη is strictly productive and not concerned with action (e.g. *Eth. Nic.* 1140a16-17).

[93] By way of further elaboration: this art (τέχνη) is concerned with cultivating a good state (εὐεξία) in the soul (ψυχή) and this good state (εὐεξία) may be identified with excellence (ἀρετή). This transformation of the soul is automatically expressed in actions (ἔργα), these actions (ἔργα) being the tangible 'product' (ἔργον) of the art (τέχνη) and the means by which this change in the soul is assessed. Thus this art (τέχνη) – identified with philosophy – transforms both soul (ψυχή) and way of life (βίος) simultaneously. As we shall see below in Chapter 3 § 7, a similar schema can be seen with the Stoics.

[94] As Foucault has put it, with Socrates we have a conception of philosophy that cannot be reduced to the mere awareness of a principle (see *The Use of Pleasure*, p. 72; *L'usage des plaisirs*, pp. 97-98).

[95] Note the way in which the range of meanings of ἔργα contributes to the analogy. The 'works' of the philosopher are his 'actions', his philosophical way of life. See also Chapter 3 §4 below.

Socratic sense insofar as their ἔργα are not yet in harmony with their λόγοι. The philosophical expert, on the other hand, will express his mastery in his actions and not just in his words. Moreover, the analogy with the craftsman suggests that what we have here is a form of knowledge that is *primarily* expressed in an individual's actions. Although an expert in a τέχνη will be able to give a rational account of what he is doing, this remains secondary to the practice of the τέχνη itself.[96] As Epictetus reminds his students, a builder does not offer to discourse on the art of building; rather he builds, thereby showing his mastery of his art.[97] Socrates' conception of philosophy as a τέχνη rather than simply a matter of λόγος means that an individual's actions (ἔργα) and way of life (βίος) may often be a better indication of an individual's philosophy than any written or spoken account (λόγος). As such, this conception of philosophy gives a philosophical significance to biography that philosophy conceived as simply a matter of λόγος cannot. Indeed, Xenophon reports that before his trial Socrates said to his companions that there was no need for him to prepare a lengthy written defence, for his behaviour throughout his life constituted the best defence he could possibly have.[98]

It is important to stress, however, that with Socrates this image of philosophy as an art concerned with one's way of life is only hinted at and is by no means developed into a fully-fledged concept. Socrates' comments serve merely as suggestive ways in which to think about the issues involved. It was only later, in the hands of the Stoics, that the concept of an art of living (τέχνη περὶ τὸν βίον) was developed. Nevertheless Socrates can be credited with being probably the first to examine in any detail the various components from which that concept was formed. In the next chapter I shall examine how the Stoics did just this, creating a conception of philosophy able to deal adequately with the idea that philosophy is something primarily expressed in one's way of life.

---

[96] In his *Of Art and Wisdom*, Roochnik argues that Plato rejects the τέχνη analogy because it is unable to offer an adequate model for knowledge of ἀρετή. In its place Roochnik suggests that Plato held on to a non-technical conception of knowledge and one of the few characteristics that he assigns to this is a harmony between deeds and words (see pp. 97, 105, 107, 125, 176). Yet this is precisely one of the key characteristics of a technical conception of knowledge and the technical model offers an ideal framework within which to understand such a harmony. It offers a model of knowledge that is *primarily* expressed in actions but also necessarily involves the ability to explain the skill in words. Of course there is a sense in which such knowledge is not *necessarily* expressed in actions; the builder must choose to build before anyone can see that he possesses the art of building. However, once he has chosen to build (excepting deliberate intent or external interference) he will *necessarily* build good houses if he possesses the art. Compared to Aristotle's reading of Socrates' position, the τέχνη model offers an excellent framework for understanding a form of knowledge in which there is no gap between λόγος and ἔργον, *pace* Roochnik.

[97] See Epictetus *Diss.* 3.21.4.

[98] See Xenophon *Apol.* 3.

Chapter 3

The Stoic Conception of the Art of Living

1. The Phrase 'Art of Living'

With Socrates, one can see all of the components necessary for the construction of a concept of an art of living. Although it is clear that he conceived of an art (τέχνη) concerned with one's way of life (βίος) involving both rational principles (λόγοι) and training (ἄσκησις), Socrates does not appear to have constructed a fully-fledged concept of an art of living (τέχνη περὶ τὸν βίον).

In ancient philosophical sources the idea of an 'art of living' is primarily associated with the Stoics. In Greek sources the phrase τέχνη περὶ τὸν βίον (or variations upon it) occurs most often in the works of Sextus Empiricus who, as we shall see in the next chapter, discussed this concept in some detail and made a number of objections to it.[1] As he reports,

> the Stoics say straight out that practical wisdom (φρόνησιν), which is knowledge of things which are good and bad and neither, is an art relating to life (τέχνην ὑπάρχειν περὶ τὸν βίον), and that those who have gained this are the only ones who are beautiful, the only ones who are rich, the only ones who are sages.[2]

Beyond the works of Sextus Empiricus there are seven other occurrences in the Greek sources, four of which have explicit Stoic provenance, of which three are relevant

---

[1] As I have already noted in the Introduction, versions of this phrase appear in ancient Greek literature a total of 41 times. Of these, 34 derive from the works of Sextus Empiricus. The Latin equivalents *ars vitae* and *ars vivendi* are less frequent. The former appears in Cicero *Fin.* 3.4, 4.19, 5.18, *Tusc. Disp.* 2.12, Seneca *Epist.* 95.7, 95.8. The latter appears in Cicero *Fin.* 1.42, 1.72, 5.16, *Acad.* 2.23, Seneca *Epist.* 95.9. Note also Seneca fr. 17 Haase *apud* Lactantius *Div. Inst.* 3.15.1 (*PL* 6.390-91). The occurrences in Seneca's *Epist.* appear in a passage that will be discussed in § 5 below. The occurrences in Cicero attest that this concept became commonplace but they do not add much to our understanding of its precise nature. However they do not support the claim that this concept was used by *all* of the post-Aristotelian philosophical schools, *contra* Reid, *M. Tulli Ciceronis Academica*, p. 203.

[2] Sextus Empiricus *Adv. Math.* 11.170 (= *SVF* 3.598; trans. Bett modified).

here.[3] The first of these, by Epictetus, has already been quoted in the Introduction but it may be helpful to repeat it again here:

> Philosophy does not promise to secure anything external for man, otherwise it would be admitting something that lies beyond its proper subject matter (ὕλης). For just as wood is the material (ὕλη) of the carpenter, bronze that of the statuary, so each individual's own life (ὁ βίος αὐτοῦ ἑκάστου) is the material (ὕλη) of the art of living (τῆς περὶ βίον τέχνης).[4]

The important point here is not merely the idea that the subject matter (ὕλη) of the art of living (τῆς περὶ βίον τέχνης) is each individual's own life (ὁ βίος αὐτοῦ ἑκάστου) but also that this is conceived as something that is not external to the individual. In other words, an individual's way of life (βίος) is what Epictetus will characterize elsewhere as something within our power or 'up to us' (ἐφ' ἡμῖν) and as such one of the few things that should be the proper object of our concern.[5] This focus upon what is internal to the individual or a proper concern for the individual can also be seen in the second passage. In his epitome of Stoic ethics preserved by Stobaeus, the doxographer Arius Didymus reports that the Stoics conceived human excellence or ἀρετή as the art concerned with the whole of life (περὶ ὅλον οὖσαν τὸν βίον τέχνην).[6] For the Stoics, ἀρετή was conceived as an internal mental state, a

---

[3] The fourth explicitly Stoic instance (which I shall not discuss) is Chrysippus *apud* Galen *Plac. Hipp. Plat.* 3.8.16 (5.352 Kühn = 226.25-29 De Lacy = *SVF* 2.909, 911). The words περὶ τῶν κατὰ τὸν βίον τέχνη occur within the context of an allegorical interpretation of the gods and consequently this example does not bear on the subject under discussion here. However it is the only one explicitly credited to the early Stoa. The three not explicitly Stoic occurrences are Philo *Leg. Alleg.* 1.57 (although still excerpted by von Arnim as *SVF* 3.202), Plutarch *Quaest. Conv.* 613b, Clement of Alexandria *Paed.* 2.2 (*PG* 8.420a). None of these merit any further comment.

[4] Epictetus *Diss.* 1.15.2, with commentary in Dobbin, pp. 156-57. At *Diss.* 4.8.12 the material (ὕλη) of philosophy is said to be an individual's reason (λόγος). Note also *Diss.* 1.26.7 where Epictetus uses τὰ βιωτικά in analogy with τὰ μουσικά (Wolf and Upton translate τὰ βιωτικά as *artem vivendi*, Carter and Oldfather as 'the art of living') and *Diss.* 4.1.63 where he refers to ἡ ἐπιστήμη τοῦ βιοῦν, perhaps following Musonius Rufus fr. 3 (10.6-7 Hense = 40.13-14 Lutz).

[5] See e.g. Epictetus *Ench.* 1.1 which is discussed further in Chapter 6 § 2 (a). This concern with βίος in Stoicism can also be seen in the fragmentary remains of Chrysippus' Περὶ βίων (see *SVF*, vol. 3, p. 194). Note also *POxy* 3657 (= *CPF* I 1, 100.5), esp. 2.13-15, which appears to propose βίος as a Stoic τόπος (with the commentary by Sedley in *The Oxyrhynchus Papyri*, vol. 52, p. 54; also *CPF* I 1***, p. 802).

[6] Arius Didymus 2.7.5b10 (2.66.14-67.4 WH = *SVF* 3.560). Arius Didymus has been identified with the Alexandrian philosopher Arius of the first century BC (see Pomeroy, *Arius Didymus*, pp. 1-3), although this claim has been called into question by Göransson (see *Albinus, Alcinous, Arius Didymus*, pp. 203-18). Note also the passage at 2.7.5b4 (2.62.15-17 WH = *SVF* 3.278) which, if Hirzel's emendation of τελείας to τέχνας is adopted (*contra* Wachsmuth, von Arnim, and Pomeroy), reads ταύτας μὲν οὖν τὰς ῥηθείσας ἀρετὰς τέχνας εἶναι λέγουσι περὶ τὸν βίον καὶ συνεστηκέναι ἐκ θεωρημάτων, 'so they say that the above-mentioned virtues are arts

disposition of the soul (ψυχή).[7] The third passage derives from the geographer Strabo, himself a Stoic and an associate of Posidonius, who characterizes both geography and philosophy as the art of living and happiness (τῆς περὶ τὸν βίον τέχνης καὶ εὐδαιμονίας).[8]

Drawing these remarks together we can see that the art of living is, on the one hand, identified with the internal mental state of ἀρετή and, on the other hand, concerned with one's βίος, which is also characterized as something in some sense internal or properly belonging to the individual. It is also in some way concerned with one's well-being or happiness (εὐδαιμονία). There is a sense, then, in which the art of living may be seen to be self-reflexive, echoing Socrates' idea of taking care of oneself (ἐπιμελεῖσθαι ἑαυτοῦ).[9]

This reflects some of the central tenets of Stoic ethical theory, which it may be helpful to outline in brief here. The point of departure for Stoic ethics is the theory of οἰκείωσις.[10] According to this theory the principal desire of all animals and humans is for self-preservation.[11] The thing most important to any animal is its own constitution. Thus it will reject whatever will harm that constitution and pursue what will benefit it. Moreover, an animal's constitution forms its primary object of experience and so any encounters with external objects will always be with reference to its constitution. All animals, insofar as they possess the power to do so, strive to preserve themselves and to avoid anything that may harm them. This constitutes each individual animal's own internal nature. It is, then, according to nature (one's own nature, itself part of cosmic nature) that one strives to persevere, selecting what is beneficial and rejecting what is harmful.

For an irrational animal, these beneficial objects are fairly obvious; food, shelter, the opportunity to procreate, and so on. What about for a rational animal though? For an infant, this concern for self-preservation simply manifests itself in a desire for food. In a philosopher, however, who is aspiring to the perfect rational life, this

---

concerning life and are comprised from rules of behaviour' (trans. Pomeroy modified). Hirzel's suggestion is recorded in the 'Corrigenda et Addenda' to WH, vol. 1, p. xxxix.

[7] See e.g. Diogenes Laertius 7.89 (= *SVF* 3.39), Sextus Empiricus *Adv. Math.* 11.23 (= *SVF* 3.75), Arius Didymus 2.7.5b1 (2.60.7-8 WH = *SVF* 3.262), with Inwood & Donini in *CHHP*, pp. 714-24.

[8] Strabo 1.1.1 (= Posidonius test. 75 EK), with Kidd, *Posidonius, The Commentary*, pp. 60-62. For Strabo's Stoic credentials see e.g. 1.2.34 where he writes 'our Zeno'.

[9] This is a characteristic noted by Foucault: 'No technique, no professional skill can be acquired without exercise; nor can one learn the art of living, the *technē tou biou*, without an *askēsis* that must be understood as a training of the self by the self (*un entraînement de soi par soi*)' ('L'écriture de soi', in *Dits et écrits*, vol. 4, p. 417; *Essential Works*, vol. 1, p. 208). I shall return to this passage in Chapter 5 § 2 (b).

[10] On this concept see Pembroke, 'Oikeiōsis'; Striker, 'The Role of *Oikeiōsis* in Stoic Ethics'; Inwood, *Ethics and Human Action in Early Stoicism*, pp. 184-201; Engberg-Pedersen, *The Stoic Theory of Oikeiosis*; Inwood and Donini in *CHHP*, pp. 677-82. The term is notoriously difficult to translate: Inwood suggests 'orientation'; LS suggest 'appropriation'.

[11] The principal sources here are Diogenes Laertius 7.85-86 (= *SVF* 3.178 = LS 57 A), Cicero *Fin.* 3.16 (= *SVF* 3.182), Hierocles *Elementa Ethica* 1.34-2.9 (= LS 57 C).

changes. For a rational being, the fundamental characteristic will be its rational soul, rather than its animalistic impulses. Thus, when a rational being seeks to preserve its own constitution *qua* rational being, it will seek to preserve its rationality, that is, to take care of its soul. The continual pursuit of sensual gratification, although the appropriate primary impulse for an irrational animal, will conflict with this insofar as it will reinforce irrational desires. What is in accord with the constitution of a rational being, then, is rational behaviour. To preserve and cultivate its own constitution, the rational being will cultivate the excellence (ἀρετή) of its soul (ψυχή). Thus, for the rational being – i.e. the philosopher – only this excellence (ἀρετή) is judged to be good. Those objects of one's primary impulses such as food or health or wealth, although apparently beneficial to every human being, do not contribute to the preservation of a rational being *qua* rational being. They only contribute to its survival *qua* animal.[12]

This theory forms the basis for the famous Stoic claim that only virtue or excellence (ἀρετή) is good and that all other apparently beneficial entities are strictly speaking indifferent.[13] Although the philosopher may prefer to be healthy and wealthy than not – hence their status as 'preferred indifferents' – these things are not strictly speaking good because they do not contribute to the preservation of his own constitution insofar as he is a rational being. Only excellence (ἀρετή) – that is, an excellent disposition of the soul – contributes to the continuing self-preservation of a philosopher *qua* philosopher. Thus, the aspiring Stoic philosopher is not concerned with wealth or social standing; like Socrates, his only concern is to take care of his soul. It is to this end that the art of living is directed.

Although these explicit references to an art of living and these brief remarks concerning Stoic ethical theory shed some light on the issues at hand, they do not give us enough information to understand fully the precise nature of this conception of philosophy. In order to do that it will be necessary to draw upon a number of related discussions. In the next section I shall consider the way in which the Stoics presented their philosophy as primarily concerned with transforming one's life (βίος) and, in particular, modelling one's life upon the example set by Socrates. Then I shall consider the way in which the Stoics adopted and developed Socrates' medical analogy between arts that take care of the body and arts that take care of the soul. In the light of this analogy with the art of medicine I shall examine Stoic definitions and discussions of τέχνη to see how well this analogy works. I shall then turn to an important discussion by Seneca that deals with the relationship between philosophical doctrines (*decreta*) and precepts (*praecepta*), a discussion that can be seen to develop Socrates' remarks concerning the relationship between λόγος and ἄσκησις. Finally, I shall attempt to reconcile this image of Stoic philosophy with some of the more traditional portraits in which it is presented as a systematic and highly structured body

---

[12] See Cicero *Fin.* 3.21 (= *SVF* 3.188 = LS 59 D).

[13] For further discussion see Kidd, 'Stoic Intermediates and the End for Man'; Inwood and Donini in *CHHP*, pp. 690-99. It is also worth noting that some Stoics – one example being Posidonius – did not take this theory to be the basis for Stoic ethics; see Striker, 'The Role of *Oikeiōsis* in Stoic Ethics', p. 292.

of knowledge comprised of the three components of logic, physics, and ethics. Once these tasks have been completed I shall attempt to offer a definition of the Stoic conception of philosophy.

2. The Ideal of the Sage

As with Socrates, for Stoics such as Epictetus the subject matter (ὕλη) of philosophy is one's own life (βίος). In this, as in many other things, the Stoics may well have consciously followed the example set by Socrates. According to the Epicurean Philodemus, some Stoics actually wanted to be called 'Socratics'.[14] Embarrassed by the behaviour of some of the Cynics to whom their school's founder Zeno was so closely linked – and for that matter by some of the Cynic-inspired attitudes of Zeno and Chrysippus themselves – these later Stoics, it is claimed, hoped to redeem the Cynic dimension within Stoicism by transforming it into a stepping stone in a genealogy extending back to Socrates.[15] Faced with the succession Diogenes–Crates–Zeno, these later Stoics expanded it into Socrates–Antisthenes–Diogenes–Crates–Zeno, in effect proposing Socrates' companion Antisthenes as a key link between the disreputable Diogenes and the respectable Socrates.[16] Whether one decides to choose Diogenes or Socrates as the point of departure for such a Stoic genealogy, either way it seems likely that the early Stoics would have considered themselves to be continuing a Socratic tradition which conceived of philosophy as a matter of 'deeds not words' (ἔργα οὐ λόγοι).[17] One need only note that Zeno was first inspired to study philosophy after reading an account of Socrates in Xenophon's *Memorabilia* and chose to study with the Cynic Crates as he was the closest approximation to the Socrates he had read about that he could find.[18] It was probably within this context, then, that the early Stoics constructed their philosophy. Remaining faithful to Cynic and Socratic philosophy, Stoicism was constructed around a practical goal, namely,

---

[14] Philodemus *De Stoicis* (*PHerc* 155 & 339) 13.3-4 Dorandi (not in *SVF*): Σωκρατικοὶ καλεῖσθαι θέ[λ]ουσιν. For the relationship between the Stoics and Socrates see Long, 'Socrates in Hellenistic Philosophy'; Striker, 'Plato's Socrates and the Stoics'.

[15] Some of the 'Cynic inspired' ideas of Zeno and Chrysippus will be discussed below in Chapter 4 § 2 (e). A variety of ancient sources attest to a perceived closeness between Stoicism and Cynicism; see e.g. Cicero *Off.* 1.128, Juvenal *Saturae* 13.122, Diogenes Laertius 7.121 (= *SVF* 3 Apollod. 17), Arius Didymus 2.7.11s (2.114.24-25 WH = *SVF* 3.638).

[16] For criticism of the subsequent 'Cynicized' portrait of Antisthenes see Dudley, *A History of Cynicism*, pp. 1-16, with the more recent discussion in Goulet-Cazé, 'Who Was the First Dog?'.

[17] Note that even if one were to place Diogenes at the beginning of the Stoic genealogy, he himself was reportedly described by Plato as a 'Socrates gone mad' (Σωκράτης μαινόμενος); see Diogenes Laertius 6.54, Aelian *Varia Historia* 14.33 (both *SSR* V B 59). This may perhaps be glossed as Socrates' philosophy pushed to its logical extreme.

[18] See Diogenes Laertius 7.2 (= *SVF* 1.1), Eusebius 15.13.8 (816c = *SVF* 3 Z.T. 1).

not merely to know the nature of excellence (ἀρετή) and wisdom (σοφία), but rather
to live a life shaped by excellence and wisdom – to become a sage (σοφός).[19]

The Stoic conception of the sage was nothing less than the ideal of a perfect
individual, an individual described in terms that were usually reserved only for the
gods.[20] The sage is described in a variety of sources as one who does everything that
he undertakes well, one who is never impeded in what he does, one who is infallible;
he is more powerful than all others, richer, stronger, freer, happier; he alone is the
only individual worthy of the title 'king'.[21] The doxographer Arius Didymus adds the
following:

> The virtuous man (σπουδαῖον) is great, powerful, eminent, and strong. [...] Consequently
> he is neither compelled by anyone nor does he compel another, neither prevented by nor
> preventing anyone else, neither forced by another nor forcing anyone else, neither
> dominating nor dominated, neither doing harm to another nor suffering harm from anyone
> else [...]. He is particularly happy, prosperous, blessed, fortunate, pious, dear to the gods,
> meritorious, a king, a general, a politician, good at managing the household and at making
> money.[22]

Not surprisingly, there was considerable doubt as to whether any examples of such an
individual existed, ever existed, or could ever exist. Neither Zeno nor Chrysippus ever
appear to have described themselves as sages.[23] Chrysippus went further, stating that
he had never even known one.[24] Alexander of Aphrodisias described the Stoic sage as
rarer than an Ethiopian phoenix.[25] However, the ever practical Seneca seems to have

---

[19] Terms used for the sage, seemingly interchangeably, include σοφός and σπουδαῖος (and in
Latin, *sapiens*). See Tsekourakis, *Studies in the Terminology of Early Stoic Ethics*, pp. 124-38.
[20] See Jagu, *Zénon de Cittium*, p. 30; Long, 'Dialectic and the Stoic Sage', p. 103.
[21] For accounts of the sage see Arius Didymus 2.7.5-12 (2.57.13-116.18 WH), Cicero
Tusc. Disp. 3.10-21 (= *SVF* 3.570), *Parad. Stoic.* 33-52, *Fin.* 3.26 (= *SVF* 3.582), 3.75
(= *SVF* 3.591), *Rep.* 1.28 (= *SVF* 3.600), Diogenes Laertius 7.121-25, Plutarch *Comp. Arg.
Stoic.* 1057d-e, 1058b-c, *Comm. Not.* 1063d (= *SVF* 3.759). For discussion see Kerferd, 'What
Does the Wise Man Know?'; Edelstein, *The Meaning of Stoicism*, pp. 1-18.
[22] Arius Didymus 2.7.11g (2.99.12-100.6 WH = *SVF* 3.567; trans. Pomeroy modified).
[23] For Zeno see Decleva Caizzi, 'The Porch and the Garden', pp. 317, 320; for Chrysippus see
Diogenianus *apud* Eusebius 6.8.16 (264c = *SVF* 3.668) and the next note. Sextus Empiricus,
Adv. Math. 11.181, objected that if the Stoics did not claim to be sages themselves, then they
admitted that they did not possess wisdom and thus that they did not possess precisely what
they claimed to teach. This objection will be discussed further in Chapter 4 § 2 (b).
[24] See Plutarch *Stoic. Rep.* 1048e (= *SVF* 3.662, 668).
[25] Alexander of Aphrodisias *Fat.* 199.16-20 (= *SVF* 3.658 = LS 61 N): 'Of men, the greatest
number are bad, or rather there are one or two whom they [the Stoics] speak of as having
become good men as in a fable, a sort of incredible creature as it were and contrary to nature
and rarer than the Ethiopian phoenix; and the others are all wicked and are so to an equal
extent, so that there is no difference between one and another, and all who are not wise are alike
mad' (trans. Sharples). See also Seneca *Epist.* 42.1: 'For one [man] of the first class perhaps
springs into existence, like the phoenix, only once in five hundred years' (trans. Gummere).

been a little more optimistic, proposing Cato as a concrete example of such an individual.[26]

In contrast to this image of a perfect individual, the Stoics characterized everyone else as 'fools' (φαῦλοι).[27] The foolish are, in the words of a summary by Plutarch, 'madmen and fools, impious and lawless, at the extremity of misfortune and utter unhappiness'.[28] They are slaves and children, and are often dismissed as sub-human, with only the wise deserving of the title 'men' (ἄνθρωποι).[29] Yet, if the sage is as rare as he is said to be, then the implication is that almost everybody falls into this somewhat unflattering category.[30]

This conception of the sage and the distinction between the wise and the foolish had already been made by the Cynics.[31] Diogenes described the majority of humankind as mad and slaves, sub-human even.[32] In contrast he described good men as godlike.[33] The Cynic conception of the wise person is, like that of the Stoic sage, of someone who is free and happy regardless of the circumstances in which they might find themselves. Indeed, Diogenes is often cited by later Stoics as an example of such an individual himself,[34] and it is reported that the Stoic sage will himself follow the Cynic way of life (κυνικὸς βίος), a way of life characterized as a short cut to virtue (σύντομον ἐπ' ἀρετὴν ὁδόν).[35]

Other ancient sources tend to refer to one or two examples of the sage only; see e.g. Diogenianus *apud* Eusebius 6.8.13 (264b = *SVF* 3.668).

[26] See Seneca *Const. Sap.* 7.1; also Rist, 'Seneca and Stoic Orthodoxy', p. 2012. Seneca's optimism was criticized by his otherwise devoted admirer Justus Lipsius in *Manuductio* 2.8 (1604 edn, pp. 82-84; trans. in Kraye, *Cambridge Translations*, pp. 200-02).

[27] See Arius Didymus 2.7.11g (2.99.3-5 WH = *SVF* 1.216 = LS 59 N): 'It is the view of Zeno and his Stoic followers that there are two races of men, that of the worthwhile (σπουδαίων), and that of the worthless (φαύλων)' (trans. Pomeroy). As well as 'wise' and 'foolish', and 'worthwhile' and 'worthless', Long & Sedley propose 'excellent' and 'inferior'. Beyond φαῦλος, the word ἄφρων is also often used (and in Latin, *insipiens* and *stultus*).

[28] Plutarch *Stoic. Rep.* 1048e (= *SVF* 3.662, 668). See also Arius Didymus esp. 2.7.11k (2.103.24-106.20 WH = *SVF* 3.677), Cicero *Parad. Stoic.* 27-32, with further references in *SVF* 3.657-84.

[29] Cicero uses the term 'man' in this restricted sense in *Rep.* 1.28: 'while others are *called* men (*homines*), only those who are skilled in the specifically human arts are worthy of the name' (trans. Rudd). See also Epictetus *Diss.* 2.24.19-20, Marcus Aurelius 11.18.10. The Greek and Latin are, of course, gender neutral.

[30] This distinction between the wise and the foolish seems to be more important to the Stoa than the universal respect for human rationality often attributed to it (e.g. Nussbaum, *The Therapy of Desire*, pp. 325, 331, 343).

[31] See Jagu, *Zénon de Cittium*, p. 31. For a Cynic example of the restricted use of 'man' (ἄνθρωπος) see Diogenes *apud* Diogenes Laertius 6.41 (= *SSR* V B 272).

[32] See e.g. Diogenes Laertius 6.33 (= *SSR* V B 76), 6.71 (= *SSR* V B 291).

[33] See Diogenes Laertius 6.51 (= *SSR* V B 354).

[34] See the idealized portrait in Epictetus *Diss.* 3.22; note also Marcus Aurelius 8.3.

[35] See Diogenes Laertius 6.104 (not in *SVF*), 7.121 (= *SVF* 3 Apollod. 17), Arius Didymus 2.7.11s (2.114.24-25 WH = *SVF* 3.638).

This conception of the sage shared by the Stoics and Cynics derives ultimately from Socrates. As we have already seen, it is reported that Zeno turned to philosophy after reading about Socrates in Xenophon's *Memorabilia*, and became a student of the Cynic Crates because Crates was the closest thing he could find to the example of Socrates.[36] The image of the Stoic sage was thus not a hypothetical ideal,[37] but rather based upon an idealized image of actual individuals, an image that functioned as an exemplar or role model.[38] Names often cited include Antisthenes and Diogenes, but ultimately the Stoic sage is based upon the figure of Socrates.[39]

Socrates himself was often described by his contemporaries in terms similar to those later reserved for the Stoic sage. For example, in the *Symposium* Plato makes Alcibiades describe Socrates as a 'godlike and extraordinary man',[40] while in the *Memorabilia* Xenophon describes him as 'the perfect example of goodness and happiness'.[41] The name of Socrates appears throughout later Stoic authors as the

---

[36] See Diogenes Laertius 7.2 (= *SVF* 1.1), Eusebius 15.13.8 (816c = *SVF* 3 Z.T. 1).

[37] The sage is often presented as just this, especially by philosophers since the Renaissance. See e.g. Erasmus, *Praise of Folly*, pp. 45-46, and Justus Lipsius, *Manuductio* 2.8 (1604 edn, p. 84), despite the contrary claims of his beloved Seneca in *Const. Sap.* 7.1. More famous is Kant's judgement, in which the sage is characterized as an ideal, an archetype existing in thought only. Indeed, Kant goes so far as to say that even to attempt to depict this ideal in a romance is impracticable, let alone in reality (*Critique of Pure Reason* A569-70, B597-98). One notable, if early, exception to this modern tendency is Angelo Politian who, in his *Epistola ad Bartolomeo Scala*, argued that if just one example could be found, that would be enough to affirm the reality of the sage. Then, following Cicero and Seneca, he cites Cato as his example. For translations of Politian and Lipsius see Kraye, *Cambridge Translations*, pp. 192-99 & 200-09 respectively.

[38] Hadot, 'La figure du sage dans l'Antiquité gréco-latine', pp. 15-18, argues that the image of the sage is not a theoretical construction but rather a reflection upon an outstanding individual, whether it be Plato reflecting upon Socrates or Seneca reflecting upon Cato. See also his *Philosophy as a Way of Life*, p. 147 (but apparently contradicted at p. 57). Note also Hicks, *Stoic and Epicurean*, p. 88, and the discussion of *exempla* in Seneca by Newman, '*Cotidie meditare*', pp. 1491-93.

[39] In an interesting paper entitled 'Philosophical Allegiance in the Greco-Roman World', David Sedley has drawn attention to what he calls 'a virtually religious commitment to the authority of a founder figure' in the Hellenistic philosophical schools (see also Brunschwig, 'La philosophie à l'époque hellénistique', p. 512). He goes on to note that, while none of the later Stoics can be seen to criticize their founder Zeno, in Zeno's own day it would have been Socrates who stood as the great authority figure for the Stoa (pp. 97-99). Although I am also not aware of any criticism of Zeno, I have not noticed much eulogy either. In fact, for a later Stoic like Epictetus it is Socrates who stands out as the great role model, followed by Diogenes the Cynic. In the light of Philodemus' claim that some Stoics wanted to be called Socratics (*De Stoicis* (*PHerc* 155 & 339) 13.3-4 Dorandi) and my suggestion here that the sage is an idealized image of Socrates, it is tempting to suggest that throughout the history of Stoicism Socrates may well have been seen as the ultimate founder of the Stoic tradition, with Zeno occupying a slightly lesser position.

[40] Plato *Symp.* 219c.

[41] Xenophon *Mem.* 4.8.11.

finest example of wisdom.[42] If only one or two sages ever existed, then Socrates is almost always cited as one of them. The status of Socrates as the fundamental Stoic role model is captured by Epictetus when he says:

> Even if you are not yet a Socrates, you must live as if you wish to become a Socrates.[43]

There is a very real sense, then, in which one might define the goal of Stoic philosophy – the attainment of wisdom (σοφία), the aspiration to become a sage (σοφός) – as the task of becoming like Socrates.[44]

In between these two classes of the foolish majority (φαῦλοι) and the rare sage (σοφός), there is a third group, those who are 'making progress' (προκοπή).[45] Individuals in this intermediate group may be described as lovers of wisdom, as philosophical 'apprentices', as those who admire the figure of the sage and aspire to become like him, but nevertheless are strictly speaking still classed as foolish. This is illustrated by the image of man drowning just below the surface:

> Just as in the sea the man a cubit from the surface is drowning no less than the one who has sunk 500 fathoms, so neither are they any the less in vice who are approaching virtue (ἀρετή) than they who are a long way from it [...] so those who are making progress (οἱ προκόπτοντες) continue to be stupid and depraved until they have attained virtue (ἀρετή).[46]

This third group may be seen to correspond to Socrates' description of himself as one who has become aware of his own ignorance but does not yet possess wisdom.[47] Yet for a number of the Stoics, Socrates is himself said to be one of the wise, perhaps the only obvious and uncontroversial example. This paradox might be explained by suggesting that their judgement was based upon what he did rather than what he said, that is, on his ἔργα rather than his λόγοι.[48]

---

[42] See Döring, *Exemplum Socratis*, pp. 18-42 (on Seneca), pp. 43-79 (on Epictetus).

[43] Epictetus *Ench.* 51.3 (trans. Boter), with comment in Jagu, *Épictète et Platon*, pp. 47-62; Hijmans, Ἄσκησις, pp. 72-77; Long, 'Socrates in Hellenistic Philosophy', pp. 150-51. See also the list of references to Socrates in Epictetus gathered together in *SSR* I C 530.

[44] See Long, 'Socrates in Hellenistic Philosophy', pp. 160-64.

[45] This notion is particularly prominent in Epictetus, e.g. *Ench.* 12, 13, 48. See also the discussion in Seneca *Epist.* 75.8-18 where this intermediate category is itself divided into three sub-categories. However, note Diogenes Laertius 7.127 (= *SVF* 3.536) where this intermediate category is characterized as Peripatetic and explicitly said not to be Stoic. Thus it may have been an innovation of the middle or late Stoa.

[46] Plutarch *Comm. Not.* 1063a (= *SVF* 3.539; trans. Cherniss); see also ibid. 1062e, Diogenes Laertius 7.120 (= *SVF* 3.527), Cicero *Fin.* 3.48 (= *SVF* 3.530).

[47] See e.g. Plato *Apol.* 21c-d.

[48] Of course, the ideal for Socrates is harmony between ἔργα and λόγοι, to be able to act well and give a rational account of that behaviour. Given the Stoic claim that only the sage possesses knowledge (ἐπιστήμη), one would assume that their ideal would also involve such a harmony. In that case, Socrates would fail the test.

Members of this third group are philosophers in the etymological sense of the word.[49] They are lovers of wisdom or, to be more precise, they aspire to become like the image of the sage. In this sense they are primarily lovers of the idealized σοφός rather than abstract σοφία. For the Stoics, philosophy is that which transforms φιλόσοφοι into σοφοί. As such, the subject matter (ὕλη) of philosophy is one's way of life (ὁ βίος αὐτοῦ ἑκάστου);[50] its task is to transform one's way of life into the life of a sage, to become like Socrates. Just as we have already seen with Socrates, then, the primary concern of Stoic philosophy is βίος.[51]

3. An Art Concerned with the Soul

With Socrates we saw that the idea of an art (τέχνη) concerned with one's life (βίος) was closely connected to the idea of an art concerned with taking care of one's soul (ψυχή), although the precise relationship between these two ideas was not made explicit. This idea of an art concerned with taking care of the soul analogous to medicine as the art concerned with taking care of the body was developed by a number of Stoics,[52] but in particular by Chrysippus. Two extended reports drawing upon Chrysippus' use of this analogy survive, the first by Cicero, the second by Galen. By examining each of these accounts in turn hopefully it will be possible to reconstruct a basic understanding of how the Stoics used and developed this Socratic analogy.

(a) The Medical Analogy in Cicero's Tusculan Disputations

The first of these accounts can be found in Cicero's *Tusculan Disputations*.[53] Scholars have suggested a number of works by Chrysippus as the source for this account,

---

[49] Seneca offers an account of Stoic philosophy beginning with this etymological distinction in *Epist.* 89.4. See also Gourinat, *Premières leçons sur le Manuel d'Épictète*, pp. 19-20.

[50] See Epictetus *Diss.* 1.15.2-3, quoted above, § 1.

[51] A notable exception to this generalization is Posidonius who, displaying the influence of Aristotle, defines the goal as 'to live contemplating (θεωροῦντα) the truth and order of all things' (Posidonius fr. 186 EK *apud* Clement of Alexandria *Strom.* 2.21 (*PG* 8.1076a) = LS 63 J). As with Aristotle, this 'theoretical life' is still a mode of life. However, as Edelstein notes, 'The Philosophical System of Posidonius', pp. 314-15, this is a considerable shift from the more orthodox Stoic position.

[52] See the extended discussion in Pigeaud, *Le maladie de l'âme*, pp. 245-371, and note in particular the account in Arius Didymus 2.7.5b4 (2.62.15-20 WH = *SVF* 3.278): 'For just as the health of the body is a correct mixture of the hot, cold, dry, and wet elements in the body, so too the health of the soul (τὴν τῆς ψυχῆς ὑγίειαν) is a correct mixture of the beliefs in the soul. And likewise, just as bodily strength is an adequate tension in the sinews, so mental strength is adequate tension when deciding and acting or not' (trans. Pomeroy). The idea of tension in the soul will be discussed further in Chapter 5 § 4.

[53] See Cicero *Tusc. Disp.*, in particular 3.1-21 and 4.9-33. I have used the editions by King (LCL) and Dougan & Henry. The context is a discussion concerning whether the sage can be

including his Περὶ παθῶν and Θεραπευτικός.[54] Cicero opens his account, just as Socrates does in the *Gorgias*, by drawing a distinction between the soul and the body, and proposing that just as there is health and sickness of the body, so there is health and sickness of the soul.[55] Again, just like Socrates, Cicero suggests that the diseases of the soul are in many ways more dangerous than those of the body.[56] Yet despite this he notes that, in general, little attention has been paid to the idea of a medicine for the soul (*animi medicina*) analogous to medicine for the body.[57] Nevertheless Cicero does think that such an art exists and that that art is philosophy.[58] The primary task for the philosopher, then, is to treat the diseases of the soul (*animi morbum*). However, unlike the physician, he will not attempt to treat other people but rather he will focus his attention upon himself.[59] The philosopher is thus one who concerns himself with the diseases of his own soul.

After this general introduction to what he takes to be the nature and function of philosophy, Cicero turns to the details of the Stoic analogy between diseases (*morbi*) of the body and the soul.[60] He begins by drawing attention to the claim that no foolish individual is free from such diseases.[61] Only the sage is free from the diseases of the soul as only he has mastered philosophy conceived as the art that treats these diseases. Wisdom (*sapientia*, σοφία) is thus defined simply as a healthy soul (*animi sanitas*).[62]

---

totally free from emotions (the Stoic position) or subject to some moderate emotions (the Peripatetic position). For an outline of the argument in these sections of the text see Dougan & Henry, vol. 2, pp. ix-xxi; MacKendrick, *The Philosophical Books of Cicero*, pp. 149-63. For further discussion of Cicero's treatment of this material see Pigeaud, *La maladie de l'âme*, esp. pp. 245-315; Nussbaum, *The Therapy of Desire*, pp. 316-58; Sorabji, *Emotion and Peace of Mind*, pp. 29-54. Note also the recent commentary in Graver, *Cicero on the Emotions*.

[54] For a survey of opinions concerning Cicero's sources see Dougan & Henry, vol. 2, pp. xxx-xlvii. For Chrysippus' Περὶ παθῶν (of which the Θεραπευτικός may have been one book) see *SVF* 3.456-90. Von Arnim includes a number of passages from *Tusc. Disp.* as *testimonia* for Περὶ παθῶν; see *SVF* 3.483-88.

[55] See *Tusc. Disp.* 3.1.

[56] See *Tusc. Disp.* 3.5.

[57] See *Tusc. Disp.* 3.1.

[58] See *Tusc. Disp.* 3.6: *est profecto animi medicina, philosophia*.

[59] See *Tusc. Disp.* 3.6. This reflects the nature of Socrates' own project to take care of himself (ἐπιμελεῖσθαι ἑαυτοῦ) and is developed later by Epictetus, for whom the philosopher can treat only himself (see e.g. *Diss.* 1.15.1-2).

[60] At *Tusc. Disp.* 3.7 Cicero proposes *morbus* as a translation for πάθος (note also 3.23, 4.10). However it might be more accurate to translate πάθος as *perturbatio* (as Cicero himself does in *Fin.* 3.35), saving *morbus* for νόσος. See Dougan & Henry, vol. 2, p. 9; also Adler in *SVF* 4, pp. 172-73.

[61] See *Tusc. Disp.* 3.9: *omnium insipientium animi in morbo sunt*. At 3.10 Cicero explicitly says that in this the Stoics followed Socrates.

[62] See *Tusc. Disp.* 3.10: *ita fit ut sapientia sanitas sit animi*. The Stoic characterization of the foolish as 'insane' is thus not mere rhetoric but in fact quite literal, for they were thought to have unhealthy (*insanitas*) minds.

Only by submitting oneself to the therapy of philosophy can this state of health be reached.[63]

Cicero notes that the Stoics, and Chrysippus in particular, devoted much space to the analysis and definition of the various disturbances of the soul.[64] These disturbances are emotions (*perturbationes*, *morbi*), in particular the emotions of anger, covetousness, distress, compassion, and envy, all of which are said to imply or presuppose one another.[65] The Stoic analysis of these emotions focused upon four principal types produced by beliefs in something either good or evil, either currently present or expected to happen in the future.[66] The task of philosophy, then, is to enable one to overcome these unwelcome mental states. Only by doing this will one be able to approach the ideal of the sage. The key to this, Cicero suggests, is to trace the origins of these mental disturbances just as a doctor might diagnose sicknesses affecting the body.[67] Only then will it become possible to overcome these diseases of the soul. Again, Cicero notes that Chrysippus in particular devoted considerable attention to the development of this analogy.[68] As Cicero develops his Stoic inspired diagnosis he suggests that the origins of these disturbances are to be found in an individual's beliefs or opinions (*in opinione*).[69] The emotions are thus merely the symptoms of mental disturbance. The underlying causes are these beliefs (*opiniones*).[70] The task of philosophy – directed towards the cultivation of wisdom

---

[63] *Tusc. Disp.* 3.13.

[64] See *Tusc. Disp.* 4.9 (= *SVF* 3.483): 'Chrysippus and the Stoics in discussing disorders of the soul have devoted considerable space to subdividing and defining them' (trans. King).

[65] See *Tusc. Disp.* 3.19-21, note also 4.16-22. The emotions listed here are anger (*ira*), covetousness (*concupisco*), distress (*aegritudo*), compassion (*miseratio*), and envy (*invidia*).

[66] See *Tusc. Disp.* 3.24-25 (= *SVF* 3.385), 4.11-14. These four types are delight (*laetitia*), lust (*libido*), distress (*aegritudo*), and fear (*metus*). Note the summary at 4.14 (= *SVF* 3.393): *aegritudo opinio recens mali praesentis … laetitia opinio recens boni praesentis … metus opinio impendentis mali … libido opinio venturi boni*. The relationship between these four is best illustrated by means of a table (following Dougan & Henry, vol. 2, pp. xi & xxxi):

		praesentis –	*laetitia* (ἡδονή)	–	belief in present good
	boni				
		absentis –	*libido* (ἐπιθυμία)	–	belief in future good
perturbationes (πάθη)					
		praesentis –	*aegritudo* (λύπη)	–	belief in present evil
	mali				
		absentis –	*metus* (φόβος)	–	belief in future evil

[67] See *Tusc. Disp.* 3.23.

[68] See *Tusc. Disp.* 4.23 (= *SVF* 3.424): 'far too much attention is devoted by the Stoics, principally by Chrysippus, to drawing an analogy between diseases of the soul and diseases of the body' (trans. King).

[69] *Tusc. Disp.* 3.24.

[70] These beliefs are, in turn, the product of judgements. There appears to have been a dispute in the early Stoa concerning whether emotions should be characterized as judgements or the

(*sapientia*), understood as the health of the soul (*animi sanitas*) – is to treat these beliefs or opinions which cause the disturbances of the soul.[71]

(b) The Medical Analogy in Galen's On the Doctrines of Hippocrates and Plato

Cicero's account may be supplemented by turning to Galen who, in Book Five of his *On the Doctrines of Hippocrates and Plato*, discusses an argument between Chrysippus and Posidonius concerning certain details of this analogy between diseases of the mind and diseases of the body.[72] According to Galen, both men agreed that such disturbances (πάθη) do not occur in the soul of 'the better sort of men' (τῶν ἀστείων),[73] probably a reference to the sage. However, Galen reports disagreement between Chrysippus and Posidonius with regard to what goes on in the souls of the foolish majority (ἡ τῶν φαύλων ψυχή). According to Chrysippus, their souls are best described as analogous to a body which is prone to become ill due to a small and chance cause (ἐπὶ μικρᾷ καὶ τυχούσῃ προφάσει).[74] Posidonius questioned this analogy, arguing that it would be wrong to compare a diseased soul with a healthy body which was not at present ill but merely prone to illness.[75] Galen goes on to offer his own account of the analogy:

> The souls of virtuous men (τὰς τῶν σπουδαίων ψυχὰς) ought to be compared to bodies immune from disease, [...] the souls of those making progress (προκοπτόντων) should be compared to bodies of robust constitution, souls of intermediate persons to bodies that are healthy without being robust, souls of the multitude of ordinary men (φαύλων) to bodies that become ill at a slight cause, and souls of men who are angry or enraged or in any affected state whatever to bodies that are actually diseased.[76]

Galen is keen to emphasize that this analogy between the health of the body (ἡ τοῦ σώματος ὑγίεια) and the health of the soul (ἡ τῆς ψυχῆς ὑγίεια) was of particular importance for the Stoics, hence their concern with and occasional disputes over precisely how it should be conceived. The reason for this attention is not too difficult to discern for, as we have already seen in Cicero's account, the Stoic definition of philosophy as that which cultivates the health of the soul depends upon it. Galen is well aware of this and quotes the following from Chrysippus:

---

product of judgements. The former position is attributed to Chrysippus, the latter to Zeno. I shall return to this in Chapter 7 § 2.
[71] As Epictetus will later say, 'it is not things themselves (τὰ πράγματα) that disturb men, but their judgements (δόγματα) about these things' (*Ench.* 5). This definition of philosophy as the treatment of opinions or judgements will become central in Chapter 7.
[72] The relevant passage is Galen *Plac. Hipp. Plat.* 5.1-2 (5.428-445 Kühn = 292.4-304.32 De Lacy). I have relied upon the edition with translation by De Lacy.
[73] *Plac. Hipp. Plat.* 5.2.2 (5.432 Kühn = 294.31 De Lacy; trans. De Lacy).
[74] See *Plac. Hipp. Plat.* 5.2.3 (5.432 Kühn = 294.33-36 De Lacy = *SVF* 3.465).
[75] See *Plac. Hipp. Plat.* 5.2.4-12 (5.432-435 Kühn = 294.36-296.36 De Lacy = Posidonius fr. 163 EK).
[76] *Plac. Hipp. Plat.* 5.2.9 (5.434 Kühn = 296.21-27 De Lacy; trans. De Lacy modified).

It is not true that whereas there is an art (τέχνη), called medicine, concerned with the diseased body (περὶ τὸ νοσοῦν σῶμά), there is no art (τέχνη) concerned with the diseased soul (περὶ τὴν νοσοῦσαν ψυχήν), or that the latter should be inferior to the former in the theory and treatment of individual cases.[77]

For Chrysippus, this art is philosophy and the philosopher is 'the physician of the soul' (ὁ τῆς ψυχῆς ἰατρός).[78]

* * *

In the light of these two accounts concerning the nature and function of philosophy, both of which claim the authority of Chrysippus, we can see that the Stoics held the task of the philosopher to be the cultivation of the health of the soul (ἡ τῆς ψυχῆς ὑγίεια, *anima sanitas*), 'to take care of one's soul' (ἐπιμελεῖσθαι τῆς ψυχῆς) as Socrates would have put it. Two points deserve noting here. The first is the claim that the philosopher cannot treat others but rather must focus upon himself, that is, upon the diseases (πάθη, *perturbationes*) within his own soul. The second is that the underlying cause of these diseases (πάθη, *perturbationes*) are one's beliefs or opinions (δόξαι, *opiniones*).[79] However, our present concern is with the analogy between the art that takes care of the soul and the art that takes care of the body, medicine. These passages suggest that the Stoics placed particular emphasis upon this medical analogy: philosophy is the art that takes care of the soul analogous to the way in which medicine is the art that takes care of the body, an art that Cicero aptly calls 'Socratic medicine' (*Socratica medicina*).[80] In many ways this analogy appears to work well. Medicine is an art that involves complex theoretical knowledge yet is clearly orientated towards a practical goal. It appears to offer an excellent model for a conception of philosophy involving both complex theory (λόγος) and practical exercise (ἄσκησις) directed towards the transformation of one's life (βίος), for this is precisely what medicine attempts to achieve with respect to the body. However, in order to test this model and to see just how well it works in the specific context of the Stoics' philosophy, we must return to the question concerning the nature of τέχνη.

4. Stoic Definitions of τέχνη

In order to understand the analogy between philosophy and medicine better it will be necessary to consider the precise nature of the art of medicine and the way in which it

---

[77] *Plac. Hipp. Plat.* 5.2.22 (5.437 Kühn = 298.28-31 De Lacy = *SVF* 3.471; trans. De Lacy).

[78] *Plac. Hipp. Plat.* 5.2.23 (5.437 Kühn = 298.33 De Lacy = *SVF* 3.471).

[79] I note again the dispute between early Stoics concerning the precise nature of the relationship between opinions or judgements (δόξαι, κρίσεις) and emotions (πάθη), such as that between Zeno and Chrysippus reported in Galen *Plac. Hipp. Plat.* 5.1.4 (5.429 Kühn = 292.17-20 De Lacy = *SVF* 1.209, 3.461). I shall return to this in Chapter 7 § 2.

[80] Cicero *Tusc. Disp.* 4.24 (= *SVF* 3.424).

might differ from other arts, something that we have already discussed in the previous chapter. However, before doing this it might be helpful to begin by considering some more general attempts by the Stoics to define τέχνη.

According to Olympiodorus, Zeno defined an art (τέχνη) as 'a system of apprehensions unified by practice for some goal useful in life'.[81] By 'system of apprehensions' (σύστημα ἐκ καταλήψεων) we can understand a systematic body of knowledge made up of apprehensions, these being assents to 'adequate impressions' (φαντασία καταληπτική).[82] These apprehensions should be understood as secure instances of empirical knowledge. This system is 'unified by practice' (συγγεγυμνασμένων), that is, brought together into a system through training or exercise, as in the case of an apprentice who brings together all of the principles that he has learned into a real body of knowledge only when he engages in practical training. This systematic body of knowledge is 'directed towards a useful goal or a good purpose' (πρός τι τέλος εὔχρηστον),[83] a formulation that recalls the distinction in the *Gorgias* between arts which aim at something good and mere empirical knacks which aim at short-term pleasure.[84] Finally, the useful goal to which an art is directed is 'within life' (τῶν ἐν τῷ βίῳ), a point which serves simply to underscore the practical nature of an art.

There is nothing in this definition that is immediately controversial.[85] An art (τέχνη) is a systematic body of knowledge, based upon empirically derived principles but also requiring practice or training, with some specific practical goal. Any Stoic conception of an art concerned with the health of the soul will presumably conform to this definition. As we have already noted, this art is identified with human excellence

---

[81] Olympiodorus *In Gorg.* 12.1 (= *SVF* 1.73 = LS 42 A): Ζήνων δέ φησιν ὅτι τέχνη ἐστὶ σύστημα ἐκ καταλήψεων συγγεγυμνασμένων πρός τι τέλος εὔχρηστον τῶν ἐν τῷ βίῳ. See the detailed analysis in Sparshott, 'Zeno on Art', pp. 284-90. Other ancient sources that report this definition, although often without attribution, include Lucian *De Parasito* 4 (= *SVF* 1.73), Sextus Empiricus *Adv. Math.* 2.10 (= *SVF* 1.73), and Ps.-Galen *Def. Med.* 7 (19.350 Kühn = *SVF* 2.93).

[82] Alternatively, an objective, cognitive, recognizable, or convincing impression (or presentation). For comments on the translation of this term see Sandbach, 'Phantasia Kataleptike', p. 10; Hadot, *The Inner Citadel*, p. 104. For discussion of this concept and Stoic epistemology in general see Sandbach, 'Phantasia Kataleptike'; Frede, 'Stoics and Skeptics on Clear and Distinct Impressions', pp. 157-70; Frede in *CHHP*, pp. 300-16; Rist, *Stoic Philosophy*, pp. 133-51; Striker, 'Κριτήριον τῆς ἀληθείας', pp. 51-68, 73-76; Hankinson, 'Natural Criteria and the Transparency of Judgement', pp. 168-70; Watson, *The Stoic Theory of Knowledge*, pp. 34-36. This concept will be discussed further in Chapter 4 § 2 (c) and Chapter 7 § 2 (c).

[83] Sparshott, 'Zeno on Art', p. 289, notes that the precise meaning of εὔχρηστος is difficult to determine and suggests that 'useful' or 'serviceable' (LSJ) does not do justice to the presence of the εὐ prefix. He proposes 'of good use'. However it is perhaps also worth noting that some Stoic sources appear to use this term to describe 'preferred indifferents'; see e.g. Plutarch *Stoic. Rep.* 1038a (= *SVF* 3.674), *Comm. Not.* 1070a (= *SVF* 3.123).

[84] See Plato *Gorg.* 464b-465a.

[85] However, as we shall see in Chapter 4 § 2 (c), Sextus Empiricus will object to its reliance upon the idea of an 'adequate impression'.

(ἀρετή) and with wisdom (σοφία, φρόνησις).[86] Human excellence or wisdom, then, is an art, a systematic body of knowledge directed towards the cultivation of the health of the soul. However, one important question that this definition does not address is the relationship between the practice of this art and the goal to which it is directed. This is, in effect, the same as the question of whether the possession of expertise in an art is, on its own, a sufficient condition for securing that towards which the art is directed. If the goal (τέλος) of the art of living is the cultivation of well-being (εὐδαιμονία), then will expertise in that art guarantee well-being? In order to consider this question it might be helpful to begin by returning to some of the distinctions made in the previous chapter between different types of τέχνη.

As we have seen in the previous chapter, it is possible to outline a number of different types of art or craft (τέχνη). Here I shall focus upon just three types; the *productive* (ποιητική), the *performative* (πρακτική), and the *stochastic* (στοχαστική).[87] As we have already seen, a *productive* art is one that produces a product (ἔργον). An example of this sort of art would be shoemaking. In this case the product is clearly distinct from the process that produces it. The goal of shoemaking is to make shoes and so the goal (τέλος) of this type of art may be identified with the product (ἔργον) produced. The expert shoemaker can easily be identified by his ability to make good shoes. A *performative* art is one in which the goal of the art is identical with the performance of the art itself. An example of this sort of art would be dancing. In this case, the art aims at nothing beyond its own activity, and the actions (ἔργα) that constitute this activity are its 'product' (ἔργον). A possessor of this type of art can be identified simply by their ability to practise the art well. A *stochastic* art is one that does not produce a distinct physical product but instead aims at a goal clearly distinguishable from the practice of the art itself.[88] Examples of this sort of art would include medicine and navigation. In this case, the goal (τέλος) of the art – in the example of medicine, health – is not a separate physical product. It is also important to note that the possession of expertise in this sort of art is not necessarily enough to guarantee the desired result. If a so-called shoemaker failed to make a good pair of shoes then it would be reasonable to conclude that, in fact, the individual in question did not possess the art of shoemaking. Yet if a doctor failed to save a patient one would not necessarily assume that the doctor had not performed well. In other words, although a practitioner of a stochastic art may be an expert in their art, that expertise will not on its own always guarantee achievement of the goal of the art (in

---

[86] See Arius Didymus 2.7.5b10 (2.66.14-67.4 WH = *SVF* 3.560); also Alexander of Aphrodisias *Mant.* 159.33-34 (= *SVF* 3.66), Sextus Empiricus *Adv. Math.* 11.170 (= *SVF* 3.598), Cicero *Acad.* 2.23 (= *SVF* 2.117). It is important to note that, unlike Aristotle, the Stoics tend to use the terms σοφία and φρόνησις synonymously. See Tsekourakis, *Studies in the Terminology of Early Stoic Ethics*, pp. 128-31.

[87] The other types of τέχνη mentioned in the last chapter – the *acquisitive* (κτητική) and the *theoretical* (θεωρητική) – although important for Plato are not relevant here.

[88] 'Stochastic' from στοχαστικός, 'skilful in aiming at', 'able to hit' (LSJ); deriving from στοχάζομαι, 'to aim'. Sometimes τέχναι στοχαστικαί is translated as 'conjectural arts' (e.g. Barnes, *et al.*, *Alexander of Aphrodisias, On Aristotle Prior Analytics 1.1-7*).

this example, the health of the patient). This is due to the role played by external factors outside of the practitioner's control.[89] Instead, the expert in a stochastic art will only be successful 'for the most part' (ἐπὶ τὸ πολὺ).[90]

Of these three types of τέχνη it would be reasonable to suppose that the art that is concerned with the health of the soul is a stochastic art. This appears to be implicit in the analogy with medicine which, as we have seen, was taken quite seriously. Unfortunately this is the most complex of the three types. It is clear that the goal of a productive art is the physical product that is produced, while the goal of a performative art is the activity or practice of the art itself. A good shoemaker is one who makes good shoes; a good dancer is one who gives a good performance. In each case, successful achievement of the goal (τέλος) can be evaluated with reference to the ἔργον, the product or performance. With a stochastic art, however, this is not the case. As we have already seen, an excellent doctor may consistently practice the art of medicine without error and yet in some instances he will not be able to cure all of his patients due to external factors beyond his control. One is faced with the paradox of an expert who does not always achieve the goal of the art that he is practising, in this case health. If we accept the medical analogy, then, insofar as it is like medicine, the art concerned with the health of the soul – the art of living – will also face this problem.

In order to overcome this problem, the Stoic Antipater – who did conceive the art of living as stochastic – suggested that in the case of such arts the goal (τέλος) should be understood not as a specific desired outcome but rather as a correct performance of the art itself, defining the goal (τέλος) as doing everything within one's power (πᾶν τὸ καθ᾽ αὑτὸν ποιεῖν) to attain the desired outcome.[91] The advantage of this formulation is that, as in the case of productive and performative arts, the goal becomes that by which one can assess the ability of a practitioner. Thus, a good doctor is not one that produces health in his patients but rather one that does all that he can within his power to produce health in his patients. Similarly, a good archer is

---

[89] See Striker, 'Following Nature', p. 244.

[90] See Alexander of Aphrodisias *In An. Pr.* 165.8-15 (trans. Mueller & Gould). Here Alexander follows Aristotle *Eth. Nic.* 1112a30-1112b11, esp. 1112b8-9. Aristotle puts this down to the indeterminate subject matter of the arts in question rather than to the role of external factors. Alexander lists both of these as defining characteristics of a stochastic art (*Quaest.* 61.1-28). However the first of these cannot be right (*pace* Roochnik, *Of Art and Wisdom*, p. 52) and may be seen to reflect Aristotle's somewhat rigid distinction between arts and sciences, and the inferior status that he assigns to the former.

[91] See Arius Didymus 2.7.6a (2.76.11-15 WH = *SVF* 3 Ant. 57) with discussion in Long, 'Carneades and the Stoic *telos*', p. 81; Inwood, 'Goal and Target in Stoicism', pp. 550-52; Striker, 'Antipater, or The Art of Living', pp. 306-11; 'Following Nature', pp. 243-44. Antipater's formulation appears to have been in response to criticism from the Academic Carneades who objected to Antipater's revised formulation of the Stoic τέλος as selecting certain primary natural things and rejecting other non-natural things (also reported in Arius Didymus). For ancient criticism of Antipater's τέλος formulation see Alexander of Aphrodisias *Mant.* 164.3-9 (part in *SVF* 3.193 = LS 64 B), who also reports Antipater's formulation (without naming him) at 161.5-6 (not in *SVF*).

not necessarily one that always hits his target but, rather, one that does all that is in his power to hit the target.[92] The archer's goal (τέλος), on this account, is to shoot well; whether he hits the target or not will depend upon a number of external factors outside of his control. Similarly, whether a doctor saves his patient or not will depend not merely upon his own expertise but also upon a number of external factors. It is the role played by these external factors that leads to the distinction between goal (τέλος) and function or product (ἔργον) in stochastic arts and not any indeterminacy with regard to the subject matter or the expert's actions.[93]

We now have two distinct conceptions of a stochastic art. In the first of these it was admitted that occasionally an expert will not always reach the goal (τέλος) of the art. The doctor, for example, will not always save his patients. In the second conception – attributed to Antipater – the goal (τέλος) is redefined as 'making every effort' or 'doing everything within one's power' (πᾶν τὸ καθ' αὑτὸν ποιεῖν) to achieve the desired outcome.[94] The goal of medicine would thus become not cultivating health but 'making every effort' to cultivate health. In a passage by Alexander of Aphrodisias both of these conceptions of a stochastic art are discussed and both are rejected.[95] We have already noted the problems with the first conception, namely that it becomes difficult to assess whether someone has expertise in their art or not. The problem with the second conception is that, although an expert will always be said to have reached the goal by 'making every effort', the idea that the goal of medicine is *not* cultivating health and the goal of archery is *not* hitting targets fails to do justice to the nature of these arts. Although achieving these goals is, to a certain extent, independent of mastery of the art in question due to the role that external factors will play in determining the outcome, nevertheless these goals *remain* the reason why one would choose to learn one of these arts in the first place.[96] To say that the goal (τέλος) of medicine – the goal being that to which all actions can be referred – was a correct performance of medical technique, rather than the restoration of the health of the patient, would fail to explain a number of things typically done when practising the art of medicine.

---

[92] This example comes from Cicero *Fin.* 3.22 (= *SVF* 3.18).

[93] See Ierodiakonou, 'Alexander of Aphrodisias on Medicine as a Stochastic Art', pp. 481-82, *contra* Inwood, 'Goal and Target in Stoicism', pp. 549-50, and Roochnik, *Of Art and Wisdom*, p. 52.

[94] See Arius Didymus 2.7.6a (2.76.11-15 WH = *SVF* 3 Ant. 57).

[95] See Alexander of Aphrodisias *Quaest.* 61.1-28 (ll. 4-23 = *SVF* 3.19, although there is no explicit reference to the Stoa), translated in Sharples, *Alexander of Aphrodisias, Quaestiones 2.16-3.15*. Note also Alexander of Aphrodisias *In Top.* 32.12-34.5, *In An. Pr.* 39.30-40.5, 165.8-15. For discussion see Ierodiakonou, 'Alexander of Aphrodisias on Medicine as a Stochastic Art', p. 475; Roochnik, *Of Art and Wisdom*, pp. 54-55; Inwood, 'Goal and Target in Stoicism', pp. 549-50; Striker, 'Following Nature', p. 244.

[96] See e.g. Plutarch's criticisms of Antipater's position in *Comm. Not.* 1071b-c: 'If someone should say that an archer in shooting does all that in him lies not for the purpose of hitting the mark but for the purpose of doing all that in him lies, it would be thought that he was spinning some monstrous and enigmatic yarns' (trans. Cherniss). Note also Cicero *Fin.* 3.22 (= *SVF* 3.18).

In order to overcome these problems Alexander offers a third option.[97] He suggests that in a stochastic art it is necessary to make a clear distinction between the goal (τέλος) of the art and its function, action, or product (ἔργον). Thus, in the case of medicine, the goal (τέλος) – that for the sake of which every effort is made – would remain health, but the proper task or function (ἔργον) would become to make every effort towards achieving that goal.[98] This is clearly better than Antipater's paradoxical formulation. Alexander suggests that emphasizing this distinction between goal (τέλος) and function (ἔργον) is necessary due to the role played by external factors in stochastic arts. According to this third formulation, an expert in a stochastic art will always achieve the ἔργον of his art, as in the other arts, and this may form a basis for judging his expertise.[99] However, due to the role of external factors he will not always achieve the τέλος of his art.[100] The expert doctor, for example, will not always manage to cultivate health (the τέλος), but – if he *is* an expert – he will always make every effort towards cultivating health (the ἔργον).

As one can see, the question concerning the nature of stochastic arts in general, and medicine in particular, is very complex. However, our primary concern here is not with the nature of the art of medicine itself but rather with the status of the analogy between the art of medicine and the art of living. This analogy appears to imply that one should conceive the art of living as a stochastic art. However, if one conceives the Stoic art of living as a stochastic art one immediately faces a problem. It is reported that the goal (τέλος) of the Stoic art of living is the cultivation of well-being or happiness (εὐδαιμονία).[101] If one conceives the art of living as a stochastic art then this goal of εὐδαιμονία – like health in the case of medicine – will *not* necessarily follow from a correct performance of that art. Instead it will be dependent upon other external factors. This *must be wrong* insofar as the Stoic art of living (identified with ἀρετή) is repeatedly said to be a sufficient condition for happiness (εὐδαιμονία) by itself (this is precisely what distinguishes it from the Peripatetic

---

[97] This appears at *Quaest.* 61.23-28, omitted in *SVF* 3.19.

[98] To a certain extent Alexander follows Aristotle here, as one might expect. See esp. Aristotle *Top.* 101b5-10 and *Rhet.* 1355b12-14. In the former Aristotle suggests that expertise in medicine should be evaluated with reference to a practitioner using all of the available means. In the latter he suggests that the function (ἔργον) of medicine is not simply to create health but to move the patient as far towards health as is possible in the circumstances.

[99] It is important to note the various ways in which the notion of ἔργον functions in the three types of τέχνη. In a productive art the ἔργον is the physical product, the pair of shoes made by the shoemaker. In a performative art the ἔργον is the action 'produced' by the artist, the performance itself (this was the sense in which the term was understood in Chapter 1). In a stochastic art the ἔργον becomes the task or function of the art, that which the doctor does with reference to the τέλος. Thus the 'product' (ἔργον) of medicine is not health (which is in fact the τέλος) but rather those actions which are directed towards cultivating health. See Alexander of Aphrodisias *In Top.* 32.27-33.4, discussed in Roochnik, *Of Art and Wisdom*, p. 54.

[100] In productive and performative arts the ἔργον and τέλος always coincide.

[101] See e.g. Arius Didymus 2.7.6e (2.77.16 WH = *SVF* 3.16). This is, in turn, identified with living in accordance with excellence (ἀρετή) and with nature (φύσις).

position).[102] If it *were* a stochastic art, expertise would *not* be sufficient to guarantee the goal, εὐδαιμονία.

We are left, then, with two other alternatives. The first would be to characterize the art of living as a productive art, in which case one would have to say that it is an art that produces happiness (εὐδαιμονία), this being its 'product'.[103] The second would be to characterize it as a performative art, in which case well-being or happiness (εὐδαιμονία) would have to be identified with the performance of the art itself. In either of these alternatives εὐδαιμονία would be both the τέλος and the ἔργον of the art, for these coincide in these two types of art, and in either case expertise in the art would guarantee attainment of the τέλος. The question, then, becomes whether the Stoics conceived εὐδαιμονία as a product or as an activity.[104] According to Cicero, at least some Stoics adopted the second of these options:

> We do not consider that wisdom resembles navigation or medicine, but it is more like the gestures just mentioned, and like dancing, in that the actual exercise (*effectio*) of the skill is in itself, and does not aim at an external object.[105]

This suggests that wisdom – identified elsewhere with the art of living and characterized as that which guarantees εὐδαιμονία – is a performative art like dancing, acting, or music, and not like the stochastic arts of medicine and archery.[106]

---

[102] *Pace* Dobbin, *Epictetus, Discourses Book 1*, p. 156, who, on the basis of the reports concerning Antipater, suggests that all Stoics held the art of living to be stochastic. This is clearly not the case for someone like Epictetus (Dobbin's primary subject) for whom the art of living is concerned only with what is within one's own power (ἐφ' ἡμῖν) and for whom success in that art is in no way dependent upon external factors. For the distinction between the Stoic and Peripatetic positions see Cicero *Tusc. Disp.* 5.40-41 (= LS 63 L), Aulus Gellius 18.1.1-14 (part in *SVF* 3.56).

[103] This is suggested in Alexander of Aphrodisias *Mant.* 159.33-34 (= *SVF* 3.66): 'excellence is an art that produces happiness' (ἡ δὲ ἀρετὴ τέχνη κατ' αὐτοὺς εὐδαιμονίας ποιητική), an account that may implicitly assume Aristotle's restricted conception of τέχνη as essentially ποιητική τέχνη (see Aristotle *Eth. Nic.* 1140a1-23). As I have noted in the previous chapter, this is also the way in which Irwin attempts to explain the relationship between τέχνη and εὐδαιμονία in the early Platonic dialogues (see his *Plato's Moral Theory*). However he has been criticized because this reduces ἀρετή to something purely instrumental rather than an end in itself (see Vlastos, *Socrates: Ironist and Moral Philosopher*, pp. 6-10).

[104] Alternatively one might ask how the Stoics understood ἔργον in this particular context, ἔργον covering both 'product' and 'action'.

[105] Cicero *Fin.* 3.24 (= *SVF* 3.11; trans. Wright); see also 3.32. The word *effectio* should be understood similarly to ἔργον, that is as referring to the 'product' of an art. In a performative art the performance itself is the 'product' (ἔργον, *effectio*). This is distinct from the attempt in *Fin.* 3.22 to characterize the art of living as a stochastic art using the analogy with an archer. That analogy only works with reference to the desire to secure 'primary natural objects' (τὰ πρῶτα κατὰ φύσιν, *princpia naturae*).

[106] See Long, 'Carneades and the Stoic *telos*', pp. 83-84, for the same conclusion. For the identification between the art of living and wisdom see Cicero *Fin.* 1.42, Sextus Empiricus *Adv. Math.* 11.181, and the discussion in § 7 below.

It is primarily an *activity* that is not directed towards any further goal beyond the activity itself. It is the very performance of the art of living that constitutes εὐδαιμονία, itself conceived as an activity,[107] just as the satisfaction gained from the performing arts is to be found in the very act of the performance itself.

What does this account of the different τέχναι contribute to our understanding of the concept of an art of living? We are now in a position to say that this art (τέχνη) is a systematic body of knowledge based upon empirically derived principles and brought together through practice. It is directed towards a goal (τέλος) which we have seen described as the health of the soul (τὴν τῆς ψυχῆς ὑγίειαν) and as εὐδαιμονία, which may be understood to be synonymous.[108] Finally, this goal is identical to the activity of practising the art of living itself (rather than a distinct product produced by it or something contingent upon other external factors). As a performative art, then, one can see the limits of the analogy between the Stoic art of living and medicine. Yet nevertheless one can also understand why this analogy came to be so common in ancient discussions concerning the nature and function of philosophy. Philosophy treats the soul analogously to the way in which medicine treats the body; however, the *way* in which it achieves this is, for the Stoics at least, subtly different.[109]

5. The Relationship between ἄσκησις and λόγος

An important element in Zeno's definition of τέχνη is the reference it makes to the role of practice. As we have seen, an art, according to Zeno, is a systematic body of knowledge that is brought into its systematic unity by way of practice (συγγεγυμνασμένων). One can immediately see how this echoes Socrates' claim in the *Gorgias* that the development of expertise in an art will require not just an understanding of the relevant principles (λόγοι) but also training (ἄσκησις). For Zeno, then, as well as Socrates, τέχνη involves both λόγος and ἄσκησις. A number of other early Stoic sources also make reference to the importance of ἄσκησις.[110] But what exactly is the role of ἄσκησις in the Stoic concept of an art of living? It should

---

[107] Aristotle famously characterized εὐδαιμονία as an activity (see e.g. *Eth. Nic.* 1176a30-1176b9), with which the Stoics would agree. See Long, 'Stoic Eudaimonism', p. 82.

[108] Note the etymological meaning of εὐδαιμονία as having a good daimon or spirit and the resonance between this and the idea of a healthy soul.

[109] The prevalence of this analogy even among Stoics presumably reflects the influence of Socrates who hints at the analogy but who would not have engaged in the careful analysis of different types of τέχνη begun by Plato (in his evaluation of the status of rhetoric) and taken to its heights in later authors such as Galen and Alexander of Aphrodisias (in their evaluations of the status of medicine). Of course, for a Peripatetic the medical analogy *does* work in all of its details for they would be happy to acknowledge the role played by external factors in the cultivation of εὐδαιμονία (see e.g. Aristotle *Eth. Nic.* 1178b33-1179a9).

[110] See e.g. Aristo *apud* Clement of Alexandria *Strom.* 2.20 (*PG* 8.1052b = *SVF* 1.370). Note also the references in Diogenes Laertius to two works entitled Περὶ ἀσκήσεως by the Stoics Herillus (7.166 = *SVF* 1.409) and Dionysius (7.167 = *SVF* 1.422). Further references can be found in Chapter 5 § 1.

be clear from what has already been said that this question will be of central importance for the creation of a conception of philosophy that can adequately deal with the idea that philosophy is primarily expressed in one's way of life (βίος).

No extended early Stoic source dealing with this topic survives. However, it is addressed in a pair of letters by Seneca which include a number of references to the idea of an *ars vitae*.[111] The first of these letters deals with the question of whether philosophical doctrines (*decreta*) are sufficient on their own without precepts (*praecepta*) for the art of living. The second deals with the question of whether precepts (*praecepta*) are sufficient without doctrines (*decreta*). By *decreta* we can understand doctrines, principles, or opinions; by *praecepta* we can understand precepts, teachings, instructions, written rules, exercises, or maxims directed towards the transformation of an individual's behaviour.[112] Although the notion of *praecepta* may be slightly broader than that of ἄσκησις, Seneca's discussion bears directly upon the relationship between λόγος and ἄσκησις insofar as it deals with the question of whether either philosophical theory or practical advice are, on their own, sufficient for transforming one's behaviour.[113]

Seneca opens the first of these two letters by noting that, on the one hand, there are those who have claimed that precepts are the only significant component within philosophy, abstract theory being unnecessary insofar as it is of no practical import, while, on the other hand, there are those who think that precepts are of little use and that doctrines are by themselves sufficient for living well.[114] The second of these positions was held by the Stoic Aristo, and Seneca begins by considering Aristo's arguments. Aristo argues that precepts will be of no use to someone who lacks the appropriate understanding for that ignorance will cloud whatever they do. Only those free from such ignorance can benefit from precepts (*praecepta*). However, precepts are totally superfluous to such individuals who, being free from error, do not need any instruction; 'to one who knows, it is superfluous to give precepts; to one who does not know, it is insufficient'.[115] According to Aristo, only the doctrines (*decreta*) of philosophy can make any difference to someone's way of life; precepts (*praecepta*) are pointless.[116] There are two points that need to be noted here. The first is that Aristo holds a position similar to the intellectualist reading of Socrates in which

---

[111] These letters are Seneca *Epist.* 94 and 95. I have used the editions by Reynolds (OCT) and Gummere (LCL). As we shall see, these letters include a number of Latin translations from earlier Stoics including Aristo (*SVF* 1.358-359) and Cleanthes (*SVF* 1.582).

[112] See the respective entries in *OLD*. With regard to *praecepta*, Newman has argued that it is artificial to try to distinguish between, on the one hand, the notion of a philosophical exercise and, on the other, its written or rhetorical expression. Instead, he suggests that, for the later Stoics at least, philosophical texts were themselves seen to be central to such exercises, whether they be in the form of instructions directed towards students or texts produced by students themselves ('*Cotidie meditare*', pp. 1478-82). I shall return to this point in Chapter 5 § 5.

[113] For a discussion of these letters in relation to the role of techniques (exercises) and analysis (theory) in Stoic cognitive therapy see Sorabji, *Emotion and Peace of Mind*, pp. 161-63.

[114] See *Epist.* 94.1-3.

[115] *Epist.* 94.11 (= *SVF* 1.359): *praecepta dare scienti supervacuum est, nescienti parum.*

[116] See *Epist.* 94.13.

theoretical understanding alone is thought to guarantee excellence (ἀρετή). The second is that Aristo holds on to the orthodox Stoic distinction between the wise (σοφοί) and the non-wise (φαῦλοι), characterizing the non-wise as mad or insane (*insania*).[117] However, he does not appear to consider the possibility of a third intermediate category, namely those who are 'making progress' (προκοπή), philosophers in the etymological sense of the word.

In his response to Aristo, Seneca is happy to acknowledge the central importance of philosophical doctrines (*decreta*) but questions Aristo's outright rejection of the role that precepts (*praecepta*) might play. For Seneca, precepts do not teach but they do reinforce teaching already received: 'advice is not teaching; it merely engages the attention and rouses us, and concentrates the memory, and keeps it from losing grip'.[118] Thus precepts (*praecepta*) are not for the sage who already enjoys secure knowledge, but rather for those who are 'making progress' (προκοπή, *proficientes*), those who in one sense already know but who have not yet fully assimilated that knowledge and have not yet translated that knowledge into actions. Seneca responds to the claim that precepts only work with reference to the theoretical arguments that underpin them by saying that precepts act to remind one of those arguments and to assist in their digestion.[119] Just like the training undertaken by the apprentice craftsman, Seneca suggests that precepts (*praecepta*) serve as a form of training for one who has already studied philosophical doctrines (*decreta*).[120] Precepts are thus an often useful complement to doctrines, at least for those who are 'making progress' (προκοπή, *proficientes*).[121]

The question that follows naturally, and which is dealt with in the second of these letters, is whether such precepts are sufficient on their own to transform an individual's way of life. Following Aristo, Seneca acknowledges that precepts can be of little help to a disturbed mind.[122] Moreover, although precepts can indeed bring about a change in behaviour, they cannot do so alone. For Seneca, philosophy is both theoretical and practical (*contemplativa et activa*); it involves both doctrines and precepts (*decreta et praecepta*).[123] In order to illustrate this inter-dependency Seneca draws a number of analogies: doctrines (*decreta*) are like the branches of a tree while precepts (*praecepta*) are like the leaves, the latter depending upon the former for their existence, the strength of the former only being seen in the display of the latter. Alternatively, doctrines are like the roots of a tree and precepts are like the leaves, the

---

[117] See *Epist.* 94.17.

[118] *Epist.* 94.25 (trans. Gummere): *non docet admonitio sed advertit, sed excitat, sed memoriam continet nec patitur elabi.*

[119] I shall develop this idea of 'digestion' of philosophical doctrines in Chapter 5 § 3 (b).

[120] See *Epist.* 94.32. Recalling points that I have already discussed in Chapter 1 § 3, Seneca goes on here (*Epist.* 94.40-42) to suggest that the best form of *praeceptum* is association with a living role model and suggests that *praecepta* are in effect substitutes for direct contact with a philosophical mentor.

[121] Seneca is explicit on this point at *Epist.* 94.50. For Seneca's own understanding of the intermediate category of those 'making progress' (*proficientes*) see *Epist.* 75.8-18.

[122] See *Epist.* 95.4; also 95.38.

[123] See *Epist.* 95.10.

former being the hidden foundation for the latter, the latter being the outward expression of the strength of the former. Again, doctrines are like the heart of a living being while precepts are like the actions of the limbs, the former being hidden and only known to the world via the movements of the latter, which depend upon the former for their power of movement.[124]

In each of these analogies the doctrines (*decreta*) are the necessary but concealed foundation of the precepts (*praecepta*). The precepts form the outward and visible expression of the doctrines, without which the doctrines would remain hidden. Seneca's conclusion, then, is that both doctrines and precepts are necessary for the acquisition of wisdom (*sapientia*, σοφία).[125] The *praecepta* of Seneca, although perhaps broader in scope than the notion of ἄσκησις, are similar to the training undertaken by an apprentice implicit in Socrates' discussion of τέχνη. While both Socrates and Seneca clearly affirm that an understanding of the relevant doctrines or principles (*decreta*, λόγοι) is a necessary condition for the acquisition of expertise, both also acknowledge the role that some form of exercise or exhortation (*praecepta*, ἄσκησις) might play in that acquisition. Although neither would want to say that such exercise or training could ever be a sufficient condition on its own, both appear to lean towards the claim that it may be a necessary condition alongside a grasp of the relevant principles.

6. The Stoic Division of Philosophy

The account so far of a conception of philosophy as an art (τέχνη) concerned with one's way of life (βίος) and involving two components, philosophical theory (λόγος) and philosophical exercise (ἄσκησις), is relatively straightforward. However, what is not so immediately clear is how this might be reconciled with the common image of Stoic philosophy as a highly structured system divided into the three components of logic, physics, and ethics. According to the summary of Stoic philosophy by Diogenes Laertius,

> they [the Stoics] say that philosophical discourse (τὸν κατὰ φιλοσοφίαν λόγον) has three parts, one of these being physical (φυσικόν), another ethical (ἠθικόν), and another logical (λογικόν).[126]

---

[124] See *Epist.* 95.59, 95.64.
[125] Doctrines (*decreta*) are clearly a necessary condition. They may in certain circumstances be a sufficient condition but, in general, Seneca tends to doubt this. Precepts (*praecepta*) may in certain circumstances be a sufficient condition but again, in general, Seneca tends to doubt this. However, whether precepts are a necessary condition is not so clear. Seneca appears to be inclined to say yes. Nevertheless, for Seneca *decreta* retain a certain priority over *praecepta*.
[126] Diogenes Laertius 7.39 (= *SVF* 2.37 = Posidonius fr. 87 EK = LS 26 B; trans. LS). For commentary see Kidd, *Posidonius, The Commentary*, pp. 350-52. A full survey of the various ancient divisions can be found in Sextus Empiricus *Adv. Math.* 7.2-23.

It is interesting to note that it is not philosophy that is divided into these three parts but rather philosophical discourse (τὸν κατὰ φιλοσοφίαν λόγον). Elsewhere, in Plutarch, we are told that it is philosopher's theorems (τῶν τοῦ φιλοσόφου θεωρημάτων) that are divided.[127] It is also interesting to note that according to Diogenes Laertius this division was first made by Zeno, and then restated by Chrysippus, in works both called *On Discourse* (Περὶ λόγου).[128] It seems, then, that this division was primarily conceived as a division of *philosophical discourse*, not of *philosophy* itself.[129] As for philosophy proper, Diogenes Laertius reports the following:

> They compare philosophy to a living being (εἰκάζουσι δὲ ζῴῳ τὴν φιλοσοφίαν), likening logic (τὸ λογικόν) to bones and sinews, ethics (τὸ ἠθικόν) to the fleshier parts, and physics (τὸ φυσικόν) to the soul. They make a further comparison to an egg: logic is the outside, ethics is what comes next, and physics the innermost part; or to a fertile field: the surrounding wall corresponds to logic, its fruit to ethics, and its land or trees to physics; or to a city which is well fortified and governed according to reason.[130]

Elsewhere, in Sextus Empiricus, the first of these similes is credited to Posidonius and his preference for this one in particular is explained:

> Posidonius differed: since the parts of philosophy are inseparable from each other, yet plants are thought of as distinct from fruit and walls are separate from plants, he claimed that the simile for philosophy should rather be with a living being, where physics is the blood and flesh, logic the bones and sinews, and ethics the soul.[131]

These passages suggest that, for the Stoics, philosophy itself was conceived as a unified entity with three parts that could only be divided from one another in discourse.[132] Just as a living animal is composed of flesh, bones, and soul that can

---

[127] See Plutarch *Stoic. Rep.* 1035a (= *SVF* 2.42).

[128] See Diogenes Laertius 7.39 (= *SVF* 2.37). For ancient references to these works see the lists in *SVF*, vol. 1, p. 71, and vol. 3, p. 201. All but one derive from Diogenes Laertius.

[129] For further discussion see Hadot, 'Philosophie, Discours Philosophique, et Divisions de la Philosophie chez les Stoïciens'; Gourinat, *La dialectique des Stoïciens*, pp. 19-34; Ildefonse, *Les Stoïciens I*, pp. 23-29. That the Stoics drew a sharp distinction between philosophy and philosophical discourse is made clear in Epictetus' analogy with the art of building: just as the builder does not discourse about building but builds, so the philosopher does not engage only in discourse about wisdom but also endeavours to become wise (see *Diss.* 3.21.4).

[130] Diogenes Laertius 7.40 (= *SVF* 2.38 = LS 26 B; trans. LS). Note that in each case physics is in some sense foundational, logic gives strength or protection, while ethics is the largest or most visible part.

[131] Posidonius fr. 88 EK *apud* Sextus Empiricus *Adv. Math.* 7.19 (= LS 26 D; trans. Kidd, modified). Note that physics and ethics have changed places when compared with the version in Diogenes Laertius.

[132] See Hicks, *Stoic and Epicurean*, pp. 54-55; Hadot, 'Les divisions des parties de la philosophie dans l'Antiquité', pp. 208-11.

only be distinguished from one another as component parts in abstraction, so philosophy can only be divided into the component parts of logic, physics, and ethics in abstraction. Philosophy proper has no parts.

Philosophy itself, an activity directed towards the cultivation of wisdom (σοφία), involves all three of these elements. It is not that practical ethics utilizes the theoretical arguments of physics and logic.[133] Rather one might say that each of these three parts is both theoretical and practical, and that they are interdependent with one another. Moreover, this interrelation means that expertise in one will always involve expertise in the others. For example, someone who understands the organization and structure of the cosmos will at the same time know how to act within the cosmos.[134] The sage will thus simultaneously practise all three aspects of philosophy in his life. He will practise logic by analysing his judgements, practise physics by locating himself as but one part of the larger cosmic system, and practise ethics in his actions. Thus Cicero notes that for the Stoics there are not only ethical virtues (*virtutes*) but also physical and logical virtues.[135] As one might expect, following the Socratic doctrine of the unity of virtue or human excellence (ἀρετή), the Stoics held these three types of virtues to be one.[136] This might be glossed by saying that there is a single corporeal state or disposition of the soul (ψυχή) that, when possessed, is expressed in a variety of different ways, which may be classified according to the tripartite division of philosophical discourse.

The Stoic position is thus very different from Aristotle's account of the different parts of philosophy. Rather than three mutually dependent components, Aristotle divides the theoretical from the practical and proposes a hierarchy of sub-parts within each.[137] Theoretical philosophy, for example, is divided into three parts arranged in a specific order depending upon their relation with impermanent matter, the highest of the theoretical sciences being theology (θεολογική), also called first philosophy (πρώτη φιλοσοφία). Logic is rejected as a science in its own right and is relegated to the status of a tool or instrument (ὄργανον).[138] In contrast, for the Stoics philosophy is a unified whole without any internal hierarchy and Posidonius' comparison with a living being is in many ways the most appropriate of those proposed. Their organic conception of philosophy as three interdependent components of equal status might be

---

[133] For the Stoics, logic is no mere organon or tool as it was for Aristotle; rather it is an essential part of philosophy itself (see Christensen, *An Essay on the Unity of Stoic Philosophy*, p. 39). This seems to have been emphasized in particular by Posidonius (see Kidd, *Posidonius, The Commentary*, pp. 352-55).
[134] See Bréhier, *The Hellenistic and Roman Age*, p. 37; Hadot, *The Inner Citadel*, pp. 77-82; 'La philosophie antique: une éthique ou une pratique?', pp. 25-26.
[135] See Cicero *Fin.* 3.72 (= *SVF* 3.281).
[136] See Schofield 'Ariston of Chois and the Unity of Virtue'; for Socrates see Penner 'The Unity of Virtue'.
[137] See Aristotle *Metaph.* 1025b3-1026a32, with Guthrie, *History*, vol. 6, pp. 130-34; Hadot, 'Les divisions des parties de la philosophie dans l'Antiquité', pp. 202-08; 'Philosophie, Discours Philosophique, et Divisions de la Philosophie chez les Stoïciens', pp. 207-08.
[138] This term was applied to Aristotle's logic by Alexander of Aphrodisias *In Top.* 74.29-30; see Guthrie, *History*, vol. 6, p. 135.

said to reflect the Stoic theory of a single immanent rational principle (λόγος) underpinning each part of their system,[139] while Aristotle's hierarchy of parts is clearly a reflection of the priority that he gives to that which is unchanging, with the most important part of philosophy being that which comprehends substance understood as the unchanging substrate of all existing things. Moreover, in contrast to Aristotle's division between the theoretical sciences of physics and theology on the one hand, and the practical sciences of ethics and politics on the other, for the Stoics all three aspects of philosophy are at once both theoretical and practical.[140] For them, if a division is to be made between theory and practice it must be made *within* each part of philosophy and not *between* them.

Returning to Diogenes Laertius' account of the various similes for philosophy, he continues his report by adding:

> On the statements of some of them [the Stoics], no part is given preference over another but they are mixed together.[141]

The division into three parts and the various arguments over the relative order of those parts seems to have been primarily a debate concerning the teaching of philosophy and the order in which students should be introduced to the different subjects of philosophical discourse.[142] Thus the Stoic debate concerning the relative order of the parts is not a question of a fundamental hierarchy, as it would have been for Aristotle, but rather merely a question of different teaching methods. For philosophy conceived as the cultivation of excellence (ἀρετή), there is neither a hierarchy nor a division. Indeed, those Stoics who affirmed the essentially mixed nature of philosophy are also said to have taught philosophy in a mixed form in order to emphasize this.[143]

7. Towards a Definition of Philosophy

We are now in a position to bring together these various Stoic ideas concerning the nature and function of philosophy and to offer a preliminary definition of philosophy

---

[139] Here, λόγος should be understood differently to the way in which it has been used thus far. In this context it refers to a single rational principle within nature responsible for the order of the cosmos, often referred to as the σπερματικὸς λόγος (see e.g. Diogenes Laertius 7.136 = *SVF* 1.102). This conception clearly owes much to Heraclitus (see e.g. fr. 1 DK). I shall touch upon this again in Chapter 7 § 2 (a).

[140] See Hadot, 'La philosophie antique: une éthique ou une pratique?', p. 25. However, as Hadot himself notes, pp. 31-32, with Aristotle the matter is, as always, significantly more complex (see e.g. Aristotle *Pol.* 1325b16-21).

[141] Diogenes Laertius 7.40 (= *SVF* 2.41 = LS 26 B; trans. LS).

[142] For differing orders see e.g. Plutarch *Stoic. Rep.* 1035a-f (part in *SVF* 2.42), Diogenes Laertius 7.40-41 (part in *SVF* 2.38, 43), Sextus Empiricus *Adv. Math.* 7.20-23 (part in *SVF* 2.44). See also Ildefonse, *Les Stoïciens I*, p. 24.

[143] See Diogenes Laertius 7.40 (= *SVF* 2.41).

as conceived by the Stoics. But first it is important to be clear concerning the distinction between philosophy (φιλοσοφία) and wisdom (σοφία). With Socrates, as we have already seen, philosophy was conceived as an art concerned with the *cultivation* of wisdom (σοφία) or human excellence (ἀρετή). Socrates was thus a philosopher in the etymological sense of the word, he searched for wisdom but he did not possess it himself. There is for Socrates, then, a clear distinction between philosophy (φιλοσοφία) and wisdom (σοφία); the former is that which searches for the latter.

With the Stoics, the matter is unfortunately not so clear. This is due to the tendency in some sources to move between the words philosophy (φιλοσοφία) and wisdom (σοφία) as if they were synonymous.[144] Seneca, for one, holds on to the etymological definition of philosophy, describing wisdom (*sapientia*) as the ultimate good and philosophy (*philosophia*) as the love of that good and the attempt to attain it.[145] Yet, as we have seen, insofar as the art of living (τέχνη περὶ τὸν βίον) is an art (τέχνη), it is, for the Stoics, a form of secure knowledge (ἐπιστήμη). As such, it is a form of knowledge reserved for the sage (σοφός). Thus one might be tempted to identify the possession of the art of living with wisdom (σοφία) itself. On this account, philosophy would not be the art of living but rather that which *desires* or *cultivates* the art of living. However, as we have also already seen, Epictetus does not understand philosophy in this way and he identifies the art of living with philosophy (φιλοσοφία) rather than wisdom (σοφία).[146]

Before attempting to offer a solution to this problem, it may be helpful to note two important points which have a direct bearing on this question. The first is the characterization of the art of living as a performative art not directed towards any goal beyond the performance itself. The second is the emphasis upon philosophy as a unified entity that, strictly speaking, cannot be divided into the distinct parts of logic, physics, and ethics. In order for this unified entity to exist it must, according to Stoic ontology, exist as a physical body.[147] Thus philosophy must in some sense be corporeal (σώματος), while philosophical discourse, as something 'sayable' (λεκτός), would be classified as incorporeal (ἀσώματος).[148] The only plausible place where

---

[144] See Ierodiakonou, 'The Stoic Division of Philosophy', pp. 60-61.

[145] See Seneca *Epist.* 89.4: *Sapientia perfectum bonum est mentis humanae; philosophia sapientiae amor est et adfectatio.*

[146] See Epictetus *Diss.* 1.15.2.

[147] According to Stoic ontology only bodies (σώματα) exist; see e.g. Plutarch *Comm. Not.* 1073e (= *SVF* 2.525).

[148] See Ierodiakonou, 'The Stoic Division of Philosophy', p. 61. For the ontological distinction between σώματος and ἀσώματος see e.g. Alexander of Aphrodisias *In Top.* 301.19-25 (= *SVF* 2.329 = LS 27 B), Sextus Empiricus *Adv. Math.* 10.218 (= *SVF* 2.331 = LS 27 D), Seneca *Epist.* 58.13-15 (= *SVF* 2.332 = LS 27 A), with Brunschwig, 'The Stoic Theory of the Supreme Genus and Platonic Ontology'. For the ontological status of λεκτά as ἀσώματα see e.g. Sextus Empiricus *Adv. Math.* 7.38 (= *SVF* 2.132), with Bréhier, *La théorie des incorporels dans l'ancien Stoïcisme*, pp. 14-36. According to Stoic ontology there are two categories of entity under the common heading of 'something' (τι). These are corporeals (σώματα) and incorporeals (ἀσώματα). Strictly speaking only the former 'exist'; the latter merely 'subsist'

either philosophy or wisdom could conceivably have a physical existence is inside the material soul (ψυχή) of its possessor.[149] For the Stoics, then, for philosophy to exist it must do so as a corporeal state or disposition of the soul (διάθεσις τῆς ψυχῆς).[150] Yet as we have already seen, philosophy as the art of living is *also* conceived as a performative art and, as such, an activity or way of life. How can it be both?

In order to understand the relationship between these two characteristics attributed to philosophy, it may be helpful to turn to Chrysippus' famous cylinder analogy.[151] In this analogy Chrysippus draws attention to the fact that when one pushes a cylinder, although the movement is initiated by the push, the *way* in which the cylinder moves is due to its own internal nature or form, namely its circular cross-section. Chrysippus uses this analogy to illustrate a distinction between what might be called internal and external causes,[152] a distinction necessary for his account of freedom and determinism. The initial push that starts the cylinder rolling is an external cause but the nature or shape of the cylinder that determines the *way* in which it moves is an internal cause. In the case of humans, it is the internal disposition of one's soul (διάθεσις τῆς ψυχῆς) that determines the *way* in which one responds to external events. As in the case of the cylinder, this internal nature directly impacts upon the way in which a thing behaves. Any alteration in this internal cause will have a direct and necessary impact upon an individual's behaviour. In other words, philosophy, conceived as a disposition of the soul (διάθεσις τῆς ψυχῆς), will have a direct and necessary impact upon an individual's behaviour. Philosophy is thus both this internal corporeal disposition of the soul and an activity or way of living, the latter being the necessary expression of the former.

The Stoic art of living is directed towards transforming this internal cause, namely the physical disposition of one's soul (διάθεσις τῆς ψυχῆς). This may be identified with the cultivation of wisdom (σοφία) or human excellence (ἀρετή), these also being corporeal dispositions. As such, there appears to be a distinction between this art

---

(ὑφεστάναι). For further discussion see Goldschmidt, *Le système stoïcien et l'idée de temps*, pp. 13-25; Rist, *Stoic Philosophy*, pp. 152-59; Pasquino, 'Le statut ontologique des incorporels dans l'ancien Stoicisme'; Sedley in *CHHP*, pp. 395-402.

[149] For Stoic materialist psychology, see Long, 'Soul and Body in Stoicism', pp. 34-57; Long in *CHHP*, pp. 560-84; Annas, *Hellenistic Philosophy of Mind*, pp. 37-70.

[150] See Diogenes Laertius 7.89 (= *SVF* 3.39), where ἀρετή is described as a disposition of the soul; also Plutarch *Virt. Mor.* 441b-c (= *SVF* 3.459), Sextus Empiricus *Adv. Math.* 11.23 (= *SVF* 3.75 = LS 60 G).

[151] See Aulus Gellius 7.2.11 (= *SVF* 2.1000 = LS 62 D), Cicero *Fat.* 42 (= *SVF* 2.974 = LS 62 C), with discussion in Bobzien, *Determinism and Freedom in Stoic Philosophy*, pp. 258-71. Note also Alexander of Aphrodisias *Fat.* 181.26-30 (= *SVF* 2.979).

[152] Many scholars have identified these internal and external causes with the 'perfect and principal' (*perfectae et principales*) and 'auxiliary and proximate' (*adiuvantes et proximae*) causes in Cicero *Fat.* 41 (= *SVF* 2.974 = LS 62 C) and the 'self-sufficient' (αὐτοτελής) and 'initiatory' (προκαταρκτικός) causes in Plutarch *Stoic. Rep.* 1056b (= *SVF* 2.997). However, recently Bobzien, 'Chrysippus' Theory of Causes', has argued forcefully that these terminological distinctions relate to a distinction between sufficient and non-sufficient causes, and cannot be mapped onto the cylinder analogy.

(τέχνη) that *cultivates* wisdom (σοφία) and wisdom itself, just as we have already seen with Socrates. This, in turn, implies that philosophy (φιλοσοφία) conceived as this art (τέχνη) should be understood in its etymological sense as that which desires wisdom (σοφία), again following Socrates. However, in order to accept this conclusion one would have to understand the art of living *qua* art quite loosely, for strictly speaking an art (τέχνη) is, for the Stoics, a body of secure knowledge (ἐπιστήμη) and as such is reserved for the sage (σοφός). In order to overcome this difficulty one would have to define philosophy as the *desire* for the art of living or that which *cultivates* the art of living. This is clearly somewhat cumbersome and one can understand why this formulation was not used. Yet, strictly speaking, the art of living should not be identified with philosophy (φιλοσοφία) but rather with what philosophy aims at, namely the ideal mental disposition that is wisdom (σοφία) and human excellence (ἀρετή). Such difficulties do not apply to Socrates' position whose art is not itself excellence (ἀρετή) but rather the art that *cultivates* excellence (ἀρετή). In practice, however, the distance between these two accounts is slight, for if one truly masters philosophy conceived as the art that *cultivates* wisdom (σοφία) then one will soon possess wisdom itself. According to the Stoic definition of a τέχνη, philosophy in its etymological sense cannot be the art of living but rather the activity of learning the art of living, a process that culminates in the possession of σοφία.

8. Summary

In this chapter we have seen how the Stoics took up and developed a number of themes from Socrates, including the idea of an art (τέχνη) concerned with one's life (βίος) and a (slightly problematic) analogy between that art and the art of medicine, and how they developed these into a fully fledged concept of philosophy as an art of living (τέχνη περὶ τὸν βίον). Yet despite the problems with the medical analogy, it is important to acknowledge the resonances between medicine and philosophy (as it is conceived here). Not only does the philosopher take care of the soul in a manner analogous to the way in which the doctor takes care of the body, but also the doctor's art is one primarily devoted to a practical outcome and yet involves a substantial body of theoretical understanding. As such, the doctor – as serious scholar whose study is devoted to a practical vocation – forms the perfect model for the Stoic philosopher. It is understandable, then, why the medical analogy should prove so seductive, both then and now.

We have also seen how Seneca in particular developed the idea that the acquisition of the art of living may involve not merely an understanding of the relevant principles or theories (λόγοι, *decreta*) but also some form of practical training or teaching (ἄσκησις, *praecepta*). It is this philosophical training or exercise – analogous to the training that transforms an apprentice into a master craftsman – that translates philosophical theories (λόγοι) into philosophical actions (ἔργα), transforming one's way of life (βίος). Only by supplementing the study of philosophical theory with practical philosophical training will it be possible to transform the internal disposition of one's soul (διάθεσις τῆς ψυχῆς) and attain the philosophical knowledge and understanding (ἐπιστήμη, σοφία) that will necessarily transform one's life into that of the sage.

In Part II I shall explore the relationship between philosophical theory and training further. However, in order to complete our discussion of the idea of an art concerned with one's life, I shall first turn to consider what must be the single most important text dealing with this idea, namely the extended polemic against the possibility of the existence of such an art made by Sextus Empiricus.

Chapter 4

Sceptical Objections

In the last chapter we saw how the Stoics adopted a number of Socratic ideas concerning an art (τέχνη) directed towards the transformation of one's life (βίος) and developed these into a fully-fledged concept of an art of living (τέχνη περὶ τὸν βίον). For Stoics such as Epictetus, the subject matter (ὕλη) of an individual's philosophy is their own life (ὁ βίος αὐτοῦ ἑκάστου).[1] In the second century AD Epictetus was particularly well known and it is from this period that a text of particular importance derives.[2] Writing during this time when Epictetean Stoicism was immensely popular, Sextus Empiricus wrote a detailed discussion of, and series of arguments against, the Stoic concept of an art of living.[3] This discussion is important for a number of reasons. Firstly, it contains significantly more instances of the phrase 'the art of living' (τέχνη περὶ τὸν βίον), or variations upon it, than any other ancient text; secondly, it contains much doxographical information concerning this Stoic concept; thirdly, it offers a series of important objections to this concept that may help to shed light on the precise way in which it was presented by the Stoics.

In this chapter I shall consider Sextus' arguments against the very idea of such a thing called an art of living.[4] The first section offers a brief outline of Sextus'

---

[1] See Epictetus *Diss.* 1.15.2, already quoted and discussed in Chapter 3 § 1.

[2] For Epictetus' fame in this period see e.g. Celsus *apud* Origen *Cont. Cels.* 6.2 (*PG* 11.1289 = test. 26 Schenkl), Aulus Gellius 1.2.6 (= test. 8 Schenkl), Fronto *Epist.* (2.52 Haines), Galen *Lib. Prop.* 11 (19.44 Kühn = test. 20 Schenkl).

[3] As I have already noted in the Introduction, Bett, *Sextus Empiricus, Against the Ethicists*, p. ix, suggests that Sextus' polemic was directed towards philosophers who 'lived centuries before his own time'. However, it has been argued (with regard to Plotinus' polemic against the Gnostics in *Enn.* 2.9 and Simplicius' polemic against the Manichaeans in *In Ench.* 35) that such polemics were usually a response to direct contact with adherents of the philosophical position under attack (see Tardieu, 'Sabiens coraniques et "Sabiens" de Harran', pp. 24-25 n. 105; Hadot, 'The Life and Work of Simplicius', p. 287). It makes more sense to suppose that Sextus' polemic was inspired by direct contact with contemporary followers of Epictetus (who no doubt would have laid great stress on the idea of an art of living) than with written texts that would have been centuries old.

[4] These arguments occur in two works: *Pyrr. Hyp.*, esp. 3.239-249, and *Adv. Math.*, esp. 11.168-215. I shall focus upon the account in *Pyrr. Hyp.* but shall refer continually to the parallel discussion in *Adv. Math.* 11, also known as *Adversus Ethicos*. The *Pyrr. Hyp.* survive in three books; *Adv. Math.* survives in eleven. Book 1 of *Pyrr. Hyp.* contains a methodological overview of Pyrrhonian Scepticism while Books 2 and 3 argue against the claims of other dogmatic philosophers in the fields of logic, physics, and ethics. The material discussed in Books 2 and 3 is also discussed in *Adv. Math.* 7-11 in an extended form (*Adv. Math.* 1-6 are

sceptical methodology, the second section considers each of Sextus' objections in turn, and the third section attempts to bridge the apparent distance between Sextus and the Stoics by drawing attention to common elements in their philosophical projects.

1. The Sceptical Method

Sextus' discussion of the idea of an art of living forms part of his general sceptical project of undermining the claims of those he calls the dogmatists (οἱ δογματικοί).[5] Immediately before dealing with the art of living Sextus proposes a number of arguments against the claims of dogmatic ethicists and, in particular, against the claim that certain things are good or bad by nature (φύσει).[6] In order to do this he adopts two strategies. His first is to place side by side the conflicting opinions of the dogmatists concerning what is and is not said to be good.[7] This unresolvable disagreement, he argues, should lead any impartial observer to suspend their judgement (ἐποχή). His second strategy is to propose arguments in favour of positions opposed to the specific claims of the dogmatists in order to counter-balance the positive arguments made by the dogmatists, thereby creating a state of equipollence (ἰσοσθένεια). Faced with equally plausible arguments on both sides, Sextus suggests that the rational response will again be to suspend judgement (ἐποχή) or, to be more precise, he suggests that when faced with such balanced arguments one will simply find oneself in a state of ἐποχή.[8]

As a supplement to these more general arguments against the claims of dogmatic ethicists, Sextus then introduces his arguments against the possibility of any such thing called an art of living (ἡ περὶ τὸν βίον τέχνη).[9] While his more general attack is

---

probably from a completely different work). For the Greek texts I have relied upon the LCL edition by Bury which is based upon Bekker's 1842 edition. For the *Pyrr. Hyp.* I have also consulted the BT edition by Mutschmann & Mau. Note also the translations by Annas & Barnes (*Sextus Empiricus, Outlines of Scepticism*) and Bett (*Sextus Empiricus, Against the Ethicists*). For a general introduction see Allen 'The Skepticism of Sextus Empiricus'.

[5] As Annas & Barnes note (*The Modes of Scepticism*, pp. 1-2), the Greek term does not involve the pejorative tone associated with the English equivalent. An ancient dogmatist was simply someone who held certain opinions or dogmas.

[6] See *Pyrr. Hyp.* 3.168-238, esp. 3.179, 3.190, 3.235, *Adv. Math.* 11.42-140.

[7] See *Pyrr. Hyp.* 3.180-82.

[8] One does not choose ἐποχή; rather it simply happens as a consequence of ἰσοσθένεια. See Barnes, 'The Beliefs of a Pyrrhonist', pp. 58-59.

[9] As I have already noted, these are in *Pyrr. Hyp.* 3.239-249 and *Adv. Math.* 11.168-215. Traditionally it has been thought that the *Pyrr. Hyp.* is the earlier of these two works. However recently it has been argued that this may in fact be the later of the two, being an abridged and slightly rewritten version of material already discussed in *Adv. Math.*; see Bett, *Against the Ethicists*, pp. xxiv-xxviii; Striker, '*Ataraxia*: Happiness as Tranquillity', p. 191.

aimed at all dogmatists, it is clear that this second attack is directed specifically against the Stoics and their account of the nature and function of philosophy. [10]

2. Sextus Empiricus' Objections to an Art of Living

In Book 3, Chapter 25 of the *Outlines of Pyrrhonism* Sextus asks the question 'Is there an art of living?' (εἰ ἔστι τέχνη περὶ βίον). [11] He opens this chapter by saying that it should already be clear from his arguments up to that point that such an art cannot exist. [12] Despite this, he proceeds to offer five distinct arguments directed against its very possibility. [13] In order to consider each of these arguments I shall quote them in turn as they appear in the *Outlines of Pyrrhonism* (occasionally supplementing that version with the slightly longer accounts of the same material in *Against the Ethicists*) to see if they offer any decisive arguments against the Stoic conception of philosophy.

(a) Competing Arts of Living

> Since the dogmatists do not agree in laying down a single art of living (τέχνην περὶ τὸν βίον), [14] but rather some hypothesize one and some another, they land in dispute and in the 'argument from dispute' (τῷ ἀπὸ τῆς διαφωνίας λόγῳ) which we have propounded in what we said about the good. [15]

Sextus' first objection is based upon the claim that the various dogmatic schools of philosophy – Stoics, Epicureans, Peripatetics – are unable to agree upon the precise nature of the art of living. Each school proposes its own account of what this might be. [16] This conflict, Sextus suggests, calls the entire notion into question, landing them

---

[10] Although the attack beginning at *Adv. Math.* 11.168 is formally directed towards the dogmatists (δογματικοί) in general (and Epicurus is named in particular at *Adv. Math.* 11.169), the bulk of the text addresses specifically Stoic doctrines and it is clear that the Stoics are Sextus' principal target (see esp. *Adv. Math.* 11.170). See Bett, *Against the Ethicists*, p. 187.

[11] The parallel section in *Adv. Math.* (Book 11 Chapter 6) is entitled εἰ ἔστι τις περὶ τὸν βίον τέχνη (τὸν omitted by Bury). Bekker's edition omits the subtitles.

[12] See *Pyrr. Hyp.* 3.239.

[13] In *Adv. Math.* 11 there are a total of seven arguments; see the list and analysis in Bett (*Against the Ethicists*, p. 182 & pp. 191-224 respectively). The arguments omitted in *Pyrr. Hyp.* are much weaker than those common to both texts. Consequently I am inclined to agree with Bett that the *Pyrr. Hyp.* is the later of the two works, being a revised version in which the less sound arguments have been dropped.

[14] Bekker, Bury (LCL): τέχνην περὶ τὸν βίον, Mutschmann & Mau (BT): τέχνην περὶ βίον.

[15] *Pyrr. Hyp.* 3.239 (trans. Annas & Barnes modified); see also *Adv. Math.* 11.173-77, with Bett, *Against the Ethicists*, pp. 191-94, 262-63.

[16] It is interesting to note here that Sextus implies that *each* of the dogmatic schools proposed its own art of living. As we have seen, ancient uses of this phrase are primarily connected to the Stoa, and it seems unlikely that Peripatetics would have conceived philosophy as an art. I take it

in the 'argument from dispute' (διαφωνία).[17] The problem, he argues, is that if the various dogmatic schools propose mutually exclusive arts directed towards the cultivation of happiness (εὐδαιμονία), then it will be impossible to follow them all. The only other alternative is to select just one art and follow that. However, before one can do that one must first decide which conception one will follow. Assuming that this will not be an arbitrary decision, there must be some grounds upon which one of the conflicting conceptions may be chosen. In the discussion of this objection in *Against the Ethicists* Sextus proposes that the only way in which one of these conceptions can be selected is by using some other art or expertise.[18] Yet this other art, Sextus argues, will itself need to be justified, and so on, into an infinite regress. He concludes that insofar as one cannot follow them all *and* one has no grounds for preferring any one over any other, the only rational course of action is to reject them all. The conflict between the various conceptions of an art of living proposed by the dogmatists should lead one to suspend judgement (ἐποχή).

Sextus' principal argument here rests upon the assumption that the choice of any one art of living over any other must be made using some other art or skill (τέχνη). That is to say that the process of evaluation of the different conceptions proposed by the dogmatists must involve another art that will require its own justification. However, there are no obvious grounds for this claim. An alternative way in which one might attempt to evaluate the various conceptions of an art of living would be with reference to their relative success. If each of these arts (τέχναι) claims to offer the best way in which one can cultivate happiness (εὐδαιμονία), then the most reasonable mode of evaluation would be to see which of them does in fact cultivate happiness. Such an assessment could be made either by attempting to put into practice each of the competing arts (τέχναι) or by examining the lives of those who have been reported to have prospered while following one of these arts (τέχναι). Either way, it is far from clear that an infinite regress of justification is inevitable. If the aim of each of these arts is to cultivate well-being or happiness (εὐδαιμονία), and this happiness is a state observable by third persons, then the process of relative evaluation should be fairly straightforward.

It is of course far from clear that Sextus would accept this as a criterion. Bett suggests that 'some form of reasoning or experience', including presumably the experience of happiness (εὐδαιμονία), could be proposed as a criterion of selection.[19] Yet he concludes that even to this Sextus could simply raise the question concerning *its* credentials, preserving his argument from dispute (διαφωνία). However, it is by no means obvious that Sextus would necessarily respond in this way. If one turns to

---

that here Sextus is simply referring to the fact that each of the dogmatic schools proposed its own ethical philosophy directed towards the cultivation of εὐδαιμονία, each based upon a different set of claims to secure knowledge.

[17] This is the first of the Five Modes of Agrippa; see Diogenes Laertius 9.88, *Pyrr. Hyp.* 1.165, with discussion in Hankinson, *The Sceptics*, pp. 182-92.

[18] See *Adv. Math.* 11.176-77.

[19] See Bett, *Against the Ethicists*, pp. 192-93.

other passages where he discusses the nature of the sceptical philosophical project one
can find two important types of claim which are relevant here.

The first of these relates to the claim that the goal (τέλος) of sceptical philosophy
is tranquillity (ἀταραξία).[20] In a number of passages Sextus suggests, albeit
obliquely, that the tranquillity which accompanies the repeated suspension of
judgement itself constitutes happiness (εὐδαιμονία):

> If someone should say that a certain thing is not more by nature to be chosen than to be
> avoided, nor more to be avoided than to be chosen, [...] he will live happily and without
> disturbance (βιώσεται μὲν εὐδαιμόνως καὶ ἀταράχως) [...] freed from the trouble
> associated with the opinion that something bad or good is present.[21]

In other words, Sextus himself proposes a philosophical method directed towards the
cultivation of happiness (εὐδαιμονία). In this, he follows a number of earlier
Sceptics, and in particular Timon, who affirmed that Scepticism was the only sure
path to the happy life.[22] In the words of Photius, 'he who philosophizes after the
fashion of Pyrrho (κατὰ Πύρρωνα) is happy (εὐδαιμονεῖ)'.[23] Passages such as these
suggest that both Sextus and earlier Sceptics acknowledged the existence of happiness
(εὐδαιμονία) and that, on at least this issue, they did not suspend judgement. If this is
the case then the presence or absence of happiness could, in principle, form the
foundation for a Sceptical comparative analysis of the various arts of living proposed
by the dogmatists.

The second type of claim made by Sextus that is relevant here – one that may also
help to clarify the first – relates to physical experiences of sensations such as pleasure
or pain. Although Sextus claims that the suspension of judgement will bring
tranquillity, he does not claim that the Sceptic will be completely undisturbed. Certain
things, Sextus says, will continue to force themselves upon the Sceptic, who will feel
cold and hunger and pain just like anybody else.[24] The suspension of judgement
cannot overpower the experience (πάθος) of physical pain; what it can do is
overcome the belief (δόξα) that that pain is something bad.

The Sceptic will not of course make any substantial claims concerning the status
of the content of these experiences, but he will nevertheless acknowledge them *as*
experiences. As Timon is reported to have said, 'I do not lay it down that honey is
sweet, but I admit that it appears (φαίνεται) to be so'.[25] In other words, the Sceptic

---

[20] See *Pyrr. Hyp.* 1.12, 1.25-30. This will be discussed in further detail in § 3 below.

[21] *Adv. Math.* 11.118 (trans. Bett). See also *Adv. Math.* 7.158, 11.140, 11.141, 11.147, with
discussion in Striker, '*Ataraxia*: Happiness as Tranquillity', pp. 188-91.

[22] See e.g. Aristocles *apud* Eusebius 14.18.1-4 (758c-d = test. 2 *PPF* = LS 1 F). The *testimonia*
and *fragmenta* for Timon are collected in *PPF*.

[23] Photius *Bibl.* cod. 212 (169b26-29 = LS 71 C; trans. LS).

[24] See *Pyrr. Hyp.* 1.29-30, 1.13, 3.235-36, with Burnyeat, 'Can the Sceptic Live his
Scepticism?', p. 43.

[25] Timon *apud* Diogenes Laertius 9.105 (= fr. 74 *PPF* = LS 1 H; trans. Hicks).

simply acknowledges what happens to him, acknowledges the presence of those sensations which are forced upon him.[26]

There appears to be no reason why a Sceptic could not acknowledge the presence of happiness (εὐδαιμονία) in precisely this way. Clearly the Sceptic would not claim that happiness (εὐδαιμονία) was an objectively observable state but nevertheless he could acknowledge that he himself was experiencing something that might best be described as happiness (εὐδαιμονία), just as he could describe or report other experiences that happened to him. Indeed, this seems to be the only plausible way in which a Sceptic could justify his claim that the suspension of judgement (ἐποχή) will bring tranquillity (ἀταραξία), which as we have seen is itself identified with happiness (εὐδαιμονία). There is no obvious reason, then, why Sextus could not accept the presence or absence of the experience of happiness (εὐδαιμονία) as a criterion for evaluating the various arts of living proposed by the dogmatic schools of philosophy. His principal argument here fails, even for one who holds onto the basic principles of Scepticism.

(b) The Art of Living Cannot be Taught

> Since wisdom (φρόνησίς) is a virtue (ἀρετή), and only the sage has virtue, the Stoics – not being sages – will not possess the art of living (τὴν περὶ τὸν βίον τέχνην), *and not having this, neither will they teach it to others.*[27]

Here, Sextus argues that in order for the Stoics to be able to teach their art of living they must first possess it. However, insofar as they reserve this virtue or excellence (ἀρετή) for the sage and do not themselves claim to be sages, they do not possess it and thus they cannot teach it. Even if the Stoic art of living did exist in the one or two sages that may or may not have lived at one time, the typical Stoic preacher who claims to be able to teach it cannot.

This argument draws upon the Stoics' own comments concerning the rarity of the sage and a number of passages where leading Stoics denied that they themselves had achieved wisdom.[28] The paradox that Sextus seizes upon here – that someone without

---

[26] This issue is closely related to the question concerning the *extent* of Sextus' scepticism. This question has been presented in terms of 'rustic' versus 'urbane' Scepticism, the former involving ἐποχή regarding all beliefs and the latter involving ἐποχή only regarding philosophical and scientific theories. In general, I am inclined to interpret Sextus as a 'rustic' Sceptic and my appeal here to experiences does not involve an appeal to non-scientific beliefs. For further discussion see in particular Barnes, 'The Beliefs of a Pyrrhonist', pp. 61-62, with Burnyeat, 'Can the Sceptic Live his Scepticism?'; Frede, 'The Sceptic's Beliefs'; Hankinson, *The Sceptics*, pp. 273-78.

[27] *Pyrr. Hyp.* 3.240 (trans. Annas & Barnes modified), with the final clause in italics added from *Adv. Math.* 11.181 (μὴ ἔχοντες δὲ ταύτην οὐδὲ ἄλλους διδάξουσιν). Note also that in *Adv. Math.* 11.181 the relationship between wisdom and the art of living is made more explicit: 'For if the art of living – being wisdom – is a virtue, and only the sage has virtue, the Stoics – not being sages – will not possess wisdom nor any art of living'.

[28] See the references in Chapter 3 § 2.

wisdom could nevertheless teach it to others – captures something of the essentially Socratic flavour of Stoic thought concerning human excellence (ἀρετή). Insofar as Sextus' objection challenges the essentially Socratic position of the Stoics it also challenges Socrates himself, echoing an objection often raised against him, namely that he is himself unable to teach goodness or excellence (ἀρετή) if at the same time he declares that he knows nothing.[29] Socrates' identification of such excellence (ἀρετή) with knowledge (ἐπιστήμη) implies that he must know what is good before he can teach it to others. Indeed, it also implies that he must know what is good before he can be good himself. Sextus' objection against the Stoics is, in effect, also an objection against this Socratic position.

In order to clarify Sextus' objection to the Stoics it may be helpful to begin by considering the Socratic version of the same problem. Yet, as ever, the Socratic position is more complex than it at first appears to be. Nevertheless, it is possible to sketch the outline of a solution. The problem may be stated thus: on the one hand Socrates sincerely proclaims his ignorance; on the other hand he has an unsurpassed reputation for wisdom and appears to attempt to teach others. Yet at the same time one of his few positive doctrines is the claim that virtue or excellence (ἀρετή) is a form of knowledge (ἐπιστήμη), that all virtuous behaviour is the product of knowledge, and that all vice is the product of ignorance.[30] If Socrates does not possess this knowledge himself, he can neither be virtuous himself nor teach it to others.

The beginnings of a response to this paradox may be drawn from a passage from Xenophon:

> At the same time he [Socrates] never undertook to teach how this could be done [to become good]; but by obviously being such a person, he made those who spent their time with him hope that, if they followed his example (μιμουμένους), they would develop the same character.[31]

According to Xenophon, Socrates possesses virtue or excellence (ἀρετή) and this is evident to all insofar as it is expressed in his behaviour (ἔργα). By associating with him and watching the way in which he acts, others can learn from his example. However Socrates is sincere when he says that he does not know what human excellence (ἀρετή) is. He cannot claim to know what it is because he is unable to give a rational account (λόγος) of it. Socrates' excellence (ἀρετή) is thus unarticulated. By observing his behaviour (ἔργα) others can see that he possesses such excellence (ἀρετή) but that is very different from him being able to offer a rational account

---

[29] For Socrates' profession of ignorance see e.g. Plato *Apol.* 21b, *Meno* 71b, *Theaet.* 150c-d, Aristotle *Soph. Elench.* 183b7-8 (= SSR I B 20), Aeschines *Alcibiades* fr. 11c Dittmar *apud* Aristides *Rhet.* 1.74 (162.2-7 Lenz & Behr = SSR VI A 53), Cicero *Acad.* 1.16 (= SSR I C 448). For further discussion see Brickhouse & Smith, *Plato's Socrates*, pp. 30-38; Vlastos, 'Socrates' Disavowal of Knowledge'; Guthrie, *History*, vol. 3, pp. 442-49.

[30] For discussion see Guthrie, *History*, vol. 3, pp. 450-59.

[31] Xenophon *Mem.* 1.2.3 (trans. Tredennick).

(λόγος) of this behaviour.[32] Thus Socrates is at once both virtuous but also without knowledge (ἐπιστήμη) of what this virtue or excellence (ἀρετή) is.[33] As such, he is unable to teach it in the conventional sense of passing on a systematic body of knowledge (ἐπιστήμη). The teaching that he is able to undertake consists of undermining other people's claims to knowledge (ἐπιστήμη) and provoking them into enquiry themselves.[34] Yet, as Xenophon makes clear, he can also teach by example, insofar as excellence (ἀρετή) is for him a matter of deed not words (ἔργα οὐ λόγοι).[35] That is, he can show others what it might mean to act virtuously but he cannot explain to them precisely what virtue or excellence (ἀρετή) is. That is why he continues in his search for such knowledge (ἐπιστήμη) despite his unsurpassed reputation for wisdom (σοφία).

This tentative attempt to explain Socrates' paradoxical position may help us to understand the Stoic position. As Sextus notes, the Stoics do not claim to possess virtue or excellence (ἀρετή) themselves, yet nevertheless at the same time they claim to be able to teach the art of living that cultivates such excellence. As in the case of Socrates, a number of the leading Stoics had reputations for wisdom (σοφία) and in particular wisdom expressed in their actions (ἔργα) and way of life (βίος).[36] If those same Stoics denied having reached the state of perfection reserved for the sage, that may well have been due to their inability to offer a full rational account (λόγος) of that wisdom. Nevertheless, they would still have been able to 'teach' by way of practical example and by undermining the presuppositions of their students, just as Socrates did.[37] Thus they could act not so much as teachers, but rather as fellow, if more advanced, students. As such advanced students, they would inquire with, rather than instruct, more junior students.[38] In response to his criticisms, one might say that Sextus assumes a too narrow conception of what could constitute philosophical teaching.

---

[32] The argument here is similar in certain respects to that at the beginning of Plato's *Meno* (see 71d-72c) where although Meno can point to examples of virtue (ἀρετή) he is unable to offer an account of what it is that makes them virtuous. Similarly, Socrates can possess virtue (ἀρετή) – can point to himself as an example so to speak – but nevertheless cannot offer a rational account (λόγος) of the nature of that virtue (ἀρετή).

[33] On this point my position shares much in common with Brickhouse & Smith, *Plato's Socrates*, p. 38. Socrates may be convinced of the truth of any number of ethical propositions, yet he cannot claim to know any of them if he is unable to give a rational account (λόγος) of them. Hence his strong conviction yet sincere profession of ignorance.

[34] See Vlastos, *Socrates: Ironist and Moral Philosopher*, p. 32. However, whether this was an example of what Vlastos calls 'complex irony' is a question too complex to address here.

[35] As I have already noted in Chapter 1 § 2, the ideal is a harmony between deeds and words.

[36] See e.g. Diogenes Laertius 7.10-11 (= *SVF* 1.7-8).

[37] In reply to a similar objection concerning his ability to teach rhetoric, Isocrates is reported to have described himself as a whetstone that can sharpen but cannot cut; see Plutarch *Vit. Dec. Orat.* 838e, *Gnom. Vat.* no. 356; also Rosenthal, *The Classical Heritage in Islam*, p. 264.

[38] See Hicks, *Stoic and Epicurean*, p. 88.

(c) The Art of Living Presupposes Adequate Impressions

If, then, for there to be an art of living there must first be art (τέχνην), and if for art to exist apprehensions (κατάληψιν) must first exist, and if for apprehensions to exist assent to an adequate impression (καταληπτικῇ φαντασίᾳ) must first have been apprehended (κατειλῆφθαι), and if adequate impressions are undiscoverable, then the art of living is undiscoverable.[39]

This argument is directed against the specifically Stoic definition of an art (τέχνη). As we have already seen in Chapter 3, according to the Stoics an art or skill (τέχνη) is defined as a 'system of apprehensions' (σύστημα ἐκ καταλήψεων), an apprehension being assent to an adequate impression (κατάληψιν δὲ καταληπτικῇ φαντασίᾳ συγκατάθεσιν).[40] Sextus' argument here is with the notion of an 'adequate impression' (φαντασία καταληπική).[41] In Stoic epistemology this term is used to refer to the criterion of truth.[42] It is defined as an impression that is caused by an object and stamped upon the mind in accordance with the nature of that object in such a way that it could not have been produced by a non-existing object.[43] It is an impression that is so clear, distinct, vivid, and obvious that it is its own guarantee of its accuracy and clarity.[44] This guaranteed accuracy may be understood in terms of its causal history; that is, in terms of the physical conditions of all of the elements involved in its production. If the sense organs, the object in question, and all the other variables are not obstructed or in an abnormal state, then the resulting impression will be 'adequate' (καταληπική).[45]

Although at first glance this concept appears somewhat obscure, a number of ancient examples may help to clarify it. Epictetus attempts to do just this by proposing that in the middle of the day one should attempt to hold the belief that it is in fact the middle of the night.[46] He suggests that one just cannot do this. He concludes that during the day the impression 'it is daytime' is so powerful that it must be an

---

[39] *Pyrr. Hyp.* 3.242 (trans. Annas & Barnes modified); see also *Adv. Math.* 11.182, with Bett, *Against the Ethicists*, pp. 198-202, 263-64. In order to be consistent I have here, as elsewhere, translated φαντασία καταληπτική as 'adequate impression'. However, in this particular passage this obscures the connection between this concept and κατάληψις 'apprehension' and κατειλῆφθαι 'apprehended'. Annas & Barnes use 'apprehensive appearance' in order to emphasize this connection.

[40] See *Pyrr. Hyp.* 3.241, 3.188 (= *SVF* 2.96), *Adv. Math.* 11.182 (= *SVF* 2.97). Note also Olympiodorus *In Gorg.* 12.1 (= *SVF* 1.73 = LS 42 A) and the discussion in Chapter 3 § 4.

[41] For a note on the translation of this term and references to further discussions see above Chapter 3 § 4.

[42] See e.g. *Adv. Math.* 7.227 (= *SVF* 2.56), Diogenes Laertius 7.54 (= *SVF* 2.105 = LS 40 A).

[43] See e.g. *Adv. Math.* 7.248, Cicero *Acad.* 2.18, 2.77 (all *SVF* 1.59), Diogenes Laertius 7.45-46 (*SVF* 2.53), 7.50 (= *SVF* 2.60).

[44] See Frede in *CHHP*, pp. 312-13.

[45] See *Adv. Math.* 7.424, with Frede, 'Stoics and Skeptics on Clear and Distinct Impressions', esp. pp. 157-58.

[46] See Epictetus *Diss.* 1.28.2-3; also *Adv. Math.* 7.242-43 (= *SVF* 2.65 = LS 39 G).

'adequate impression' (φαντασία καταληπτική). One might say that impressions of this sort demand assent.[47] If, on the other hand, one found that one *could* hold the opposing impression then this would immediately call into question the validity of the initial impression, and this might lead one to withhold one's assent. For example, the impression that the number of stars in the night sky is even is no more self-evident or obviously correct than the impression that the number is odd.[48] Thus, in a manner similar to Sextus' own Scepticism, Epictetus proposes that in such a scenario one would be forced to withhold one's assent and to suspend judgement (ἐποχή).[49]

It is not too surprising to find that Sextus has little time for this concept which functions for the Stoics as a criterion of truth, in effect underwriting their dogmatism to which he objects. Indeed, it is his principal target in the attack he makes upon Stoic epistemology elsewhere.[50] His argument there concerns the question of how one is supposed to distinguish between an adequate impression and an ordinary unreliable impression. The Stoic claim that this is simply self-evident carries little weight with him. Sextus argues that as a matter of fact it is impossible to distinguish between these two sorts of impressions. Being itself the criterion of truth, the Stoics cannot appeal to any further criterion in order to underwrite the reliability of an adequate impression. If they attempt to do that, they will simply fall into circularity.[51] As such, Sextus argues that it is impossible to know if one ever has an adequate impression.[52] Insofar as the Stoic concept of an art is built upon such impressions, any such art will be equally undiscoverable.

Sextus was not the first to raise this sort of objection. Earlier Academic sceptics such as Arcesilaus and Carneades argued that there would always be a risk of mistaking false impressions for true ones.[53] Indeed, Sextus was well aware of these earlier arguments and he is an important source for our knowledge of them. He also reports the way in which later Stoics modified their definition of 'adequate impression' in response to these earlier criticisms, adding that it forms the criterion of truth 'provided that it has no obstacle' (καὶ τὸ μηδὲν ἔχουσαν ἔνστημα).[54] In other

---

[47] See *Adv. Math.* 7.257, Cicero *Acad.* 2.38, with Burnyeat, 'Can the Sceptic Live his Scepticism?', pp. 46-47 n. 38.

[48] See Epictetus *Diss.* 1.28.3; also *Adv. Math.* 7.243, 7.393, 8.147, 8.317.

[49] See Epictetus *Diss.* 1.28.2-3, with Burnyeat, 'Can the Sceptic Live his Scepticism?', p. 44. For other reports of the Stoic attitude towards suspension of judgement see Sextus Empiricus *Adv. Math.* 7.155 (= LS 41 C), Cicero *Acad.* 2.57 (= LS 40 I). For further discussion of the relationship between Pyrrhonian and Stoic suspension of judgement see Allen, 'The Skepticism of Sextus Empiricus', pp. 2596-97.

[50] This is in *Adv. Math.* 7.401-35; see esp. 7.427-29.

[51] They will 'fall into the circular (διάλληλον) mode of difficulty (ἀπορίας)' (*Pyrr. Hyp.* 3.242). This is a reference to the fifth of the Five Modes of Agrippa; see Diogenes Laertius 9.88, *Pyrr. Hyp.* 1.169, with discussion in Hankinson, *The Sceptics*, pp. 182-92.

[52] It should noted that here (in *Pyrr. Hyp.*) Sextus does not argue that there is no such thing as an adequate impression (as he does in *Adv. Math.* 11.182) but rather that such impressions are undiscoverable (ἀνεύρετος).

[53] See *Adv. Math.* 7.159-65 (= LS 70 A); also Cicero *Acad.* 2.77 (= *SVF* 1.59 = LS 40 D).

[54] *Adv. Math.* 7.253 (= LS 40 K).

words, later Stoics responded to sceptical objections by acknowledging that in certain circumstances it *is* possible to mistake a false impression for an adequate impression. However, adequate impressions will remain self-evident in more typical conditions, when an individual's sense organs are functioning properly and there are no external obstructions to the senses.

For instance, individuals rarely mistake two-dimensional representations of three-dimensional objects for real three-dimensional objects, unless those representations are of the highest quality. Even then, such representations mislead only initially and their true nature is soon found out after closer scrutiny. Moreover, the sceptical objection that it is possible to be mistaken *sometimes* with regard to adequate impressions does not force one to the conclusion that one can *never* be sure. While it is certainly possible sometimes to be mistaken, this is not enough to support the claim that when a rational being experiences a true impression under normal conditions that he will *never* be able to recognize it as such. If he can, then adequate impressions survive the sceptical attack. However, in those circumstances when one cannot be sure, a Stoic would acknowledge that the most prudent option would be to suspend judgement.

With regard to everyday examples of claims to secure knowledge, the example of an adequate impression proposed by Epictetus – 'it is daytime' – is not particularly controversial. Indeed, it does not appear to be the sort of impression with which Sextus would have any particular argument. Sextus makes this clear himself:

> When we say that Sceptics do not hold beliefs (μὴ δογματίζειν), [...] they would not say, when heated or chilled, 'I think I am not heated (or chilled)'. Rather we say that they do not hold beliefs in the sense in which some say that belief (δόγμα) is assent to some unclear object of investigation in the sciences (ἐπιστήμας); for Pyrrhonists do not assent to anything unclear (ἀδήλων).[55]

The Sceptic, then, should not necessarily have any difficulty with Epictetus' adequate impression 'it is daytime'.[56] Moreover, as we have already noted, neither would the Stoic have any difficulty with the idea of refusing to assent to anything unclear. The distance between Scepticism and Stoicism here is perhaps not as great as one might at first suppose.

(d) The Art of Living Produces no Distinctive Actions

> Every art (τέχνη) appears to be apprehended from the actions (ἔργων) delivered specifically by it. But there is no action specific to the art of living. Whatever anyone might

---

[55] *Pyrr. Hyp.* 1.13 (trans. Annas & Barnes).
[56] Of course, Sextus would certainly not call such an experience an 'adequate impression' or even a belief. Rather, as we have already seen in § 2 (a) above, he would only be able to acknowledge or report such an experience *as an experience*, without making any further claim about it. This issue is closely related to the debate concerning the difference between 'rustic' and 'urbane' Scepticism, on which see the note in § 2 (a).

say to be its action will be found common to ordinary people too (e.g. honouring your parents, returning loans, and all the rest). There is therefore no art of living.[57]

Here Sextus argues that there are no acts peculiar to the sage who possesses the art of living that could not be performed by anyone else. In effect, he argues against the conception of virtue (ἀρετή) or wisdom (σοφία) as primarily a disposition concerned with *how* someone acts, as opposed to a conception concerned with *what* an individual does. Sextus implicitly claims that if one were to accept this account of what it means to possess the art of living then it would become impossible to distinguish between those who do and those who do not possess it.[58] In such a situation it would become empty to claim that any art of living exists. In short, Sextus argues that for an art of living to exist in any meaningful sense it must enable its possessor to do certain things that otherwise he would not be able to do.

The immediate Stoic response to this objection would be to argue that wisdom (σοφία) is not to be found in a specific set of actions (ἔργα) performed but rather in the motivation for any action performed, the disposition standing behind an action.[59] To this Sextus responds that a problem with this Stoic argument is that it still makes distinguishing between those who do and do not possess the art of living impossible.[60] A Socratic response to this would be to say that the key difference between one who does and one who does not possess an art (τέχνη) is the ability of the former to give a rational account (λόγος) of what he or she is doing.[61] While the lucky amateur who has a certain empirical knack (ἐμπειρία, τριβή) may be able to emulate the acts of a professional, he will nevertheless be unable to explain *why* it is that he is able to achieve the results that he does.[62] One who possesses the art of living, on the other hand, will be able to offer an account of *why* he does what he does, thereby making manifest the internal disposition which constitutes his wisdom (σοφία).[63] Despite Sextus' objection, this functions as a very clear way of distinguishing between those who do and do not possess any art, including the art of living.

A corollary to this is that one who possesses the art of living will not only be able to offer an account (λόγος) of his actions but also will be more consistent in his

---

[57] *Pyrr. Hyp.* 3.243 (trans. Annas & Barnes modified). See also *Adv. Math.* 11.197-209, with Bett, *Against the Ethicists*, pp. 210-20 & 265.
[58] A similar objection could be made against Sextus himself if the life of tranquillity that *he* advocates is indistinguishable from the lives of other people; see Annas & Barnes, *The Modes of Scepticism*, pp. 169-71.
[59] Sextus was well aware of this Stoic counter argument; see *Adv. Math.* 11.200.
[60] See *Pyrr. Hyp.* 3.244, *Adv. Math.* 11.203, with Bett, *Against the Ethicists*, p. 215.
[61] See esp. Plato *Gorg.* 465a, with discussion in Chapter 2 § 3.
[62] Thus Socrates is himself merely a 'lucky amateur' insofar as he cannot give a rational account (λόγος) of his virtuous behaviour. He has wisdom in 'deeds not words' (ἔργα οὐ λόγοι) but not the ideal harmony of 'deeds and words' (ἔργα καὶ λόγοι).
[63] As Bett suggests (*Against the Ethicists*, p. 215), the appropriate disposition 'could be revealed by what they [the wise] say about them rather than by any feature intrinsic to the actions themselves'.

actions and more successful than the lucky amateur.[64] Although this will not be a property of any particular action, being something only observable over a series of actions, it nevertheless forms another way in which the presence or absence of an art may be discerned by an observer.

A secondary part of Sextus' argument here (although only in *Against the Ethicists* and not the *Outlines of Pyrrhonism*) is the claim that if someone did follow such an art and act according to a single rational account (λόγος) then this would surely be noticeable in their behaviour:

> If the wise person (ὁ φρόνιμος) had a single and determinate order of life, he would have been plainly apprehended even from this by those who are not wise; but he is not apprehended by these people; therefore the wise person is not to be grasped from the order of his actions (ἐκ τῆς τάξεως τῶν ἔργων).[65]

Here Sextus concedes a number of points to the Stoics without realizing it. The rarity of those who have managed to perfect the art of living is precisely the basis for the Stoic claim concerning the rarity of the sage. That such individuals would be immediately recognizable would be affirmed by the Stoics,[66] who would no doubt point to specific examples – such as Socrates and Diogenes – as instances of individuals who *did* follow such a way of life and *were* noticed by both their contemporaries and later generations. The fact that only these and perhaps one or two others have been noticed is precisely the reason why they should be held up as examples and role models to the rest of humankind, the Stoics would argue. The rarity of such figures is no argument against the existence of an art of living as such; it merely serves to underline its value and importance.[67]

(e) The Art of Living Cannot be Put into Practice

> Most of what the philosophers say is like this – but they would never dare to put it into action (διαπράττεσθαι) unless they were fellow-citizens of the Cyclopes of the Laestrygonians. But if they never perform these actions […] then there is no action (ἔργον) specific to those people suspected of possessing the art of living.[68]

Sextus' final argument is based upon the scandalous nature of a number of the often Cynic inspired Stoic doctrines. The passage here follows immediately after a series of quotations from Zeno and Chrysippus which describe a number of these sorts of

---

[64] Sextus touches on this at *Adv. Math.* 11.206-07; see Bett, *Against the Ethicists*, p. 218.

[65] *Adv. Math.* 11.209 (trans. Bett).

[66] See e.g. Plutarch *Stoic. Rep.* 1042e-f (= *SVF* 3.85), Cicero *Nat. Deo.* 2.145.

[67] As has been noted in Chapter 3 § 2, Politian (in his *Epistola ad Bartolomeo Scala*) argued that if just one example could be found, that would be enough to affirm the reality of the sage; he then cites Cato as his example (see Kraye, *Cambridge Translations*, pp. 192-99, esp. p. 196).

[68] *Pyrr. Hyp.* 3.249 (trans. Annas & Barnes modified). See also *Adv. Math.* 11.188-96, with Bett, *Against the Ethicists*, pp. 205-10 & 264-65.

ideas, including bisexualism, masturbation, incest, and cannibalism.[69] Sextus argues that insofar as these doctrines go against the established customs and laws of almost all countries, they can never be put into practice. As such, the Stoic art of living is worthless because, if it involves such actions, it can never be put into practice. If it is never put into practice and it does not produce any actions (ἔργα) then it is, for all practical purposes, redundant.

The argument that Sextus makes here is not that an art of living as such does not or cannot exist but rather that the specifically Stoic art of living is useless insofar as it can never be practised.[70] The precise relationship between these scandalous ideas and the concept of an art of living is not made clear by Sextus and it is likely that he uses this material purely to shock. It is far from obvious that eating one's dead parents has any bearing upon the existence or non-existence of an art of living. It is also far from obvious that any Stoic claimed that one who practised the Stoic art of living would, as a matter of course, eat their dead parents.

The shock that Sextus attempts to produce by quoting this material betrays a certain respect for traditional custom and law that is perhaps surprising from a Sceptic. It would certainly have carried little weight with the Stoics, to whom this objection is addressed. One need only be reminded that, after Socrates, Diogenes the Cynic is one of the most cited examples of a Stoic sage.[71] His acts of public masturbation and other celebrated indecencies paid little respect to the established customs and laws of the Athenians.[72] Acts such as these were actually praised by Stoics, including Chrysippus,[73] praise which later earned harsh criticism from opponents such as Philodemus.[74]

In order to place this material within the appropriate context, it must be remembered that Stoic ethics is grounded upon the Sophistic and Cynic distinction

---

[69] See *Pyrr. Hyp.* 3.245-248 (= *SVF* 1.250, 1.256, 3.745, 1.254, 3.752). Sextus mentions similar Stoic material at 3.199-201 (= *SVF* 1.585), 3.205-207 (= *SVF* 1.256). This sort of material is particularly associated with Zeno's Πολιτεία which is reported to have been written when he was still under the influence of his teacher Crates the Cynic (see Diogenes Laertius 7.4 = *SVF* 1.2; fragments collected in Baldry, 'Zeno's Ideal State'). It reappears in Chrysippus' Περὶ πολιτείας (this being one of the sources quoted by Sextus) which may have been a commentary upon Zeno's text (fragments listed in *SVF*, vol. 3, pp. 202-03). The attempt to discredit Stoicism by drawing attention to its affinity with Cynicism appears to have been a common tactic used by ancient critics and is particularly prominent in Philodemus' *De Stoicis* (*PHerc* 155 & 339). For further discussion of the relationship between Cynicism and Stoicism see Rist, *Stoic Philosophy*, pp. 54-80.
[70] See Bett, *Against the Ethicists*, p. 206.
[71] See e.g. Seneca *Tranq. An.* 8.4-5, *Ben.* 5.4.3-4, Marcus Aurelius 8.3, and in particular the important passage in Epictetus *Diss.* 3.22.
[72] For Diogenes' indecency see e.g. Diogenes Laertius 6.46, 6.69 (both *SSR* V B 147).
[73] See Plutarch *Stoic. Rep.* 1044b (= *SVF* 3.706). Chrysippus comments that he wished that the desire for food could be relieved so easily by simply rubbing one's stomach.
[74] See Philodemus *De Stoicis* (*PHerc* 155 & 339) *passim* but e.g. 11.9-13 Dorandi. The Cynic tendencies of the early Stoa also appear to been a source of embarrassment for some later Stoics such as Panaetius (see e.g. fr. 55 van Straaten *apud* Cicero *Fin.* 4.79).

between what is in accordance with nature (κατὰ φύσιν) and what is merely in accordance with custom (κατὰ νόμον).[75] Implicit within the Stoic ideal of living in accordance with nature (τὸ ὁμολογουμένως τῇ φύσει ζῆν) is the rejection of a way of life subordinate to custom (νόμος).[76] It is likely that it was within this context that Zeno and Chrysippus discussed acts such as incest and cannibalism; they were less positive proposals and more reflections upon the distinction between νόμος and φύσις. Indeed, such acts would have been strictly speaking 'indifferent' (ἀδιάφορον) according to the Stoic classification of things good, bad, and indifferent, and thus not positively recommended at all.[77] The purpose of a discussion of these topics would not have been to recommend them as regular practices but rather to argue that, insofar as they are only prohibited by arbitrary customs (νόμοι) and are not bad in themselves, they may be appropriate in certain exceptional circumstances (κατὰ περίστασιν).[78] Such acts play no essential role within the Stoic conception of an art of living and were not proposed by the Stoics as everyday practices. Although the sage – like Diogenes – may be said to engage in such practices in certain circumstances,[79] this has little bearing upon the possibility of an art of living.

(f) Summary

These, then, are Sextus' principal arguments against the Stoic conception of an art of living.[80] None of them are decisive. In many of them Sextus appears to be quite categorical in his claim that an art of living does not exist, a categorical claim that appears to go against the Sceptical method of the suspension of judgement (ἐποχή). To be fair to Sextus, however, his aim here may be not to express his own opinion but rather to offer a number of arguments *against* the existence of an art of living in order to counter-balance the arguments of the dogmatists *for* such an art. His intention may have been to create the appropriate balance of arguments on both sides (ἰσοσθένεια)

---

[75] See the note on this distinction in Chapter 1 § 1.

[76] For the Stoic ideal of living in accordance with nature (τὸ ὁμολογουμένως τῇ φύσει ζῆν) see Arius Didymus 2.7.6a (2.75.11-76.15 WH = LS 63 B), Diogenes Laertius 7.87 (= *SVF* 1.179, 3.4), Cicero *Fin.* 4.14 (= *SVF* 1.179, 3.13), Epictetus *Diss.* 3.1.25, Marcus Aurelius 3.4.4, with discussion in Bonhöffer, *Die Ethik des Stoikers Epictet*, pp. 163-88 (= *The Ethics of the Stoic Epictetus*, pp. 209-38).

[77] See e.g. *Pyrr. Hyp.* 1.160 where Sextus reports that Chrysippus held incest to be 'indifferent' (ἀδιάφορον). For discussion of the classification 'good, bad, indifferent' see Kidd, 'Stoic Intermediates and the End for Man'.

[78] See Diogenes Laertius 7.121, 7.109 (= *SVF* 3.496), with Bett, *Against the Ethicists*, p. 209.

[79] As Bett notes (*Against the Ethicists*, p. 209), many of these scandalous ideas derive from Stoic political works which dealt primarily with the conduct of the sage rather than ordinary people (e.g. Zeno's Πολιτεία and Chrysippus' Περὶ Πολιτείας). To propose that a sage in some form of ideal community might commit such acts in exceptional circumstances is very different from proposing such acts as part of everyday behaviour for students of philosophy.

[80] As I have already noted, there are two further arguments in *Adv. Math.* 11 but these are weaker than the five common to *Adv. Math.* and *Pyrr. Hyp.*.

that would lead a reasonable individual to suspend judgement (ἐποχή).[81] Although Sextus appears to argue forcefully against the existence of an art of living, his own attitude may well have been one of agnosticism consistent with the general sceptical method.[82] However, if we conclude that Sextus' arguments against the notion of an art of living do not work, then he will have failed to create the balance of arguments required to generate suspension of judgement.

3. Philosophy and Biography in Scepticism

Whether Sextus' objections to the notion of an art of living stand or not, what they appear to illustrate is a sceptical attack upon a certain conception of philosophy, an attack upon a conception of philosophy which claims that philosophy is an art that can transform one's way of life (βίος). It may appear, then, as if Sextus and the sceptical tradition to which he belongs form an important exception to the general claim made in Chapter 1 that in Hellenistic and Graeco-Roman antiquity philosophy was primarily concerned with the way in which one lived. However, although this may appear to be the case, in fact it is not so.

A number of ancient sources make it quite clear that sceptical philosophers thought that philosophy – their philosophy – would transform their way of life (βίος) just as much as any Stoic or Epicurean thought that their philosophy would transform their lives.[83] In particular they conceived sceptical philosophy as a pursuit directed towards the cultivation of tranquillity (ἀταραξία) or, to be more precise, a pursuit inspired by 'the hope of becoming tranquil' (τὴν ἐλπίδα τοῦ ἀταρακτήσειν).[84] Their argument with the dogmatists in general, and the Stoics in particular, was not about *whether* philosophy was concerned with transforming one's way of life but rather was simply at the level of *how* they thought philosophy would transform one's life.

As we have already seen, the Sceptical philosophical method involved responding to dogmatic philosophical claims by propounding equally convincing counter-claims. Their objective was to cloud the issue in question by making both sides of any argument equally compelling. When faced with two sets of equally convincing arguments in equipollence (ἰσοσθένεια), the Sceptics claimed that one would soon find oneself in a state of suspended judgement (ἐποχή) and one would not be able to hold any positive belief at all.

---

[81] See Hankinson 'Values, Objectivity, and Dialectic', pp. 66-68. As he notes, Sextus' negative dogmatic conclusions are 'only half the story'.

[82] Thus Sextus' arguments must be considered alongside important passages such as *Pyrr. Hyp.* 1.13-15 and in particular the distinction between Academic and Pyrrhonist scepticism at 1.3. However, as Bett notes (*Against the Ethicists*, p. 189), there is no indication in *Adv. Math.* 11 that this is the approach Sextus is taking. Yet this may simply reflect the fact that the opening sections of that work (equivalent to *Pyrr. Hyp.* 1), which would have placed the later arguments in context, have been lost.

[83] See e.g. *Adv. Math.* 11.110-18, with Annas & Barnes, *The Modes of Scepticism*, pp. 166-71; Morrison, 'The Ancient Sceptic's Way of Life'.

[84] *Pyrr. Hyp.* 1.12 & 1.25.

The Sceptics claimed that the repeated experience of such suspended judgement (ἐποχή) would bring untroubledness or tranquillity (ἀταραξία).[85] This, the Sceptics suggested, could not be worked towards in any direct sense, but rather would be the inevitable consequence of one's consistent suspension of judgement. It would be something that would simply happen to the Sceptic.[86] Sextus illustrates the way in which tranquillity comes to the Sceptic only when he gives up searching for it with an anecdote about a painter called Apelles. It is said that Apelles was trying to paint a picture of a horse and wanted to represent the lather on the horse's mouth. He was unable to achieve the desired effect, gave up, and threw his sponge at the painting in disgust. When the sponge hit the painting it produced a perfect representation of the lather of the horse's mouth.[87] In just the same way, Sextus suggests, the Sceptic achieves tranquillity as soon as he gives up his search and suspends judgement (ἐποχή). Once he does this, it appears of its own accord.[88]

In particular, the Sceptics appear to have believed that this tranquillity (ἀταραξία) was the only true path to well-being or happiness (εὐδαιμονία).[89] In other words the Sceptics, just as much as the Stoics or Epicureans or any other dogmatists, affirmed that philosophy – in this case the Sceptical philosophical method of suspending judgement (ἐποχή) – was the key to happiness (εὐδαιμονία), the key to living well. Despite their objections to the Stoic concept of an art of living, the Sceptics also held that philosophy was the key to living well. In particular they characterized philosophy as a therapy for the soul, employing a medical analogy not dissimilar to those used by both Socrates and the Stoics:

> Sceptics are philanthropic and wish to cure by argument (ἰᾶσθαι λόγῳ), as far as they can, the conceit and rashness of the Dogmatists. Just as doctors for bodily afflictions have remedies which differ in potency [...] so Sceptics propound arguments which differ in strength.[90]

Their argument with the Stoics may be seen, then, as an argument between two competing schools of philosophy concerning the precise way in which the study of philosophy would bring about well-being or happiness (εὐδαιμονία), and not an

---

[85] See *Pyrr. Hyp.* 1.26. The word ἀταραξία (from ταραχή) means literally 'un-disturbed' or 'un-troubled'. Striker notes ('*Ataraxia*: Happiness as Tranquillity', pp. 183-84) that the Latin *tranquilitate* was often used to translate εὐθυμία rather than ἀταραξία (e.g. Cicero *Fin.* 5.23). Nevertheless 'tranquillity' captures the meaning of ἀταραξία as Sextus uses the word.

[86] See *Pyrr. Hyp.* 1.26 & 1.28. Barnes, 'The Beliefs of a Pyrrhonist', p. 59, emphasizes the causal nature of this sequence: investigation leads to opposed arguments, which leads to equipollence (ἰσοσθένεια), which leads to suspension of judgement (ἐποχή), which, in turn, leads to tranquillity (ἀταραξία).

[87] See *Pyrr. Hyp.* 1.28. For an ancient account of Apelles see Pliny *Nat. Hist.* 35.79-97.

[88] See Burnyeat, 'Can the Sceptic Live his Scepticism?', p. 29.

[89] See the arguments in *Adv. Math.* 11.110-67, with Burnyeat, 'Can the Sceptic Live his Scepticism?', p. 30.

[90] *Pyrr. Hyp.* 3.280 (trans. Annas & Barnes). The latter part of this passage is Sextus' apology for the varying quality of the arguments that he deploys.

argument about whether or not it could. On this latter point, the Sceptics are at one with the Stoics and the other dogmatists.[91] Although Sceptics such as Sextus may have had doubts about the *way* in which the Stoics claimed that philosophy could transform one's way of life, they did not have any doubts that their own philosophical method would transform their own lives. Despite his objections, there is a sense in which Sextus' scepticism may itself be loosely characterized as an art of living, or at least a philosophical method primarily concerned with living well.

4. Summary

In this chapter I have considered a number of objections against the idea of an art (τέχνη) concerned with one's life (βίος) made by Sextus Empiricus. I have also suggested that, despite making these objections, Sextus' own philosophy can be seen to be directed towards the transformation of one's way of life (βίος). Sextus' polemic against the Stoic concept of an art of living (τέχνη περὶ τὸν βίον) forms the largest single document concerning this concept and that is why it has been considered in some detail. Hopefully this has shed further light upon this Stoic conception of philosophy and has developed and qualified the discussion in Chapter 3.

This draws to an end the discussion of the idea of a τέχνη concerned with βίος. In Part II we shall move forward to examine the role of the two components of such a τέχνη that we have uncovered in the accounts of both Socrates and the Stoics, namely λόγος and ἄσκησις. As we saw in Chapter 2, the role of exercise (ἄσκησις) was held to be of particular importance by Socrates in the *Gorgias*, forming an essential component alongside rational discourse (λόγος) in his conception of an art (τέχνη). In Socrates' technical conception of philosophical knowledge (ἐπιστήμη), such knowledge cannot be identified merely with rational understanding (λόγος) but will also involve exercise or training (ἄσκησις). We have also seen how the Stoics developed this technical conception of philosophical knowledge and how Stoics such as Seneca placed particular emphasis upon the essential role of both λόγος and ἄσκησις in philosophy. In Part II, then, I shall focus upon the relationship between these two components of philosophy conceived as a τέχνη. In particular, I shall develop the idea of a philosophical ἄσκησις insofar as this is the key component distinguishing the technical conception of philosophy from those conceptions which characterize philosophy simply as a matter of rational discourse (λόγος).

---

[91] See Annas & Barnes, *The Modes of Scepticism*, p. 170. In antiquity only the Cyrenaics were not eudaimonists; see Annas, *The Morality of Happiness*, p. 322.

PART II
λόγος and ἄσκησις

Chapter 5

Philosophical Exercises

1. The Relationship between ἄσκησις and λόγος

In Part I I have attempted to outline a certain conception of philosophy as an art or craft (τέχνη) concerned with one's life (βίος). As we have seen, central to this conception is the role played by some form of training or exercise (ἄσκησις).[1] In the *Gorgias*, for example, we saw Socrates emphasize the need not only for the mastery of the principles (λόγοι) behind an art or craft (τέχνη) but also the need for some form of practical training (ἄσκησις). It is not enough for the apprentice shoemaker to grasp the theoretical principles (λόγοι) behind his chosen craft; he must also train (ἀσκέω) in order to translate that theoretical understanding into practical ability. For in the case of a craft (τέχνη) such as shoemaking, one can only claim to have knowledge (ἐπιστήμη) of that craft if one can produce the appropriate works (ἔργα) identified with that craft's goal (τέλος), in this case a good pair of shoes.

Philosophy conceived as an art (τέχνη), then, will involve both rational principles (λόγοι) and practical training (ἄσκησις), and its goal (τέλος) will be to produce the works (ἔργα) appropriate to it. With this conception, philosophical knowledge (ἐπιστήμη) will directly impact upon one's life (βίος) because such knowledge will necessarily lead to philosophical actions (ἔργα).[2] This is the essential difference

---

[1] As I have noted in Chapter 2, ἄσκησις (from ἀσκέω) may be translated as training, exercise, or practice. Also there are μελέτη (practice, exercise, care (from μελετάω) which covers a range of meanings overlapping both ἄσκησις and ἐπιμέλεια) and γυμνάζω (suggesting an athletic metaphor). I shall not attempt to draw any important distinction between these terms and I take them to be broadly synonymous (although note the discussion and distinctions drawn in Foucault, *L'herméneutique du sujet*, p. 339). All three of these terms appear in Epictetus (see e.g. Epictetus *Diss.* 2.9.13, 3.12.7-8, with discussion in Hijmans, Ἄσκησις, pp. 64-77, who also notes the term ἐκπονεῖν. The Latin equivalent for ἄσκησις would be *exercitatio* (as used by Seneca and also by Wolf and Schweighäuser in their Latin translations of Epictetus), but note also *meditatio* (also used by Seneca and adopted by Newman in his 'Cotidie meditare') and *studium* (used by Wolf to translate μελέτη). That ἄσκησις was considered to be an important philosophical topic is illustrated by the existence of a number of texts entitled Περὶ ἀσκήσεως (*De Exercitatione*), including works by the Stoics Herillus and Dionysius (Diogenes Laertius 7.166 & 167 = *SVF* 1.409 & 422), Musonius Rufus (fr. 6 = pp. 22-27 Hense), Epictetus (*Diss.* 3.12; note also 3.2, 3.3), and a text attributed to Plutarch and preserved only in Syriac (see Gildemeister & Bücheler, 'Pseudo-Plutarchos περὶ ἀσκήσεως').

[2] In this technical conception of philosophy is it important to stress again that knowledge (ἐπιστήμη) is conceived not merely in terms of rational understanding (λόγος) but rather as a technical expertise based upon both rational understanding (λόγος) and practical training

between philosophy conceived as an art (τέχνη) and philosophy conceived simply as a matter of developing a rational understanding (λόγος) in which there is no necessary connection between knowledge (ἐπιστήμη) and actions (ἔργα). The fundamental difference between these two conceptions of philosophy is clearly the role played by training or exercise (ἄσκησις) in philosophy conceived as an art (τέχνη). As in the case of shoemaking, in order for the philosophical apprentice to master his art – the art of living (τέχνη περὶ τὸν βίον) – he will have to undergo some form of philosophical training (ἄσκησις) after he has learnt the basic principles (λόγοι) of his art. Only once such practical training has been successfully completed will he be able to claim mastery of that art. Thus, in the Stoic art of living, ἄσκησις is the key to transforming a philosopher (φιλόσοφος) into a sage (σοφός).[3]

However, it is important to stress that despite the central role of practical training (ἄσκησις) in philosophy conceived as an art (τέχνη) this does not imply any rejection or devaluation of philosophical discourse or theory (λόγος). Rather, philosophical exercise should be understood as a supplement to such theory. Philosophy conceived as an art (τέχνη) involves both theory (λόγος) and practice (ἄσκησις).

In order to illustrate the nature of this relationship between λόγος and ἄσκησις it may be instructive to consider some passages from Epictetus. The first of these derives from a chapter entitled 'What is the Rule of Life?' (τίς ὁ βιωτικὸς νόμος).[4] Here Epictetus draws attention to the idea that philosophy is not merely a matter of theory or words (θεωρία, λόγοι) but rather is something primarily expressed in one's way of life (βίος):

> The philosophers first exercise us in theory (θεωρίας), where there is less difficulty, and then after that lead us to the more difficult matters; for in theory there is nothing which

---

(ἄσκησις). As we have seen in Chapter 2, this is where Aristotle's criticisms of Socrates fall down.

[3] For a general discussion of ἄσκησις in Stoicism see Goulet-Cazé, *L'ascèse cynique*, esp. pp. 159-91. For references to ἄσκησις in the early Stoa see Aristo *apud* Clement of Alexandria *Strom.* 2.20 (*PG* 8.1052b = *SVF* 1.370), Diogenes Laertius 7.166 (= *SVF* 1.409), Diogenes Laertius 7.167 (= *SVF* 1.422), Aetius *Plac.* 1.Prooem.2 (*DG* 273a13-14 = *SVF* 2.35), Arius Didymus 2.7.5b4 (2.62.15-20 WH = *SVF* 3.278); note also Clement of Alexandria *Strom.* 7.16 (*PG* 9.536c = *SVF* 3.490 although no explicit reference to the Stoa is made). For Posidonius on ἄσκησις see Galen *Plac. Hipp. Plat.* 5.6.13-14 (5.471 Kühn = 328.21-7 De Lacy = fr. 150 EK), 5.6.19-22 (5.472 Kühn = 330.6-21 De Lacy = fr. 168 EK). Note also his appearance in Seneca's discussion of *praecepta* and *decreta* in *Epist.* 94.38 (= fr. 178 EK). For Seneca (who uses *exercitatio* and *meditatio*) see e.g. *Epist.* 15.5, 16.1, 70.18, 82.8, 90.46, with further examples in Delatte *et al.*, *Seneca Opera Philosophica Index Verborum*, pp. 222 & 430. The role of ἄσκησις in Epictetus and Marcus Aurelius will be discussed in Chapters 6 and 7. The other late Stoic text worthy of note is Musonius Rufus' Περὶ ἀσκήσεως (fr. 6 = pp. 22-27 Hense), preserved in Stobaeus 3.29.78 (3.648.1-651.21 WH). The text, along with a translation into English, can also be found in Lutz, 'Musonius Rufus: The Roman Socrates', pp. 52-57. I shall discuss this text in § 2 (a) below.

[4] See Epictetus *Diss.* 1.26.

holds us back from following what we are taught, but in the affairs of life (τῶν βιωτικῶν) there are many things which draw us away.[5]

It is relatively easy, Epictetus suggests, to master philosophical theorems (θεωρήματα); the difficult task is to translate those philosophical ideas into philosophical actions (ἔργα). Yet, as his teacher Musonius Rufus put it, just as medical theories (λόγοι) are useless unless they are used to cultivate health in the body, so philosophical theories (λόγοι) are useless unless they are used to cultivate the excellence (ἀρετή) of the soul.[6] However, this should not lead one to devalue such theory. On the contrary, Epictetus makes this point precisely to draw attention to the need for such theoretical education *before* one attempts such actions. It is the preparation or necessary condition for the philosophical life.[7] Thus training or exercise (ἄσκησις) alone will never be enough. As with other arts and crafts (τέχναι), mastery will require both practice (ἄσκησις) and a grasp of the relevant theoretical principles (λόγοι).

The necessity of philosophical λόγοι is the subject of another passage from Epictetus, a chapter concerned with the question of the necessity of the art of reasoning (τὰ λογικά).[8] While Epictetus stresses the need for the study of logic, an interlocutor – one of his students perhaps – interrupts by saying, 'Yes, but the therapy [of one's judgement] is a much more pressing need [than the study of logic]'.[9] Epictetus responds to this by saying that before one can engage in that practical project of therapy (θεραπεία) one must first be able to understand and to define what it is that one hopes to cure. He notes that not only do early Stoics such as Zeno and Chrysippus acknowledge this but also a so-called 'Cynic' like Antisthenes.[10] According to Epictetus, for Antisthenes – just as it was for Socrates – philosophical education begins with the examination of terms (τῶν ὀνομάτων ἐπίσκεψις).[11]

This discussion between Epictetus and his student illustrates two points. The first is the attitude of the student which suggests the existence in certain philosophical circles of an emphasis upon exercise in antiquity at the *expense* of theory, an attitude probably connected to the image of the pseudo-philosopher who sports a philosopher's dirty cloak and beard, but no philosophical actions (ἔργα) based upon rational principles (λόγοι); one who plays at being a philosopher but has not yet

---

[5] Epictetus *Diss.* 1.26.3 (trans. Oldfather modified); see also *Diss.* 2.9.13.
[6] See Musonius Rufus fr. 3 (12.15-19 Hense = 42.19-22 Lutz).
[7] See e.g. Epictetus *Diss.* 4.4.11: 'is not the reading of books a kind of preparation for the act of living?' (trans. Oldfather).
[8] See Epictetus *Diss.* 1.17, esp. 4-12.
[9] Epictetus *Diss.* 1.17.4 (trans. Oldfather modified). The precise meaning of this passage is based upon a conjecture first made by Wolf (Cologne edn (1595), vol. 3, p. 471, and reprinted in both Upton and Schweighäuser). The portions of the translation in brackets are based upon Wolf's gloss who understands 'therapy' (θεραπεία) as 'therapy of judgement' (θεραπεία τῆς ὑπόληψεως).
[10] For Antisthenes' status as a 'Cynic' see Dudley, *A History of Cynicism*, pp. 1-16, and more recently Goulet-Cazé, 'Who Was the First Dog?'.
[11] See Epictetus *Diss.* 1.17.12 (= Antisthenes fr. 38 DC = *SSR* V A 160 & I C 530).

developed the necessary understanding.[12] The second is Epictetus' clear affirmation of the necessity of both exercise (ἄσκησις) and theory (λόγος) for philosophy. Philosophical exercises cannot replace theory; rather they supplement theory.[13] Theory – such as the ethical theory one finds in Hierocles' treatise the *Elements of Ethics*, roughly contemporary with Epictetus – remains a necessary condition and, for Epictetus, the point of departure for philosophical education.[14] Yet theory alone is not enough for one to make proper philosophical progress. For that, both λόγος and ἄσκησις are required.[15]

2. The Concept of a Spiritual Exercise

We have already seen that some form of ἄσκησις will be necessary for philosophy conceived as an art (τέχνη). However, nothing has been said concerning the precise nature of this philosophical exercise. As we have already seen, for Socrates philosophy is an art that takes care of the soul (ἐπιμελεῖσθαι τῆς ψυχῆς) analogous to gymnastics (γυμναστική), the art that takes care of the body.[16] These philosophical exercises must thus be conceived as in some sense exercises for the soul analogous to exercises for the body. Indeed, we have already come across this idea in a passage by Xenophon which is worth repeating:

> I notice that as those who do not train the body (μὴ τὰ σώματα ἀσκοῦντας) cannot perform the functions proper to the body, so those who do not train the soul (μὴ τὴν ψυχὴν ἀσκοῦντας) cannot perform the functions of the soul.[17]

Just as the health of the body requires physical training, so the health of the soul (ἡ τῆς ψυχῆς ὑγίεια) will require some form of 'mental training', what we might call 'exercise for the soul' (ἄσκησις τῆς ψυχῆς).

---

[12] However, Dobbin, *Epictetus, Discourses Book 1*, p. 163, takes it to be a swipe at Epictetus himself, given Epictetus' own emphasis upon practice over theory elsewhere.

[13] This is a point upon which Nussbaum (*The Therapy of Desire*, p. 353) has criticized Foucault and 'affiliated writers' (by which she seems to mean Pierre Hadot). I shall discuss this in § 2 (b) below.

[14] See e.g. Epictetus *Diss.* 3.23.1-3 where he makes clear that before one can engage in the training necessary to an art or craft one must first understand the precise nature of the goal of that art.

[15] The necessity of ἄσκησις for Epictetus is noted by Hijmans, *Ἄσκησις*, p. 67.

[16] Epictetus also uses this analogy, often employing the verb γυμνάζω and related terms in his discussions of philosophical training. See e.g. *Diss.* 3.3.14, 3.8.1, 3.20.9. That Epictetus would have been familiar with Socrates' use of this analogy in the *Gorgias* is evidenced by his use of the *Gorgias* in the *Dissertationes* (see e.g. *Diss.* 2.12.5, with Jagu, *Épictète et Platon*, esp. pp. 136-37, and his list of parallel passages on p. 161).

[17] Xenophon *Mem.* 1.2.19 (trans. Marchant).

(a) Hadot on Spiritual Exercises

The concept of an exercise for the soul (ἄσκησις τῆς ψυχῆς) has recently been developed by Pierre Hadot who proposes the phrase 'spiritual exercise' (*exercice spirituel*).[18] Hadot suggests that one should consider an ancient philosophical position not merely in terms of a set of written doctrines but also as a series of practices or exercises directed towards the transformation of one's entire way of being (*manière d'être*).[19] The phrase 'spiritual exercise' used by Hadot derives from Ignatius of Loyola who defines it thus:[20]

> The term 'spiritual exercises' (*exercitiorum spiritualium*) denotes every way of examining one's conscience, of meditating, contemplating, praying vocally and mentally, and other spiritual activities, as will be said later. For just as strolling, walking, and running are exercises for the body (*exercitia quaedam corporalia*), so 'spiritual exercises' (*spirituale exercitium*) is the name given to every way of preparing and disposing one's soul to rid herself of all disordered attachments (*praeparandi et disponendi animum ad expellendos omnes inordinatos affectus*), so that once rid of them one might seek and find the divine will in regard to the disposition of one's life for the good of the soul.[21]

---

[18] See Hadot, *Exercices spirituels et philosophie antique*. I have only been able to consult the 1st edition. The translation into English under the title *Philosophy as a Way of Life* is based upon the 2nd edition which includes further material. See also his 'La philosophie antique: une éthique ou une pratique?', pp. 7-18; *Qu'est-ce que la philosophie antique?*, pp. 276-333; Gourinat, 'Vivre la philosophie', pp. 236-39. Hadot cites two works that inspired this concept: Rabbow, *Seelenführung*, and I. Hadot, *Seneca und die griechisch-römische Tradition der Seelenleitung*. He also notes the use of this phrase by Vernant in relation to Pythagoreanism (see *Mythe et pensée chez les Grecs*, vol. 1, p. 96; *Myth and Thought among the Greeks*, p. 87).

[19] See Hadot, *Exercices spirituels*, p. 60; *Philosophy as a Way of Life*, p. 127. Jonathan Barnes has questioned the language that Hadot occasionally uses to describe spiritual exercises, such as 'a practice designed to effect a radical change of being (*un changement radical de l'être*)' (*Qu'est-ce que la philosophie antique?*, p. 271), and suggests that in fact the notion is very straightforward: 'the notion of intellectual ἄσκησις, of "mental gymnastics", is at bottom a pretty down-to-earth sort of thing; and in most ancient texts ἄσκησις aims at nothing so high-falutin' as a change of being. After all, the idea of training or practice is hardly esoteric or religious (or even remarkable): it is a piece of ordinary, robust, common sense that if you want to ride a bike, then you should get pedalling' (*Logic and the Imperial Stoa*, p. 47 n. 101). The context of Hadot's remark indicates that he is referring to a *transformation du moi* conceived as a change in one's *habitus*. Nevertheless, I agree with Barnes that the idea of intellectual ἄσκησις should be understood as a piece of ordinary common sense.

[20] Here Hadot follows Rabbow who appears to have been the first to turn to Ignatius as a model for understanding ancient philosophical practices. See Hadot, *Exercices spirituels*, p. 59; *Philosophy as a Way of Life*, p. 126; Rabbow, *Seelenführung*, pp. 56-80.

[21] Ignatius of Loyola, *Exercitia Spiritualia*, Annotationes 1. This translation is by Munitiz & Endean in *Personal Writings*, p. 283, and is based upon the Spanish 'autograph' manuscript, two early versions of a Latin translation known as the 'versio prima' (which may be by Ignatius himself), and the first printed edition known as the 'versio vulgata' (see ibid., pp. 281-82). All four versions are printed in the 'Monumenta Historica Societatis Iesu' edition by Calveras & de

For Ignatius, a spiritual exercise is an exercise for the soul just as a physical exercise is an exercise for the body. Although at first glance it might seem anachronistic to apply this sixteenth-century Christian concept to an ancient philosophical position, Hadot argues that in fact the spiritual exercises of Ignatius stand within a Christian tradition that stretches back to antiquity and that is indebted to ancient philosophical practice.[22] As one might expect, Hadot explicitly identifies 'exercise' (*exercice*) with ἄσκησις,[23] and Ignatius' 'spiritual exercise' (*exercitium spiritualis*) with ἄσκησις τῆς ψυχῆς, a phrase used by Clement of Alexandria:

> The cure (θεραπεία) of self-conceit (as of every ailment (πάθους)) is threefold: [1] the ascertaining of the cause and [2] the mode of its removal, and thirdly, [3] the training of the soul (ἡ ἄσκησις τῆς ψυχῆς) and accustoming it (ἐθισμός) to assume a right attitude towards the judgements come to.[24]

In this brief analysis of the therapy of mental disturbances or emotions (πάθη) by Clement, the first two stages may be characterized as some form of philosophical analysis, namely a theoretical examination of the causes of mental disturbances and a proposed cure. Both of these are purely a matter of λόγοι. The third stage is the training or exercise (ἄσκησις) of the soul, namely the process by which the proposed cure of the passions is put into practice. This three stage analysis is in fact very similar to the two stage account of philosophical education made by Epictetus in which an initial period of studying philosophical principles (λόγοι) precedes a period of engaging in philosophical exercises (ἀσκήσεις). In both cases the final stage is an ἄσκησις directed towards the translation of λόγοι into ἔργα.

Beyond Clement of Alexandria, two further examples of the phrase ἄσκησις τῆς ψυχῆς can be found, one by Musonius Rufus, the other by Diogenes the Cynic. In an essay devoted to this topic entitled *On Exercise* (Περὶ ἀσκήσεως),[25] Musonius Rufus

---

Delmases, pp. 140-43. The Latin excerpts follow the texts of the two versions of the 'versio prima' which differ little at this point in the text.

[22] The Latin phrase *exercitium spiritualis* is used in the fourth century in Rufinus *Historia Monachorum* 7 (*PL* 21.410d) & 29 (*PL* 21.453d). For discussion of early Christian use of this concept see Leclercq, 'Exercices spirituels'. One should perhaps also note the medieval use of adapted versions of the *Enchiridion* of Epictetus, for which see Spanneut, *Permanence du Stoïcisme*, pp. 202-05, with texts in Boter, *The Encheiridion of Epictetus and its Three Christian Adaptations*, pp. 351-411.

[23] See Hadot, *Exercices spirituels*, p. 60; *Philosophy as a Way of Life*, p. 128. He also notes μελέτη and takes this to be synonymous with ἄσκησις.

[24] Clement of Alexandria *Strom.* 7.16 (*PG* 9.536c = *SVF* 3.490, although there is no explicit reference to the Stoa). The notion of 'accustoming' or 'habituating' (ἐθισμός) will be developed further in § 3 (a) below.

[25] This text is Musonius Rufus fr. 6 *apud* Stobaeus 3.29.78 (22.6-27.15 Hense = 52.7-56.11 Lutz). For comment see Geytenbeek, *Musonius Rufus and Greek Diatribe*, pp. 40-50, who describes Musonius' account of ἄσκησις as 'truly Stoic' (p. 44), and Hadot, *Qu'est-ce que la philosophie antique?*, pp. 289-91. Versions of the phrase ἄσκησις τῆς ψυχῆς appear at 25.4-5 & 25.14-15 Hense (54.10 & 54.18 Lutz).

suggests that, since a human being is neither just soul (ψυχή) nor just body (σῶμα) but rather some form of synthesis of the two, each individual will need to take care (ἐπιμελεῖσθαι) of both parts.[26] Musonius says that there are thus two kinds of exercise or training (ἄσκησις), one which is appropriate for the soul and one which is appropriate for the body but also impacts upon the soul at the same time.[27] According to Musonius, all physical training falls into the second of these groups and in fact always involves an element of spiritual exercise.[28] An example of this would be training one's body to cope with extremes of heat or cold, the famous example being Diogenes' practice of hugging statues in the middle of winter, an activity that would also strengthen one's soul.[29] As for purely spiritual exercises, Musonius says the following:

Training which is peculiar to the soul (τῆς ψυχῆς ἄσκησις) consists first of all in seeing that the proofs (ἀποδείξεις) pertaining to apparent goods as not being real goods are always ready at hand (προχείρους) and likewise those pertaining to apparent evils as not being real evils, and in learning to recognize the things which are truly good and in becoming accustomed (ἐθίζεσθαι) to distinguish them from what are not truly good. In the next place it consists of practice (μελετᾶν) in not avoiding any of the things which only seem evil, and in not pursuing any of the things which only seem good; in shunning by every means those which are truly evil and in pursuing by every means those which are truly good.[30]

This shares much in common with Clement's account which presented a spiritual exercise as that which puts into practice a theoretical analysis of the causes and remedies of the emotions (πάθη). Here, a spiritual exercise is that which translates proofs concerning what is good and bad into behaviour based upon those proofs. It is that which translates philosophical λόγοι into philosophical ἔργα.

A second example of the use of the phrase ἄσκησις τῆς ψυχῆς beyond Clement may be attributed to Diogenes the Cynic. According to the report of Diogenes Laertius, Diogenes the Cynic distinguished between two types of exercise (ἄσκησις), that for the soul and that for the body (τὴν μὲν ψυχικήν, τὴν δὲ σωματικήν), and claimed both of these types of exercise to be essential.[31] In particular, Diogenes is reported to have drawn upon the analogy with training in an art or craft:

---

[26] See Musonius Rufus fr. 6 (24.9-14 Hense = 54.2-7 Lutz).

[27] See Musonius Rufus fr. 6 (25.4-6 Hense = 54.10-11 Lutz).

[28] The same point is made by Musonius' pupil Epictetus in *Diss.* 3.12.16.

[29] See Musonius Rufus fr. 6 (25.6-14 Hense = 54.11-18 Lutz). For Diogenes' statue hugging see Diogenes Laertius 6.23 (= *SSR* V B 174). For a further example of this type of exercise see Epictetus *Ench.* 47.

[30] Musonius Rufus fr. 6 (25.14-26.5 Hense = 54.18-25 Lutz; trans. Lutz). The notion of 'becoming accustomed' (ἐθίζεσθαι) will be discussed in § 3 (a) below; the idea of keeping proofs 'ready to hand' (πρόχειρος) will be developed in Chapter 6 § 1.

[31] See Diogenes Laertius 6.70 (= *SSR* V B 291) with detailed treatment in Goulet-Cazé, *L'ascèse cynique*, pp. 195-222. I say '*may* be attributed to Diogenes the Cynic' because the text

Take the case of flute players and of athletes: what surpassing skill they acquire by their own incessant toil; and, if they had transferred their efforts to the training of the soul (τὴν ἄσκησιν καὶ ἐπὶ τὴν ψυχήν), how certainly their labours would not have been unprofitable or ineffective.[32]

Thus, the student of philosophy who wants to master the art of living and to cultivate excellence (ἀρετή) will need to train in a manner analogous to the way in which the athlete or the craftsman must train.

It is clear, then, that Ignatius' distinction between spiritual exercises and physical exercises was already explicit in antiquity.[33] Thus, far from being anachronistic, Hadot's use of Ignatius' phrase 'spiritual exercise' is useful to capture what Clement, Musonius, and Diogenes all call ἄσκησις τῆς ψυχῆς, and to distinguish this from physical exercise.[34]

However, it is important to stress that Hadot's use of the phrase 'spiritual exercise' does not imply any substantial claim concerning the nature of the soul (ψυχή) as such.[35] The Stoics and the Epicureans, for example, both proposed materialist accounts of the soul and yet both schools can be seen to have engaged in spiritual exercises.[36] A good example of an Epicurean spiritual exercise can be found in Epicurus' *Letter to Menoeceus*:

Accustom yourself (συνέθιζε) to the belief that death is nothing to us (μηδὲν πρὸς ἡμᾶς). For all good and evil lie in sensation, whereas death is the absence of sensation.[37]

Here Epicurus is not merely making a doctrinal claim that death is 'nothing to us' (μηδὲν πρὸς ἡμᾶς) but rather is proposing that one accustoms oneself (συνέθιζε) to this thought in a way that will transform one's attitude towards death and thus impact upon one's life (βίος).[38] By engaging in this meditation upon the nature of death the hope is that one will be able to overcome both the fear of death and the belief that

---

that survives appears to be a paraphrase by Diogenes Laertius and consequently it is difficult to attribute a specific phrase to his subject.

[32] Diogenes Laertius 6.70 (= *SSR* V B 291; trans. Hicks modified).

[33] A further ancient example of this distinction between exercises for the body and for the soul can be found in Ps.-Plutarch *De Exercitatione*, preserved only in Syriac. See Gildemeister & Bücheler, 'Pseudo-Plutarchos περὶ ἀσκήσεως', pp. 524-25, with comment in Geytenbeek, *Musonius Rufus and Greek Diatribe*, p. 43.

[34] Newman, '*Cotidie meditare*', pp. 1507 n. 66 & 1515, criticizes Hadot for trying to impose a strict definition to a practice that varied considerably. Although Newman may be correct to emphasize the ways in which ancient philosophers engaged in different forms of spiritual exercise, Hadot's phrase remains a helpful general characterization. Newman himself opts for the Latin *meditatio* and appears to oscillate between using it in an equally broad way and using it in a more limited sense to refer to 'reflecting ahead of time what evils may come' (p. 1477).

[35] See Gourinat, 'Vivre la philosophie', p. 237.

[36] For Epicurean and Stoic materialist psychology see Annas, *Hellenistic Philosophy of Mind*.

[37] Epicurus *Epist. ad Men.* (*apud* Diogenes Laertius 10) 124 (= LS 24 A; trans. LS).

[38] The notion of accustoming oneself (συνέθιζε) will be developed further in § 3 (a) below.

death is something inherently bad. That this transformation of one's attitude is Epicurus' aim – not just here but in his philosophy as a whole – is made explicit at the beginning of the same letter where he identifies the study of philosophy with the cultivation of happiness (εὐδαιμονία) and the health of the soul:

> Let no one either delay philosophizing when young, or weary of philosophizing when old. For no one is too young or too old for health of the soul (τὸ κατὰ ψυχὴν ὑγιαῖνον).[39]

That Epicurus engages in these exercises of the soul directed towards the cultivation of mental health, yet at the same affirms the soul to be corporeal, indicates that the phrase 'spiritual exercise' does not contain any presupposition concerning the nature of the soul (ψυχή) as such.[40] The phrase 'mental exercise' might be seen to be more appropriate. The term 'spiritual' does indeed have a number of unhelpful connotations but so does the term 'mental'.[41] Alternative phrases such as 'mental exercise' or 'mental training' suggest to a modern reader something akin to psychotherapy. Although there may be some points of contact between ancient exercises of the soul and modern psychotherapy, there are just as many points of departure.[42] On balance, Hadot's phrase 'spiritual exercise' is well suited, has ancient precedent in the ἄσκησις τῆς ψυχῆς of Clement, Musonius, and Diogenes, and can be clearly defined so that the careful reader will not be confused.

(b) Hadot, Foucault, and Nussbaum on the Nature of Philosophy

In the light of the extended discussion concerning τέχνη in Part I, there are, however, certain features of Hadot's use of the phrase 'spiritual exercise' about which one should be cautious. According to Hadot, 'it is *philosophy itself* that the ancients

---

[39] Epicurus *Epist. ad Men.* (*apud* Diogenes Laertius 10) 122 (= LS 25 A; trans. LS modified). For further discussion see Nussbaum, *The Therapy of Desire*, pp. 102-39.

[40] See Urmson, *The Greek Philosophical Vocabulary*, pp. 144-45, on ψυχή. Anything alive has a ψυχή and thus the Greek word is significantly broader than either 'soul' or 'mind'. A more cumbersome alternative occasionally proposed is 'life-force'. Another suggestion has been 'animator' (see Barnes, *Aristotle*, p. 65). However Urmson, *The Greek Philosophical Vocabulary*, pp. 144-45, offers a number of reasonable arguments in favour of 'soul' rather than 'mind'.

[41] This problem of translation is of course merely a corollary to the more general problem of finding a suitable English equivalent for ψυχή (see the previous note). If one follows Urmson's arguments in favour of 'soul' rather than 'mind', then it would follow that in this context 'spiritual' would be better than 'mental'.

[42] See in particular the material discussed in Chapter 7 § 2. The relationship between the individual and the cosmos outlined there would hardly fit under the modern label 'psychotherapy'. However, perhaps one could, following Panizza, 'Stoic Psychotherapy in the Middle Ages and Renaissance', p. 40, use 'psychotherapy' in its strictly etymological sense. For further discussion of the relationship between ancient philosophy and modern psychotherapy see Gill, 'Ancient Psychotherapy', pp. 316-23.

thought of as a spiritual exercise'.[43] Yet as we have seen, this is not strictly speaking correct. For the Stoics, at least, philosophy is an art in which such exercises form but one part.[44] If philosophy were simply a series of exercises for the soul, then it would be nothing more than a process of habituation that would not involve the development of a rational understanding of what was being learned. In other words, it would *not* be based upon an understanding of the λόγοι underpinning philosophy conceived as a τέχνη. If, for example, the medical student did not first study the principles underpinning the art of medicine and launched straight into simply copying the behaviour of others, one would hardly claim that he would be likely to master his chosen art. The same applies to philosophy conceived as an art. Philosophy for the Stoics is not merely a series of spiritual exercises; rather these exercises serve to train the apprentice philosopher in the art of living, to translate his doctrines (λόγοι) into actions (ἔργα), to transform his life (βίος) into that of a sage. But, as Epictetus emphasizes, before such exercises can begin the apprentice must first learn his doctrines and master philosophical theory. Exercises alone are not enough. In his attempt to emphasize the importance of ἄσκησις in ancient philosophy Hadot has, it seems, forgotten the role of λόγος.

It has often been claimed that Michel Foucault's account of what he calls techniques or technologies of the self (*techniques de soi, technologies de soi*) – an account that explicitly draws upon the work of Hadot – suffers from the same problem, namely an emphasis upon ἄσκησις at the expense of λόγος.[45] In particular,

---

[43] Hadot, *Philosophy as a Way of Life*, p. 126 (emphasis added by translator); *Exercices spirituels*, p. 59: 'C'est la philosophie elle-même que les Anciens se sont représentés comme un exercice spirituel'. Note also *Philosophy as a Way of Life*, p. 273. Hadot's claim is based upon references to two texts, Aetius *Plac.* 1.Prooem.2 (*DG* 273a13-14 = *SVF* 2.35 = LS 26 A) and Ps.-Galen *Hist. Phil.* 5 (19.231 Kühn = *DG* 602.19-603.1). However, these texts do not define philosophy as an exercise (ἄσκησις), but rather as the exercise (ἄσκησις) of an art (τέχνη), a phrase one might gloss as an art put into practice. Hadot's claim appears, then, to be based upon a misreading of these two relatively unimportant texts.

[44] At one point Hadot appears to assume that for the Stoics an exercise and an art amount to the same thing; see *Exercices spirituels*, pp. 15-16, *Philosophy as a Way of Life*, pp. 82-83, 'The Stoics, for instance, declared explicitly that philosophy, for them, was an 'exercise' (*exercice*). In their view, philosophy did not consist in teaching an abstract theory – much less in the exegesis of texts – but rather in the art of living (*un art de vivre*)'.

[45] Foucault introduces this concept in his 1980-81 lecture course entitled *Subjectivité et vérité* (not yet published); see *Dits et écrits*, vol. 4, p. 213; *Essential Works*, vol. 1, p. 87. His earliest discussion in print can be found in his general introduction to the last two volumes of his *Histoire de la sexualité*, first published separately as 'Usage des plaisirs et techniques de soi' (1983); see *Dits et écrits*, vol. 4, p. 545, and *The Use of Pleasure*, pp. 10-11 (*L'usage des plaisirs*, pp. 18-19). This is also where he acknowledges his debt to Hadot; see *Dits et écrits*, vol. 4, p. 542, and *The Use of Pleasure*, p. 8 (*L'usage des plaisirs*, p. 15). The concept is developed further in 'Technologies of the Self', in *Dits et écrits*, vol. 4, pp. 783-813; *Essential Works*, vol. 1, pp. 223-51. For further discussion of Foucault's engagement with ancient philosophy see Davidson, 'Ethics as Ascetics: Foucault, the History of Ethics, and Ancient Thought'; Miller, 'From Socrates to Foucault'; Nehamas, *The Art of Living*, pp. 157-88; note also Part III of Davidson, *Foucault and his Interlocutors*, entitled 'Foucault and the Ancients'.

Martha Nussbaum has criticized both Hadot and Foucault for obscuring what she takes to be the essential role of reason and rational argument in ancient philosophy.[46] She suggests that if one does not emphasize the role of reason in ancient philosophy then an ancient philosophical way of life will become indistinguishable from ancient religious ways of life. On her account, Hadot and Foucault are unable to account for the difference between the sorts of ascetic exercises undertaken by, say, the Desert Fathers, and a properly philosophical exercise. As she puts it,

> Stoicism is indeed, as Michel Foucault and other affiliated writers [i.e. Hadot] have recently insisted, a set of techniques for the formation and shaping of the self. But what their emphasis on habits and *techniques du soi* too often obscures is the dignity of reason. [...] What sets philosophy apart from popular religion, dream-interpretation, and astrology is its commitment to rational argument. [...] For all these habits and routines are useless if not rational.[47]

Whilst Nussbaum is surely correct to emphasize the role of rational argument in ancient philosophy in general, and Stoicism in particular, she is herself far from clear concerning how one should understand the relationship between such rational arguments and the philosophical techniques which she also acknowledges to be vital. She appears to say that Stoicism is indeed a series of such habits, routines, or techniques, but then qualifies this by characterizing these as *rational* exercises ('Stoicism is indeed [...] a set of techniques [... which are] useless if not rational'). Yet as we have seen, for the Stoics, philosophy is an art (τέχνη) comprised of two components, rational argument (λόγος) and practical exercise or training (ἄσκησις), both being necessary components of this art concerned with transforming one's way of life (βίος). Indeed, this is in fact precisely how Foucault understands the matter. Despite Nussbaum's account of his position, Foucault's characterization of ancient philosophy as a technique *cannot* be identified with Hadot's characterization of philosophy as spiritual exercise. Foucault writes,

> No technique, no professional skill can be acquired without exercise; nor can one learn the art of living, the *technē tou biou*, without an *askēsis* that must be understood as a training of the self by the self.[48]

---

[46] See Nussbaum, *The Therapy of Desire*, pp. 5, 353-54. On p. 5 she claims that Foucault characterizes ancient philosophy as simply 'a set of *techniques du soi*' and understands these techniques as something similar to Hadot's spiritual exercises. In fact, as we shall see, Foucault is careful not to identify his *techniques* with such exercises.

[47] Nussbaum, *The Therapy of Desire*, p. 353.

[48] Foucault, 'L'écriture de soi', in *Dits et écrits*, vol. 4, p. 417: 'Aucune technique, acune habileté professionelle ne peut s'acquérir sans exercice; on ne peut non plus apprendre l'art de vivre, la *technē tou biou*, sans une *askēsis* qu'il faut comprendre comme un entraînement de soi par soi'; trans. in *Essential Works*, vol. 1, p. 208.

Here Foucault's position is clear; acquisition of a technique *requires* exercise, τέχνη *requires* ἄσκησις. In other words, when Foucault talks about techniques or technologies of the self (*techniques de soi, technologies de soi*) he uses these terms in the strictly etymological sense of a τέχνη and, despite Nussbaum's account, he does not identify these techniques with ἄσκησις.[49] Rather, for Foucault, ancient philosophy is a τέχνη that *involves* ἄσκησις. His 'techniques of the self' (*techniques de soi*) should thus be understood as 'arts of the self' rather than 'exercises of the self'.[50] As arts, Foucault's techniques do not devalue the role of rational argument as Nussbaum claims but rather will involve λόγος alongside ἄσκησις as an essential component. Thus Foucault's position is clearly very different from Hadot's, a difference overlooked by Nussbaum who appears to assume that Foucault's techniques of the self (*techniques de soi*) can be identified with Hadot's spiritual exercises (*exercices spirituels*).[51]

The important point to note here is that one should not identify spiritual exercises with philosophy itself. As we have already seen, such exercises are merely the second, although essential, stage of philosophical education coming after an initial stage devoted to philosophical principles (λόγοι). Although Nussbaum is correct to emphasize the essential role of rational argument (λόγος), her implicit qualification of the idea of philosophy as 'technique' to 'rational technique' in her discussion of Foucault is far from clear. Instead, following the τέχνη analogy, Stoic philosophy should be understood as an art (τέχνη) grounded upon rational principles (λόγοι) which are only expressed in one's behaviour (ἔργα, βίος) after a period of practical training (ἄσκησις). Both λόγος and ἄσκησις are necessary components of philosophy conceived as a τέχνη but neither can be identified with philosophy itself.

3. The Function of Spiritual Exercises

This conception of a spiritual exercise as one component of philosophy conceived as an art (τέχνη) will be central to distinguishing between this technical conception of philosophy and philosophy conceived simply as an activity concerned with rational

---

[49] A number of other passages appear to confirm that Foucault understood *technique* in its etymological sense; see e.g. *The Use of Pleasure*, p. 11 (*L'usage des plaisirs*, p. 18); *Dits et écrits*, vol. 4, pp. 545, 671; *L'herméneutique du sujet*, p. 428.

[50] See esp. 'L'écriture de soi', in *Dits et écrits*, vol. 4, p. 415; *Essential Works*, vol. 1, p. 207, where he uses precisely this phrase; 'les arts de soi-même'. That Foucault understood ancient philosophy as an art rather than an exercise or practice is also made clear in *The Care of the Self*, p. 44 (*Le souci de soi*, p. 62).

[51] Nussbaum does in fact note that Hadot offers a 'different account' to Foucault (*The Therapy of Desire*, p. 353 n. 34). However her explication of Foucault's position fails to make this clear. The same mistake is also made by Davidson, 'Ethics as Ascetics: Foucault, the History of Ethics, and Ancient Thought', p. 123: 'For Foucault himself philosophy was a spiritual exercise'. Hadot himself distinguishes his position from Foucault in *Philosophy as a Way of Life*, pp. 206-07, but with regard to a totally different issue, namely, Foucault's reliance upon what Hadot considers to be an anachronistic conception of 'self'.

explanation. In order to understand the significance of this distinguishing component we must consider exactly how it was thought to function. As we have already noted, the purpose of these exercises is to enable one to express one's philosophical principles (λόγοι) in one's actions (ἔργα), thereby transforming one's way of life (βίος). In a text that may well have been influenced by Epictetus, Galen writes,

> All we must do is keep the doctrine (δόγμα) regarding insatiability and self-sufficiency constantly at hand (πρόχειρον), and commit ourselves to the daily exercise (ἄσκησιν) of the particular actions (ἔργων) which follow from these doctrines.[52]

In other words, the function of these daily exercises recommended by Galen is to translate doctrines (δόγματα, λόγοι) into one's actions and behaviour (ἔργα, βίος). In a number of the ancient accounts concerning exactly how this is to be done there are two themes which emerge: habituation (ἐθισμός) and digestion (πέψις).

(a) Habituation

We have already come across the idea of accustoming or habituating oneself in passing in passages from Clement, Musonius, and Epicurus.[53] For Clement, spiritual exercise consists in accustoming (ἐθισμός) the soul to make correct judgements.[54] For Musonius, spiritual exercise consists in becoming accustomed (ἐθίζεσθαι) to distinguish between real and apparent goods.[55] In both cases we might say that the function of a spiritual exercise is to accustom or to habituate (ἐθίζω) the soul

---

[52] Galen *Aff. Dign.* 9 (5.52 Kühn = 34.24-26 de Boer; trans. Singer modified). A number of features of this text suggest the influence of Epictetus, including not only the emphasis upon daily exercise and transforming doctrines into actions but also the use of certain terminology such as 'up to us' (ἐφ' ἡμῖν) and 'at hand' (πρόχειρον). Galen himself reports that he wrote on Epictetus although the text in question is lost; see *Lib. Prop.* 11 (19.44 Kühn = test. 20 Schenkl). He was also personal physician to Marcus Aurelius, who was certainly well acquainted with Epictetus (see Chapter 7 § 1 below).

[53] See Clement of Alexandria *Strom.* 7.16 (*PG* 9.536c = *SVF* 3.490), Musonius Rufus fr. 6 (25.14-26.5 Hense = 54.18-25 Lutz), and Epicurus *Epist. ad Men.* (*apud* Diogenes Laertius 10) 124 (= LS 24 A), all cited above. The term translated as 'habituation' or 'accustoming' (ἐθισμός) derives from the verb 'to accustom' (ἐθίζω), which in turn derives from 'custom' or 'habit' (ἔθος). This is itself related to 'character' or 'disposition' (ἦθος), as Aristotle notes in *Eth. Nic.* 1103a17-18. It is important to note that in this context ἐθίζω should be understood not as unthinking habit but rather as a conscious learning process (see Urmson, *The Greek Philosophical Vocabulary*, p. 62). Other ancient references to the importance of habituation (ἐθισμός) include e.g. Plato *Phaedo* 67c (with further references in Brandwood, *A Word Index to Plato*, p. 285), Aristotle *Eth. Nic.* 1103a14-23 (who acknowledges its necessity in the acquisition of both ἀρετή and τέχνη at 1103a31-32 and 1105b9-18, where a medical analogy is used), Plotinus *Enn.* 1.3.2, 1.6.9 (with further references in Sleeman & Pollet, *Lexicon Plotinianum*, col. 287).

[54] See Clement of Alexandria *Strom.* 7.16 (*PG* 9.536c = *SVF* 3.490), quoted above.

[55] See Musonius Rufus fr. 6 (25.14-26.5 Hense = 54.18-25 Lutz), quoted above.

according to philosophical doctrines or principles (λόγοι), to absorb philosophical ideas into one's character (ἦθος) which, in turn, will determine one's habitual behaviour. We have also seen this idea in action in Epicurus' phrase 'accustom yourself (συνέθιζε) to the belief that death is nothing to us'.[56] It can also be seen in a number of Stoic texts such as the following; the first from Epictetus, the second and third from Marcus Aurelius:

> At everything that happens to you remember to turn to yourself and find what capacity you have to deal with it. If you see a beautiful boy or girl, you will find self-control as the capacity to deal with it; if hard labour is imposed on you, you will find endurance; if abuse, you will find patience. And when you make a habit of this (καὶ οὕτως ἐθιζόμενόν), the impressions will not carry you away.[57]

> Accustom yourself (ἔθισον) in the case of whatever is done by anyone, so far as possible to inquire within yourself: 'to what end does this man do this?' And begin with yourself and first examine yourself.[58]

> Contemplate continually all things coming to pass by change, and accustom yourself (ἐθίζου) to think that Universal Nature loves nothing so much as to change what is and to create new things in their likeness.[59]

This process of accustoming oneself is something that Marcus in particular suggests can be achieved only by repeated reflection. In order to illustrate this he characterizes the process in terms of 'dyeing' one's soul just as a piece of cloth might be dyed a new colour:

> As are your repeated imaginations so will your mind be, for the soul is dyed (βάπτεται) by its imaginations. Dye it, then, in a succession of imaginations like these.[60]

Thus Marcus' *Meditations* often repeat certain themes again and again, reflecting the repetitive nature of spiritual exercises. This is something also emphasized by Marcus' physician, Galen, who characterizes the beginning of such exercises (ἡ τῆς ἀσκήσεως ἀρχή) as the repetition of propositions to oneself two or three times.[61]

---

[56] See Epicurus *Epist. ad Men.* (*apud* Diogenes Laertius 10) 124, quoted above. At the end of the same letter (135) Epicurus also emphasizes the the need for daily exercise.

[57] Epictetus *Ench.* 10 (trans. Boter). For further references to habituation in Epictetus see e.g. *Diss.* 2.9.10, 2.9.14, 2.18.4, 3.8.4, 3.12.6, 3.25.10.

[58] Marcus Aurelius 10.37 (trans. Farquharson).

[59] Marcus Aurelius 4.36 (trans. Farquharson).

[60] Marcus Aurelius 5.16 (trans. Farquharson); see also 3.4: 'dyed with justice to the core' (δικαιοσύνη βεβαμμένον εἰς βάθος). In his commentary Farquharson claims that this image is original to Marcus (see p. 658). However, as Newman notes ('*Cotidie meditare*', p. 1507), it had already been used by Seneca (e.g. *Epist.* 71.31).

[61] See Galen *Aff. Dign.* 5 (5.21 Kühn = 15.16-18 de Boer); note also ibid. 5 (5.24-25 Kühn = 17.11-22 de Boer), 6 (5.30 Kühn = 21.3-10 de Boer), 9 (5.52 Kühn = 34.24-26 de Boer,

A spiritual exercise is, then, a form of practical training directed towards the incorporation of philosophical doctrines into one's everyday habits. This habituation (ἐθισμός) involves a transformation of one's character (ἦθος) which in turn transforms one's behaviour.[62] As such, this process will enable the translation of doctrines (λόγοι) into actions (ἔργα). It is the second stage of philosophical education once the study of theory has been completed. It is the means by which the philosophical apprentice completes his education in philosophy conceived as a τέχνη.

(b) Digestion

Alongside this theme of habituation one also finds the use of an analogy with the digestion of food. Epictetus writes the following:

> Do not, for the most part, talk among laymen about your philosophical principles (περὶ τῶν θεωρημάτων), but do what follows from your principles. […] For Sheep, do not bring their fodder to the shepherds and show how much they have eaten, but they digest (πέψαντα) their food within them, and on the outside produce wool and milk. And so do you, therefore, make no display to the laymen of your philosophical principles (τὰ θεωρήματα), but let them see the results (τὰ ἔργα) which come from the principles when digested (πεφθέντων).[63]

For Epictetus, this process of philosophical 'digestion' (πέψις) is essential.[64] Too many of his students, he suggests, 'throw up' (ἐξεμέω) what they have heard before having given themselves an opportunity to digest (πέσσω) it. They repeat philosophical ideas before they have assimilated them and thus they are unable to act in accordance with them, creating a disharmony between their actions and words. Such undigested principles are, for Epictetus, simply 'vomit' (ἔμετος).[65]

---

already quoted above). Note also the following from the first book of Galen's *De Moribus* (Περὶ ἠθῶν), preserved only in an Arabic epitome: 'a character is developed through being constantly accustomed to things that man sets up in his soul and to things that he does regularly every day' (p. 241 Mattock; also in Rosenthal, *The Classical Heritage in Islam*, p. 91). For further discussion of this text see Walzer, 'New Light on Galen's Moral Philosophy'.

[62] As we have already seen in Chapter 3 § 7, for the Stoics this will be a corporeal transformation of the dispositions of the soul (διαθέσεις τῆς ψυχῆς).

[63] Epictetus *Ench.* 46 (trans. Oldfather modified). The key term here is the verb 'digest' (πέσσω) which is used three times (lines 8, 11, & 13 Boter, in the forms ἔπεψας, πέψαντα, and πεφθέντων respectively). Note also the use of ἔργα here and the way in which it functioned in Chapter 3 § 4; only once principles have been digested will the appropriate ἔργα – results, products, actions – be produced.

[64] For further examples of 'philosophical digestion' in Epictetus see *Diss.* 3.21.1-4, 2.9.18. Another image used by Epictetus closely related to digestion is that of a ripening fruit (see e.g. *Diss.* 1.15.6-8, 4.8.36). A fruit must be given time to ripen – to digest what it needs – before it is ready to eat and the same applies to the philosophical development of the soul.

[65] This imagery can also be found in an extended passage in *Diss.* 3.21.1-4: 'Those who have learned the principles (θεωρήματα) and nothing else are eager to throw them up (ἐξεμέσαι)

This analogy with digestion also appears in Seneca's advice to Lucilius concerning the art of reading:

> Be careful lest this reading of many authors and books of every sort may tend to make you discursive and unsteady. You must linger among a limited number of master-thinkers and digest their works (*innutriri oportet*) [...] for food does no good and is not assimilated into the body if it leaves the stomach as soon as it is eaten, and nothing hinders a cure so much as frequent change of medicine. [...] Each day [...] after you have run over many thoughts, select one to be thoroughly digested (*concoquas*) that day.[66]

Philosophical principles only attain value once they have been digested. Just as food transforms and becomes part of the body only once it has been digested, so philosophical nourishment must be digested before it can become part of the soul,[67] transforming one's character (ἦθος) and ultimately one's behaviour (ἔργα, βίος).[68] Spiritual exercises are directed towards this process of philosophical digestion, a process that transforms the soul (ψυχή, ἦθος) and translates theoretical principles (θεωρήματα, λόγοι) into actions (ἔργα).

---

immediately, just as persons with a weak stomach throw up their food. First digest (πέψον) your principles, and then you will surely not throw them up (ἐξεμέσῃς) this way. Otherwise they are mere vomit (ἔμετος), foul stuff and unfit to eat. But after you have digested these principles, show us some change in your governing principle (ἡγεμονικοῦ) that is due to them; as the athletes show their shoulders as the results of their exercising (ἐγυμνάσθησαν) and eating, and as those who have mastered the arts (τέχνας) can show results of their learning. The builder does not come forward and say, "Listen to me deliver a discourse about the art of building"; but he takes a contract for a house, builds it, and thereby proves that he possesses the art (τέχνην)' (trans. Oldfather).

[66] Seneca *Epist.* 2.2-4 (trans. Gummere modified). As one can see, here Seneca uses both *concoquo* and *innutrio* but in general he prefers *concoquo* which, when used in this context, the *OLD* glosses as 'to absorb into the mind'. See also *Epist.* 84.5-8, with comment in Foucault, 'L'écriture de soi', in *Dits et écrits*, vol. 4, pp. 422-23; *Essential Works*, vol. 1, pp. 213-14.

[67] See Simplicius' comment on *Ench.* 46, the chapter quoted above (*In Ench.* 64.27-30 Hadot): 'For as meats, when they are duly concocted, distribute themselves into the several parts and mix with the vital juices and blood to nourish and strengthen the body, so do maxims and doctrines, when well digested, convert into nourishment and make the soul healthful and vigorous' (trans. Stanhope).

[68] This link between character and an individual's habitual actions is noted by Galen in the first book of his *De Moribus* (Περὶ ἠθῶν), preserved only in an Arabic epitome. According to Galen, an individual's character (ἦθος) generates actions without further reflection and thus any substantial transformation of behaviour will involve transforming one's character (pp. 236, 241 Mattock; see also Rosenthal, *The Classical Heritage in Islam*, pp. 85 & 91, with comment in Walzer, 'New Light on Galen's Moral Philosophy', p. 85). Elsewhere Galen suggests that the transformation of one's ἦθος will involve both ἄσκησις and δόγματα (see Galen *Aff. Dign.* 7 = 5.37 Kühn = 25.21-24 de Boer). The same point is made by Plotinus in *Enn.* 2.9.15: justice (δικαιοσύνη) is developed in one's character (ἦθος) by reasoning (λόγος) and training (ἄσκησις).

* * *

These processes of habituation (ἐθισμός) and digestion (πέψις) form the function of spiritual exercises. They aim at the assimilation of philosophical principles into one's soul (ψυχή) that will, in turn, transform one's way of life (βίος). Like the apprentice craftsman who has learned the principles (λόγοι) of his art but has not yet mastered the necessary practical technique, so the student of this technical conception of philosophy will not be able to claim philosophical knowledge (ἐπιστήμη) on the basis of his understanding of philosophical principles (λόγοι) alone. According to this technical conception of philosophy, knowledge (ἐπιστήμη) conceived as technical expertise will also require this process of assimilation. Like the apprentice craftsman, this training may take some time and will in some sense never be fully completed. Just as the master craftsman will continue to improve his technique as he works, so the philosopher will continue to improve himself and his life. As Galen puts it, in order to become a perfected individual one must engage in exercises throughout the whole of one's life.[69]

4. The Mechanism of Spiritual Exercises

Although it is relatively clear *what* a spiritual exercise attempts to achieve, namely the digestion of principles and habituation of the soul, it is less clear precisely *how* this might be achieved. So far, the discussion of the idea of a spiritual exercise – an ἄσκησις of the ψυχή – has not made reference to any specific conception of the ψυχή. Although ancient philosohers may, in general, agree on the *purpose* of spiritual exercises, their diverging conceptions of the soul (ψυχή) will clearly lead to quite different accounts of the *way* in which such exercises might work. In the broadest terms, ψυχή may be understood to refer to the principle of life or animation within a living being.[70] However, in order to develop an account of how a specifically Stoic spiritual exercise might function it will be necessary to consider briefly the Stoic conception of the soul (ψυχή).

---

[69] See Galen *Aff. Dign.* 4 (5.14 Kühn = 11.15-16 de Boer); note also ibid. (5.16 Kühn = 12.9-10 de Boer), 5 (5.25 Kühn = 18.4-8 de Boer). A similar point is made in Aristotle *Eth. Nic.* 1147a21-22 where he suggests that the digestion of words and their transformation into genuine knowledge takes time.

[70] In the discussion in *De Anima* Aristotle presents the ψυχή as the first principle of living things (ἀρχὴ τῶν ζῴων), as that by virtue of which something is alive, and as that by virtue of which a thing has movement (κίνησις) and perception (αἴσθησις). See Aristotle *De Anima* 402a6-7, 413a20-22, and 403b25-27 respectively. With these general claims the Stoics would agree; see e.g. Diogenes Laertius 7.156-57 (= *SVF* 1.135, 2.774, 3 Ant. 49, Posidonius fr. 139 EK).

(a) The Stoic Conception of ψυχή

The Stoics' materialist conception of the soul (ψυχή) can only be understood within the broader context of their physics.[71] According to Stoic physics, all physical objects involve two basic principles (ἀρχαί), matter (ὕλη) and breath (πνεῦμα).[72] This breath (πνεῦμα), itself material, pervades all physical objects and the qualities of any particular object are due to the tension (τόνος) of the breath (πνεῦμα) within it.[73] The solidity of a stone, for example, is due to the tension of the breath (ὁ τόνος τοῦ πνεύματος) within it, a tension (τόνος) that generates stability.[74]

Different degrees of tension (τόνος) in the breath (πνεῦμα) pervading an object will generate different qualities. In the case of the stone, the tension (τόνος) of the breath (πνεῦμα) may be said to give the stone a certain state of cohesion (ἕξις). A higher degree of tension would generate more complex qualities such as self-movement. In fact, the Stoics outline four distinct categories of pneumatic tension: a state of cohesion (ἕξις), nature or growth (φύσις), soul (ψυχή), and rational soul (λογικὴ ψυχή).[75] The first of these is the type of tension found in inanimate physical objects such as stones, the second is that found in plants, the third that found in animals, and the fourth that found in rational adult humans.[76] There is no substantial

---

[71] For general accounts of the Stoic conception of ψυχή see Long, 'Soul and Body in Stoicism'; Inwood, *Ethics and Human Action in Early Stoicism*, pp. 18-41; Annas, *Hellenistic Philosophy of Mind*, pp., 37-87; Gourinat, *Les stoïciens et l'âme*, pp. 17-35; Long in *CHHP*, pp. 560-84.

[72] Translating πνεῦμα is difficult. It is often rendered as 'breath', 'spirit', 'vital breath', 'vital spirit', or simply transliterated. I use 'breath' following Long & Sedley, and Gourinat's *souffle*. For general accounts of the two ἀρχαί, the concept of πνεῦμα, and its total blending with matter, see Samburgky, *Physics of the Stoics*, pp. 1-48; Todd, *Alexander of Aphrodisias on Stoic Physics*, pp. 29-73; Gould, *The Philosophy of Chrysippus*, pp. 93-102; Sorabji, *Matter, Space, and Motion*, pp. 83-98. For more on the two ἀρχαί see Chapter 7 § 2 (a) below.

[73] For τόνος as the source of qualities see Nemesius *Nat. Hom.* 2 (18.2-10 Morani = LS 47 J). For τόνος as source of cohesion of bodies see Alexander of Aphrodisias *Mixt.* 223.34-36 (= *SVF* 2.441 = LS 47 L). It has been suggested that τόνος could be understood as 'wavelength'; see Long in *CHHP*, p. 566. For further comment see Voelke, *L'idée de volonté dans le stoïcisme*, pp. 11-18.

[74] See e.g. Alexander of Aphrodisias *Mixt.* 223.34-36 (= *SVF* 2.441 = LS 47 L), Plutarch *Comm. Not.* 1085d (= *SVF* 2.444 = LS 47 G).

[75] For this fourfold division see Philo *Quod Deus Imm.* 35-36 (= *SVF* 2.458 = LS 47 Q), *Leg. Alleg.* 2.22-23 (= *SVF* 2.458 = LS 47 P), Themistius *De Anima* 1.5 (2.64.25-28 Spengel = *SVF* 1.158), Ps.-Galen *Intro. Med.* 13 (14.726 Kühn = *SVF* 2.716 = LS 47 N). In some of the ancient sources the last of these, λογικὴ ψυχή, is replaced by νοῦς.

[76] The first of these is exemplified by physical coherence and stability. The second supplements this with self-movement. The third adds to these impressions and impulses. Finally, the fourth adds rational judgements as a mediator between those impressions and impulses. For further discussion see Annas, *Hellenistic Philosophy of Mind*, pp. 50-56.

difference in kind between these four types of physical entity and the hierarchy is purely one of increasing degrees of tension (τόνος).[77]

The soul (ψυχή) of an individual human being is thus simply the breath (πνεῦμα) present in that individual at a certain level of tension (τόνος).[78] The rational soul of the sage will be that same breath (πνεῦμα) in an increased state of tension (τόνος).

(b) Transformation of the ψυχή

In the light of this, one can see that a specifically Stoic spiritual exercise will be directed towards the transformation of the disposition of the soul (διάθεσις τῆς ψυχῆς), a transformation achieved by an alteration in its tension (τόνος). Just as a physical exercise will improve the tension in one's muscles, so a spiritual exercise will improve the tension in one's soul.[79] It is reported that a soul in poor condition – that is, one with relatively weak tension – will be one subject to mental disturbances or emotions (πάθη).[80] These are the products of beliefs that, in turn, are the product of judgements.[81] A soul in good condition will be free from such emotions and this will reflect a correct use of judgements. There is, then, a correlation between weak tension and poor judgements on the one hand, and strong tension and sound judgements on the other.

What we have in a specifically Stoic context, then, are two parallel descriptions of a single process concerned with the improvement of one's soul (ψυχή). A Stoic spiritual exercise will be concerned with examining one's judgements and rejecting

---

[77] Alternatively the distinction is characterized in terms of density and fineness, with inanimate objects having the densest πνεῦμα and rational souls having the finest. See the account of the transformation of πνεῦμα in the process of birth in Hierocles *Elementa Ethica* 1.12-28 (= LS 53 B). See also Plutarch *Stoic. Rep.* 1052f (= *SVF* 2.806) who presents the transformation from φύσις to ψυχή as one of 'cooling' (ψῦξις), although he is apparently contradicted in Galen *Quod Animi Mores* 4 (4.783-84 Kühn = *SVF* 2.787) who suggests that the πνεῦμα of ψυχή is drier and hotter than that of φύσις. As I have already noted, Long suggests that the difference may be understood in terms of 'wave-length'. I am inclined to conceive it in terms of increasing organizational and functional complexity (see Lewis, 'The Stoics on Identity and Individuation', p. 99).

[78] See the excerpts from Chrysippus preserved (in Latin) in Calcidius *In Tim.* 220 (232.16-19 Waszink = *SVF* 2.879 = LS 53 G). This conception of the ψυχή as πνεῦμα in a certain state owes a debt to Heraclitus who is reported to have characterized the ψυχή as an 'exhalation' (ἀναθυμίασις). See Aristotle *De Anima* 405a25-26 (= Heraclitus test. 15 DK) and, in particular, Arius Didymus *Epit. Phys.* fr. 39 (*DG* 470.25-471.2 = *SVF* 1.141, 1.519 = Heraclitus fr. 12 DK) where Cleanthes reports that, on this, Zeno followed Heraclitus. For further comment see Kahn, *The Art and Thought of Heraclitus*, pp. 259-60.

[79] See Arius Didymus 2.7.5b4 (2.62.24-63.1 WH = *SVF* 3.278). As I have already noted 'improve' may be characterized as an increase in the tension or the fineness of the πνεῦμα.

[80] See e.g. Diogenes Laertius 7.158 (= *SVF* 2.766) where emotions are described as a variation in πνεῦμα. Sleep is also presented as a slackening of tension.

[81] Note however the dispute between early Stoics on the nature of the relationship between beliefs and emotions; see e.g. Galen *Plac. Hipp. Plat.* 5.1.4 (5.429 Kühn = 292.17-20 De Lacy = *SVF* 1.209, 3.461). I shall return to this in Chapter 7 § 2 (b).

those bad judgements that lead to emotions (πάθη). The process of transforming one's judgements and overcoming such emotions (πάθη) may also be described in purely physical terms as a transformation of the tension (τόνος) of one's soul (ψυχή).[82] Thus, the *way* in which a Stoic spiritual exercise will work is by an increase in the tension (τόνος) of the breath (πνεῦμα) that constitutes the material soul (ψυχή). As we have already noted in Chapter 3, this transformation of the disposition of the soul (διάθεσις τῆς ψυχῆς) will necessarily involve a transformation in one's way of life (βίος).[83]

5. The Form of Spiritual Exercises

Having considered *what* a spiritual exercise attempts to achieve and the *way* in which it might achieve this, there remains the question of the *form* that such exercises might take. In the case of an art or craft such as shoemaking, training will take the form of repeated practice. In order to master his chosen profession the apprentice shoemaker will have to try his hand at making shoes, knowing full well that despite his grasp of the principles behind the art it will be some time before he is able to produce a decent pair of shoes and claim to possess the knowledge that constitutes technical expertise. With the art of living, the precise *form* of the necessary exercises or training is less clear. Fortunately a number of examples can be found in the ancient literature. One that we have already encountered is Epicurus' meditation upon the thought that death is 'nothing to us'.[84] Yet, in general, these spiritual exercises do not appear to have been done *in abstracto*. Instead they were often associated with a written text.[85]

Philosophical texts come in a variety of forms but the most obvious are perhaps those of the treatise, such as those produced by Aristotle, Chrysippus, or Hierocles, and the commentary, such as those produced by Alexander of Aphrodisias or Simplicius. Yet alongside these works containing philosophical theory (λόγος) there are also texts comprised of philosophical exercises (ἀσκήσεις) which serve a very

---

[82] Note also Seneca *Epist.* 16.3 where philosophy is characterized as that which moulds and constructs the soul (*animum format et fabricat*).

[83] See Chapter 3 § 7.

[84] See Epicurus *Epist. ad Men.* (*apud* Diogenes Laertius 10) 124 (= LS 24 A), quoted and discussed above. Further examples drawn from a wide variety of ancient sources are discussed in Sorabji, *Emotion and Peace of Mind*, pp. 211-52. Particular examples of Stoic exercises will be discussed further in Chapters 6 and 7.

[85] See the discussions in Newman, '*Cotidie meditare*', pp. 1478-82, and Foucault, 'L'écriture de soi', in *Dits et écrits*, vol. 4, pp. 415-30; *Essential Works*, vol. 1, pp. 207-22. Nehamas, *The Art of Living*, p. 8, suggests that what he calls the art of living is primarily practised in writing. Yet by this he appears to mean that a philosophical life will be one devoted to writing and that the texts produced will be the lasting monument to that life. Yet this is surely the life of an author, and not necessarily that of a philosopher (although these may of course be combined). The significance attached to written texts for the art of living as conceived here is, as we shall see, only insofar as they function as philosophical exercises directed towards the digestion of λόγοι and the transformation of one's βίος.

different function. An example of this latter form of text would be the *Handbook* of Epictetus.[86] This text is devoted to the process of philosophical habituation and digestion, that is, to spiritual exercises conceived as an essential second stage of philosophical education. As such, its form and its function are quite different from those of the philosophical treatise. Yet, in the light of what we have seen, it can nevertheless be seen to be a thoroughly philosophical text.

We have, then, two distinct forms of philosophical text corresponding to the two components of philosophy conceived as a τέχνη; texts devoted to λόγοι and texts devoted to ἀσκήσεις. Texts concerned with spiritual exercises may themselves by subdivided into different types. In particular, two distinct literary forms of exercise may be noted. The first type, exemplified by the *Handbook* of Epictetus, is primarily an instructional text directed towards training the student of philosophy who has already completed his preliminary education in philosophical theory.[87] The second, exemplified by the *Meditations* of Marcus Aurelius, is a text produced by a student where the very act of writing itself can be seen to constitute the exercise.[88]

These two examples of two different types of text concerned with spiritual exercises – the *Handbook* and the *Meditations* – are perhaps the most important surviving texts relating to Stoic ἄσκησις.[89] The former is a guidebook for philosophical apprentices; the latter is a text produced by an apprentice. These texts are examples of the *form* of the exercises which complete the Stoic art of taking care of one's soul. First the theory is studied and understood, then texts such as these are studied or written in order to aid the digestion of those theories.

---

[86] For Hadot, Plato's dialogues would also fall into this latter category, being forms of written exercise designed to provoke the reader rather than merely to instruct. See *Philosophy as a Way of Life*, p. 91.

[87] Hankinson, *The Sceptics*, pp. 305-06, suggests that Sextus Empiricus' *Pyrr. Hyp.* should also be conceived in this way, namely as 'a handbook for other apprentice Sceptics'.

[88] At *Diss.* 2.1.29-33 Epictetus explicitly recommends this form of philosophical writing to his students, in contrast to merely rhetorical prose aimed at nothing more than securing the praise of one's readers. He also implies that Socrates wrote in this way, upsetting the assumption that Socrates wrote nothing. In a note on this passage Oldfather (LCL, vol. 1, p. 222) suggests that it is possible that Socrates engaged in much of this sort of private writing, none of which would have been intended for circulation (like Marcus' *Meditations*). For further discussion of this form of written spiritual exercise see Foucault, 'L'écriture de soi', in *Dits et écrits*, vol. 4, pp. 415-30; *Essential Works*, vol. 1, pp. 207-22.

[89] A third example would be Seneca's *Epist.*, described by Nussbaum as 'the greatest body of surviving Stoic therapeutic writing' (*The Therapy of Desire*, p. 337). For general discussion see Newman '*Cotidie meditare*', pp. 1483-95. For the way in which correspondence may function as a written spiritual exercise see Foucault, 'L'écriture de soi', in *Dits et écrits*, vol. 4, pp. 423-30; *Essential Works*, vol. 1, pp. 214-21. Newman also proposes Ps.-Seneca *De Remediis Fortuitorum* (alongside Marcus Aurelius) as one of the few literary examples of the *meditatio* in action (pp. 1477 n. 6, 1495-96). This text does not appear in the more recent editions of Seneca but it can be found in Haase (BT) and Palmer, *Seneca's De Remediis Fortuitorum and the Elizabethans*, pp. 28-65. Palmer argues that this is a genuine work of Seneca, although it only survives in a mutilated form, perhaps being an epitome of an originally longer work (p. 20).

In the remaining two chapters I shall consider these two Stoic texts as examples of the two types of text devoted to spiritual exercise. Chapter 6, devoted to the *Handbook* of Epictetus, will examine how this second stage of philosophical education was conceived and will consider the relationship between different types of spiritual exercise and the different parts of philosophical discourse. Chapter 7, devoted to the *Meditations* of Marcus Aurelius, will focus upon the way in which these same spiritual exercises are united in a text written by a philosophical apprentice, albeit an eminent one. Once we have considered the way in which these texts function we should have a clearer idea of both the form and the function of spiritual exercises and the role that they play in philosophy conceived as the art of living.

Chapter 6

Exercises in the *Handbook* of Epictetus

In the last chapter I began to develop the idea of a philosophical exercise that, alongside philosophical discourse or theory, would form an essential component of philosophy conceived as a τέχνη. In this chapter I shall continue to develop this concept of a philosophical ἄσκησις or spiritual exercise by focusing upon a text devoted to such exercises, the *Handbook* of Epictetus.[1] The aim of this chapter is twofold. The first is to consider in more detail the relationship between ἄσκησις and λόγος, the two components of philosophy conceived as a τέχνη. The second is to present the *Handbook* as an example of one of the two types of philosophical text associated with spiritual exercises that I outlined at the end of the last chapter.[2] In order to complete these tasks it will be necessary to explore the internal structure of the *Handbook* and to see precisely how it functions as a philosophical text devoted to ἄσκησις. But first, some introductory remarks.

1. Introduction to the *Handbook*

The *Handbook* of Epictetus – described by Justus Lipsius as the soul of Stoic philosophy – is in many ways the archetypal example of a form of writing appropriate

---

[1] For comment on the text of both the *Enchiridion* and *Dissertationes* of Epictetus see Additional Note 3. For the *Enchiridion* I have relied upon the texts in Oldfather (LCL) and Boter, and have consulted the translations by Oldfather, Boter, and White. The most important studies of Epictetus remain the works of Adolf Bonhöffer and, in particular, *Epictet und die Stoa* and *Die Ethik des Stoikers Epictet*, the second of which has recently been translated into English as *The Ethics of the Stoic Epictetus*. Also worthy of note are Colardeau, *Étude sur Épictète*; Xenakis, *Epictetus: Philosopher-Therapist*; Hijmans, *Ἄσκησις: Notes on Epictetus' Educational System*; More, *Hellenistic Philosophies*, pp. 94-171; Hadot, *The Inner Citadel*, pp. 73-100; Dobbin, *Epictetus, Discourses Book 1* (a translation with commentary); Gourinat, *Premières leçons sur le Manuel d'Épictète*; Long, *Epictetus*; with further references in Hershbell, 'The Stoicism of Epictetus: Twentieth Century Perspectives'. Useful notes on the text can be found in Upton (vol. 2, pp. 271-87) and in Schweighäuser (*Epicteteae Philosophiae Monumenta*, vol. 3, pp. 139-70, but *not* in his 1798 edition of the *Enchiridion* which contains primarily textual notes). A substantial introduction can be found in Hadot, *Arrien, Manuel d'Épictète*, pp. 11-160.

[2] Chapter 7 will attempt to do the same for the other type of philosophical text associated with spiritual exercises by examining the *Meditations* of Marcus Aurelius.

to philosophy conceived as an art of living.[3] According to the sixth-century commentary by the Neoplatonist Simplicius,[4] the *Handbook* was compiled by Arrian from his accounts of Epictetus' lectures now known as the *Discourses*.[5] It takes the form of a collection of passages from the *Discourses* short enough to be easily reproduced, carried around, or even memorized.[6] Its title, Ἐγχειρίδιον, suggests something that is, in the words of Musonius, always ready at hand (πρόχειρος),[7] a point noted by Simplicius in his commentary:

> It is called *Encheiridion* (Ἐγχειρίδιον) because all persons who are desirous to live as they ought, should be perfect in this book, and have it always ready at hand (πρόχειρον); a book of as constant and necessary use as the sword (which commonly went by this name, and from whence the metaphor seems to be taken) is to a soldier.[8]

As Simplicius indicates, the word ἐγχειρίδιον can also mean sword. It can also refer to a variety of handheld tools, such as those used for cutting stone.[9] What these different meanings share in common is indicated by the root 'hand' (χείρ); they are all things that one keeps 'ready to hand' (πρόχειρος). Thus Arrian's choice of ἐγχειρίδιον as a title suggests a text conceived as a guidebook or manual designed to be used in some form of practical activity.[10]

---

[3] See Lipsius *Manuductio* 1.19 (1604 edn, p. 63): *Enchiridion sane egregium, & Stoicae moralis philosophie velut anima.*

[4] For discussion of Simplicius' commentary, including when and where it was written (recently a subject of debate), see Ilsetraut Hadot's *Le problème du néoplatonisme alexandrin*, 'The Life and Work of Simplicius in Greek and Arabic Sources', and her Introduction in *Simplicius, Commentaire sur le Manuel d'Épictète*.

[5] See Simplicius *In Ench*. Praef. 4-7 Hadot, with further discussion of Arrian and Epictetus in Stadter, *Arrian of Nicomedia*, pp. 19-31. The *Dissertationes* probably existed in eight books originally so the *Enchiridion* in theory summarizes the four books now lost as well as the four still extant (see Additional Note 3 for further information). Schenkl and Boter both supply references to the parallels between the *Enchiridion* and passages in the *Dissertationes*. As Barnes notes (*Logic and the Imperial Stoa*, p. 24), nothing in the *Enchiridion* suggests that the lost books of the *Dissertationes* contained anything substantially different from the content of the surviving books, which are themselves to a certain degree repetitive.

[6] Boter notes that there are relatively few direct excerpts from the *Dissertationes* in the *Enchiridion* (see p. xiii). However, one can be found in § 29 which is an almost word for word reproduction of *Diss*. 3.15.1-13 (first noted by Upton, vol. 2, p. 277) and thus bracketed as an interpolation by Boter (see his discussion, p. 127).

[7] See Musonius Rufus fr. 6 (25.14-26.5 Hense = 54.18-25 Lutz), already quoted above in Chapter 5 § 2 (a).

[8] Simplicius *In Ench*. Praef. 18-20 Hadot (trans. Stanhope modified).

[9] See the examples listed in LSJ, p. 475.

[10] The title Ἐγχειρίδιον is usually translated into English as *Manual* or *Handbook*. In French it is usually translated as *Manuel*, but to translate it as *Pensées* (e.g. Brun, ed., *Les Stoïciens*, p. 114) would obscure the primarily practical connotations associated with the title. I prefer *Handbook* to *Manual* insofar as it reflects the presence of χείρ in ἐγχειρίδιον. Gourinat, *Premières leçons sur le Manuel d'Épictète*, p. 40, has suggested that as this would still have

Each chapter of the *Handbook* contains what might broadly be characterized as practical advice rather than substantial philosophical argument. In his commentary, Simplicius is explicit that what we have here is primarily a book of spiritual exercises:

> For as the body (σῶμα) gathers strength by exercise (γυμνάζεταί), and frequently repeating such motions as are natural to it; so the soul (ψυχή) too, by exerting its powers, and the practice of such things as are agreeable to nature, confirms itself in habits, and strengthens its own natural constitution.[11]

This account of the function of the *Handbook* as a text clearly shares much in common with Socrates' conception of an art (τέχνη) concerned with taking care of the soul (ψυχή). Indeed, Simplicius explicitly proposes that Epictetus was inspired by the example of Socrates as he is presented in *Alcibiades I*.[12] Simplicius' reason for making this connection may have been part of a deliberate Neoplatonic educational strategy rather than a desire to shed light upon Epictetus,[13] but nevertheless the resonance is clear: the *Handbook* is a book designed to be used to exercise (γυμνάζειν, ἀσκεῖν) the soul (ψυχή) analogous to the way in which one might exercise the body.[14]

---

been the era of the papyrus roll as opposed to the codex (on which see Kenyon, *Books and Readers in Ancient Greece and Rome*, p. 98), in certain respects a rolled up copy of the *Enchiridion* would have literally resembled a handheld tool or sword.

[11] Simplicius *In Ench.* Praef. 87-90 Hadot (trans. Stanhope). At Praef. 51-52 Simplicius characterizes the contents of the *Enchiridion* as all expressions of one τέχνη, namely that of amending man's life (τὴν διορθωτικὴν τῆς ἀνθρωπίνης ζωῆς).

[12] See Simplicius *In Ench.* Praef. 82-87 Hadot, a claim repeated in the Renaissance by Politian (*Angeli Politiani pro Epicteto Stoico ad Bartholomeu Scala Epistola*, in his *Opera Omnia*; translated in Kraye, *Cambridge Translations*, pp. 192-99). For Epictetus' use of *Alcibiades I* in the *Dissertationes* see Jagu, *Épictète et Platon*, pp. 137-38, 161.

[13] In the Neoplatonic syllabus, philosophical education began with *Alcibiades I*, a text described by Proclus in his commentary on it as 'the beginning (ἀρχή) of all philosophy' (see Proclus *In Alc. I* 11.3 Westerink). Later in the same text (11.11-15), Proclus credits the priority given to *Alcibiades I* to Iamblichus, although it actually dates back to the Middle Platonist Albinus (see Mansfeld, *Prolegomena*, pp. 84-97; Dillon, *The Middle Platonists*, pp. 304-06). Note also the *Proleg. Phil. Plat.* in which it is said that of the Platonic dialogues 'the first to be explained is the *Alcibiades*, because it teaches us to know ourselves, and the right course is to know oneself before knowing external things, for we can scarcely understand those other things so long as we are ignorant of ourselves' (26.18-20 Westerink). By connecting the *Enchiridion* with *Alcibiades I*, then, Simplicius may be seen to be proposing *Alcibiades I* as the next philosophical text to read after the *Enchiridion*, in effect drawing readers of Epictetus into a Neoplatonic reading list and thus away from Stoicism.

[14] As such, the *Enchiridion* resonates not just with Socrates' position (discussed in Chapter 2) but also with the discussion in Cicero's *Tusc. Disp.* (discussed in Chapter 3). This latter resonance was noted by the Renaissance Humanist Niccolo Perotti in § 7 of the 'Praefatio' to his Latin translation of the *Enchiridion* (*c.* 1450), both edited and published for the first time in Oliver, *Niccolo Perotti's Version of The Enchiridion of Epictetus* (see pp. 65-69).

But to whom was the *Handbook* directed? Broadly speaking there are two possible groups of philosophical readers and, as we shall see, this question will bear upon that concerning the relationship between λόγος and ἄσκησις.

Simplicius suggests that the *Handbook* should be read by the philosophical beginner in need of preliminary moral instruction before commencing the study of philosophy proper, that is, the study of Platonic philosophy.[15] One might suggest that, beyond the uses to which it may have been put in the Neoplatonic educational syllabus, the *Handbook* should indeed be understood as a text devoted to preliminary moral training (ἄσκησις) designed to prepare a beginner for the study of philosophical theory (λόγος). This implies that a philosophical beginner will use this text of spiritual exercises on its own, without recourse to philosophical theory, and that he or she will do so successfully (for otherwise there would be no point). It implies, then, that these written philosophical exercises will, on their own, be sufficient to overcome the emotions (πάθη) and transform the soul (ψυχή).

Alternatively, one might conceive the *Handbook* as a text for more advanced philosophical students. There are, I propose, two reasons why this may be a better approach.

Firstly, there is the question concerning why Arrian would have produced this epitome of the *Discourses*. Throughout the *Discourses* Epictetus advises his students to keep their philosophical principles 'ready to hand' (πρόχειρος).[16] As a student of Epictetus himself, Arrian may have composed the *Handbook* not so much as an introduction to Epictetus for beginners but rather as a *aide mémoire* for himself,[17] a small digestible summary of Epictetus' philosophy that he could carry with him and always keep 'ready to hand' (πρόχειρος).[18] This would certainly explain the choice of title.

Secondly, there is Epictetus' account of philosophical education which, as we have already seen, is comprised of, first, a thorough study of philosophical principles and, second, a series of exercises designed to digest those principles and transform

---

[15] See Simplicius *In Ench.* Praef. 61-81 Hadot. For discussion see I. Hadot, *Le problème du néoplatonisme alexandrin*, pp. 160-64; 'The Spiritual Guide', p. 451; also Mansfeld, *Prolegomena*, p. 70. Hadot suggests that the commentary itself should also be seen as an example of a written series of spiritual exercises (see *Le problème du néoplatonisme alexandrin*, pp. 164-65).

[16] See e.g. *Diss.* 1.1.21, 1.27.6, 2.1.29, 2.9.18, 3.10.1, 3.10.18, 3.11.5, 3.17.6, 3.18.1.

[17] Simplicius, *In Ench.* Praef. 7-9 Hadot, reports that Arrian addressed the book to his friend Messalinus, already an admirer of Epictetus. Either way, I suggest that it would have been conceived for someone already familiar with Epictetus' philosophy.

[18] A similar procedure can be seen in the letters of Epicurus. See e.g. *Epist. ad Pyth.* (*apud* Diogenes Laertius 10) 84 and *Epist. ad Herod.* (*apud* Diogenes Laertius 10) 35 where he presents these letters as summaries of his larger philosophical works specifically designed as aids to memory for more advanced students. For a table outlining the correspondences between these letters and Epicurus' *On Nature* see Sedley, *Lucretius and the Transformation of Greek Wisdom*, p. 133.

one's behaviour.[19] In short, Epictetus proposes first the study of λόγοι and then, only once these have been mastered, a series of ἀσκήσεις designed to digest those λόγοι. In the light of this, we might conceive the *Handbook* as a text for relatively advanced students, for those who have already mastered philosophical doctrines in the classroom and are now ready to attempt to put those doctrines into practice via a series of spiritual exercises. For students such as these, the *Handbook* would serve as a series of exercises to study and a distilled summary and reminder of all that they had learned in the classroom. The *Handbook* would thus function as a text for the second stage of philosophical education, just as the theoretical treatise would have functioned as a text for the first stage.[20] As such, it would not present any philosophical content with which the student would not already be familiar, but rather would repeat familiar material in a form specifically directed towards its digestion (πέψις).

Given that the *Handbook* is a collection of spiritual exercises, if it were used by a beginner who had not yet studied philosophical theory, it would in effect be a series of ἀσκήσεις without λόγοι. Yet as we have already seen, for Epictetus ἀσκήσεις must come *after* the study of λόγοι, for their function is the digestion of those λόγοι.[21] Arrian would surely have been well aware of this point and thus it seems more likely that he conceived the *Handbook* as a text for more advanced philosophical students. As for Simplicius' claim that it is a text for beginners, that has more to do with how he thought the text could be appropriated to function within the Neoplatonic educational syllabus rather than how it might function within the context of Epictetus' own account of philosophical education.

2. Three Types of Spiritual Exercise

Having considered the way in which the *Handbook* may be used as a text devoted to spiritual exercises, we now need to consider its contents. At first glance the 53 chapters or sections of the text do not appear to be in any particular order.[22] However, it has been argued that it is possible to discern some form of structure within the

---

[19] See *Diss.* 1.26.3, 1.17.4-12, with the discussion in Chapter 5 § 1 above.

[20] I have already noted in Chapter 1 that Epictetus may well have engaged in close readings of treatises such those by Chrysippus as part of his classroom teaching. See e.g. *Diss.* 2.21.11, with More, *Hellenistic Philosophies*, p. 98; Long, 'Epictetus, Marcus Aurelius', p. 993.

[21] See Chapter 5 § 1. As we have seen in Chapter 3 § 5, this point had already been made by Seneca in *Epist.* 94.25-26. For further general discussion of the theme of ἄσκησις in Epictetus see Hijmans, *Ἄσκησις*, pp. 64-77; Colardeau, *Étude sur Épictète*, pp. 115-48; Xenakis, *Epictetus: Philosopher-Therapist*, pp. 70-84.

[22] The division into 53 sections used by Schenkl, Oldfather, and Boter, derives from Schweighäuser's 1798 edition. This was itself built upon Upton's division of the text into 52 sections in his 1739 edition. Before Upton, the text was often divided into 79 sections, most notably by Wolf (1560, repr. 1595, 1655, 1670). This older division of the text corresponds to its division in many editions of Simplicius' commentary (e.g. Heinsius 1640, Stanhope's translation of 1694), although the latest edition by I. Hadot departs from this.

text,[23] a structure that is implicitly introduced in the opening section. Although the presence of this structure has been contested, it nevertheless forms a useful point from which to begin. By examining this structure we shall be able to see precisely how the *Handbook* focuses upon a number of different types of spiritual exercise (ἄσκησις), and how each of these types of exercise relates to philosophical discourse or theory (λόγος).

(a) Section 1: Three τόποι

The key to the structure of the *Handbook* as a whole can be found in the very first section where the three central themes are announced:

> Of things, some are up to us (ἐφ᾽ ἡμῖν), and some are not up to us (οὐκ ἐφ᾽ ἡμῖν). Up to us are [1] opinion (ὑπόληψις), [2] impulse (ὁρμή), [3] desire [and] aversion (ὄρεξις, ἔκκλισις), and, in a word, all our actions (ἔργα). Not up to us are our body (σῶμα), possessions (κτῆσις), reputations (δόξαι), offices (ἀρχαί), and, in a word, all that are not our actions.[24]

Following Socrates' exhortation in the *Apology* for his fellow citizens to take care of their souls rather than their possessions, the *Handbook* opens with this distinction between what is and what is not 'up to us' (ἐφ᾽ ἡμῖν) or in our control,[25] and proposes that the only things truly within one's control are four activities of the soul, namely opinion (ὑπόληψις), impulse (ὁρμή), desire (ὄρεξις), and aversion (ἔκκλισις). The last two of these may be taken together insofar as they express opposing forms of the same activity, giving three categories of things within one's control: opinion (ὑπόληψις), impulse (ὁρμή), desire and aversion (ὄρεξις καὶ ἔκκλισις).[26] These

---

[23] See e.g. (in chronological order) Pohlenz, *Die Stoa*, vol. 2, p. 162; P. Hadot 'Une clé des *Pensées* de Marc Aurèle', pp. 71-72; Stadter, *Arrian of Nicomedia*, p. 29; I. Hadot, *Simplicius, Commentaire*, pp. 149-51; Gourinat, *Premières leçons sur le Manuel d'Épictète*, pp. 45-53; P. Hadot, *Arrien, Manuel d'Épictète*, pp. 36-140. For a similar attempt to discern an implicit structure in Book 1 of the *Dissertationes*, see De Lacy, 'The Logical Structure of the Ethics of Epictetus'.

[24] *Ench.* 1.1.

[25] This distinction between what is and is not 'up to us' (ἐφ᾽ ἡμῖν) may be seen to draw upon the earlier Stoic theory of internal and external causes, illustrated in Chrysippus' cylinder analogy. See Chapter 3 § 7 above, with discussion in Bobzien, *Determinism and Freedom in Stoic Philosophy*, pp. 330-38.

[26] These are the powers of an individual's προαίρεσις, an Aristotelian term which in Epictetus refers to an individual's faculty of choice. For further discussion see Dobbin, 'Προαίρεσις in Epictetus'; Voelke, *L'idée de volonté dans le stoïcisme*, pp. 142-60; Inwood, *Ethics and Human Action in Early Stoicism*, pp. 240-42; Rist, *Stoic Philosophy*, pp. 228-29.

three areas of study (τόποι) announced in the first section of the text may be seen to introduce the three central themes of the rest of the *Handbook*.[27]

The precise nature of these three areas of study (τόποι) is discussed at greater length in the *Discourses*, a discussion which this opening section would no doubt recall to the mind of the advanced student already familiar with Epictetus' philosophy. The following passage gives probably the clearest account of this threefold distinction:

> There are three areas of study (τόποι), in which a person who is going to be noble (καλόν) and good (ἀγαθόν) must be trained (ἀσκηθῆναι):
> [1.] That concerning desires and aversions (ὀρέξεις καὶ ἐκκλίσεις), so that he may neither fail to get what he desires nor fall into what he would avoid.
> [2.] That concerning the impulse to act (ὁρμάς) and not to act (ἀφορμάς), and, generally, appropriate behaviour (καθῆκον); so that he may act in an orderly manner and after due consideration, and not carelessly.
> [3.] The third is concerned with freedom from deception (ἀνεξαπατησίαν) and hasty judgement (ἀνεικαιότητα), and, generally, whatever is connected with assents (συγκαταθέσεις).[28]

The three areas (τόποι) of training (ἄσκησις) outlined here are the same three areas introduced in the opening section of the *Handbook* but presented in reverse order. As we shall see, each of these types of ἄσκησις may be seen to correspond to one of the three parts of Stoic philosophical discourse (τὸν κατὰ φιλοσοφίαν λόγον) outlined by Diogenes Laertius; the physical (φυσικόν), the ethical (ἠθικόν), and the logical (λογικόν).[29] Following their order in this passage from the *Discourses*, the first type of exercise concerning desires and aversions (ὀρέξεις καὶ ἐκκλίσεις) may be seen to correspond to 'physics', the second type concerning impulse (ὁρμή) may be seen to correspond to 'ethics', and the third type concerning opinion (ὑπόληψις) and assent (συγκατάθεσις) may be seen to correspond to 'logic'.[30] Although this correlation has been questioned,[31] as we shall see, a case can be made to connect the three parts of

---

[27] For further discussion of this threefold distinction see e.g. Bonhöffer, *Die Ethik des Stoikers Epictet*, pp. 16-126 (= *The Ethics of the Stoic Epictetus*, pp. 30-165); More, *Hellenistic Philosophies*, pp. 107-53; Hadot, *The Inner Citadel*, pp. 82-98.

[28] *Diss.* 3.2.1-2. This division into three types of ἄσκησις can be found throughout the *Dissertationes*; see e.g. 1.4.11, 2.8.29, 2.17.15-18 & 31-33, 3.12.1-17, 4.4.16, 4.10.1-7 & 13.

[29] See Diogenes Laertius 7.39 (= *SVF* 2.37), with the discussion in Chapter 3 § 6 above.

[30] For this correlation between the three τόποι and the three parts of philosophical discourse see Bonhöffer, *Epictet und die Stoa*, pp. 22-28; *Die Ethik des Stoikers Epictet*, pp. 46-49 & 58-60 (= *The Ethics of the Stoic Epictetus*, pp. 78-85); More, *Hellenistic Philosophies*, pp. 107-08; Pohlenz, *Die Stoa*, vol. 1, pp. 328-29; Hadot, 'Philosophie, Discours Philosophique, et Divisions de la Philosophie chez les Stoïciens', p. 218; *The Inner Citadel*, pp. 89-98.

[31] Doubts have been expressed by Dobbin, *Epictetus, Discourses Book 1*, and Barnes, *Logic and the Imperial Stoa*. Dobbin suggests that 'it is vain to look for a complete correlation' (p. 94) and that they 'do not completely correspond' (p. 164). However, his discussion appears, to me at least, to be a little unclear. He claims that the three τόποι do not correspond

philosophical discourse with these three areas (τόποι) of training or exercise
(ἄσκησις). What we have with the *Handbook*, then, is a text devoted to three types of
spiritual exercise, each of which is concerned with the digestion and assimilation of
one of the three types of philosophical discourse.

After the opening section of the *Handbook* which introduces the three τόποι, the
remainder of the text can be seen to divide loosely into groups of chapters concerned
with the three types of exercise.[32] Whether this was an intentional device planned by
Arrian is not important here. Nor are arguments concerning precisely where one
divides the text in order to form these different groups. What is important is that by
approaching the text with such an internal structure in mind one can gain a clearer
understanding of the three types of exercise proposed by Epictetus. Assuming a
correlation between these three types of exercise (ἄσκησις) and the three types of
philosophical discourse (λόγος) hopefully will also be instructive; what follows will
attempt to flesh out that correlation.

(b) Sections 2-29: Physical Exercises

The first of the three types of exercise dealt with in the *Handbook* is concerned with
exercises for one's desires and aversions (ὀρέξεις καὶ ἐκκλίσεις),[33] and this type of
exercise may be seen to correspond to 'physics'.[34] Spiritual exercises of this type are

---

completely to the three parts of philosophical discourse and discusses the case of logic,
apparently to support this claim. Despite this he then admits that the third τόπος *does* represent
the study of logic (p. 164). He suggests that any inconsistency is due to Epictetus' use of two
distinct conceptions of logic, one expansive (including epistemology), the other restrictive
(limited to dialectic). Yet it is far from clear that Epictetus does use two different conceptions
of logic. Rather, he simply follows the standard Stoic conception of logic which is significantly
broader than merely dialectic, but sometimes refers to dialectic as logic, of which it is
obviously a part, without necessarily implying that it is the *only* part. Barnes, arguing against
Bonhöffer and Hadot, claims that 'the three τόποι here are not the three traditional parts of
philosophy' (p. 34). Yet Hadot's claim is not that these are the *same* but rather that they
correspond to one another (see e.g. 'Une clé des *Pensées* de Marc Aurèle', p. 69). I suggest that
one think not in terms of a correspondence between three areas of study and three parts of
philosophy, but rather a correspondence between three types of philosophical *exercise* and three
types of philosophical *discourse*.
[32] In what follows I broadly follow the division of the *Enchiridion* outlined by Gourinat,
Premières leçons sur le Manuel d'Épictète, pp. 45-48. This differs slightly from the earlier
accounts such as those in Pohlenz, *Die Stoa*, vol. 2, p. 162; P. Hadot, *The Inner Citadel*,
pp. 326-27; I. Hadot, *Simplicius, Commentaire*, pp. 149-51 (since Gourinat note also P. Hadot,
Arrien, Manuel d'Épictète, pp. 36-142). I do not want to suggest that Gourinat's analysis is
definitive. Rather I simply want to draw attention to the presence of a structure within the
Enchiridion based around the three types of exercise which correspond to the three parts of
philosophical discourse, a point agreed upon by all those noted above.
[33] For discussion of these terms and the extent to which Epictetus' use of them differs from the
early Stoa see Inwood, *Ethics and Human Action in Early Stoicism*, pp. 115-26.
[34] See e.g. Bonhöffer, *Die Ethik des Stoikers Epictet*, pp. 18-49 (= *The Ethics of the Stoic
Epictetus*, pp. 32-81) who characterizes this τόπος as 'desire according to nature'.

directed towards transforming one's desires and aversions so that one only wills that which is in accordance with nature (κατὰ φύσιν).[35] Many of the passages in this first section of the *Handbook* focus upon the order of nature and what is appropriate to desire in light of an understanding of that order. For example:

> Do not seek events to happen as you want (θέλεις), but want (θέλε) events as they happen, and your life will flow well (εὐροήσεις).[36]

The aim of this type of exercise is to train one's desires and aversions, to accustom oneself to desire whatever happens, to bring one's will into harmony with the will of the cosmos conceived as a living being.[37] In Stoic physics, the individual is understood as but one component within a cosmos conceived as a complex network of interconnected causes.[38] This network of causes was called 'fate' (εἱμαρμένη).[39] Within this network of causes, early Stoics such as Chrysippus distinguished between two types of fated things, 'simple' (*simplicia*) and 'conjoined' (*copulata*).[40] For Chrysippus, simple-fated things are necessary and the product of the essence of a thing, such as the fact that all mortal beings will die. Conjoined-fated things involve both internal and external causes and it is by way of the role played by internal causes in conjoined-fated things that the Stoics introduce the notion of freedom into their deterministic system.[41] For example, 'Socrates will die' is a simple-fated thing by

---

[35] In this context I use φύσις to refer to the order of universal nature, the cosmos. Epictetus also uses φύσις to refer to the nature of a particular species and to the nature of an individual. See Hijmans, 'A Note on φύσις in Epictetus', p. 282.

[36] *Ench.* 8: μὴ ζήτει τὰ γινόμενα γίνεσθαι ὡς θέλεις, ἀλλὰ θέλε τὰ γινόμενα ὡς γίνεται, καὶ εὐροήσεις. Note the etymological connection between γίνεσθαι (i.e. γίγνεσθαι) and τὰ γινόμενα. In order to capture this one might translate as 'do not seek occurrences to occur as you want, but want occurrences as they occur, and your life will flow well'. Regarding the use of εὐροήσεις, note Zeno's εὐδαιμονία δ' ἐστὶν εὔροια βίου (Arius Didymus 2.7.6e = 2.77.21 WH = *SVF* 1.184). For parallels to this passage see e.g. *Diss.* 1.12.15, 2.14.7, 2.17.17-18, 4.1.89-90, 4.7.20.

[37] For this conception of the cosmos see e.g. the extended account in Cicero *Nat. Deo.* 2.16-44, esp. 2.22 (= *SVF* 1.112-114), with further references in *SVF* 3.633-645.

[38] For Stoic physics and cosmology see Sambursky, *Physics of the Stoics*; Hahm, *The Origins of Stoic Cosmology*; Sedley in *CHHP*, pp. 382-411; Furley in *CHHP*, pp. 432-51.

[39] See Diogenes Laertius 7.149 (= *SVF* 2.915), Aetius *Plac.* 1.28.4 (*DG* 324a1-3 = *SVF* 2.917 = LS 55 J), Aulus Gellius 7.2.3 (= *SVF* 2.1000 = LS 55 K), Cicero *Div.* 1.125 (= *SVF* 2.921 = LS 55 L). For discussion see Gould, 'The Stoic Conception of Fate'; Long, 'Stoic Determinism and Alexander of Aphrodisias *De Fato* (i-xiv)'; Bobzien, *Determinism and Freedom in Stoic Philosophy*, pp. 16-58.

[40] See Cicero *Fat.* 30 (= *SVF* 2.956), with further discussion in Bobzien, *Determinism and Freedom in Stoic Philosophy*, pp. 199-233.

[41] This formed part of the Stoic response to the 'lazy argument' (ἀργὸς λόγος), namely the claim that within a deterministic account of the cosmos it would become pointless for an individual to act towards any specific goal insofar as the outcome must already be predetermined; see Cicero *Fat.* 28-29, Origen *Cont. Cels.* 2.20 (*PG* 11.837-40 = *SVF* 2.957). For Chrysippus' distinction between internal and external causes see e.g. Cicero *Fat.* 41-42

virtue of the fact that Socrates is a mortal being, but 'Socrates will die today' is not simply-fated insofar as various other factors will contribute to the outcome, such as whether one chooses to call out a doctor or not, if he is ill.[42] Chrysippus uses this distinction between simple-fated and conjoined-fated things to argue that even within a determinist conception of the cosmos an individual's decision to act can still contribute to the outcome of events. Epictetus, however, is keen to stress the role of external causes in conjoined-fated things and to remind his students that the outcome of these things is far from being within one's control, even though they involve an element that is 'up to us' (ἐφ' ἡμῖν). An individual's desire and effort is but one causal factor among many in a conjoined-fated thing and consequently one can in no way control the final outcome. Thus Epictetus warns his students not to make their happiness or well-being (εὐδαιμονία) dependent upon the outcome of such things.

The alternative proposed by Epictetus is to bring one's own desires into harmony with the desires of the cosmos, to overcome the boundary between the individual and the cosmos so that one's own desire is in harmony with cosmic fate.[43] According to Stoic physics, any individual entity will act according to its own nature unless hindered by some external cause. From the perspective of the individual there are a whole series of external causes which hinder one's desires and actions. These external causes are other individual entities acting in accordance with their own internal natures. But cosmic nature includes everything that exists and thus has nothing external to it. In his account of Stoic cosmology Cicero writes:

> the various limited modes of being may encounter many external obstacles to hinder their perfect realization, but there can be nothing that can frustrate nature as a whole, since she embraces and contains within herself all modes of being.[44]

Only the cosmos as a whole has complete freedom. It always acts according to its own nature and can never be hindered insofar as there are no external causes to interrupt its actions. From a cosmic perspective, then, the distinction between internal

---

(= *SVF* 2.974), Aulus Gellius 7.2.11 (= *SVF* 2.1000), Plutarch *Stoic. Rep.* 1055f-1057c (part in *SVF* 2.994), with further discussion in Chapter 3 § 7 above.

[42] This example derives from Cicero *Fat.* 30 (= *SVF* 2.956), modified in the light of Diogenianus *apud* Eusebius 6.8.35 (267a-b). Another example of a conjoined-fated thing is 'Laius will have a son Oedipus' which will of course depend upon 'Laius will have intercourse with a woman' (see Origen *Cont. Cels.* 2.20 (*PG* 11.837-40) = *SVF* 2.957). In this example the two events are not only conjoined (*copulata*) but also co-fated (*confatalis*), one being a necessary condition of the other. See also Diogenianus *apud* Eusebius 6.8.25-29 (265d-266b) = *SVF* 2.998).

[43] Sorabji expresses this point perfectly: 'it is not a matter of gritting your teeth. It is about seeing things differently, so that you do not need to grit your teeth' (*Emotion and Peace of Mind*, p. 1).

[44] Cicero *Nat. Deo.* 2.35 (not in *SVF* but see 1.529; trans. Rackham): *Etenim ceteris naturis multa externa quo minus perficiantur possunt obsistere, universam autem naturam nulla res potest impedire, propterea quod omnis naturas ipsa cohibit et continet.* See also Plutarch *Stoic. Rep.* 1050c-d (= *SVF* 2.937), Marcus Aurelius 8.7, 10.33.

and external causes falls away. The distinction between such causes is thus always only *relative* to the perspective of a particular individual.[45] Epictetus appears to have overcome this always only relative distinction between internal and external causes, and to experience himself in agreement with the network of causes that constitutes fate. By 'willing' whatever happens, Epictetus identifies his own will with the will of the cosmos. In effect, he expands his conception of his own will to include and encompass all causes, both internal and external to himself.[46] What Epictetus proposes, then, is a transformation of one's way of life based upon a detailed understanding of the nature of causes.

We are now in a position to understand how Epictetus' exercises concerning desire and aversion (ὄρεξις καὶ ἔκκλισις) can be seen to relate to Stoic physical theory. Such theory postulates that the cosmos as a whole is a unified system of causes and that the individual is but one part of that system. Epictetus' exercises concerning desire and aversion attempt to assimilate and digest that theory so that it will transform one's behaviour. What we might call the practical implication of Stoic physical theory is the thought that, as a part of the system of nature, one should not conceive oneself as an isolated entity surrounded by external causes, but rather as a single element within a larger unified physical system. Epictetus' 'physical exercises' are directed towards the transformation of one's desires in the light of this. They attempt to put into practice Stoic physics. This is how Stoic physical theory relates to Epictetus' first τόπος.

(c) Sections 30-41: Ethical Exercises

The second of the three types of exercise in the *Handbook* is concerned with one's impulse (ὁρμή).[47] Insofar as these impulses are impulses towards action, this type of exercise may be seen to correspond to 'ethics'.[48] Spiritual exercises of this type are directed towards transforming one's impulses so that one only engages in 'appropriate

---

[45] See Botros, 'Freedom, Causality, Fatalism, and Early Stoic Philosophy', p. 287.

[46] Compare this with the way in which the distinction between what is and is not 'up to us' (ἐφ' ἡμῖν) is often cited as an example of the way in which Epictetus limits his conception of the individual and isolates it from both its own body and the rest of the external world (see e.g. Kahn, 'Discovering the Will', p. 253). Although there is a sense in which such a characterization is correct, the physical exercise in *Ench.* 8 appears to suggest this other tendency in which the individual expands his conception of himself to include all the actions of the cosmos.

[47] The introduction of the second τόπος at *Ench.* 30 is one point upon which commentators generally agree as this section opens with the words τὰ καθήκνοτα.

[48] See Bonhöffer, *Die Ethik des Stoikers Epictet*, pp. 58-109 (= *The Ethics of the Stoic Epictetus*, pp. 82-158), who characterizes this τόπος as 'action according to nature'. The connection is made explicit in Diogenes Laertius 7.84 (= *SVF* 3.1) where ὁρμή is presented as part of ethics.

actions' (καθήκοντα), namely actions that are appropriate to one's own nature, to one's place in society, or the particular situation in which one may find oneself.[49]

According to Stoic ethical theory, of the impulses towards action, the primary impulse (πρώτη ὁρμή) is towards self-preservation.[50] This leads one to select things that are in accordance with one's own nature (κατὰ φύσιν), such as food or anything else conducive to one's health. Any action that is in accordance with one's nature (κατὰ φύσιν) may be said to be an 'appropriate action' (καθῆκον).[51] Many actions inspired by this primary impulse are common to animals, infants, and adults. However, for a rational adult the only properly appropriate actions will be those which are the product of rational impulses, namely an impulse with a rational justification.[52] Thus they will be actions that are appropriate to one's nature not merely as a biological entity but also as a rational being.[53] Some of these appropriate actions will be unconditional; others will vary according to circumstance.[54]

In the *Handbook*, Epictetus deals with three different types of appropriate action (καθῆκον) – social, religious, and personal – examples of which would include what is appropriate behaviour towards one's brother, towards the gods, and towards oneself.[55] In particular, Epictetus discusses these in relation to what would constitute appropriate behaviour for a philosopher. For example:

---

[49] The term 'appropriate' (καθῆκον) is glossed by Zeno in Diogenes Laertius 7.108 (= *SVF* 1.230, 3.493 = LS 59 C) and translated into Latin by Cicero as *officium* in *Fin.* 3.20 (= *SVF* 3.188 = LS 59 D). It is defined as an action that is in accordance with one's nature (κατὰ φύσιν) and has been understood as 'function', 'proper function', 'task', or 'duty'. It is applied to infants, animals, even plants (see Diogenes Laertius 7.107), so it clearly cannot be understood as 'duty' in any narrow moral sense. For further discussion see Bonhöffer, *Die Ethik des Stoikers Epictet*, pp. 193-233 (= *The Ethics of the Stoic Epictetus*, pp. 244-89); Rist, *Stoic Philosophy*, pp. 97-111; Tsekourakis, *Studies in the Terminology of Early Stoic Ethics*, pp. 1-60; Inwood, *Ethics and Human Action in Early Stoicism*, pp. 200-01. That appropriate actions (καθήκοντα) fall under the heading of 'ethics' along with impulse (ὁρμή) is made explicit in Diogenes Laertius 7.84 (= *SVF* 3.1).
[50] See e.g. Diogenes Laertius 7.85 (= *SVF* 3.178), Aulus Gellius 12.5.7 (= *SVF* 3.181), with the discussion in Chapter 3 § 1 above.
[51] See Diogenes Laertius 7.108 (= *SVF* 3.493).
[52] See Diogenes Laertius 7.86 (= *SVF* 3.178), 7.108 (= *SVF* 3.495). Compare with Aristotle *Eth. Nic.* 1097b33-1098a18 where the function of man is characterized as an activity of the soul according to reason (κατὰ λόγον).
[53] For the rational adult, to act according to one's nature (κατὰ φύσιν) is to act according to reason (κατὰ λόγον). See Diogenes Laertius 7.86 (= *SVF* 3.178).
[54] The well-known example of a Stoic appropriate action dependent upon circumstance is suicide; see e.g. Diogenes Laertius 7.130 (= *SVF* 3.757), Plutarch *Stoic. Rep.* 1042d (= *SVF* 3.759), Cicero *Fin.* 3.60 (= *SVF* 3.763), with Rist, *Stoic Philosophy*, pp. 233-55.
[55] These three types can be seen in *Ench.* §§ 30 (social), 31-32 (religious), and 33-35 (personal). Epictetus appears to have emphasized the role of social καθήκοντα perhaps more than was done in the early Stoa. This reflects his use of the analogy between one's social position and the role given to an actor in a play (see e.g. *Ench.* 17).

When you are about to meet someone, especially one of the people enjoying high esteem, ask yourself what Socrates or Zeno would have done in such circumstances, and you will not be at a loss to deal with the situation properly.[56]

Here Epictetus presents the behaviour of these two philosophers as examples of the sort of behaviour to which the apprentice philosopher should aspire. Just as one might say that what is appropriate behaviour for an infant will differ from what is appropriate for an adult, so Epictetus suggests that what is appropriate for a typical person will not necessarily be appropriate for a philosopher. If one attempts to follow a philosophical way of life – to adopt the role of the philosopher – then one must acknowledge that this will affect what will and will not be appropriate for one to do. In order to discover what sort of behaviour *is* appropriate to the philosopher, Epictetus suggests that one should examine the lives of role models such as Zeno or Socrates. A study of their lives will soon reveal that the philosopher must be indifferent to external circumstances, unconcerned with material possessions, and undisturbed when faced with death. These attitudes will determine the actions that are appropriate to the philosopher who aspires to a completely rational way of life.

We can now see that exercises concerned with one's impulse (ὁρμή) and with what sort of behaviour is appropriate (καθῆκον) will vary depending upon the individual concerned. In the *Handbook*, a text for philosophical apprentices, the focus is clearly on actions appropriate for an aspiring student of philosophy. These 'ethical exercises' can be seen to attempt to put into practice Stoic ethical theory concerned with how one should act. Although, unlike physical theory, the practical implications of such theory may seem obvious, nevertheless the student of philosophy will still need to engage in a series of exercises designed to aid its digestion so that he or she will be able not merely to *say* how the sage should act but also to *act* as the sage should act. Thus, 'ethical exercises' are essential.

(d) Sections 42-45: Logical Exercises

The third of the three types of exercise dealt with in the *Handbook* is concerned with one's judgement (ὑπόληψις) and one's assents (συγκαταθέσεις).[57] As has been suggested, this type of exercise may be seen to correspond to 'logic'.[58] Epictetus is himself the first to note the apparent irrelevance of the study of the form of logical arguments to daily life.[59] Nevertheless he repeatedly affirms the need for this type of

---

[56] *Ench.* 33.12 (trans. Boter).
[57] These terms will be discussed further in Chapter 7 § 2 (b) below.
[58] See Bonhöffer, *Die Ethik des Stoikers Epictet*, pp. 122-26 (= *The Ethics of the Stoic Epictetus*, pp. 158-65) who characterizes this τόπος as 'judgement according to nature'. This clearly presupposes a conception of 'logic' much broader than that common today; see Barnes in *CHHP*, pp. 65-67; LS, vol. 1, pp. 188-89. It also involves a conception of logic broader than that presupposed by Xenakis, 'Logical Topics in Epictetus', p. 94.
[59] See e.g. *Diss.* 1.7.1, with Barnes, *Logic and the Imperial Stoa*, pp. 38-42, 62-70.

spiritual exercise.[60] Such exercises are directed towards transforming the way in which one judges impressions (φαντασίαι), training oneself to give assent (συγκαταθέσις) only to those that are 'adequate impressions' (φαντασίαι καταληπτικαί).[61] Central to this is the role played by judgements (ὑπολήψεις, δόγματα). For example:

> Someone bathes quickly: do not say, 'he bathes badly', but 'he bathes quickly'. Someone drinks much wine: do not say, 'he drinks badly', but 'he drinks much'. For before knowing his judgement (δόγμα), how do you know that it is bad? In that way it will not happen to you that you receive adequate impressions (φαντασίας καταληπτικάς) of some things but give your assent (συγκατατίθεσθαι) to others.[62]

Here Epictetus illustrates an important distinction between what is given in an impression (φαντασία) and what is added to that impression by the individual. In this case, the addition is the value-judgement concerning someone else's behaviour. The third type of exercise concerned with judgement (ὑπόληψις) and assent (συγκαταθέσις) is designed to train the individual to assent only to those impressions which have not been supplemented by an unwarranted value-judgement. In other words, they involve using logical analysis concerning what is true, what is false, and what is doubtful, in relation to one's judgements and the beliefs based upon those judgements. This, Epictetus suggests, is the only real reason to study logic.[63]

There is a sense in which this third type of exercise is the most important of the three, insofar as it underwrites the other two. One's judgements will always, to a certain extent, determine one's desires and impulses. It may seem odd, then, that according to the analysis of the structure of the *Handbook* that has been outlined it is relegated to relatively few sections towards the end of the text. However, this theme – the analysis of one's judgements – can be seen to run throughout the text of the *Handbook* and, for example, it appears at the very beginning of the text in the discussion of desires and aversions.[64] Yet in these later sections the idea of a 'logical exercise' takes centre stage, exercises designed to digest logical and epistemological theory so that these seemingly abstract subjects can contribute to the task of transforming one's way of life.[65]

---

[60] He also affirms the need to study logical theory; see e.g. Epictetus *Diss.* 2.25.1-3.

[61] For more on 'adequate impressions' see Chapter 4 § 2 (c) and Chapter 7 § 2 (c).

[62] *Ench.* 45 (trans. Boter modified).

[63] Epictetus mocks one of his students by saying, 'It is as if, when in the sphere of assent (συγκαταθετικοῦ τόπου) surrounded with impressions (φαντασιῶν), some of them adequate (καταληπτικῶν), and others not adequate (ἀκαταλήπτων), we should not wish to distinguish between them, but to read a treatise *On Comprehension* (Περὶ καταλήψεως)' (*Diss.* 4.4.13; trans. Oldfather modified).

[64] See e.g. *Ench.* 3 & 5.

[65] As I have already noted, the Stoic conception of logic (λογική) was significantly broader than the modern conception, including not only dialectic, but also rhetoric, and what today would be called epistemology. See LS, vol. 1, pp. 188-89; Barnes in *CHHP*, pp. 65-67.

(e) Sections 46-52: The Philosophical βίος

After these three groups of chapters dealing with the three types of spiritual exercise corresponding to the three types of philosophical discourse, the structure implicit in the *Handbook* appears to break down. However, the chapters that constitute the final part of the text can be seen to have a theme of their own; the philosophical life (βίος).[66] In particular, these chapters focus upon how a philosopher should act, the difference between a non-philosopher or layman (ἰδιώτης) and someone who is making progress (προκοπή), and how to train oneself to become a philosopher.[67] To this part of the *Handbook* belongs the analogy between the digestion of philosophical principles and the digestion of food by sheep.[68] This is followed by a reminder concerning the function of philosophical discourse, for example, the function of a commentary on the philosophical works of Chrysippus:

> If I am impressed by the explaining (ἐξηγεῖσθαι) itself, what have I done but ended up a grammarian (γραμματικὸς) instead of a philosopher (φιλοσόφου), except that I am explaining Chrysippus instead of Homer. Instead when someone says to me 'read me some Chrysippus' I turn red when I am unable to exhibit actions (τὰ ἔργα) that match and harmonize (σύμφωνα) with his words (τοῖς λόγοις).[69]

Passages such as this in the final part of the *Handbook* serve to emphasize the practical nature of the text by focusing on the idea that the product of philosophy is constituted by actions (ἔργα) rather than words (λόγοι). The three τόποι do not form yet another mode of theoretical analysis of Stoic doctrine; rather they are the means by which such doctrine is put into practice. This series of chapters at the end of the *Handbook* remind the philosophical apprentice of this, the apprentice who – when faced with a series of complex physical, ethical, and logical theories – may occasionally lose sight of the reason why they began to study philosophy in the first place.

(f) Section 53: Maxims

The final chapter of the *Handbook* is comprised of four short quotations. These texts, capturing the central themes of the *Handbook*, may be seen as maxims to be learnt by the student, and Epictetus (or, more likely, Arrian) suggests that these should be kept

---

[66] Although this is clearly a departure from the three τόποι outlined by Epictetus, note the fragmentary text in *POxy* 3657 (= *CPF* I 1, 100.5), esp. 2.13-15, which appears to propose βίος as a Stoic τόπος (see the commentary by Sedley in *The Oxyrhynchus Papyri*, vol. 52, p. 54, and in *CPF* I 1***, p. 802).

[67] See *Ench.* §§ 46-47, 48, and 51-52 respectively. Note that the three τόποι outlined in § 52 do not appear to correlate to the main set of τόποι with which we have been concerned here. However see I. Hadot, *Simplicius, Commentaire*, p. 150 n. 22.

[68] See *Ench.* 46, quoted and discussed in Chapter 5 § 3 (b) above.

[69] *Ench.* 49.

at hand (πρόχειρα). The first pair – from Cleanthes and Euripides – focus upon the Stoic goal of living in harmony with nature:

[1] 'Lead me on, Zeus, both you and Destiny,
wherever you assign me to go,
for I will follow without hesitation; but if I do not want,
being bad, I will follow all the same'.

[2] 'Whoever has complied well with necessity,
is wise according to us and knows the things of the gods'.[70]

The second pair – both quotations attributed to Socrates – highlight his status as the ultimate philosophical role model and the figure behind the idealized image of the Stoic sage:[71]

[3] 'But, Crito, if it pleases the gods like this, it must happen like this'.
[4] 'Anytus and Meletus can kill me, but they cannot harm me'.[72]

Simplicius notes in his commentary that the second of these quotations from Socrates – the final line of the *Handbook* – brings us back to the very beginning of the text insofar as it emphasizes again the claim that the individual should not place value upon those things that are not 'up to us' (ἐφ' ἡμῖν).[73] The behaviour of Socrates at his trial forms a powerful example of an attitude of indifference towards those things that are not within one's control. It also illustrates the sort of transformation in attitude and behaviour towards which the spiritual exercises in the *Handbook* are directed. From beginning to end, then, the *Handbook* is a text designed to instruct the philosophical apprentice how to put into practice the doctrines that he or she has learned with the ambitious goal of developing an attitude of calm (ἀπάθεια) and tranquillity (ἀταραξία) inspired by Socrates.

---

[70] *Ench.* 53.1-2. These are by Cleanthes (= *SVF* 1.527) and Euripides (= fr. 956 Nauck; *not* fr. 965 listed by Schenkl, Oldfather, and Boter).
[71] Note in particular *Ench.* 51.3: 'Even if you are not yet a Socrates, you must live as if you wish to become a Socrates' (trans. Boter), with comment in Jagu, *Épictète et Platon*, pp. 29-33, 47-62; Hijmans, *Ἄσκησις*, pp. 72-77; Long, 'Socrates in Hellenistic Philosophy', pp. 150-51. A list of references to Socrates as a Stoic role model in Epictetus can be found in *SSR* I C 530 but, in particular, note *Diss.* 4.1.159-69 (= *SSR* I C 524).
[72] *Ench.* 53.3-4. These are from Plato *Crito* 43d and Plato *Apol.* 30c. They both differ slightly from the texts preserved in the Platonic MS tradition.
[73] See Simplicius *In Ench.* 71.44-47 Hadot.

3. Summary

In this chapter I have developed the discussion concerning the relationship between λόγος and ἄσκησις by examining Epictetus' account of three τόποι in which he suggests one should be trained. I have suggested that it is possible to sketch a correspondence between these three areas of philosophical training or exercise and the three parts of Stoic philosophical discourse. Each type of training may be seen to be designed to digest and to assimilate the ideas expressed in the corresponding part of discourse and, together, these exercises form the second stage required in the study of philosophy conceived as a τέχνη.

The introduction of this account of the three τόποι has be described as Epictetus' single important innovation and contribution to Stoic philosophy.[74] It is also often presented as a division *within* ethics.[75] However, as we have seen, this is not the case. Epictetus does *not* neglect physics and logic in favour of ethics. His is a 'practical philosophy' rather than merely 'practical ethics', embodying not only practical ethics but also what one might call 'practical physics' and 'practical logic'. If he neglects anything it is philosophical theory, which, in the texts that survive at least, he downplays in favour of philosophical exercise. As I have already noted, this may simply reflect the literary genres of the surviving texts,[76] and there is evidence to suggest that the study of complex philosophical theories formed an important part of Epictetus' classroom teaching. The occasionally excessive emphasis upon philosophical training should not be taken to be a rejection or devaluation of philosophical theory or discourse, but rather as a reminder that such theory does not on its own constitute philosophy conceived as an art or craft (τέχνη). As with the apprentice shoemaker, an education in theory (λόγος) forms only the first stage towards mastery of one's chosen art, an education that must be supplemented with a second stage comprised of training or exercise (ἄσκησις) designed to transform one's character and habitual behaviour in the light of that theoretical understanding. Epictetus' innovation, in the form of his introduction of the three τόποι, may be seen as an attempt to emphasize the importance of such exercises by subjecting them to a detailed analysis similar to that already performed on philosophical discourse by members of the early Stoa. Yet, as we have already seen in the case of discourse, such a division was probably designed as an educational device rather than a substantial claim concerning the nature of philosophy as such, which was conceived as a unified entity and activity. Consequently it should not be assumed that this threefold analysis breaks down if, occasionally, the boundaries between the three types of exercise appear blurred.[77]

---

[74] See e.g. More, *Hellenistic Philosophies*, p. 107.

[75] Ibid.

[76] See the discussion of the *Dissertationes* within the context of the ancient literary genre of the diatribe (διατριβή) in Souilhé (CUF), vol. 1, pp. xxii-xxx.

[77] It is inevitable that analyses of our judgements, desires, and impulses, will to a certain extent overlap with one another, and that some accounts of philosophical exercises will involve more

I have followed a number of commentators in suggesting that Epictetus' threefold division of philosophical exercises can be seen to structure the text of the *Handbook*. There are clearly limits to the extent to which such a claim can be pushed. Nevertheless, I have found it helpful to follow this suggestion insofar as it enables us to examine the three types of spiritual exercise present in the *Handbook* and to emphasize the way in which this text is devoted to such exercises. The *Handbook* may be read as a text devoted to the second stage of philosophical education, a guide for students who have finished their study of philosophical theory in the classroom and are now ready to embark on the significantly harder task of putting that theory into practice. Although it may not take the traditional form of philosophical writing embodied by the complex theoretical treatise or commentary, I suggest that, insofar as it is devoted to these essential philosophical exercises, the *Handbook* is nevertheless an important philosophical text.

In the final chapter I shall move on to examine another Stoic text devoted to philosophical exercise, the *Meditations* of Marcus Aurelius. Although all three of Epictetus' τόποι may be found within the *Meditations*, there is clearly no attempt to present these in any systematic manner. Instead, one finds a written philosophical exercise emphasizing the interconected nature of the three types of Stoic spiritual exercises. By examining the *Meditations* hopefully we shall develop further our understanding of the relationship between λόγος and ἄσκησις.

---

than one of these and consequently be difficult to categorize according to this threefold schema. However, this does not diminish the benefit gained from such an analysis.

Chapter 7

Exercises in the *Meditations* of Marcus Aurelius

In the last chapter I outlined Epictetus' division of philosophical exercises into three types corresponding to the three parts of philosophical discourse. In this chapter I shall consider the relationship between λόγος and ἄσκησις further by turning to examine the *Meditations* of Marcus Aurelius.[1] As we have already seen in Chapter 5, it is possible to discern two types of text concerned with spiritual exercises, and, as we have seen in Chapter 6, the *Handbook* may be seen as an example of the first type of text, that is, as a guide to be used by philosophical apprentices. In this chapter we shall focus upon the *Meditations* as an example of the second type of text, that is, a text written by a philosophical apprentice whilst engaged in spiritual exercises.

In particular, I shall focus upon the ways in which seemingly abstract and technical parts of Stoic epistemological theory might be understood within the context of the conception of philosophy as a τέχνη outlined in Part I. In order to do this I shall focus upon a central theme in the *Meditations* – namely reflections upon the idea of a 'point of view of the cosmos' – and examine the way in which this is underpinned by Stoic epistemological theory borrowed from Epictetus.

1. The Literary Form of the *Meditations*

The *Meditations* of Marcus Aurelius are the Philosopher-Emperor's personal reflections compiled during his apprenticeship in the Stoic art of living.[2] If the *Handbook* may be characterized as a guide to spiritual exercises to be used by students, then the *Meditations* of Marcus Aurelius may be described as an example of a text produced by a student engaged in such exercises. Indeed, it is tempting to

---

[1] For comment on the text of the *Meditations* see Additional Note 4. I have relied primarily upon Farquharson's edition. Book length studies of the *Meditations* include Rutherford, *The Meditations of Marcus Aurelius*, and Hadot, *The Inner Citadel*. Shorter studies worthy of note include Brunt, 'Marcus Aurelius in his *Meditations*'; Asmis, 'The Stoicism of Marcus Aurelius'; Hadot 'Une clé des *Pensées* de Marc Aurèle'; Rist, 'Are You a Stoic? The Case of Marcus Aurelius'. A detailed textual commentary can be found in vol. 2 of Farquharson's edition. Detailed textual notes can also be found in Crossley's edition of Book 4 of the *Meditations*.

[2] There are a number of oblique references to philosophy being a τέχνη analogous to other τέχναι in the *Meditations*; see e.g. 4.2, 5.1, 6.16, 6.35, 7.68, 11.5.

speculate that Marcus may have had a copy of the *Handbook* with him when he wrote the *Meditations*.[3] The traditional Greek title of the *Meditations* – τὰ εἰς ἑαυτόν, literally 'to himself' – indicates the personal nature of this text.[4] The *Mediations* were written as a private notebook by Marcus, probably never intended for public circulation, in which he meditates upon specific philosophical ideas in order to transform his own attitudes and habitual responses. In doing this he, in effect, follows the advice given by Seneca in his *On Anger*:

> This [the soul] should be summoned to give an account of itself every day. Sextius had this habit, and when the day was over and he had retired to his nightly rest, he would put these questions to his soul: 'What bad habit have you cured today? What fault have you resisted? In what respect are you better?' Anger will cease and become more controllable if it finds that it must appear before a judge every day. [... In the evening] I scan the whole of my day and retrace all my deeds and words. I conceal nothing from myself, I omit nothing.[5]

This practice, Marcus says in Book 1, was something he learned from his Stoic mentor Rusticus.[6]

With the exception of Book 1, the *Meditations* do not seem to have any implicit structure in the way that the *Handbook* can be seen to have.[7] As we have seen, it is possible to discern within the *Handbook* a division into distinct sections each focusing upon a different type of spiritual exercise. Although the *Meditations* do not display any similar structure, Marcus can nevertheless be seen to follow Epictetus' account of

---

[3] The influence of Epictetus on Marcus is well documented; see e.g. Long, 'Epictetus, Marcus Aurelius', pp. 986-89; Hadot, *The Inner Citadel*, pp. 54-72. Although it is unclear whether Marcus had a copy of the *Enchiridion*, he does refer to the *Dissertationes*; at 1.7 Marcus says that he borrowed a copy of the 'memoirs' of Epictetus (τοῖς Ἐπικτητείοις ὑπομνήμασιν) from his teacher Rusticus (Arrian also uses ὑπομνήματα at *Diss.* Praef. 2), and he often quotes them (see e.g. 4.41, 11.33-38).

[4] The title was probably added later and the earliest recorded mention is *c.* AD 900 by Arethas, *Schol. in Lucianum* 50 (207.6-7 Rabe): Μάρκος ὁ καῖσαρ ἐν τοῖς εἰς ἑαυτὸν Ἠθικοῖς. Earlier, the text was referred to by Themistius in AD 364 (see *Orationes* 6.81c) as the *Precepts* or *Admonitions* of Marcus (τῶν Μάρκου παραγγελμάτων). See Farquharson, pp. xiii-xix, 433-34; Hadot, *The Inner Citadel*, pp. 23-25; Birley, *Marcus Aurelius*, p. 212.

[5] Seneca *De Ira* 3.36.1-3 (trans. Basore).

[6] See Marcus Aurelius 1.7: 'From Rusticus: to get an impression of need for reform and treatment of character (θεραπείας τοῦ ἤθους)', with Farquharson, p. 443. For Rusticus' status as a Stoic (who, as I have already noted, is said to have lent Marcus a copy of Epictetus' *Dissertationes*) see Dio Cassius 72.35.1.

[7] The order of the text may simply follow the order of composition but one cannot be certain. With regard to Book 1, Rutherford notes that § 6.48 appears to outline a plan for it and that it may have been composed as a separate work but preserved with the rest of the *Meditations* in the manuscript tradition. See his Introduction to the new edition of Farquharson's translation, p. xvi; also Brunt, 'Marcus Aurelius in his *Meditations*', p. 18; Birley, *Marcus Aurelius*, p. 212.

the three types of spiritual exercise corresponding to the three parts of philosophical discourse:[8]

Wipe out impression (φαντασίαν): check impulse (ὁρμήν): quench desire (ὄρεξιν): keep the governing self in its own control.[9]

Continually and, if possible, on the occasion of every impression, test it by physics, by ethics, by logic.[10]

'Impressions', 'impulses', and 'desires', are clearly references to Epictetus' three τόποι which, as we have seen, correspond to the three parts of philosophical discourse; logic, ethics, and physics. The *Meditations* can also be seen to share with the *Handbook* the idea that philosophical doctrines should always be ready to hand (πρόχειρος). In one passage Marcus emphasizes this with particular reference to Epictetus' three τόποι:

These three thoughts keep always ready to hand (πρόχειρα):
First, in what you do that your act be not without purpose and not otherwise than Right (Δίκη) itself would have done […].
The second, to remember the nature of each individual from his conception to his first breath until he gives back the breath of life […].
The third, to realize that if you could be suddenly caught up into the air and could look down upon human life and all its variety you would disdain it […].[11]

The first of these is concerned with actions and impulses, and corresponds to 'ethics'. The second is concerned with the true nature of individuals and corresponds to 'physics'. The third is concerned with the analysis of impressions (φαντασίαι) and value-judgements (ὑπολήψεις) and thus corresponds to 'logic'. To a certain extent these three thoughts are inevitably interconnected. In the passage here, Marcus imagines a perspective 'above' the everyday world of human affairs and this imagery recurs throughout the *Meditations*. Such passages may be seen to enact both a 'physical' and a 'logical' exercise, with ethical implications not far behind. In the remainder of this chapter I shall focus upon this theme in Marcus' written spiritual exercises and, in particular, its relation with Stoic logical theory in order to develop further our understanding of the relationship between λόγος and ἄσκησις. This, in turn, will contribute to our understanding of philosophy conceived as a τέχνη.

---

[8] See Hadot 'Une clé des *Pensées* de Marc Aurèle', pp. 65-83; *The Inner Citadel*, pp. 69-70.
[9] Marcus Aurelius 9.7.
[10] Marcus Aurelius 8.13. Farquharson translates φυσιολογεῖν, παθολογεῖν, and διαλεκτικεύεσθαι as 'natural science', 'psychology', and 'logic', but in his commentary (p. 759) acknowledges that this is an attempt to express the Stoic tripartite division of philosophical discourse. Indeed, Haines (LCL) translates these as 'physics, ethics, logic'.
[11] Marcus Aurelius 12.24. For further examples of πρόχειρος see e.g. 3.13, 4.3, 5.1, 6.48, 7.1, 7.64, 9.42, 11.4, 11.18.

2. The Point of View of the Cosmos

(a) Spiritual Exercises in the Meditations

Central to the written spiritual exercises that constitute the *Meditations* is the distinction between the opinions of the foolish majority and the adequate impressions of the sage. This is the distinction between the way things appear according to human opinion (δόξα) and the way they are according to nature (κατὰ φύσιν). Marcus writes that one should not hold on to the opinions of all men, but only to those of men who live in accordance with nature.[12] Only the Stoic sage experiences things as they are according to nature, that is, as they are in themselves.[13] Throughout the *Meditations* there are numerous passage that illustrate what Marcus takes this perspective to reveal. Here are five such examples:

> Of man's life, his time is a point, his substance flowing, his perception faint, the constitution of his whole body decaying, his soul a spinning wheel, his fortune hard to predict, and his fame doubtful; that is to say, all the things of the body are a river, the things of the soul dream and delusion, life is a war and a journey in a foreign land, and afterwards oblivion.[14]

> Often consider the speed of the movement and carrying away and coming to be of existing things. For substance is like a river in perpetual flow, its activities are in continuous change, its causes are in countless turns, it is never near a standstill, and close at hand is the infinite void of past and future in which all things disappear.[15]

> Observe the courses of the stars as if revolving with them and reflect upon the continuous changes of the elements into one another; for impressions such as these are for cleansing the filth of earth-bound life.[16]

> You have the power to strip away many superfluous troubles located wholly in your judgement, and to possess a large room for yourself embracing in thought the whole cosmos, to consider everlasting time, to think of the rapid change in the parts of each thing, of how short it is from birth until dissolution, and how the void before birth and that after dissolution are equally infinite.[17]

---

[12] See Marcus Aurelius 3.4.4. This is the only place where Marcus uses this Stoic formula (τῶν ὁμολογουμένως τῇ φύσει). Elsewhere (e.g. 1.9, 3.9, 3.12, 4.1, 5.3, 5.4, 7.11, 7.56, 7.74, 8.29, 10.33, 12.1), he prefers the shorthand 'according to nature' (κατὰ φύσιν).

[13] See Kerferd, 'What Does the Wise Man Know?', p. 132.

[14] Marcus Aurelius 2.17 (reading ῥόμβος with Farquharson, Haines, and Leopold, instead of ῥεμβός in Dalfen and Theiler).

[15] Marcus Aurelius 5.23.

[16] Marcus Aurelius 7.47.

[17] Marcus Aurelius 9.32.

How little a fraction of infinite and empty time has been distributed to each individual, for quickly it is lost in the eternal; and how little of the whole substance, how little of the whole soul, and on how little a clump of the whole earth do you creep. Considering all these things, imagine nothing greater than this: to act as your nature guides, and to undergo what common nature brings.[18]

In these passages and many others like them Marcus proposes what might be called a 'point of view of the cosmos', a perspective that takes as its point of departure the large-scale processes and movements of the cosmos itself, a perspective far removed from the first person perspective of ordinary human affairs. In a number of passages Marcus reminds himself continually to 'look from above' (ἄνωθεν ἐπιθεωρεῖν).[19] From this bird's-eye view or 'point of view of the cosmos' the apparently stable and secure individual appears as merely a momentary pause in the vast flows of matter and energy that constitute the physical system of the cosmos. Marcus writes:

You came into the world as a part. You will vanish in that which gave you birth, or rather you will be taken up into its generative principle by the process of change.[20]

For Marcus and his Stoic predecessors the cosmos is organized by an immanent generative principle (σπερματικὸς λόγος), also known variously as God, the world-soul, fire, and breath (πνεῦμα).[21] Some ancient accounts of Stoic physics present this as an active principle in some form of mixture with the passive principle of matter (ὕλη).[22] However, the generative principle is itself material and this distinction between two material principles is merely formal.[23] The generative principle

---

[18] Marcus Aurelius 12.32.

[19] Marcus Aurelius 9.30; see also 7.48, 12.24. This was a common theme in Stoicism before Marcus (see e.g. Seneca *Epist.* 49.2-3, 99.10, *Nat. Quaest.* 1. Praef. 7) and not the product of drug abuse, *pace* Africa, 'The Opium Addiction of Marcus Aurelius' (note also Witke, 'Marcus Aurelius and Mandragora'). It is reported that Galen administered theriac to Marcus (see Galen *Praecog.* 11.1-2 = 14.657-58 Kühn = 126.16-28 Nutton) and Africa takes this evidence of 'drug addiction' as an explanation for Marcus' 'bizarre visions' and 'extraordinary insulation from domestic reality'. For further discussion see Hadot, *Philosophy as a Way of Life*, pp. 180-82.

[20] Marcus Aurelius 4.14; see also 4.21, 6.24.

[21] See Aetius *Plac.* 1.7.33 (*DG* 305.15-306.11 = *SVF* 2.1027 = LS 46 A), Diogenes Laertius 7.135 (= *SVF* 1.102 = LS 46 B). It has been suggested that the concept of πνεῦμα as active principle of the cosmos was introduced by Chrysippus, while Cleanthes posited heat, and Zeno fire. See Lapidge, 'ἀρχαί and στοιχεῖα', pp. 274-75; Solmsen, 'Cleanthes or Posidonius? The Basis of Stoic Physics', pp. 456-57.

[22] See Diogenes Laertius 7.134 (= *SVF* 1.85, 2.300 = LS 44 B).

[23] See e.g. Calcidius *In Tim.* 294 (297.1-2 Waszink = *SVF* 1.87). Central to discussions of this point has been a variant reading in Diogenes Laertius 7.134 (= *SVF* 2.299 = Posidonius fr. 5 EK = LS 44 B); according to the MSS the two principles are 'corporeal' (σώματα) but an alternative reading in the *Suda* (*s.v.* Ἀρχή (A 4092)) suggests 'incorporeal' (ἀσωμάτους). A number of editors have adopted the *Suda* reading (e.g. Lipsius *Physiologia Stoicorum* 2.5, von Arnim (*SVF*), Hicks (LCL), H. S. Long (OCT)) but more recently the MS reading has gained

(σπερματικὸς λόγος) or breath (πνεῦμα) is not in mixture with matter (ὕλη), but rather may be conceived as a certain quality of matter itself. Stoic physics is thus monistic, conceiving material nature as a force moving itself.[24] Within this monistic materialism, the generative principle produces all stability and form, with processes of condensation, rarefaction, solidification, and stratification generating states of pneumatic tension (τόνος τοῦ πνεύματος).[25] In this, the Stoics follow Heraclitus and his physics of continual flux organized by a single rational principle (λόγος) generating stability through processes of dynamic equilibrium.[26] What Stoic physics adds to this is a distinctively biological orientation. Their generative principle functions as a principle of nonorganic life and as such Marcus proposes that we should never cease to think of the cosmos as one living being (ἓν ζῷον τὸν κόσμον).[27] For the Stoics, this living material nature is God,[28] defined as the intelligence in matter (νοῦν ἐν ὕλῃ),[29] and, as both Cicero and Plotinus note, this is often used as a way of disposing of the concept of God altogether.[30] Thus the Stoic

---

support (e.g. LS, Sorabji, *Matter, Space, and Motion*, pp. 93-94). I understand the relationship between the principles in a similar way to Todd ('Monism and Immanence', p. 139), who characterizes the principles as primarily a logical or conceptual distinction within a physically unified system. The claim would not be that the principles are incorporeal but rather that the *distinction* between these two inseparable aspects of a single substance is an incorporeal λεκτά or proposition. In other words, the principles constitute merely a formal distinction, not an ontological one (they are never found dissociated from one another). The principles, as aspects of a single material unity, remain corporeal; only the linguistic distinction between them is incorporeal.

[24] See Diogenes Laertius 7.148 (= *SVF* 2.1132 = LS 43 A).

[25] See e.g. Diogenes Laertius 7.142 (= *SVF* 1.102 = LS 46 C), Plutarch *Stoic. Rep.* 1053f (= *SVF* 2.449 = LS 47 M), *Comm. Not.* 1085d (= *SVF* 2.444 = LS 47 G), Nemesius *Nat. Hom.* 2 (18.2-10 Morani = LS 47 J), and, for pneumatic tension, Alexander of Aphrodisias *Mixt.* 223.34-36 (= *SVF* 2.441 = LS 47 L).

[26] Much of Stoic physics can already be found within the fragments of Heraclitus, in particular a model of dynamic equilibrium based upon a theory of pneumatic tension. See e.g. fr. 8 DK *apud* Aristotle *Eth. Nic.* 1155b4-6, fr. 31 DK *apud* Clement of Alexandria *Strom.* 5.14 (*PG* 9.160a), and fr. 51 DK *apud* Hippolytus *Refutatio* 9.9 (241.19-21 Wendland). It is often claimed that this resonance may be due to a Stoicized portrait of Heraclitus used by later doxographers; however, this could not have affected Aristotle's testimony. For further discussion see Long, 'Heraclitus and Stoicism', pp. 133-56; Bréhier, *Chrysippe*, pp. 142-44. Of all the Stoics, Marcus appears to have had a particularly strong interest in Heraclitus, naming him often and preserving five of the fragments (4.46 & 6.42 are the sources for fr. 71-75 DK).

[27] Marcus Aurelius 4.40. For a contemporary explication of the concept of 'nonorganic life' see De Landa, 'Nonorganic life'.

[28] See Cicero *Nat. Deo.* 1.39 (= *SVF* 2.1077 = LS 54 B).

[29] Plutarch *Comm. Not.* 1085b (= *SVF* 2.313).

[30] See Cicero *Nat. Deo.* 1.32 (with reference to Antisthenes and so fr. 39b DC = *SSR* V A 180) and Plotinus *Enn.* 6.1.27 (= *SVF* 2.314), who says that the Stoics bring in God only for the sake of appearances (εὐπρεπείας), defining Him as matter in a certain state (ὕλη πῶς ἔχουσα).

conception of the cosmos is more biological than theological and Stoic cosmology is always 'cosmobiology'.[31]

It is this physical or scientific approach that constitutes 'the point of view of the cosmos'. From this perspective, nature is experienced as a cosmic process of continual flux punctuated with occasional points of dynamic equilibrium. It is already clear that Marcus uses this perspective in order to devalue human anxieties and concerns. The suggestion is that by placing what appears to be stable within the broader context of a cosmos defined by constant flux, one can become aware of, and open to, the inevitable change of all things – change in circumstance, change in fortune, change in health, and, above all, the change from life to death. Indeed, Marcus makes numerous references to death,[32] and in general he characterizes it as but one aspect of a more general cosmic process:

> All things are in change (πάντα ἐν μεταβολῇ), and you yourself are in continuous alteration and, in a sense, destruction. So, too, is the cosmos as a whole.[33]

Marcus supplements this kind of very abstract reflection upon death as but one expression of continual cosmic transformation with references to the deaths of powerful individuals who once occupied positions similar to his own:

> Alexander the Great and his stable boy were levelled in death, for they were either taken up into the same life-giving principles of the cosmos (τοὺς αὐτοὺς τοῦ κόσμου σπερματικοὺς λόγους) or were scattered without distinction into atoms.[34]

Although in this last passage one can see Marcus' agnostic attitude towards both Stoic and Epicurean physics, the one physical doctrine which he continually affirms is the Heraclitean doctrine of universal flux, adopted by the Stoics. The fundamental law of the cosmos is the inevitability of continual transformation and it is within this context that Marcus wants to understand death. Death is not the end but merely an internal rearrangement in a much larger cosmic system. For instance:

> I was composed of a formal and a material substance; and of these neither will pass away into nothingness, just as neither came to exist out of nothingness. Thus, every part of me will be assigned its place by change (κατὰ μεταβολὴν) into some part of the cosmos, and that again into another part of the cosmos, and so on to infinity.[35]

---

[31] I borrow this term from Hahm, *The Origins of Stoic Cosmology*, pp. 136-84; see also Annas, *Hellenistic Philosophy of Mind*, p. 43; Lapidge, 'Stoic Cosmology', p. 163.

[32] See the discussions in Rutherford, *The Meditations of Marcus Aurelius*, pp. 161-67; Hadot, *The Inner Citadel*, pp. 275-77; Newman, '*Cotidie meditare*', pp. 1509-11.

[33] Marcus Aurelius 9.19.

[34] Marcus Aurelius 6.24; see also 8.31, and comment in Newman, '*Cotidie meditare*', p. 1510.

[35] Marcus Aurelius 5.13.

Many further passages expressing this theme could also be mentioned. As we have already seen, the repetition of these ideas is central to their 'digestion' (πέψις). By reflecting over and over again on the same philosophical themes Marcus attempts to 'dye' his soul, to make himself so completely accustomed to these ideas that they transform his character and thus his habitual behaviour.[36] The motive behind this is the thought that by overcoming the limited perspective of the individual with its assumption of stability, one will be able to escape the emotional disturbances (πάθη) that occur when the only ever apparently stable is inevitably transformed.

Freeing oneself of this limited first person perspective will free one from the emotional turmoil that goes with it. From the cosmic perspective, everything is in a continual state of change and nothing is expected to remain stable for long. In this sense, the 'point of view of the cosmos' enables one to free oneself from attachment to particular external objects, to free oneself from the bad passions that accompany such attachments, and thus to cultivate well-being (εὐδαιμονία). It is this cosmic perspective that the Stoic sage is said to experience.

(b) Impressions and Judgements

How does Marcus Aurelius think that one might be able to overcome the everyday limited perspective of the individual and approach this cosmic perspective? To some extent this question has been answered insofar as we have already encountered examples of Marcus' spiritual exercises directed towards that very goal. Yet these were reflections upon the cosmic perspective itself rather than philosophical exercises directed towards cultivating that perspective. In order to cultivate the 'point of view of the cosmos', Marcus proposes another series of spiritual exercises which draw upon Stoic epistemological theory and, in particular, the Stoic theory of judgement (ὑπόληψις, δόγμα, κρίμα, κρίσις).[37] Marcus suggests that all of the problems that accompany the limited perspective of the individual are the product of human judgements:

---

[36] See the discussion in Chapter 5 § 3 (a) above.

[37] Marcus and Epictetus use a variety of terms that can all be and have been translated as either 'judgement' or 'opinion'. These include ὑπόληψις, δόγμα, κρίμα, and κρίσις. Marcus uses ὑπόληψις and δόγμα most, 25 and 21 times respectively, while Epictetus overwhelmingly prefers δόγμα, using it over 100 times (see the indexes in Dalfen (BT) and Schenkl (BT) respectively). In the index to his *Die Ethik des Stoikers Epictet* (p. 267) Bonhöffer suggests that ὑπόληψις and δόγμα can be taken to be synonymous and Epictetus uses them as such at *Diss.* 1.11.33. In his Latin translation of Epictetus, Wolf renders both ὑπόληψις and δόγμα as *opinio* (*Ench.* §§ 1 & 5 = §§ 1 & 10 in his edition) and elsewhere both δόγμα and κρίμα as *decretum* (*Diss.* 1.11.33 & 2.15.8). Crossley suggests that when Marcus uses κρίμα it should be understood to be synonymous with δόγμα (see p. 6). I shall assume that all of these terms are broadly synonymous and render all of them as 'judgement', understanding them also to involve the notions of 'opinion' or 'assumption'. Occasionally I also follow Hadot's suggestion of 'value-judgement' for ὑπόληψις (see *The Inner Citadel*, p. 83). For further comment on Epictetus' use of δόγμα see Barnes, 'The Beliefs of a Pyrrhonist', pp. 71-72.

Look at the inmost causes of things, stripped of their husks; note the intentions that underlie actions; [...] observe how man's disquiet is all of his own making, and how troubles come never from another's hand, but like all else are creatures of our own judgement (ὑπόληψις).[38]

Here Marcus follows his Stoic mentor Epictetus in suggesting that all judgements of good and evil are always a product of the perspective of the limited individual.[39] As Epictetus often repeats, what upsets people are not things themselves, which are neither good nor evil, but rather their judgements (δόγματα) about things. Compare the following two passages, the first Marcus, the second Epictetus:

If you suffer because of something external, it is not due to the thing itself (ἐκεῖνο) but your judgement (κρῖμα) of it, and this it is in your power to wipe out at once [...].[40]

It is not the things themselves (τὰ πράγματα) that disturb men, but their judgements (δόγματα) about these things. For example, death is nothing dreadful, or else Socrates too would have thought so, but the judgement (δόγμα) that death is dreadful, this is the dreadful thing. When, therefore, we are hindered, or disturbed, or grieved, let us never blame anyone but ourselves, that means, our own judgements (δόγματα).[41]

Perhaps the best surviving account of Epictetus' analysis of judgement is contained in a fragment from the now lost fifth book of the *Discourses* preserved by Aulus Gellius.[42] Aulus tells the story of a journey by sea during a storm that he once made in the company of a Stoic philosopher. As the storm became more violent Aulus says that he turned to the Stoic to see how this wise man kept his composure in the face of such danger. However, he was somewhat disappointed to see that the philosopher was as pale and frightened as everybody else. When the storm passed Aulus turned to the philosopher and asked why it was that he seemed scared even though, as a Stoic, he professed to be indifferent to all such external circumstances. The philosopher responded by taking out of his bag a copy of the fifth book of the *Discourses* of Epictetus and directing Aulus to a passage that he thought would help to explain his behaviour.

According to Aulus' Latin rendition of that passage (which retains Epictetus' Greek terminology), Epictetus argued that the impressions (φαντασίαι) that present external objects are neither voluntary nor controlled, but rather force themselves upon

---

[38] Marcus Aurelius 12.8.

[39] A similar position can be found in Sextus Empiricus *Adv. Math.* 11.68-78 who, while denying the possibility of saying that anything is in its nature good or evil, will still acknowledge that it is possible to talk about good and evil relative to a particular individual. See Bett, *Sextus Empiricus, Against the Ethicists*, p. xiv.

[40] Marcus Aurelius 8.47.

[41] Epictetus *Ench.* 5 (trans. Oldfather); see also *Diss.* 2.16.24.

[42] See Aulus Gellius 19.1.1-21. The quotation from Epictetus (in Aulus' Latin) is at 19.1.15-20 (= Epictetus fr. 9 Schenkl).

the mind.[43] However, the acts of assent (συγκατάθεσις) by which these impressions are acknowledged are voluntary and subject to the will. So, when a terrifying event occurs, such as Aulus' storm at sea, even the mind of a sage will become disturbed by a sudden impression that cannot be stopped. As Augustine glosses it in his discussion of this fragment, it is as if these passions are too quick for the intellect.[44] However, the sage will not give his assent to such an impression; instead he will reject the impression and affirm that nothing terrible has actually happened. This is where the sage differs from the foolish individual who does not question his impressions and assumes that things are in reality as terrible as they first seem to be. In other words, the fool unthinkingly assents to impressions without examining their true nature. The sage, on the other hand, examines his impressions and only assents to those that are 'adequate'.[45] It was with this account of impressions that Aulus' Stoic travelling companion attempted to justify his expression of fear during the storm, namely, that although he was momentarily overcome by the impression that something terrible was happening, he did not give his assent to that impression once he had examined it.

In order to understand this account of giving assent to impressions, it may be helpful to place it alongside what Epictetus says in those books of the *Discourses* that have survived. In a passage from the second book of the *Discourses* that also considers fear while on a sea voyage Epictetus says the following:

> Whenever I go to sea, as soon as I gaze down into the depths or look at the waters around me and see no land, I am beside myself, and imagine that if I am wrecked I must swallow all that sea. Not once does it enter my head that three pints are enough. What is it then that alarms me? The sea? No, my own judgement (δόγμα).[46]

What this passage indicates – when it is considered alongside Aulus' account – is that for Epictetus the impressions that force themselves upon the mind are not simply given. Rather, they are already composite, the product of both the external object and the mind of the individual. As with Plato, for Epictetus an impression is already a blend of perception and judgement.[47] As such, impressions are not a straightforwardly accurate perception of an external object, but rather how such an object or event *seems* to be from the perspective of a particular individual. As such, they reflect that

---

[43] In the doxographical tradition, the Stoics are said to have held that impressions are imprinted on the mind, although the precise nature of this was subject to some debate. See e.g. Aetius *Plac.* 4.11.1 (*DG* 400a4-8 = *SVF* 2.83 = LS 39 E), Diogenes Laertius 7.50 (= *SVF* 2.55 = LS 39 A).

[44] Augustine *Civ. Dei* 9.4.2 (*PL* 41.259): *tanquam his passionibus praevenientibus mentis et rationis officium.*

[45] This concept will be examined further in § 2 (c) below.

[46] Epictetus *Diss.* 2.16.22 (trans. Hard modified).

[47] Compare with Plato *Soph.* 264a-b: 'what we mean by "it appears" (φαίνεται) is a blend of perception and judgement (αἰσθήσεως καὶ δόξης)'. However elsewhere (e.g. *Theaet.* 152c) Plato tends to identify 'appearing' (φαντασία) with 'perception' (αἴσθησις).

individual's own presuppositions and beliefs.[48] These impressions are impressions *of* things appearing in a certain way, not impressions *that* things are in fact that way.[49] Affirmation to such an impression is thus not necessarily to an impression merely of what is given. Drawing these two accounts by Epictetus together, four distinct stages can be outlined in his analysis of impressions:

1. The perception of an external object.
2. An almost involuntary and unconscious judgement concerning the perception. This judgement will be shaped by an individual's presuppositions, preconceptions, and mental habits.
3. The presentation of an impression composed of both perception and judgement to the conscious mind (the ruling part of the soul or ἡγεμονικόν).[50]
4. The act of granting or denying assent (συγκατάθεσις) to this composite impression, creating a belief.

According to Aulus' account, the foolish individual will not even be aware of the second stage and will assume that his impressions are an accurate reflection of external objects. The sage, on the other hand, will subject his impressions to strict examination before giving or denying assent, analysing what is given and what is the product of his own involuntary judgement. By so doing, he will be able to overcome the emotions that are a product of these judgements.[51] In other words, the sage will use his conscious act of assent to reject his unconscious act of judgement. To be more precise, the sage will go further and actually train himself to stop adding value-judgements to what is given in perception. Marcus writes,

---

[48] See De Lacy, 'The Logical Structure of the Ethics of Epictetus', p. 114; Long, 'Representation and the Self in Stoicism', pp. 103 & 111.

[49] See LS, vol. 1, pp. 239-40.

[50] This impression is often said to be presented in propositional form; see e.g. Diogenes Laertius 7.49 (= *SVF* 2.52 = LS 39 A).

[51] There was some debate in the early Stoa concerning whether emotions should be described as judgements themselves or as the product of judgements. See e.g. Galen *Plac. Hipp. Plat.* 5.1.4 (5.429 Kühn = 292.17-20 De Lacy = *SVF* 1.209, 3.461) who reports that while Zeno held that the emotions are contractions and expansions of the soul that are the product of judgements, Chrysippus identified the emotions with the judgements themselves. According to Cicero (*Acad.* 1.39 = *SVF* 1.207), Zeno held all emotions to be voluntary and the product of a judgement. According to Diogenes Laertius (7.111 = *SVF* 3.456), Chrysippus is reported to have said that greed is simply the judgement that money is intrinsically good. Of these two positions Zeno's seems to be the more plausible, namely that the emotions are the product or consequence of judgements. Thus it would make sense to say that someone might no longer be upset that someone close to them has died, but nevertheless that they still hold the judgement that their death was a terrible thing.

Do not say more to yourself than the first impressions (αἱ προηγούμεναι φαντασίαι) report. [...] abide always by the first impressions (τῶν πρώτων φαντασιῶν) and add nothing of your own from within.[52]

These first impressions are what is given by perception before any value-judgement has been made. The task for the aspiring philosopher is to train oneself to stop at these first impressions.

According to Marcus and Epictetus all statements claiming that something is either good or bad are a product of human judgements. As Simplicius comments,

those things (τὰ πράγματα) which we apprehend to be evil [...] are really neither evil themselves, nor the true causes of any evil to us [...] all our troubles and perplexities (τὰ ταράττοντα) are entirely owing to the opinions (δόγματα) which we ourselves have entertained and cherished concerning them.[53]

Indeed, it is this addition of a value-judgement that forms the unconscious contribution that the mind makes to impressions. Thus the task of the Stoic analysis of impressions and judgements is to examine impressions and to reject any value-judgements they might contain. Its aim is to develop an experience of the world as it is in itself, that is, an experience that presents things as neither good nor bad in themselves. This, Epictetus suggests, is the key to living well:

If you have right judgements (ὀρθὰ δόγματα), you will fare well (καλῶς), and if wrong (φαῦλα), ill (κακῶς); since in every case the way a man fares is determined by his judgement (δόγμα).[54]

For Epictetus, well-being (εὐδαιμονία) is directly dependent upon a correct analysis of impressions (φαντασίαι) and judgements (δόγματα, ὑπολήψεις). This, he says, is the only thing that can properly be called good. Likewise, the only thing that can properly be called bad is an incorrect use of impressions. Thus, Epictetus proposes a thoroughly Socratic analysis of behaviour based upon two premises; the first that everyone acts according to what they believe to be good, and the second that all actions are a direct consequence of one's judgements.[55] In the case of theft, for example, Epictetus suggests that the thief genuinely believes that what he does will

---

[52] Marcus Aurelius 8.49; see also 5.26.
[53] Simplicius *In Ench.* 10.11-15 Hadot (trans. Stanhope).
[54] Epictetus *Diss.* 3.9.2 (trans. Oldfather modified). See also Musonius Rufus fr. 38 (125.1-5 Hense = 134.24-136.3 Lutz) *apud* Stobaeus 2.8.30 (2.159.25-160.11 WH) where the correct use of impressions is presented as the key to serenity, cheerfulness, constancy, and excellence. This text is also Epictetus fr. 4 Schenkl and it appears to derive from one of the lost books of the *Dissertationes* where Epictetus was presumably quoting his teacher Musonius.
[55] See De Lacy, 'The Logical Structure of the Ethics of Epictetus', pp. 120-21. A good discussion of these themes in Socrates can be found in Guthrie, *History*, vol. 3, pp. 450-62.

bring him good.[56] Just like everyone else, he desires what he thinks is in his best interest. This means that his motive cannot be criticized. If one thinks that the thief has made a mistake or done something wrong then one must show that this is due to the thief's incorrect use of his impressions. To be more precise, one must show that the error lies in his implicit assent to a value-judgement that has led to his impulse to act, combined with his failure to use his faculty of assent (συγκατάθεσις) that stands in between his impressions and impulses. This failure makes the thief no different to an animal whose impulses follow directly from impressions.[57] This is where the origin of an individual's actions must be sought.

Epictetus suggests that coming to understand that this act of assent (συγκατάθεσις) is within one's own control (ἐφ᾽ ἡμῖν) is the very essence of philosophy, and the primary task for the philosopher is to test impressions and to analyse judgements,[58] for the knowledge of what is given in perception and what is added by human judgement is the key to living well. Thus, Epictetus repeatedly defines the goal (τέλος) of his philosophy as the correct use of impressions (ὀρθὴ χρῆσις φαντασιῶν).[59] What at first glance seems like a technical epistemological question, then, is in fact the foundation of his ethics and central to his project of cultivating the art of living well. This tough Socratic stance distances Epictetus from the Platonic position which, with its tripartite theory of the soul, removes an individual's responsibility for their actions by placing their origin within an alien faculty in the soul, one that reason cannot necessarily control.[60] In contrast to this, Epictetus affirms that individuals have total power over their happiness and that the key to that happiness is the correct analysis of impressions.

(c) Adequate Impressions

The impressions assented to by the sage are impressions free from human value-judgements. Thus they are impressions that do not involve the terms 'good' and 'bad'. To repeat a key passage by Marcus Aurelius:

---

[56] See Epictetus *Diss.* 2.26.1-2, 1.18.3-6, Simplicius *In Ench.* 1.305-315 Hadot.

[57] See Kahn, 'Discovering the Will', p. 247.

[58] See De Lacy, 'The Logical Structure of the Ethics of Epictetus', pp. 118-122.

[59] See e.g. Epictetus *Diss.* 2.19.32, 1.12.34, and, in particular, 1.20.15 (= *SVF* 1.182) where he cites Zeno as an authority for this formulation of the τέλος. For further examples see Bonhöffer, *Die Ethik des Stoikers Epictet*, p. 7 (= *The Ethics of the Stoic Epictetus*, p. 19).

[60] See Frede, 'The Stoic Doctrine of the Affections of the Soul', p. 98. For early Stoic monistic psychology see Plutarch *Virt. Mor.* 441b-d & 446f-447a (both *SVF* 3.459 = LS 61 B & 65 G). Early Stoic polemics against the Platonic tripartite model of the soul and their arguments in favour of a monistic psychology can be seen as an attempt to reaffirm Socratic psychology in the face of Plato's later criticisms, and thus as an attempt to present themselves as the true heirs to Socrates (see Sedley, 'Chrysippus on Psychophysical Causality', pp. 313-14). For a detailed discussion of Stoic monistic psychology and the precise nature of its response to Platonic accounts of 'irrational' desires see Gill, 'Did Chrysippus understand Medea?'.

Do not say more to yourself than the first impressions (αἱ προηγούμεναι φαντασίαι) report. [...] abide always by the first impressions (τῶν πρώτων φαντασιῶν) and add nothing of your own from within.[61]

This passage can be taken to be Marcus' formulation of the Stoic concept of an adequate impression (φαντασία καταληπτική).[62] In Stoic epistemological discussions this term is used to refer to the criterion of truth.[63] It is defined as an impression that is caused by an object and stamped upon the mind in accordance with the nature of that object in such a way that it could not have been produced by a non-existing object.[64] It is an impression that is so clear, distinct, vivid, and obvious that it is its own guarantee of its accuracy and clarity.[65] This guaranteed accuracy may be understood in terms of its causal history – that is, in terms of the physical conditions of all of the elements involved in its production. If the sense organs, the object in question, and all the other variables are not obstructed or in an abnormal state, then the resulting impression will be adequate.[66]

Although at first glance this concept appears somewhat obscure, a number of ancient examples may help to clarify it.[67] Epictetus attempts to do just this by proposing that in the middle of the day one should attempt to hold the belief that it is in fact the middle of the night.[68] He suggests that one just cannot do this. He concludes that during the day the impression 'it is daytime' is so powerful that it must be an 'adequate impression'. One might say that impressions of this sort demand assent.[69] If, on the other hand, one found that one *could* hold the opposing impression then this would immediately call into question the validity of the initial impression, and this might lead one to withhold one's assent. For example, the impression that the number of stars in the night sky is even is no more self-evident or obviously correct than the impression that the number is odd.[70] Thus, in a manner similar to the

---

[61] Marcus Aurelius 8.49.
[62] For the translation of this term, along with references to further discussion see Chapter 3 § 4. To the alternatives listed there, note also that Crossley, pp. 20-22, proposes '*irresistible perception*'.
[63] See e.g. Sextus Empiricus *Adv. Math.* 7.227 (= *SVF* 2.56), Diogenes Laertius 7.54 (= *SVF* 2.105 = LS 40 A).
[64] See Cicero *Acad.* 2.18, 2.77, Sextus Empiricus *Adv. Math.* 7.248 (all *SVF* 1.59), Diogenes Laertius 7.45-46 (*SVF* 2.53), 7.50 (= *SVF* 2.60).
[65] See in particular Frede in *CHHP*, pp. 312-13.
[66] See Frede, 'Stoics and Skeptics on Clear and Distinct Impressions', pp. 157-58, and Sextus Empiricus *Adv. Math.* 7.424 (= *SVF* 2.68).
[67] The following paragraph repeats material already presented in Chapter 4 § 2 (c).
[68] See Epictetus *Diss.* 1.28.2-3; note also Sextus Empiricus *Adv. Math.* 7.242-43 (= *SVF* 2.65 = LS 39 G).
[69] See Sextus Empiricus *Adv. Math.* 7.257, Cicero *Acad.* 2.38, with Burnyeat, 'Can the Sceptic Live his Scepticism?', pp. 46-47 n. 38.
[70] See Epictetus *Diss.* 1.28.3, Sextus Empiricus *Adv. Math.* 7.243, 7.393, 8.147, 8.317.

Pyrrhonist sceptics, Epictetus proposes that in such a scenario one is forced to withhold one's assent and suspend judgement.[71]

According to the account of Stoic epistemology made by Sextus Empiricus, giving assent to an adequate impression is the first step away from human opinion (δόξα) and towards scientific knowledge (ἐπιστήμη) reserved for the sage.[72] This scientific knowledge has been defined as a systematic series of adequate impressions that are so secure that they are impregnable to rational persuasion (i.e. no longer open to debate).[73] This absolutely secure and organized knowledge of the world is, not surprisingly, reserved only for the sage. Adequate impressions, however, can be held by anyone and thus do not in themselves constitute such scientific knowledge.[74] They are a *necessary* condition but not a *sufficient* condition of such knowledge and are thus, as Sextus reports, half way between opinion and knowledge.

The scientific knowledge (ἐπιστήμη) held by the sage and grounded upon adequate impressions (φαντασίαι καταληπτικαί) will capture the world as it is in itself. As such, it will be an objective understanding of the world, an understanding free from value-judgements (ὑπολήψεις) about external objects, and an understanding free from anthropocentric concerns.[75] In short, it will be the perspective of physics.

However, Epictetus has only a limited interest in such strictly epistemological questions and is less concerned with the role that adequate impressions play as the criterion of truth.[76] He uses the term 'adequate impression' primarily to refer to those

---

[71] See Epictetus *Diss.* 1.28.2-3, with Burnyeat, 'Can the Sceptic Live his Scepticism?', p. 44. For other reports of the Stoic attitude towards suspension of judgement see Sextus Empiricus *Adv. Math.* 7.155 (= LS 41 C), Cicero *Acad.* 2.57 (= LS 40 I). For further discussion of the relationship between Pyrrhonian and Stoic suspension of judgement see Allen, 'The Skepticism of Sextus Empiricus', pp. 2596-97.

[72] See Sextus Empiricus *Adv. Math.* 7.151 (= *SVF* 2.90 = LS 41 C), also Cicero *Acad.* 1.42 (= *SVF* 1.60 = LS 41 B), with further discussion in Arthur, 'The Stoic Analysis of the Mind's Reactions to Presentations'.

[73] See Annas, 'Stoic Epistemology', p. 187. For secure scientific knowledge to arise they must be made impregnable to rational argument; see Arius Didymus 2.7.5l (2.73.16-74.3 WH = *SVF* 3.112 = LS 41 H), Cicero *Acad.* 1.41 (= *SVF* 1.60), with Ioppolo, 'Presentation and Assent', p. 436; LS, vol. 1, p. 257.

[74] Adequate impressions cannot constitute scientific knowledge themselves because they can be experienced by both the foolish and the wise, whereas scientific knowledge is restricted to the wise (see Sextus Empiricus *Adv. Math.* 7.152). However it should be stressed that the sage does not know more than the fool, rather he knows the same things in a more secure and systematic manner (see Kerferd, 'What Does the Wise Man Know?'). This difference may be seen as the same as that between the apprentice who knows an art or craft in theory and the master who has assimilated that theory and necessarily expresses his expertise in his actions. The expert does not know more than the apprentice but what he knows he knows 'better'.

[75] See Hadot, *The Inner Citadel*, p. 105.

[76] To be more precise, Epictetus expresses little interest in the details of epistemological theory in the *Dissertationes*. That is certainly very different from claiming that he had no interest in such matters at all. The image of Epictetus as a popular moralist with little interest in logic or physics may simply reflect the fact that our only sources are the *Dissertationes*, texts produced

impressions that present an external object free from any value-judgement, and it is only to impressions that are adequate (καταλητική) and thus not value-laden to which one should give one's assent.[77] These are the same as Marcus' first impressions (προηγούμεναι φαντασίαι), namely, those initial impressions that have not been supplemented with any value-judgement.

An important aspect of these adequate impressions is the rejection of the conception of the individual as an isolated entity detached from his surroundings. Epictetus suggests that this division is itself a judgement that does not derive from things themselves. In a discussion of what it might mean to live in accordance with nature he says the following:

> If you consider yourself as a detached being (ἀπόλυτον), it is natural (κατὰ φύσιν) for you to live to old age and be rich and healthy; but if you consider yourself as a man (ἄνθρωπον), and as part of the whole (μέρος ὅλου), it will be fitting, on account of that whole, that you should at one time be sick, at another take a voyage and be exposed to danger, sometimes be in want, and possibly – it may happen – die before your time.[78]

Epictetus suggests that if one considers oneself to be but one part of the cosmos as a whole then one will tend to approach any apparently bad things that may happen as simply a part of the broader cosmic process. In other words, one will come to realize that value-judgements of the form 'this is good' or 'this is bad' are actually shorthand for 'this is good *for me*' or 'this is bad *for me*'; that is, they implicitly presuppose a first person perspective. Epictetus' suggestion is that once such value-judgements have been rejected and replaced by adequate impressions then this first person perspective will also disappear,[79] replaced by a perspective embracing the whole of the cosmos in which nothing is in itself good or bad.[80]

The sage who regularly experiences adequate impressions will no longer experience the subject-centred world of everyday human existence surrounded by apparent stability. Instead, he will apprehend the cosmos as it is in itself, as a dynamic

---

within a specific literary genre primarily concerned with moral themes (see Souilhé (CUF), pp. xxii-xxx). One aspect of this quite common image of Epictetus is challenged in Barnes, *Logic and the Imperial Stoa*, pp. 24-125.

[77] See Epictetus *Diss.* 3.8.4.

[78] Epictetus *Diss.* 2.5.25 (trans. Hard); see also 2.5.13.

[79] This shares something in common with Pyrrhonism. The Pyrrhonist will also reject judgements concerning impressions and this will lead to a certain sort of detachment from any first person perspective. See Burnyeat, 'Can the Sceptic Live his Scepticism?', pp. 36-46. Of course, the Pyrrhonist will have no time for adequate impressions.

[80] This is clearly very different from the claim that from the cosmic perspective all things are good (see e.g. Long, *Hellenistic Philosophy*, p. 170). Such a position is also often attributed to Marcus, yet it is far from evident that he held this. His statement at 2.17 that according to nature nothing is bad in itself (οὐδὲν δὲ κακὸν κατὰ φύσιν) does not imply that everything is good. Note also his frequent expressions of agnosticism to the question 'providence or atoms?' (6.24, 7.32, 9.28, 9.39, 10.6, 12.14, 12.24), perhaps deriving from Epictetus (see Epictetus fr. 1 Schenkl *apud* Stobaeus 2.1.31 = 2.13.5-14.8 WH).

system of flows of matter and energy in a continual process of self-transformation. It is with this physical or scientific perspective in mind that Marcus proposes to re-describe everything usually held of value. From this new perspective he describes a human being as merely a mass of water, dust, bones, and stench; Europe as but a mound of earth in one corner of a vast ocean; death as merely a reorganization of a collection of material elements; and sexual intercourse as nothing more than a convulsive expulsion of mucus.[81]

(d) Epistemological Exercises

It is this theory of the analysis of impressions and judgements made by Epictetus that forms the backdrop to the *Meditations*. For Marcus the 'point of view of the cosmos' is just like this, namely a perspective free from the first person perspective and its value-judgements (ὑπολήψεις). It is one that rejects human opinion (δόξα) and approaches a purely physical or scientific perspective (ἐπιστήμη), an experience of things as they are in themselves, as they are according to nature. Marcus writes,

> Salvation in life depends on seeing everything in its entirety and its reality, in its matter (τὸ ὑλικόν), and in its cause (τὸ αἰτιῶδες).[82]

The Stoic ideal of living in accordance with nature (ὁμολογουμένως τῇ φύσει ζῆν) involves experiencing the world in precisely this way. As such, the Stoic philosophical project – despite its apparently more ethical orientation especially in later authors such as Epictetus and Marcus Aurelius – shares much in common with the Presocratic natural philosophers and their attempts to offer a naturalistic account of the cosmos. As we have already seen, Marcus' conception of the cosmos shares much in common with Heraclitus' conception of a complex dynamic physical system in which states of conflict generate harmony and apparent stability. For Marcus, just as for Heraclitus, a perspective of the cosmos in these terms is one in which value-judgements about external objects are avoided.[83] The 'point of view of the cosmos' outlined by Marcus and constituted by scientific adequate impressions is nothing other than the perspective of the Heraclitean λόγος, namely, a single rational account of a dynamic cosmos beyond value-judgements and limited first person perspectives.

---

[81] See Marcus Aurelius 9.36, 6.36, 2.17, & 6.13 respectively. See also 4.48 where life is described as a brief journey from mucus to ashes. As I have already noted, such imagery forms a part of Marcus' spiritual exercises and has nothing to do with drug abuse. Nor should it be read as an expression of personal melancholy or as being conducive to melancholy, *pace* Arnold, *Roman Stoicism*, pp. 124-26; Birley, *Marcus Aurelius*, p. 222. Rather, it is part of a properly philosophical perspective inspired by the Heraclitean doctrine of continual flux.

[82] Marcus Aurelius 12.29 (trans. Haines modified); see also 12.10, 12.18.

[83] See e.g. Heraclitus fr. 61 DK *apud* Hippolytus *Refutatio* 9.10 (243.14-16 Wendland) where Heraclitus can be seen to draw attention to the dependence of value-judgements upon limited perspectives (seawater is both good and bad depending upon whether one is a fish or a human). See also Aristotle *Top.* 159b30, *Phys.* 185b19-25.

It should thus be clear that the 'point of view of the cosmos' is very different from a transcendent perspective. As such, it can be contrasted with the theme of a 'view from above' that appears throughout ancient philosophy and literature, and is particularly associated with Platonism.[84] Within this Platonic tradition, the 'view from above' is the view of a soul that is detached from the body, either before birth or after death.[85] It thus involves a dualist conception of the individual and the possibility of a privileged transcendent perspective. In contrast to this, the Stoic 'point of view of the cosmos' affirms an immanent perspective of nature, a perspective that rejects the limited perspective of the human individual and the value-judgements upon which it is based. The Stoic cosmic perspective is thus not a 'view from above'.[86] It is not a transcendent perspective but rather an immanent perspective, or, to be more precise, an immanent non-individualistic perspective.[87]

The *Meditations* of Marcus Aurelius might best be understood as a collection of spiritual exercises directed towards the cultivation of this immanent non-individualistic perspective. As we have seen, the first step towards this perspective is the correct analysis of one's impressions. For both Epictetus and Marcus Aurelius, the analysis of impressions and the study of epistemology which fall under the heading of 'logic' are vital parts of their practical philosophical project. Although both Epictetus and Marcus Aurelius are often said to neglect physics and logic in favour of a diluted and popular ethics, we can in fact see that the exercises of Marcus Aurelius, building upon his reading of Epictetus, involve all three aspects of philosophy.[88] Rather than neglecting physics or logic it might be more accurate to say that these later Stoics value these aspects of philosophy to such an extent that they are not content merely to discuss these subjects but are determined to put what they have learned from them into practice. In order to do this, spiritual exercises such as the ones outlined here are essential.

---

[84] *Pace* Rutherford, *The Meditations of Marcus Aurelius*, pp. 155-61. For more on this theme in ancient philosophy see Hadot, *Philosophy as a Way of Life*, pp. 238-50; *Qu'est-ce que la philosophie antique?*, pp. 309-22.

[85] See e.g. Plato *Phaedrus* 246b-c.

[86] As Rutherford notes, *The Meditations of Marcus Aurelius*, pp. 155-57, Marcus quotes *Resp.* 486a in 7.35 and alludes to *Theaet.* 174d in 10.23. However, for Marcus, Heraclitus is by far the more important influence.

[87] This may seem surprising insofar as the analysis of impressions has also been cited as an important moment in the development of the modern concept of the self; see e.g. Long, 'Representation and the Self in Stoicism', p. 103; Kahn, 'Discovering the Will', p. 253.

[88] *Pace* Newman, '*Cotidie meditare*', p. 1474 n. 1; Annas, *The Morality of Happiness*, p. 160; Barnes, *Logic and the Imperial Stoa*, p. 34 n. 47. In particular, Newman refers to the use of the medical metaphor in later Stoic authors as an indication of this change, apparently unaware of its earlier use by Chrysippus and its origins with Socrates. The claim that later Stoics focused exclusively on ethics has recently been repeated by Morford (see *The Roman Philosophers*, p. 1). However, for a survey of Stoic physics in this period see Todd, 'The Stoics and their Cosmology in the First and Second Centuries AD', who also draws attention to the physical treatise of Cleomedes.

3. Summary

In this chapter I have attempted to do two things. The first task was to consider the nature of the *Meditations* as a philosophical text and to show some examples of the written spiritual exercises contained within it. As we have seen, the *Meditations* are a personal notebook containing written exercises that reflect upon a number of philosophical themes. The very act of writing these reflections can be seen to be a vital part of the process of digesting philosophical principles and habituating one's character to philosophical doctrines.

The second task was to develop our understanding of the relationship between λόγος and ἄσκησις further by examining the relationship between Marcus' clearly non-technical literary reflections and the details of Stoic epistemological theory. As we have seen, Marcus' exercises concerning impressions and judgements are an attempt to put into practice that theory. The *Meditations* may thus be seen as an example of the way in which the study of Chrysippus' logical theory *could* in fact contribute the transformation of one's way of life.[89]

In the light of this it may be possible to re-assess the status of the *Meditations* as a philosophical text. It has become commonplace to deny the *Meditations* the status of being a serious philosophical text, especially when placed alongside the works of Aristotle or the sober commentaries of Alexander of Aphrodisias.[90] Yet for philosophy conceived as a τέχνη, both philosophical theory (λόγος) and exercise (ἄσκησις) will be essential. As such, texts relevant to each of these components of philosophy will also be essential. For example, the philosophical apprentice attending the class of Epictetus will first have to complete his preliminary education in philosophy by studying theories and arguments (λόγοι), for which he will need to study theoretical treatises such as those of Chrysippus or Hierocles. Once he has mastered these, he will then move on to the more difficult task of translating his newly acquired understanding into his actions (ἔργα) by habituating his character (ἦθος). In order to complete this second stage of his philosophical education, he will require a very different type of text. He may use a guide to this process of habituation in the form of a text like Epictetus' *Handbook* (if it existed at the time). He may also write himself insofar as the act of writing may itself help him to digest the theories already studied in the classroom. If he does, these written reflections may well take a form similar to that of the *Meditations*.

It is possible, then, to distinguish between two types of philosophical text corresponding to the two components of philosophy conceived as a τέχνη. First come theoretical treatises, then texts concerned with exercises. Yet it would be a mistake to

---

[89] *Pace* Williams, 'Do Not Disturb', p. 26, who, as we have seen in the Introduction, rejected outright the idea that the logical works of Chrysippus could make any difference to an individual's behaviour. Here, however, I assume the broader conception of logic held by the Stoics which, as I noted in the previous chapter, includes not only dialectic but also rhetoric and epistemology (see Barnes in *CHHP*, pp. 65-67).

[90] This image of the *Meditations* has now been challenged by Hadot in *The Inner Citadel*. However, at present this work remains very much the exception to the rule.

conceive of the latter as simply a series of maxims, rules, or moral catchphrases. Rather, they form a compact distillation of Stoic philosophy designed to remind the student in a short digestible form of the complex theory that he has already studied in detail.[91] Although a text like the *Meditations* may not stand up to a close comparison with one of Aristotle's philosophical treatises, within the context of the Stoic conception of philosophy as a τέχνη requiring both philosophical λόγος and ἄσκησις, it can nevertheless be seen to be a serious philosophical work performing an essential function.

By examining the *Meditations* we have been able to see some specific examples of written spiritual exercises and have seen how these primarily non-technical passages relate to the more complex details of Stoic epistemological theory. Writing passages such as these in order to assimilate and digest complex philosophical theories is one form that the second stage of philosophical education may take. The existence of such forms of philosophical writing highlights the fact that for Stoics such as Epictetus and Marcus Aurelius mastery of philosophical arguments was not on its own enough. Mastery of philosophy in λόγοι must be supplemented with mastery of philosophy in ἔργα.

---

[91] See e.g. the reference to short and elemental axioms in Marcus Aurelius 4.3.1.

Conclusion

In the Introduction I raised the question concerning how one might conceive the relationship between an individual's philosophy and their way of life. For modern philosophers such as Hegel and Williams the suggestion that there is such a relationship merely indicates a weakness in the philosophical position in question. For them, philosophy should be understood as an abstract system or as a process of intellectual analysis. Although such philosophers might acknowledge that one's philosophy may have *some* impact upon one's way of life, for them this is not essential to philosophy but rather merely a consequence.

In contrast to this I suggested that in order to engage in a more constructive understanding of this relationship one would need a conception of philosophy in which philosophical ideas would be *primarily* expressed in one's way of life. In particular, I noted a number of other modern philosophers, including Nietzsche and Foucault, who can be seen to gesture towards the idea of philosophy as an activity primarily expressed in one's actions and concerned with turning one's life into a work of art. It was in order to develop this idea that I returned to ancient discussions concerning the idea that philosophy should be conceived as an art concerned with one's life.

1. Towards a Technical Conception of Philosophy

In the light of my discussion of Socratic and Stoic ideas of an art concerned with one's way of life (τέχνη περὶ τὸν βίον), it is now possible to offer a summary sketch of a conception of philosophy in which philosophical ideas are primarily expressed in actions and which consequently might form the basis for a more productive understanding of the relationship between philosophy and biography. I shall call this 'the technical conception of philosophy', understanding 'technical' in its etymological sense. However, it is important at the outset to draw attention to a subtle but important distinction between the Socratic and Stoic positions.

We have seen that, for Socrates, philosophy is an art (τέχνη) that is directed towards the *cultivation* of excellence (ἀρετή) and should *not* be identified with excellence (ἀρετή) itself. For him, philosophy conceived as an art *aspires* to excellence (ἀρετή) and wisdom (σοφία), and thus Socrates understands 'philosophy' (φιλοσοφία) in its etymological sense. With the Stoics, the matter is not so clear. According to Zeno's definition, any art (τέχνη) will be a form of secure knowledge (ἐπιστήμη). Consequently the art of living will be a form of secure knowledge (ἐπιστήμη) identifiable with wisdom (σοφία) and thus reserved for the sage. For the Stoics, then, philosophy understood in its etymological sense cannot be an art or expertise (τέχνη) but rather that which desires or cultivates such expertise. Yet, as we have seen, a number of Stoics including Epictetus appear to have understood the idea of an art of living as Socrates did, namely, as something synonymous with philosophy in its etymological sense.

These two accounts may be reconciled by turning to an example from some other art or craft. In the case of shoemaking, for instance, the beginning apprentice clearly does not possess expert knowledge yet one would still say that he is engaged in the art of shoemaking during his apprenticeship. The lowest trainee and the master craftsman are both engaged in the same activity even if only the latter can claim expertise in that activity. In this sense, both the philosophical apprentice and the Stoic sage may be said to be engaged in the art of living. In what follows I shall focus upon the art of living understood from the perspective of the apprentice.

By way of summary, then, in the technical conception of philosophy, philosophy is conceived as an art (τέχνη) directed towards the cultivation of an ideal disposition of the soul (διάθεσις τῆς ψυχῆς), a disposition that may be called excellence (ἀρετή) or wisdom (σοφία). Thus one might say that the subject matter (ὕλη) of this art is one's soul (ψυχή) and its goal (τέλος) is to transform or to take care of one's soul (ψυχή). The product (ἔργον) will be the transformed disposition of the soul (διάθεσις τῆς ψυχῆς), namely excellence (ἀρετή) or wisdom (σοφία). This transformed disposition will, insofar as it constitutes an internal cause, necessarily impact upon an individual's behaviour, expressing itself in their actions. Alternatively, one might say that this art (τέχνη) is concerned with one's life (βίος), that *this* is its subject matter (ὕλη), and that its goal (τέλος) is to transform one's life (βίος). Thus one might say that the product (ἔργον) of this art will be the actions (ἔργα) that constitute one's life, highlighting its status as a performative art (πρακτική τέχνη) in which the performance itself is the product. This product conceived as an activity may be characterized variously as a good flow of life (εὔροια βίου), as living well (εὖ ζῆν), and as well-being or happiness (εὐδαιμονία).[1] Ultimately not much hinges on this restatement for, as we have seen, both Socrates and the Stoics often use ψυχή and βίος interchangeably in their accounts, highlighting the close connection between these terms.[2]

A further characteristic worth underlining is the personal nature of philosophy conceived in this way. For Socrates, the task of taking care of oneself is fundamentally a private project. Although he may exhort others to take care of themselves, nevertheless it is something that they must do for themselves.[3] This

---

[1] For the formulations εὔροια βίου (attributed to Zeno) and εὖ ζῆν see Arius Didymus 2.7.6e (2.77.16-78.6 WH = *SVF* 1.184, 3.16). Aristotle famously characterized εὐδαιμονία as an activity (see e.g. *Eth. Nic.* 1176a30-1176b9), with which the Stoics would agree. For further discussion see Long, 'Stoic Eudaimonism', p. 82.

[2] This close connection may be emphasized by noting two points. The first that the disposition of one's soul (διάθεσις τῆς ψυχῆς) – one's character (ἦθος) – is the source of one's habitual way of behaving (ἔθος) and thus one's actions (ἔργα). The second is that ψυχή should be understood not in the limited sense of 'mind' but rather as 'that by virtue of which we are alive' (see Urmson, *The Greek Philosophical Vocabulary*, pp. 144-45).

[3] See Chapter 2 §§ 1-3 above.

becomes even clearer in Chrysippus' cylinder analogy which suggests that the only proper object of one's concern is the internal cause that is one's character.[4] Cicero also makes clear that, according to Chrysippus, the philosopher conceived as a doctor for the soul can only treat himself.[5] As Epictetus will put it later, the only proper objects of one's concern are those things that are in our power or 'up to us' (ἐφ᾽ ἡμῖν), namely desire, impulse, and judgement.[6] The perfection of these mental activities constitutes human excellence (ἀρετή), the only object to which the Stoics assign a positive value.[7] This somewhat self-centred attitude reflects the foundational role played by the theory of οἰκείωσις in Stoicism.[8] In the light of this one might say that the Socratic-Stoic art of living is *ethical* in the sense that it is concerned with one's character (ἦθος) which, in turn, determines one's habits (ἔθος).[9] However, it is not *moral* in the modern sense of offering a series of regulations concerning how one should act or what one should do, and it is certainly not concerned with specifying how others should act.[10] The art of living may form the basis for an *ethics* but not for a *morality*.[11]

* * *

---

[4] See Chapter 3 § 7 above.

[5] See Chapter 3 § 3 (a) above.

[6] See Chapter 6 § 2 (a) above and, in particular, Epictetus *Diss.* 1.15.1-5, partially quoted in the Introduction and in Chapter 3 § 1.

[7] On this see Kidd, 'Stoic Intermediates and the End for Man'.

[8] See Chapter 3 § 1 above.

[9] Here I use *ethics* in the sense of ἠθικός, that which is concerned with one's character (see Urmson, *The Greek Philosophical Vocabulary*, p. 62). Of course, *moralis* derives from Cicero's translation of ἦθος (see *Fat.* 1) and thus shares the same origin.

[10] Stoic 'eudaimonism' does not involve an 'ought' (*pace* e.g. Annas, *The Morality of Happiness*; Becker, *A New Stoicism*). It takes as its point of departure the assumption that everyone's ultimate desire is for happiness (εὐδαιμονία) – quite different from the claim that everyone *ought* to desire εὐδαιμονία – and then says 'if you want this, do *x*'. However, it cannot claim that one ought to do that *x*. Rather, it suggests that if one desires εὐδαιμονία then Stoicism offers the best method for its cultivation. Whether it does or not will be a question that can be settled by experimentation. Other 'eudaimonist' schools will make similar claims and the task of the philosophical student who does desire εὐδαιμονία will be to assess the relative merits of the competing methods on offer. However, none of the ancient schools appear to have tried to convince people that they *should* desire εὐδαιμονία. Two authors who have drawn attention to the non-moral nature of Stoicism are Schopenhauer (*The World as Will and Representation*, vol. 1, p. 86) and Foucault ('On the Genealogy of Ethics'; *Essential Works*, vol. 1, p. 254). Note also the excellent discussion in Vander Waerdt, 'Zeno's *Republic* and the Origins of Natural Law', pp. 281-89.

[11] This distinction between *ethics* and *morality* can be found in a number of philosophers (although often under different terms) but perhaps the two clearest expositions can be found in Foucault, *The Use of Pleasure*, pp. 25-32 (*L'usage des plaisirs*, pp. 36-45), and Deleuze, *Spinoza: Practical Philosophy*, pp. 17-29 (*Spinoza: Philosophie pratique*, pp. 27-43).

As we have seen, central to the conception of philosophy as an art are the roles played by the two components of λόγος and ἄσκησις. In the technical conception of philosophy, the study of philosophical arguments, theories, and doctrines (λόγοι, θεωρήματα, δόγματα) is merely the first part of a philosophical education. Once these have been mastered there will then be a period a practical training (ἄσκησις) in which the apprentice will attempt to digest this material in order to produce the actions or product (ἔργον) appropriate to their art.[12]

Although the practitioner of the art of living will, like other artists and craftsmen, be able to give a rational account (λόγος) of what it is that he is doing, it must be stressed that, as with other arts, this always remains secondary. Although the expert shoemaker can, if cross-examined, give an account (λόγος) of the principles underpinning what he is doing, his primary job is to make shoes. The same applies to the philosopher whose primary job – according to the technical conception of philosophy – is to produce philosophical actions (ἔργα), to follow a philosophical way of life (βίος). Like the shoemaker, the philosopher can, if cross-examined, give an account (λόγος) of the principles underpinning that way of life. However, that account will always remain secondary.

It has been suggested that in the Hellenistic schools following a philosophical way of life (βίος) often involved simply living according to principles (λόγοι) already developed within the philosophical school to which one was drawn and thus, in general, did not involve any independent thought of one's own.[13] I do not want to enter into a discussion of the question of whether this is a fair portrait of Hellenistic philosophical practice here. Rather, I simply note that the technical conception of philosophy in no way precludes independent or original thought. It is perfectly possible to conceive a philosophical student who studies philosophical arguments and doctrines with a view not simply to repeat the opinions of others but rather to develop his own system of philosophical doctrines based upon his own arguments.[14] What the technical conception of philosophy proposes is that any set of philosophical doctrines is not itself the final product (ἔργον) of philosophy. Those doctrines must next be digested so that they transform the soul (ψυχή) and are expressed in one's actions (ἔργα). It is these actions (ἔργα) made according to philosophical principles (κατὰ λόγον) that form the final product (ἔργον) of philosophy conceived as a performative art (πρακτική τέχνη).

---

[12] As Sorabji notes, it would be a mistake to present this as first the creation of a theory in abstract followed by the application of that theory in a somewhat automatic way (see 'Is Stoic Philosophy Helpful as Psychotherapy?', p. 209). Instead, these two elements are both constitutive of philosophy conceived as a τέχνη which is at once both theoretical and practical. The division into these two stages, as with the threefold division of philosophical discourse, is primarily an educational device rather than a substantive claim concerning the nature of philosophy.

[13] See Sedley, 'Philosophical Allegiance in the Greco-Roman World'.

[14] This is of course precisely what 'heterodox' Stoics such as Aristo or Posidonius did with respect to those parts of Stoic philosophy that they felt were untenable.

2. Two Conceptions of Philosophical Knowledge

This technical conception of philosophy conceives philosophical knowledge (ἐπιστήμη) as technical knowledge, its paradigm being the kind of knowledge found in an art or craft (τέχνη). This is clearly very different from an account of philosophy in which knowledge (ἐπιστήμη) is conceived as rational explanation or intellectual analysis (λόγος). It is particularly important to be precise here. In attempts to draw a distinction between philosophy primarily concerned with theoretical knowledge and philosophy primarily concerned with practical wisdom, an implicitly Aristotelian distinction is sometimes drawn between ἐπιστήμη and φρόνησις.[15] While the former is said to focus upon a rational understanding of the world, the latter is said to focus upon how one should act.

For the Stoics, there is no conceptual distinction between knowledge (ἐπιστήμη) and wisdom (φρόνησις, σοφία). Presenting philosophy as something concerned with one's life does not involve a rejection or devaluation of theoretical or scientific knowledge (ἐπιστήμη) but rather a different conception of such knowledge. The distinction, then, is not between knowledge (ἐπιστήμη) and wisdom (φρόνησις, σοφία) but rather between two distinct conceptions of knowledge (ἐπιστήμη). The first conceives knowledge as rational understanding primarily expressed in words; as λόγος. The second conceives knowledge as technical knowledge analogous to the expert knowledge of a craftsman; as τέχνη. As we have already seen, the second of these conceptions does not reject the first but rather incorporates it as one of its essential components, supplementing it with training or exercise (ἄσκησις) that will translate it into actions (ἔργα).

3. Philosophy and Biography

In the light of this summary, we are now in a position to return to the question concerning the relationship between philosophy and biography. With the technical conception of philosophy, philosophical ideas or doctrines are *primarily* expressed in one's behaviour. Consequently it forms an ideal foundation from which one might explore the idea that a philosopher's doctrines will be expressed in his life. Moreover, it also gives a new philosophical significance to a biographical account of a philosopher's life, for if, according to this conception, philosophy is primarily expressed in actions rather than words, then the best way in which to uncover an individual's philosophical position will be by an examination of their life. It will, in the words of Nietzsche, enable one to examine a philosopher through what he did rather than what he said, let alone what he wrote.[16]

The significance assigned to biographical information by the technical conception of philosophy is reflected, as we have seen, in the importance often attached to such

---

[15] See e.g. Critchley, *Continental Philosophy*, pp. 1-11.
[16] See Nietzsche, *Schopenhauer as Educator* § 3 (*KGW* III 1, 346; Complete Works 2, 183-84), quoted in the Introduction.

material in antiquity. A number of ancient philosophical schools attached considerable significance to biographical and anecdotal literature, and it was often thought essential to study the life of a philosopher before commencing the study of his ideas. The technical conception of philosophy offers a framework within which one might comprehend the importance attached to such literature. If philosophy conceived as an art is primarily concerned with transforming one's life (βίος) then it should not be surprising that the clearest written expression of an individual's philosophy may well be a written account of his or her life.

4. Three Different Types of Philosophical Text

One can see, then, that with the technical conception of philosophy a new philosophical significance may be attached to a written biography. In general, modern philosophical texts tend to conform to a single model which may be seen as a variation upon the ancient philosophical treatise exemplified by the surviving works of Aristotle. For some, this type of text may be supplemented with philosophical commentaries dealing with existing texts and this may be seen as a variation upon another model already present in antiquity in the works of commentators such as Alexander of Aphrodisias.

With the technical conception of philosophy, the matter is complicated somewhat. Alongside such treatises and commentaries, not only do biographies gain a new philosophical significance but also texts such as Epictetus' *Handbook* and Marcus Aurelius' *Meditations*. As we have seen, these latter texts may be characterized as texts concerned with spiritual exercises.[17] With the technical conception of philosophy, then, there are a three main types of philosophical text:

1. Literature concerned with actions (ἔργα):
    biographical literature, anecdotal material, such Xenophon's *Memorabilia* or the *Lives* of Diogenes Laertius

2. Literature concerned with arguments and doctrines (λόγοι):
    (a) theoretical treatises such as those by Aristotle, Chrysippus, or Hierocles
    (b) commentaries such as those by Alexander of Aphrodisias or Simplicius

---

[17] A number of other works have been proposed as further examples of texts devoted to spiritual exercises. These include Seneca's *Epistulae* (by Nussbaum, *The Therapy of Desire*, p. 337), Ps.-Seneca's *De Remediis Fortuitorum* (by Newman, '*Cotidie meditare*', p. 1477), Simplicius' *In Ench.* (by I. Hadot, *Le problème du néoplatonisme alexandrin*, pp. 164-65), Plato's dialogues (by P. Hadot, *Philosophy as a Way of Life*, p. 91), and Sextus Empiricus' *Pyrr. Hyp.* (by Hankinson, *The Sceptics*, pp. 305-06). Another example would be Epicurus' *Epistulae*.

3. Literature concerned with spiritual exercises (ἀσκήσεις):
   (a) texts for guiding exercises such as Epictetus' *Handbook*
   (b) texts written as exercises such as Marcus Aurelius' *Meditations*

As we have seen in Chapter 1, in later antiquity it was often suggested that philosophical education should begin with the study of a philosopher's life (βίος). Then, following Epictetus' account of philosophical education outlined in Chapter 5, the student should next study arguments and doctrines (λόγοι) before finally moving on to engage in exercises (ἀσκήσεις) designed to digest those arguments and doctrines. The final goal is of course to transform one's life into one similar to those studied at the very outset. We have, then, three main types of philosophical literature corresponding to three distinct stages in a plan for a philosophical education.

Thus the technical conception of philosophy enables one to reassess what texts may and may not be described as philosophical. As well as enabling one to reassess the philosophical significance of biographical literature, it also enables one to reassess the status of texts such as the *Handbook* of Epictetus or the *Meditations* of Marcus Aurelius. As we have seen, these texts form a compact distillation of Stoic philosophy designed to aid the student in the digestion of complex philosophical doctrines that he has already studied in detail. They function as an aide-mémoire for the student who, for instance, understands fully the principles involved in the Stoic analysis of impressions and judgements, but has not yet managed to train himself fully to assent only to adequate impressions. When approached within the context of the technical conception of philosophy, texts such as these gain a greater philosophical significance.

5. The Persistence of the Technical Conception of Philosophy

Despite the way in which the technical conception of philosophy may enable one to understand better the relationship between philosophy and biography, and the way in which it may enable one to reconsider one's assumptions concerning what constitutes a philosophical text, it has been objected that it would be pointless to attempt to revive this conception of philosophy. In particular, it has been suggested that such a conception of philosophy remains tied to the historical and cultural context in which it was produced and that the distance between that context and our own is too great.[18] Moreover, it has also been suggested that it would be idle to engage in a debate concerning the nature and function of philosophy, that philosophy as it is conceived today is neither better nor worse than it was in antiquity, just different.[19] Consequently it would be foolish to suggest that an ancient conception of philosophy could directly inform contemporary philosophical practice.

What judgements such as these fail to acknowledge is that throughout the history of Western philosophy thinkers have repeatedly returned to antiquity for inspiration

---

[18] See e.g. Williams, 'Do Not Disturb', p. 26.
[19] See e.g. Nehamas, *The Art of Living*, pp. 1-4.

and have drawn upon ancient philosophical resources to help them deal with contemporary philosophical problems and to rethink the nature of what it is that they are doing.[20] Throughout the Middle Ages, for instance, philosophers such as Peter Abelard and John of Salisbury drew upon the readily available Latin works of Cicero and Seneca not only for philosophical ideas but also for an understanding of the nature and function of philosophy as such.[21] In the Renaissance the same happened, as can be seen in a work such as Petrarch's *On the Remedies of Both Kinds of Fortune*.[22] In the sixteenth century the same occurred as part of the explicit attempt to create a 'Neostoicism' by Justus Lipsius.[23] More recently, as I have already noted in the Introduction, Nietzsche developed his own version of this conception of philosophy, drawing upon his philological education in ancient philosophy. Under the influence of Nietzsche, Foucault can also be seen to turn to this technical conception of philosophy.[24] Although one might argue that it would be a mistake to take Foucault's comments on ancient philosophy in his *A History of Sexuality* out of their genealogical context, nevertheless in a number of shorter pieces and interviews Foucault makes it clear that he had a strong personal interest in what he calls ancient technologies of the self (*technologies de soi*) and thought that they could have a contemporary relevance.[25] Although he is careful – and surely correct – to emphasize that it would be a mistake to present this ancient conception of philosophy as some

---

[20] See the survey in Domański, *La philosophie, théorie ou manière de vivre?*.

[21] For the influence of Cicero and Seneca in the Middle Ages see Spanneut, *Permanence du Stoïcisme*, pp. 190-202; Reynolds, *The Medieval Tradition of Seneca's Letters*, pp. 81-124; also Verbeke, *The Presence of Stoicism in Medieval Thought*. For Abelard see his *Dialogus inter Philosophum, Iudaeum et Christianum* (*PL* 178.1611-84, plus the recent edition by Marenbon & Orlandi under the title *Collationes*), esp. § 2 (*PL* 178.1613a), § 68 (*PL* 178.1637a-b). For John of Salisbury – Abelard's pupil in Paris – see his *Policraticus* (*PL* 199.379-822; translation by Nederman), esp. 7.8 (*PL* 199.651-53), 7.11 (*PL* 199.661).

[22] See Petrarch *De remediis utriusque fortunae* (*Opera*, vol. 1, pp. 1-254; no modern critical edition exists, extracts in *Prose*, pp. 606-45; translation by Rawski), esp. the 'Praefatio' (*Opera*, vol. 1, p. 2; Rawski, vol. 1, p. 4). In this text Petrarch draws upon Cicero's account of Stoic theories concerning the emotions and borrows his title from Ps.-Seneca's *De Remediis Fortuitorum*. For further discussion see Panizza, 'Stoic Psychotherapy in the Middle Ages and Renaissance'.

[23] See Lipsius *De Constantia* (1584, 3rd edition 1586; translation by Stradling, edited by Kirk), esp. the 'Ad Lectorem' (Kirk, p. 206), 1.10 (Kirk, p. 92). Lipsius was principally influenced by Seneca whose works he edited in 1605 and from whom he borrowed the title *De Constantia* (from Seneca's *De Constantia Sapientis*). For further discussion see Lagrée, *Juste Lipse et la restauration du stoïcisme*; Morford, *Stoics and Neostoics*, pp. 160-68; Zanta, *La renaissance du stoïcisme au XVIe siècle*, pp. 151-331; Spanneut, *Permanence du Stoïcisme*, pp. 238-55; Copenhaver & Schmitt, *Renaissance Philosophy*, pp. 260-69. Note also Moreau, ed., *Le stoïcisme au XVIe et au XVIIe siècle*.

[24] See Chapter 5 § 2 (b) above.

[25] See e.g. Foucault, 'On the Genealogy of Ethics', in *Dits et écrits*, vol. 4, pp. 392, 617; *Essential Works*, vol. 1, p. 261, and quoted in the Introduction. Note also the discussion in 'L'éthique du souci de soi comme pratique de la liberté', in *Dits et écrits*, vol. 4, pp. 708-29; *Essential Works*, vol. 1, pp. 281-301.

form of originary yet tragically forgotten conception of what philosophy truly is, Foucault is equally clear that he considers that a contemporary engagement with ancient ideas concerning the nature and function of philosophy may well be productive, so long as one remembers that the product of this encounter will itself be something contemporary.[26]

With so many reappropriations of the technical conception of philosophy in so many different historical periods, it becomes almost meaningless to characterize this conception of philosophy as 'ancient'. Like so many other things with their origins in antiquity, this conception of philosophy has become an ever present – if recently neglected – part of the Western philosophical tradition.[27] As I stressed in the Introduction, it would be a mistake to conceive the question concerning the different conceptions of philosophy outlined there as an ancient–modern dichotomy. As we have seen, in antiquity the distinction between philosophy as λόγος and philosophy as τέχνη can be seen in the respective conceptions held by Aristotle and Socrates, while more recently it can be seen with Hegel and Nietzsche.[28] What we have, then, are two alternative conceptions of philosophy, both present in antiquity and both present today. It has not been my intention to dismiss or devalue philosophy conceived as a purely theoretical enterprise, but rather to argue that philosophy has and can be conceived as something broader than just theory. To be sure, neither conception can claim superiority over the other on either originary or evolutionary grounds. Yet both exist and the aim of this study has been to contribute to the debate surrounding the nature and function of philosophy by attempting to offer a detailed account of the precise nature of philosophy conceived as a τέχνη περὶ τὸν βίον.

---

[26] See e.g. 'L'éthique du souci de soi comme pratique de la liberté' (*Dits et écrits*, vol. 4, p. 723; *Essential Works*, vol. 1, pp. 294-95), where to the question whether the classical idea of care of the self should be updated Foucault replies, 'Absolutely, but I would certainly not do so just to say, "We have unfortunately forgotten about the care of the self; so here, here it is, the key to everything". Nothing is more foreign to me than the idea that, at a certain moment, philosophy went astray and forgot something, that somewhere in its history there is a principle, a foundation that must be rediscovered. I feel that all such forms of analysis, whether they take a radical form and claim that philosophy has from the outset been a forgetting, or whether they take a much more historical viewpoint and say, "Such and such a philosopher forgot something" – neither of these approaches is particularly interesting or useful. Which does not mean that contact with such and such a philosopher may not produce something, but it must be emphasized that it would be something new'.

[27] As Nussbuam notes (*The Therapy of Desire*, p. 4), this conception of philosophy, although influential throughout the Middle Ages and Renaissance, suffered neglect in the twentieth century.

[28] Or more recently still, in the debate between Williams and Sorabji, noted in the Introduction.

Additional Notes

Additional Note 1 (on Socrates)

The problem of determining to what extent Plato's literary character 'Socrates' represents the historical Socrates is of course very complex and may well be insoluble. Putting to one side Plato's portrait of Socrates' personal characteristics, the problem may be simplified to that of determining to what extent Plato's literary character presents the philosophical views of the historical Socrates and to what extent he presents the views of Plato himself. Numerous approaches to this problem exist and it may be helpful to outline the more prominent ones very briefly (and thus inevitably somewhat crudely):

1. Everything said by Plato's character may be attributed to the historical Socrates (e.g. Burnet, *Greek Philosophy*; Taylor, *Socrates*), with the result that everything that has traditionally been called 'Platonic philosophy' is held to be 'Socratic', including the theory of Forms.
2. Plato's dialogues may be arranged on stylistic grounds into a chronological order of composition and in the earlier dialogues a distinct set of philosophical opinions can be found which reflects the ideas of the historical Socrates (e.g. Vlastos, 'Socrates'; *Socrates: Ironist and Moral Philosopher*).
3. Wherever an idea presented by Plato's character is corroborated by both Xenophon and Aristotle then that idea may be attributed to the historical Socrates (e.g. Zeller, *Socrates and the Socratic Schools*; Guthrie, *History*, vol. 3; Gulley, *The Philosophy of Socrates*).
4. The account of Socrates in Plato's *Apology* has a unique status insofar as it reports a public event and ideas presented by Plato's characters in the dialogues may only be taken to be 'Socratic' if they can also be found in the *Apology* (e.g. Kahn, *Plato and the Socratic Dialogue*).

It is clearly not possible to assess each of these approaches here or to offer a full justification for my own approach. Broadly speaking I follow the last of the approaches outlined above, taking Plato's *Apology* as my point of departure for the historical Socrates. A number of commentators have noted that, of all Plato's works, the only one that claims to report a public event is the *Apology* (see Burnet, *Plato's Euthyphro, Apology of Socrates, and Crito*, pp. 63-64; Ross, 'The Problem of Socrates', p. 36; Vlastos, 'The Paradox of Socrates', pp. 3-4; Kahn, *Plato and the Socratic Dialogue*, pp. 88-95). It has been suggested that, although still a literary re-creation, this text – and this text alone – would have been produced under certain external constraints if it were to appear convincing to Plato's contemporaries, many of whom would have been at the trial themselves or have heard first hand accounts of it.

Unlike the *Apology*, all of Plato's early dialogues present private conversations and thus would not have been subject to any comparable external constraints. Moreover, it is the only Platonic account of a conversation by Socrates at which Plato claims to have been present (see *Apol.* 34a, 38b) and, as Ross notes, this may be seen as a 'gentle hint at the historicity of this work' ('The Problem of Socrates', p. 36). On the basis of this, a 'minimal' approach to the Platonic characterization of Socrates has been proposed (by Kahn), that is, one that accepts the testimony only of the *Apology* with any measure of trust, and draws upon the early dialogues *only* when they present or elaborate ideas corroborated by the *Apology* (Hackforth expresses some doubts concerning this approach but nevertheless comes to a similar conclusion; see *The Composition of Plato's Apology*, esp. p. 146). Of course, it goes without saying that the text of the *Apology* is Plato's literary creation rather than a word for word report of what was said at Socrates' trial. Its unique status is thus not as an impeachable historical record but rather simply as the best point of departure for an understanding of the historical Socrates (recently Morrison, 'On the Alleged Historical Reliability of Plato's *Apology*', has raised some doubts concerning this approach; however, his arguments against treating the *Apology* as a straightforward report of the trial do not appear to invalidate the claim that it nevertheless remains our best point of departure).

In theory, at least, the arguments put forward by Ross, Vlastos, and Kahn concerning Plato's *Apology* should also apply to Xenophon's *Apology* (other 'apologies' now lost included one by Lysias; see Arethas *Schol. in Plat. Apol.* 18b = *SSR* I B 51). However, whereas Plato is generally agreed to have been present at the trial, Xenophon's *Apology* is based upon a second-hand account from Hermogenes (see Xenophon *Apol.* 2), although Hackforth suggests that Xenophon's may well have been written first (see *The Composition of Plato's Apology*, pp. 8-46).

Montuori has shown that a prioritization of Plato's *Apology* has repeatedly marked attempts to uncover the historical Socrates (see his *Socrates: Physiology of a Myth*, pp. 42-53). However he argues against placing too much faith in this text, suggesting that the *Apology* is a mythical and poetical creation that should be treated as a quasi-historical document. In particular he suggests that traditionally the reliability of the *Apology* has been assumed on the basis of the account it contains of the pronouncement of the Delphic oracle concerning Socrates' wisdom (pp. 47-50). Montuori argues against the historical truth of the oracle and thus refuses to grant the *Apology* a privileged position. Without wanting to comment on Montuori's complex argument concerning the oracle I simply note that this does not affect the point made by Ross, Vlastos, and Kahn concerning the public nature of the event reported in the *Apology*. In this study, then, I shall continue the tradition of prioritizing the *Apology* as a key source for the historical Socrates, but I do so only provisionally and hope to investigate the matter further at a later date.

For further discussion of what has come to be known as 'the problem of Socrates' see the works by Gulley, Guthrie, Kahn, Montuori, Ross, Taylor, and Vlastos mentioned above plus Lacey, 'Our Knowledge of Socrates', and the papers collected in vol. 1 of Prior, *Socrates: Critical Assessments*. For an historical appraisal of the development of this problem since the eighteenth century see Montuori's *De Socrate Iuste Damnato* and *The Socratic Problem: The History – The Sources*. For further comment on the status of the *Apology* as a source for the historical Socrates see Brickhouse & Smith, *Socrates on Trial*, pp. 2-10.

Additional Note 2 (on Stoicism)

The term 'Stoic' refers to the philosophical school founded by Zeno of Citium in *c.* 300 BC which continued to exert an influence at least until the time of Marcus Aurelius (d. AD 180) but probably right up until the end of the classical period (note the references in Porphyry *Vit. Plot.* 17 and Damascius *Hist. Phil.* 46d *apud* Photius *Bibl.* cod. 242 (339a17-20) = Epictetus test. 42 Schenkl). In contrast to Epicureanism, Stoicism was a philosophical school named after a place rather than a master, suggesting a less dogmatic outlook (see Brunschwig, 'La philosophie à l'époque hellénistique', p. 512). Indeed, in antiquity the Stoics appear to have been renowned for internal bickering and dispute (see e.g. Numenius *apud* Eusebius 14.5.4 (728a = *SVF* 2.20); Seneca *Epist.* 33.4; however note Sedley's reservations concerning the traditional image of Stoic liberalism in his 'Philosophical Allegiance in the Greco-Roman World', pp. 97-103). Some of these differences occasionally make generalizations concerning 'the Stoics' difficult. I shall try to avoid such problems by naming the Stoics connected with the sources that I shall use and by drawing attention to matters of internal dispute where they become relevant.

For ancient histories of the early Stoics see Book 7 of Diogenes Laertius and Philodemus' *Stoicorum Historia* (*PHerc* 1018). For modern accounts of the history of the school see Dorandi in *CHHP*, pp. 37-43; Brun, *Le stoïcisme*, pp. 7-26.

Additional Note 3 (on the texts of Epictetus)

The *Dissertationes* (Διατριβαί) of Epictetus were probably written by his pupil Arrian, as Arrian himself states in his prefatory letter, perhaps some time around the year 108 (see Millar, 'Epictetus and the Imperial Court', p. 142; Stadter, *Arrian of Nicomedia*, p. 28; Souilhé, pp. xix-xx). However, a few scholars have suggested that they may have been written by Epictetus himself (see e.g. Dobbin, pp. xxi-xxii, following Stellwag; also Souilhé, pp. xv-xvii) and some support for this suggestion might be seen in the (sometimes unreliable) *Suidae Lexicon s.v.* Ἐπίκτητος (E 2424 = test. 21 Schenkl) which claims that Epictetus wrote much (ἔγραψε πολλά). These texts appear to record Epictetus' lectures at Nicopolis and are written in Koine Greek, the popular Greek of the New Testament, in contrast to Arrian's other works which are in a more literary Attic Greek. Four books survive out of a possible total of eight (see Photius *Bibl.* cod. 58 (17b11-20 = test. 6 Schenkl who mentions eight books of Διατριβαί) and the fact that more than four books once existed is confirmed by Aulus Gellius' reference to a fifth book (See Aulus Gellius 19.1.14 = fr. 9 Schenkl, although he uses the title Διαλέξεις; see Souilhé, p. xiii). Photius also mentions another work – the *Conversations* or *Lessons* (Ὁμιλίαι) – in 12 volumes, but this is generally thought to be mistaken (see Photius *Bibl.* cod. 58 (17b11-20 = test. 6 Schenkl) &

Souilhé, p. xviii). The issue is confused further by the number of different names used by ancient authors (for further discussion see Souilhé, pp. xi-xix.). The *Enchiridion* (Ἐγχειρίδιον) was, according to Simplicius, also compiled by Arrian as a summary of the *Dissertationes*, presumably summarizing the content of the now lost books as well as those still extant (see Simplicius *In Ench.* Praef. 4-7 Hadot = test. 3 Schenkl).

The text of the surviving books of the *Dissertationes* derives from a single MS now held in the Bodleian Library, Oxford (Auct. T.4.13 = Graec. Misc. 251), from which all the other surviving MSS have been shown to derive. All of the other surviving MSS of the *Dissertationes* contain a lacuna in 1.18 where in the Bodleian MS there is a smeared ink blot (MS fol. 25r), indicating that they all ultimately derive from this single copy (see Mowat, 'A Lacuna in Arrian', pp. 60-63; Schenkl, p. lv; Souilhé, pp. lxxi-lxxii; Dobbin, p. 171). In contrast, the *Enchiridion* has been transmitted in so many MSS, including those of Simplicius' commentary and a number of Christian adaptations, that Oldfather was led to proclaim that the task of producing a new critical edition was too great compared to any likely benefit (see Oldfather (LCL), vol. 2, p. 480). This immense task has now been completed by Boter whose new edition also includes the Christian adaptations.

In general I have relied upon the LCL edition by Oldfather which is based upon Schenkl's 1916 BT edition which, in turn, is based upon the Bodleian MS. For the *Enchiridion* I have regularly consulted Boter as well. Schenkl's edition includes an invaluable Index Verborum. I have also consulted the older editions by Wolf (1595-96), Upton (1741), and Schweighäuser (1798, 1799-1800). The editions by Oldfather and Boter contain English translations. The *Handbook* is translated along with Simplicius' commentary by Stanhope (1694), and a new translation of the latter has recently appeared, by Brittain & Brennan. Note also the translations with commentaries by Dobbin (*Discourses Book 1*) and Pierre Hadot (*Manuel d'Épictète*). Fuller lists can be found in Oldfather, *Contributions Toward a Bibliography of Epictetus*, updated by *Contributions Toward a Bibliography of Epictetus: A Supplement*. A survey of recent scholarship can be found in Hershbell, 'The Stoicism of Epictetus: Twentieth Century Perspectives'.

Additional Note 4 (on the text of Marcus Aurelius)

The *Meditations* – or *To Himself* (τὰ εἰς ἑαυτόν) – were probably written while Marcus was on campaign in Europe; Books 2 and 3 are headed 'among the Quadi' (τὰ ἐν Κουάδοις) and 'at Carnuntum' (τὰ ἐν Καρνούντῳ) respectively (alternatively, these phrases may belong at the ends of Books 1 and 2). Their composition has been dated to *c.* 171-75 (see Brunt, 'Marcus Aurelius in his *Meditations*', pp. 18-19; Birley, *Marcus Aurelius*, p. 227; Farquharson, p. lxxiii). It is generally agreed that Book 1 was written last and is to a certain extent independent of the rest of the text (see Rutherford's Introduction to Farquharson's translation, p. xvi; Birley, *Marcus Aurelius*, p. 227).

The text of the *Meditations* derives primarily from two sources, a MS in the Vatican (Vat. Gr. 1950) and the relatively late *editio princeps* of 1558 by Xylander which was based upon the now lost Palatine MS (for the early editions and reception see Kraye, 'Ethnicorum omnium sanctissimus: Marcus Aurelius and his *Meditations* from Xylander to Diderot'). Other MSS supply only extracts (see Farquharson, pp. xxxii-xlii).

In general I have relied upon the edition of Farquharson but I have also always had the LCL edition by Haines at hand. Other editions worthy of note include Dalfen (BT), Leopold (OCT), and Theiler. Dalfen's edition includes a helpful Index Verborum. I have also consulted the earlier edition by Gataker (1652) and the edition of Book 4 with commentary by Crossley. The editions by Haines and Farquharson contain English translations. For further bibliographical information see Wickham Legg, 'A Bibliography of the *Thoughts* of Marcus Aurelius Antoninus', and Dalfen, pp. xxxii-xxxviii.

Glossary of Greek Words and Phrases

The following list includes only the more important Greek terms that appear in this study and focuses only upon the meanings relevant here. The obvious place for further information is Liddell and Scott's *Greek-English Lexicon* (LSJ). I have also benefited from consulting Urmson's *The Greek Philosophical Vocabulary*. Where I have referred to Latin terms I have generally specified the Greek terms to which they correspond and therefore I have not thought it necessary to list them separately here. An index of Latin to Greek correspondences can be found in volume 4 of *SVF*.

ἄνθρωπος (*anthrōpos*), pl. ἄνθρωποι (*anthrōpoi*): human being, often used in Stoicism to refer to an ideal human being and as a synonym for the sage.

ἀρετή (*aretē*), pl. ἀρεταί (*aretai*): human excellence, goodness, virtue.

ἄσκησις (*askēsis*), pl. ἀσκήσεις (*askēseis*): exercise, training, practice.

ἄσκησις τῆς ψυχῆς (*askēsis tēs psuchēs*): exercises of the soul, 'spiritual exercise'.

ἀταραξία (*ataraxia*): tranquillity, literally 'untroubled' or 'undisturbed'.

βέλτιστος (*beltistos*): the best, most excellent, that which an art aims at.

βίος (*bios*), pl. βίοι (*bioi*): way of life, manner of living, title of a written biography.

γυμναστική (*gumnastikē*): gymnastics, athletic training, the art that takes care of the body.

διάθεσις τῆς ψυχῆς (*diathesis tēs psuchēs*): a state or disposition of the soul.

δικαιοσύνη (*dikaiosunē*): justice, righteousness.

δόγμα (*dogma*), pl. δόγματα (*dogmata*): philosophical doctrine, opinion.

δόξα (*doxa*): belief, opinion.

ἐθίζω (*ethizō*): to accustom.

ἐθισμός (*ethismos*): habituation, accustoming.

ἔθος (*ethos*): habit, custom.

ἔκκλισις (*ekklisis*), pl. ἐκκλίσεις (*ekkliseis*): aversion.

ἔμετος (*emetos*): vomit; Epictetus' term for undigested philosophical doctrines.

ἐμπειρία καὶ τριβή (*empeiria kai tribē*): empirical knack or routine gained by practice rather than theoretical understanding.

ἐπιμέλεια (*epimeleia*): care, attention.

ἐπιμελεῖσθαι τῆς ψυχῆς (*epimeleisthai tēs psuchēs*): to take care of one's soul.

ἐπιστήμη (*epistēmē*): knowledge, understanding, especially scientific knowledge.

ἐποχή (*epochē*): suspension of judgement.

ἔργον (*ergon*), pl. ἔργα (*erga*): product, action, deed, work, function.

ἔργα καὶ λόγοι (*erga kai logoi*): 'deeds and words', that is, harmony between behaviour and speech.

ἔργα οὐ λόγοι (*erga ou logoi*): 'deeds not words', actions rather than theoretical explanations.

εὐδαιμονία (*eudaimonia*): well-being, prosperity, happiness.

εὐεξία (*euexia*): a good state or condition.

ἐφ' ἡμῖν (*eph' hēmin*): that which is 'up to us', in our control, in our power.

ἡγεμονικόν (*hēgemonikon*): the governing principle or most authoritative part of the soul.

ἦθος (*ēthos*): character, disposition.

θεραπεία (*therapeia*): therapy, medical treatment, cure.

θεώρημα (*theōrēma*), pl. θεωρήματα (*theōrēmata*): theory, speculation, scheme, plan.

θεωρητική τέχνη (*theōrētikē technē*): see under τέχνη.

θεωρία (*theōria*): theory, speculation, contemplation.

ἰατρική (*iatrikē*): medicine, the art that restores the good state of the body.

ἰσοσθένεια (*isostheneia*): equipollence, a state of balance.

καθῆκον (*kathēkon*), pl. καθήκοντα (*kathēkonta*): that which is appropriate, an appropriate action.

κατὰ νόμον (*kata nomon*): in accordance with custom or convention.

κατὰ φύσιν (*kata phusin*): in accordance with nature.

κτητική τέχνη (*ktētikē technē*): see under τέχνη.

λόγος (*logos*), pl. λόγοι (*logoi*): account, principle, rational explanation, theory, argument, word, literally 'something said'.

μελέτη (*meletē*): care, attention, treatment, exercise, practice.

νομοθετική (*nomothetikē*): legislative, relating to legislation.

νόμος (*nomos*): custom, convention, law.

νόσος (*nosos*): disease, sickness.

οἰκείωσις (*oikeiōsis*): orientation, appropriation.

ὁμολογουμένως τῇ φύσει ζῆν (*homologoumeōs tēi phusei zēn*): living in accordance with nature; the goal of Stoic philosophy.

ὄρεξις (*orexis*), pl. ὀρέξεις (*orexeis*): desire.

ὁρισμός (*horismos*), pl. ὅρισμοι (*horismoi*): definition.

ὁρμή (*hormē*), pl. ὁρμαι (*hormai*): impulse.

πάθος (*pathos*), pl. πάθη (*pathē*): emotion, passion, disease of the soul.

πέσσω (*pessō*): to digest; the process by which philosophical doctrines are absorbed into the soul.

πέψις (*pepsis*): digestion.

πνεῦμα (*pneuma*): breath, spirit, vital breath or spirit; one of the two principles in Stoic physics.

ποιητική τέχνη (*poiētikē technē*): see under τέχνη.

πολιτική (*politikē*): relating to citizens, political.

πρακτική τέχνη (*praktikē technē*): see under τέχνη.

προαίρεσις (*prohairesis*): an individual's faculty of choice, judgement, will, or volition.

προκοπή (*prokopē*): one who is 'making progress', especially philosophical progress towards the ideal of the sage.

πρόχειρος (*procheiros*): at hand, ready to hand, readily accessible.

σοφία (*sophia*): wisdom.

σοφός (*sophos*): one who is wise, a sage.

σπερματικὸς λόγος (*spermatikos logos*): generative principle of the cosmos.

σπουδαῖος (*spoudaios*): one who is good, excellent (opposed to φαῦλος), used in Stoicism as a synonym for sage.

στοχαστική (*stochastikē*): 'stochastic', skilful in aiming at, describes an art in which successful practice does not guarantee the goal.

στοχαστικὴ τέχνη (*stochastikē technē*): see under τέχνη.

συγκατάθεσις (*sunkatathesis*), pl. συγκαταθέσεις (*sunkatatheseis*): assent.

τέλος (*telos*): end, goal, purpose.

τεχνίτης (*technitēs*): an expert, a skilled craftsman.

τέχνη (*technē*), pl. τέχναι (*technai*): art, craft, skill, expertise. A number of distinct types of τέχνη can be distinguished:

– θεωρητικὴ τέχνη (*theōrētikē technē*): theoretical art, such as mathematics.

– κτητικὴ τέχνη (*ktētikē technē*): acquisitive art, such as fishing or hunting.

– ποιητικὴ τέχνη (*poiētikē technē*): productive art, such as building or shoemaking.

– πρακτικὴ τέχνη (*praktikē technē*): performative or active art, such as music or dancing.

– στοχαστικὴ τέχνη (*stochastikē technē*): stochastic art, such as medicine or navigation.

τέχνη περὶ τὸν βίον (*technē peri ton bion*): the art concerned with one's way of life, the art of living.

τόνος (*tonos*): tension, esp. the tension or state of the soul.

τόπος (*topos*), pl. τόποι (*topoi*): place, area; in Epictetus it is used to refer to an area or topic of study.

ὑγίεια (*hugieia*): health, soundness.

ὕλη (*hulē*): matter.

ὑπόληψις (*hupolēpsis*), pl. ὑπολήψεις (*hupolēpseis*): opinion, judgement, value-judgement.

φαντασία (*phantasia*), pl. φαντασίαι (*phantasiai*): impression, presentation, appearance.

φαντασία καταληπτικὴ (*phantasia katalēptikē*), pl. φαντασίαι καταληπτικαί (*phantasiai katalēptikai*): an adequate impression; alternatively an objective, cognitive, recognizable, or convincing impression (or presentation).

φαῦλος (*phaulos*), pl. φαῦλοι (*phauloi*): one who is simple, inferior, foolish (opposed to σπουδαῖος), the opposite of a sage.

φιλοσοφία (*philosophia*): philosophy, the love of wisdom.

φιλόσοφος (*philosophos*): a philosopher, a lover of wisdom.

φρόνησις (*phronēsis*): practical wisdom, prudence; in Stoicism synonymous with σοφία.

φύσις (*phusis*): nature, either nature as a whole or the individual nature or constitution of a thing.

χρεία (*chreia*), pl. χρεῖαι (*chreiai*): a maxim involving an anecdote used in order to make a philosophical point; literally, something of advantage or service.

ψυχή (*psuchē*): soul, mind, animating force, that by virtue of which something is alive.

Guide to Ancient Philosophers and Authors

The following list does not claim to include every ancient name that appears in this study. Dates are, of course, often far from certain. Further general biographical information can be found in the *Oxford Classical Dictionary*. Also useful is Goulet-Cazé's 'Catalogue of Known Cynic Philosophers'. However, once completed, the definitive guide to ancient philosophers will be the *Dictionnaire des Philosophes Antiques*, publié sous la direction de Richard Goulet (Paris: CNRS Éditions), of which volumes 1 'A' (1989), 2 'B-D' (1994), and 3 'E-J' (2000) are already available.

AESCHINES OF SPHETTUS (*c.* 5th-4th cent. BC): Associate of Socrates mentioned in the *Apology* and *Phaedo*; author of Socratic dialogues acknowledged in antiquity for their faithfulness to their subject. Fragments in *SSR*.

AETIUS (*c.* 1st-2nd cent. AD): Hypothetical doxographical author proposed by Diels whose anthology was constructed from the *Placita Philosophorum* attributed to Plutarch and passages in Stobaeus. Text in *DG*.

AGRIPPA (*c.* 1st cent. AD): Otherwise unknown Pyrrhonist Sceptic to whom the Five Modes of Scepticism are credited.

ALEXANDER OF APHRODISIAS (*c.* 2nd-3rd cent. AD): Holder of the Chair of Peripatetic philosophy in Athens created by Marcus Aurelius and author of scholarly commentaries on Aristotle (in *CAG*).

ANTIPATER (*c.* 2nd cent. BC): Stoic philosopher, successor to Diogenes of Babylon as head of the school, teacher of Panaetius. Fragments in *SVF*.

ANTISTHENES (*c.* 450-360 BC): Companion of Socrates who features in Xenophon's *Symposium*. Traditionally presented as a genealogical bridge between Socrates and the Cynics. Fragments in Decleva Caizzi, *Antisthenis Fragmenta*, and *SSR*.

APOLLONIUS OF TYANA (*c.* 1st cent. AD): Neopythagorean ascetic sage whose life is recounted in an extended biography by Philostratus.

ARISTO (*c.* 3rd cent. BC): Stoic philosopher with strong Cynic tendencies, pupil of Zeno. Said to have been the most famous philosopher in Athens in his day. Fragments in *SVF*.

ARISTOTLE (384-322 BC): Pupil of Plato, tutor to Alexander the Great, founder of the Lyceum and the Peripatetic tradition.

ARIUS DIDYMUS (*c.* 1st cent. BC): Doxographer whose account of Stoic ethics was included in the anthology of Stobaeus. Has been identified with the Alexandrian philosopher Arius, although some scholars doubt this.

ARRIAN (*c.* 2nd cent. AD): Pupil of Epictetus, compiler of the latter's *Dissertationes* and *Enchiridion,* and author of various historical works. Said to have modelled himself upon Xenophon.

AUGUSTINE (AD 354-430): Latin Church Father and Christian Saint who reports a number of pagan philosophical doctrines during the course of his polemics against them.

AULUS GELLIUS (*c.* AD 130-180): Author of an anthology covering a wide range of material including much relating to philosophy. Preserves a number of fragments from Epictetus and the early Stoa.

BION OF BORYSTHENES (*c.* 325-255 BC): Eclectic philosopher with strong Cynic tendencies, a pupil of Crates who also studied in the Academy and Peripatos.

CARNEADES (214-129 BC): Platonic philosopher, founder and head of the sceptical New Academy, member of the embassy of philosophers to Rome in 155 BC.

CATO THE YOUNGER (95-46 BC): Roman statesman influenced by Stoicism and often cited as an example of a Stoic sage. A biography by Plutarch survives.

CHRYSIPPUS (*c.* 280-207 BC): Stoic philosopher, third head of the Stoic school after Zeno and Cleanthes. Probably the most important and systematic of the early Stoics. Wrote extensively, almost all of which has been lost. Fragments in *SVF.*

CICERO (106-43 BC): Roman orator and statesman who presented Greek philosophy in a series of works in a form accessible to a Latin audience.

CLEANTHES (331-232 BC): Stoic philosopher, pupil of Zeno and his successor as head of the school. Fragments in *SVF.*

CLEMENT OF ALEXANDRIA (*c.* AD 150-215): Greek Church Father who reports many pagan philosophical doctrines during the course of his polemics against them.

CLEOMEDES (*c.* 1st-2nd cent. AD): Stoic philosopher of the Imperial period known only for his treatise on cosmology.

CRATES (*c.* 365-285 BC): Cynic philosopher, pupil of Diogenes, teacher of Zeno who is said to have been drawn to him due to his resemblance to Socrates. Fragments in *SSR.*

CRITOLAUS (*c.* 2nd cent. BC): Head of the Peripatetic school, member of the embassy of philosophers to Rome in 155 BC.

DAMASCIUS (*c.* 5th-6th cent. AD): Neoplatonist philosopher, teacher of Simplicius, last head of the Academy when it was closed by Justinian in AD 529.

DEMOCRITUS (b. *c.* 460 BC): Atomist philosopher from Abdera contemporary with Socrates. Fragments in DK.

DEMONAX (*c.* AD 70-170): Cynic philosopher from Cyprus who lived in Athens, a pupil of Epictetus, known primarily via the biography written by his pupil Lucian.

DIO CHRYSOSTOM (*c.* AD 40-112): Popular philosopher who travelled throughout the ancient world teaching a mixture of Cynicism and Stoicism. He was at one point a pupil of Musonius Rufus.

DIOGENES LAERTIUS (*c.* early 3rd cent. AD): Biographer and doxographer whose work is an invaluable source for ancient philosophy.

DIOGENES OF BABYLON (*c.* 240-152 BC): Stoic philosopher, pupil of Chrysippus, head of the school after Zeno of Tarsus, teacher of Panaetius, member of the embassy of philosophers to Rome in 155 BC. Fragments in *SVF*.

DIOGENES OF SINOPE (*c.* 400-325 BC): Founder of the Cynic movement famous for his scandalous behaviour, teacher of Crates. Fragments in *SSR*.

EPICTETUS (*c.* AD 55-135): Stoic philosopher, pupil of Musonius Rufus, banished from Rome by Domitian after which he set up school in Nicopolis. The *Discourses* of Epictetus preserved by Arrian form the largest surviving Stoic text in Greek.

EPICURUS (341-270 BC): Atomist and hedonist philosopher who founded the school named after him. Texts preserved in Diogenes Laertius and also in the papyri from Herculaneum.

FRONTO (*c.* AD 100-166): Marcus Aurelius' rhetoric teacher whose correspondence with Marcus was discovered in a palimpsest in the early nineteenth century.

GALEN (*c.* AD 129-210): Medical author and philosopher, personal physician to Marcus Aurelius.

HERACLITUS (*c.* 6th-5th cent. BC): Presocratic natural philosopher from Ephesus whose philosophy formed an important influence upon the development of Stoic physics. Fragments in DK.

HIEROCLES (*c.* 2nd cent. AD): Stoic philosopher, mentioned by Aulus Gellius, and the author of the ethical treatise *Elements of Ethics* preserved on papyrus.

JULIAN (AD 332-363): Roman Emperor influenced by Neoplatonism who attempted to revive pagan culture in the face of rising Christianity. Also sympathetic towards certain Cynic doctrines.

LUCIAN (*c.* AD 120-180): Satirist and one time pupil of the Cynic Demonax who often deals with philosophical themes.

MARCUS AURELIUS (AD 121-180): Roman Emperor 161-180, deeply influenced by Stoic philosophy and author of the *Meditations*.

METROCLES (*c.* 3rd cent. BC): Cynic philosopher, brother of Hipparchia and brother-in-law of Crates.

MUSONIUS RUFUS (*c.* AD 30-100): Judged variously as important Stoic philosopher or merely a popular moralizer. Occasionally appears in the works of Tacitus. Banished from Rome a number of times by different Emperors. Teacher of Epictetus. His *Diatribes* are preserved in Stobaeus.

OLYMPIODORUS (*c.* 6th cent. AD): Neoplatonist philosopher and commentator.

PANAETIUS (*c.* 185-109 BC): Stoic philosopher, pupil of Diogenes of Babylon and Antipater, teacher of Posidonius, succeeded Antipater as head of the school. Fragments in van Straaten, *Panaetii Rhodii Fragmenta*.

PHILODEMUS (*c.* 110-40 BC): Epicurean philosopher and polemecist against the Stoics, many of whose works were discovered in the Villa of Papyri at Herculaneum.

PHOTIUS (*c.* AD 810-893): Byzantine scholar, author of an important compendium concerning pagan literature.

PLATO (*c.* 430-347 BC): Follower of Socrates, teacher of Aristotle, founder of the Academy.

PLOTINUS (AD 205-270): Founder of Neoplatonism, teacher of Porphyry who wrote his biography.

PLUTARCH (*c.* AD 50-120): Philosopher and biographer primarily influenced by Platonism, author of a number of important polemical works against the Stoics.

PORPHYRY (*c.* AD 230-305): Neoplatonist philosopher, pupil and biographer of Plotinus, author of logical commentaries on Aristotle.

POSIDONIUS (*c.* 135-50 BC): Stoic philosopher, pupil of Panaetius, associate of Cicero. Fragments in EK.

PYRRHO (*c.* 360-270 BC): The first Greek sceptical philosopher after whom Pyrrhonism is named.

SENECA (*c.* 4 BC-AD 65): Stoic philosophical author, tutor to Nero, eventually forced to commit suicide.

SEXTUS EMPIRICUS (*c.* 2nd cent. AD): Sceptical philosopher and medical doctor, polemicist against all dogmatic schools of philosophy including the Stoics.

SIMON THE SHOEMAKER (*c.* 5th cent. BC): Associate of Socrates reported to have invented the Socratic dialogue.

SIMPLICIUS (*c.* 6th cent. AD): Neoplatonist and important Aristotelian commentator who also produced a commentary on Epictetus' *Enchiridion*.

SOCRATES (469-399 BC): Probably the most important philosopher in the Western tradition, put to death by the Athenian State for corrupting the youth, the first to conceive philosophy as the art of living, the inspiration for a number of diverse ancient philosophical schools. Fragments (beyond the reports of Plato and Xenophon) in *SSR*.

STOBAEUS (*c.* 5th cent. AD): John Stobaeus (Ioannes of Stobi; Skopje, Macedonia), compiler of an anthology of philosophical texts designed to aid the education of his son in Classical pagan culture. A number of ancient authors survive only thanks to their inclusion in this collection, including Arius Didymus and Musonius Rufus.

STRABO (*c.* 64 BC-AD 21): Geographer and historian, associate of Posidonius and convert to Stoicism.

TIMON (*c.* 320-230 BC): Sceptical philosopher, follower of Pyrrho. Fragments in *PPF*.

XENOPHON (*c.* 430-350 BC): Historian and 'biographer' of Socrates.

ZENO OF CITIUM (335-263 BC): Founder of Stoicism, pupil of Crates, teacher of Cleanthes. Inspired to study philosophy after reading Xenophon's portrayal of Socrates in the *Memorabilia*. Fragments in *SVF*.

Bibliography

Details concerning editions of ancient authors consulted – of which many are in the Oxford (OCT), Teubner (BT), Loeb (LCL), and Budé (CUF) series – are included in the Index Locorum. In general these are not repeated here. However, editions of ancient texts not in one of these series are included. I also include details of a number of items that have proved useful even though they have not been cited in the notes.

1. Editions and Translations of Epictetus

BOTER, G., *The Encheiridion of Epictetus and its Three Christian Adaptations*, Transmission and Critical Editions, Philosophia Antiqua 82 (Leiden: Brill, 1999)

DOBBIN, R., *Epictetus, Discourses Book 1*, Translated with an Introduction and Commentary, Clarendon Later Ancient Philosophers (Oxford: Clarendon Press, 1998)

HADOT, P., *Arrien, Manuel d'Épictète*, Introduction, Traduction et Notes (Paris: Le Livre de Poche, 2000)

HARD, R., *The Discourses of Epictetus*, Edited by Christopher Gill, The Everyman Library (London: Dent, 1995)

OLDFATHER, W. A., *Epictetus, The Discourses as Reported by Arrian, the Manual, and Fragments*, The Loeb Classical Library, 2 vols (London: Heinemann, 1925-28; repr. Harvard University Press)

SCHENKL, H., *Epicteti Dissertationes ab Arriano Digestae*, Editio Maior, Bibliotheca Scriptorum Graecorum et Romanorum Teubneriana (Leipzig: Teubner, 1916)

SCHWEIGHÄUSER, J., *Epicteti Manuale et Cebetis Tabula Graece et Latine* (Leipzig: Weidmann, 1798)

—— *Epicteteae Philosophiae Monumenta*: *Epicteti Dissertationum ab Arriano Deigestarum Libri IV eiusdem Enchiridion et ex deperditis sermonibus Fragmenta*, 3 vols in 4 (Liepzig: Weidmann, 1799); *Simplicii Commentarius in Epicteti Enchiridion accedit Enchiridion Paraphrasis Christiana et Nili Enchiridion*, 2 vols (Leipzig: Weidmann, 1800)

SOUILHÉ, J., *Épictète, Entretiens Livre I*, Collection des Universités de France publiée sous le patronage de l'Association Guillaume Budé (Paris: Les Belles Lettres, 1943; 2nd edn 1975)

STANHOPE, G., *Epictetus his Morals, with Simplicius his Comment*, Made English from the Greek (London: Richard Sare, 1694; 3rd edn 1704)

UPTON, J., *Epicteti Quae supersunt Dissertationes ab Arriano Collectae nec non Enchiridion et Fragmenta Graece et Latine*, 2 vols (London: Thomas Woodward, 1741)

WHITE, N., *Handbook of Epictetus*, Translated with Introduction and Annotations (Indianapolis: Hackett, 1983)

WOLF, H., *Epicteti Stoici Philosophi Encheiridion ... Accessere, Simplicii in eundem Epicteti libellum doctissima Scholia, Arriani commentariorum de Epicteti disputationibus libri quator*, 3 vols (Cologne: Birckmann, 1595-96)

2. Editions and Translations of Marcus Aurelius

CROSSLEY, H., *The Fourth Book of the Meditations of Marcus Aurelius Antoninus*, A Revised Text with Translation and Commentary (London: Macmillan, 1882)

DALFEN, J., *Marci Aurelii Antonini Ad Se Ipsum Libri XII*, Bibliotheca Scriptorum Graecorum et Romanorum Teubneriana (Leipzig: Teubner, 1979; 2nd edn 1987)

FARQUHARSON, A. S. L., *The Meditations of the Emperor Marcus Antoninus*, Edited with Translation and Commentary, 2 vols (Oxford: Clarendon Press, 1944); translation only repr. with Introduction and Notes by R. B. Rutherford (Oxford: Oxford University Press, 1989)

GATAKER, T., *Marci Antonini Imperatoris de rebus suis, sive de eis qae ad se pertinere censebat, Libri XII* (Cambridge: Thomas Buck, 1652)

HAINES, C. R., *The Communings with Himself of Marcus Aurelius Antoninus*, A Revised Text and a Translation into English, The Loeb Classical Library (London: Heinemann, 1916; repr. Harvard University Press)

HARD, R., *Marcus Aurelius, Meditations*, Introduction and Notes by Christopher Gill (Ware: Wordsworth, 1997)

LEOPOLD, I. H., *M. Antoninus Imperator Ad Se Ipsum*, Scriptorum Classicorum Bibliotheca Oxoniensis (Oxford: Clarendon Press, 1908)

THEILER, W., *Kaiser Marc Aurel, Wege Zu Sich Selbst* (Zürich: Artemis, 1951)

3. Other Works

ABELARD, P., *Collationes*, Edited and Translated by John Marenbon and Giovanni Orlandi, Oxford Medieval Texts (Oxford: Clarendon Press, 2001)

AFRICA, T. W., 'The Opium Addiction of Marcus Aurelius', *Journal of the History of Ideas* 22 (1961), 97-102

ALGRA, K., J. BARNES, J. MANSFELD, & M. SCHOFIELD, eds, *The Cambridge History of Hellenistic Philosophy* (Cambridge: Cambridge University Press, 1999)

ALLEN, J., 'The Skepticism of Sextus Empiricus', *ANRW* II 36.4 (1990), pp. 2582-607

ALON, I., *Socrates in Mediaeval Arabic Literature*, Islamic Philosophy, Theology, and Science 10 (Leiden: Brill & Jerusalem: The Magnes Press, 1991)

ANDERSON, G., *Sage, Saint, and Sophist: Holy Men and their Associates in the Early Roman Empire* (London: Routledge, 1994)

—— 'Alciphron's Miniatures', *ANRW* II 34.3 (1997), pp. 2188-206

ANNAS, J., 'Stoic Epistemology', in S. Everson, ed., *Epistemology*, Companions to Ancient Thought 1 (Cambridge: Cambridge University Press, 1990), pp. 184-203

—— *Hellenistic Philosophy of Mind* (Berkeley: University of California Press, 1992)

—— *The Morality of Happiness* (New York: Oxford University Press, 1993)

ANNAS, J., & J. BARNES, *The Modes of Scepticism: Ancient Texts and Modern Interpretations* (Cambridge: Cambridge University Press, 1985)

—— *Sextus Empiricus, Outlines of Scepticism* (Cambridge: Cambridge University Press, 1994)

ARMSTRONG, A. H., ed., *Classical Mediterranean Spirituality: Egyptian, Greek, Roman*, World Spirituality 15 (London: SCM, 1989)

ARNIM, H. von, *Stoicorum Veterum Fragmenta*, Volumen I Zeno et Zenonis discipuli; Volumen II Chrysippi fragmenta logica et physica; Volumen III Chrysippi fragmenta moralia, Fragmenta successorum Chrysippi; Volumen IV Quo indices Continentur, conscripsit Maximillianus Adler, 4 vols (Stuttgart: Teubner, 1903-24; repr. 1978-79)

ARNOLD, E. V., *Roman Stoicism: Being Lectures on the History of the Stoic Philosophy with Special Reference to its Development within the Roman Empire* (London: Routledge & Kegan Paul, [1911] 1958)

ARTHUR, E. P., 'The Stoic Analysis of the Mind's Reactions to Presentations', *Hermes* 111 (1983), 69-78

ASMIS, E., 'The Stoicism of Marcus Aurelius', *ANRW* II 36.3 (1989), pp. 2228-52

ATHANASSIADI, P., *Damascius, The Philosophical History*, Text with Translation and Notes (Athens: Apamea, 1999)

BALDRY, H. C., 'Zeno's Ideal State', *Journal of Hellenic Studies* 79 (1959), 3-15

BARNES, J., *Aristotle* (Oxford: Oxford University Press, 1982; rev. edn 1996)

—— 'The Beliefs of a Pyrrhonist', *Proceedings of the Cambridge Philological Society* 28 (1982); repr. in M. Burnyeat & M. Frede, eds, *The Original Sceptics: A Controversy* (Indianapolis: Hackett, 1997), pp. 58-91

—— *The Complete Works of Aristotle*, The Revised Oxford Translation, 2 vols (Princeton: Princeton University Press, 1984)

—— 'Nietzsche and Diogenes Laertius', *Nietzsche Studien* 15 (1986), 16-40

—— *Logic and the Imperial Stoa*, Philosophia Antiqua 75 (Leiden: Brill, 1997)

BARNES, J., S. BOBZIEN, K. FLANNERY, & K. IERODIAKONOU, *Alexander of Aphrodisias, On Aristotle Prior Analytics 1.1-7*, Ancient Commentators on Aristotle (London: Duckworth, 1991)

BARTON, T. S., *Power and Knowledge: Astrology, Physiognomics, and Medicine under the Roman Empire* (Ann Arbor: University of Michigan Press, 1994)

BECKER, L. C., *A New Stoicism* (Princeton: Princeton University Press, 1998)

BEKKER, I., *Aristotelis Opera*, ex recensione Immanuelis Bekkeri, edidit Academia Regia Borussica, Editio Altera quam curavit Olof Gigon, 2 vols (Berlin: De Gruyter, [1831] 1960)

—— *Sextus Empiricus* (Berlin: Reimer, 1842)

BENSON, H. H., ed., *Essays on the Philosophy of Socrates* (New York: Oxford University Press, 1992)

BETT, R., *Sextus Empiricus, Against the Ethicists*, Translation, Commentary, and Introduction, Clarendon Later Ancient Philosophers (Oxford: Clarendon Press, 1997)

BIRLEY, A. R., *Marcus Aurelius: A Biography* (London: Routledge [1966] 2000)

BLUCK, R. S., 'The Origin of the *Greater Alcibiades*', *Classical Quarterly* 3 (1953), 46-52

BOBZIEN, S., *Determinism and Freedom in Stoic Philosophy* (Oxford: Clarendon Press, 1998)

—— 'Chrysippus' Theory of Causes', in K. Ierodiakonou, ed., *Topics in Stoic Philosophy* (Oxford: Clarendon Press, 1999), pp. 196-242

BOER, W. DE, *Galeni De Propriorum Animi Cuiuslibet Affectuum Dignotione et Curatione, De Animi Cuiuslibet Peccatorum Dignotione et Curatione, De Atra Bile*, Corpus Medicorum Graecorum V 4.1.1 (Leipzig & Berlin: Teubner, 1937)

BONHÖFFER, A., *Epictet und die Stoa: Untersuchungen zur Stoischen Philosophie* (Stuttgart: Ferdinand Enke, 1890)

—— *Die Ethik des Stoikers Epictet. Anhang: Exkurse über einige wichtige punkte der Stoischen ethik* (Stuttgart: Ferdinand Enke, 1894)

—— *The Ethics of the Stoic Epictetus*, trans. W. O. Stephens (New York: Peter Lang, 1996); a translation of *Die Ethik des Stoikers Epictet*

BOTROS, S., 'Freedom, Causality, Fatalism, and Early Stoic Philosophy', *Phronesis* 30 (1985), 274-304

BRANCACCI, A., 'Dio, Socrates, and Cynicism', in S. Swain, ed., *Dio Chrysostom: Politics, Letters, and Philosophy* (Oxford: Oxford University Press, 2000), pp. 240-60

BRANDWOOD, L., *A Word Index to Plato*, Compendia 8 (Leeds: W. S. Maney & Son, 1976)

BRANHAM, R. B., & M.-O. GOULET-CAZÉ, eds, *The Cynics: The Cynic Movement in Antiquity and its Legacy* (Berkeley: University of California Press, 1996); a partial translation of M.-O. Goulet-Cazé & R. Goulet, eds, *Le Cynisme ancien et ses prolongements* (Paris: Presses Universitaires de France, 1993)

BRÉHIER, É., *Chrysippe et l'ancien stoïcisme* (Paris: Presses Universitaires de France, 1910; 2nd edn 1950)

—— *La théorie des incorporels dans l'ancien Stoïcisme*, Bibliothèque d'Histoire de la Philosophie (Paris: Vrin, 1910; repr. 1997)

—— *The Hellenistic and Roman Age*, trans. W. Baskin (Chicago: University of Chicago Press, 1965); a partial translation of *Histoire de la philosophie: L'Antiquite et le Moyen Age* (Paris: Presses Universitaires de France, 1931)

BRICKHOUSE, T. C., & N. D. SMITH, *Socrates on Trial* (Oxford: Clarendon Press, 1989)

—— *Plato's Socrates* (New York: Oxford University Press, 1994)

BRITTAIN, C., & T. BRENNAN, *Simplicius, On Epictetus Handbook 1-26*, Ancient Commentators on Aristotle (London: Duckworth, 2002)

—— *Simplicius, On Epictetus Handbook 27-53*, Ancient Commentators on Aristotle (London: Duckworth, 2002)

BROAD, C. D., *Five Types of Ethical Theory* (London: Kegan Paul, Trench, Trubner & Co., 1930; repr. 1944)

BRUN, J., *Les Stoïciens: Textes choisis* (Paris: Presses Universitaires de France, 1957)

—— *Le stoïcisme* (Paris: Presses Universitaires de France, 1958; repr. 1998)

BRUNSCHWIG, J., ed., *Les Stoïciens et leur logique: Actes du Colloque de Chantilly 18-22 Septembre 1976*, Bibliothèque d'Histoire de la Philosophie (Paris: Vrin, 1978)

—— 'The Stoic Theory of the Supreme Genus and Platonic Ontology', first published in French in J. Barnes & M. Mignucci, eds, *Matter and Metaphysics* (Naples: Bibliopolis, 1988); trans. in *Papers in Hellenistic Philosophy*, pp. 92-157

—— *Papers in Hellenistic Philosophy*, trans. J. Lloyd (Cambridge: Cambridge University Press, 1994)

—— 'La philosophie à l'époque hellénistique', in M. Canto-Sperber *et al.*, *Philosophie grecque* (Paris: Presses Universitaires de France, 1997), pp. 457-591

BRUNSCHWIG, J., & G. E. R. LLOYD, eds, *Greek Thought: A Guide to Classical Knowledge*, trans. under the direction of C. Porter (Cambridge, MA: The Belknap Press of Harvard University Press, 2000); a translation of *Le Savior Grec: Dictionnaire Critique* (Paris: Flammarion, 1996)

BRUNSCHWIG, J., & M. C. NUSSBAUM, eds, *Passions and Perceptions: Studies in Hellenistic Philosophy of Mind*, Proceedings of the Fifth Symposium Hellenisticum (Cambridge: Cambridge University Press, 1993)

BRUNT, P. A., 'Marcus Aurelius in his *Meditations*', *Journal of Roman Studies* 64 (1974), 1-20

BULLOCH, A., E. S. GRUEN, A. A. LONG, & A. STEWART, eds, *Images and Ideologies: Self-Definition in the Hellenistic World* (Berkeley: University of California Press, 1993)

BURNET, J., *Greek Philosophy: Thales to Plato* (London: Macmillan, [1914] 1961)

—— *Plato's Euthyphro, Apology of Socrates, and Crito*, Edited with Notes (Oxford: Clarendon Press, 1924)

BURNYEAT, M., 'Can the Sceptic Live his Scepticism?', in M. Schofield, M. Burnyeat, & J. Barnes, eds, *Doubt and Dogmatism: Studies in Hellenistic Epistemology* (Oxford: Clarendon Press, 1980); repr. in M. Burnyeat & M. Frede, eds, *The Original Sceptics: A Controversy* (Indianapolis: Hackett, 1997), pp. 25-57

BURNYEAT, M., & M. FREDE, eds, *The Original Sceptics: A Controversy* (Indianapolis: Hackett, 1997)

CAMP, J. M., *The Athenian Agora: Excavations in the Heart of Classical Athens* (London: Thames and Hudson, [1986] 1992)

CANTO-SPERBER, M., J. BARNES, L. BRISSON, J. BRUNSCHWIG, & G. VLASTOS, *Philosophie grecque* (Paris: Presses Universitaires de France, 1997)

CHADWICK, H., *Origen, Contra Celsum*, Translated with an Introduction and Notes (Cambridge: Cambridge University Press, 1953; repr. 1965)

CHRISTENSEN, J., *An Essay on the Unity of Stoic Philosophy* (Munksgaard: Scandinavian University Books, 1962)

CHROUST, A.-H., *Socrates Man and Myth: The Two Socratic Apologies of Xenophon* (London: Routledge & Kegan Paul, 1957)

—— 'Late Hellenistic "Textbook Definitions" of Philosophy', *Laval Theologique et Philosophique* 28 (1972), 15-25

CLAY, D., 'Lucian of Samosata: Four Philosophical Lives (Nigrinus, Demonax, Peregrinus, Alexander Pseudomantis)', *ANRW* II 36.5 (1992), pp. 3406-50

—— 'The Origins of the Socratic Dialogue', in P. A. Vander Waerdt, ed., *The Socratic Movement* (Ithaca: Cornell University Press, 1994), pp. 23-47

CLARKE, M. L., *The Roman Mind: Studies in the History of Thought from Cicero to Marcus Aurelius* (London: Cohen & West, 1956)

COLARDEAU, T., *Étude sur Épictète* (Paris: Albert Fontemoing, 1903)

COLISH, M. L., *The Stoic Tradition from Antiquity to the Early Middle Ages*, 2 vols (Leiden: Brill, 1985; repr. 1990)

COOPER, J. M., 'The *Magna Moralia* and Aristotle's Moral Philosophy', *American Journal of Philology* 94 (1973); repr. in *Reason and Emotion*, pp. 195-211

—— 'Socrates and Plato in Plato's *Gorgias*', earlier version in *Review of Metaphysics* 35 (1982); revised version in *Reason and Emotion*, pp. 29-75

—— 'Notes on Xenophon's Socrates', first published in *Reason and Emotion*, pp. 3-28

—— *Reason and Emotion: Essays on Ancient Moral Psychology and Ethical Theory* (Princeton: Princeton University Press, 1999)

COPENHAVER, B. P., & C. B. SCHMITT, *Renaissance Philosophy* (Oxford: Oxford University Press, 1992)

COTTINGHAM, J., *Philosophy and the Good Life: Reason and the Passions in Greek, Cartesian, and Psychoanalytic Ethics* (Cambridge: Cambridge University Press, 1998)

COX, P., *Biography in Late Antiquity: A Quest for the Holy Man*, The Transformation of the Classical Heritage 5 (Berkeley: University of California Press, 1983)

CRITCHLEY, S., *Continental Philosophy: A Very Short Introduction* (Oxford: Oxford University Press, 2001)

DAVIDSON, A. I., 'Ethics as Ascetics: Foucault, the History of Ethics, and Ancient Thought', in G. Gutting, ed., *The Cambridge Companion to Foucault* (Cambridge: Cambridge University Press, 1994), pp. 115-40

—— 'Pierre Hadot and the Spiritual Phenomenon of Ancient Philosophy', introduction to P. Hadot, *Philosophy as a Way of Life: Spiritual Exercises from Socrates to Foucault* (Oxford: Blackwell, 1995), pp. 1-45

—— ed., *Foucault and his Interlocutors* (Chicago: University of Chicago Press, 1997)

DECLEVA CAIZZI, F., *Antisthenis Fragmenta* (Milan: Istituto Editoriale Cisalpino, 1966)

—— 'The Porch and the Garden: Early Hellenistic Images of the Philosophical Life', in A. Bulloch, E. S. Gruen, A. A. Long, & A. Stewart, eds, *Images and Ideologies: Self-Definition in the Hellenistic World* (Berkeley: University of California Press, 1993), pp. 303-29

DE LACY, P., 'The Logical Structure of the Ethics of Epictetus', *Classical Philology* 38 (1943), 112-25

—— *Galen, On the Doctrines of Hippocrates and Plato*, Edition, Translation, and Commentary, Corpus Medicorum Graecorum V 4.1.2, 3 vols (Berlin: Akademie, 1978-84)

DE LANDA, M., 'Nonorganic Life', in J. Crary & S. Kwinter, eds, *Incorporations*, Zone 6 (New York: Zone, 1992), pp. 129-67

DELATTE, L., E. EVRARD, S. GOVAERTS, & J. DENOOZ, *Lucius Annaeus Seneca Opera Philosophica Index Verborum: Listes de Fréquence, Relevés Grammaticaux*, Alpha-Omega 41, 2 vols (Hildesheim: Olms, 1981)

DELEUZE, G., *Spinoza: Practical Philosophy*, trans. R. Hurley (San Francisco: City Lights, 1988); a translation of *Spinoza: Philosophie pratique* (Paris: Minuit, 1981)

—— *The Logic of Sense*, trans. M. Lester & C. Stivale (New York: Columbia University Press, 1990); a translation of *Logique du sens* (Paris: Minuit, 1969)

DEMAN, T., *Le témoignage d'Aristote sur Socrate* (Paris: Les Belles Lettres, 1942)

DENYER, N., *Plato, Alcibiades*, Cambridge Greek and Latin Classics (Cambridge: Cambridge University Press, 2001)

DEVINE, F. E., 'Stoicism on the Best Regime', *Journal of the History of Ideas* 31 (1970), 323-36

DIELS, H., *Doxographi Graeci*, Editio Quarta (Berlin: De Gruyter, [1879] 1965)

—— *Poetarum Philosophorum Fragmenta*, Poetarum Graecorum Fragmenta 3.1 (Berlin: Weidmann, 1901)

DIELS, H., & W. KRANZ, *Die Fragmente der Vorsokratiker*, Griechisch und Deutsch von Hermann Diels, Elfte Auflage Herausgegeben von Walther Kranz, 3 vols (Zürich & Berlin: Weidmann, 1964)

DIHLE, A., *Studien zur Griechischen Biographie*, Abhandlungen der Akademie der Wissenschaften in Göttingen, Philologisch-Historische Klasse, Dritte Folge 37 (Göttingen: Vandenhoeck & Ruprecht, 1956)

DILLON, J., *The Middle Platonists: 80 BC to AD 220* (London: Duckworth, 1977; rev. edn 1996)

DILLON, J., & A. A. LONG, eds, *The Question of "Eclecticism": Studies in Later Greek Philosophy* (Berkeley: University of California Press, 1988)

DITTMAR, H., *Aischines von Sphettos: Studien zur Lieraturgeschichte der Sokratiker*, Philologische Untersuchungen 21 (Berlin: Weidmann, 1912)

DOBBIN, R., 'Προαίρεσις in Epictetus', *Ancient Philosophy* 11 (1991), 111-35

DODDS, E. R., *Plato, Gorgias*, A Revised Text with Introduction and Commentary (Oxford: Clarendon Press, 1959)

DOMAŃSKI, J., *La philosophie, théorie ou manière de vivre? Les controverses de l'Antiquité à la Renaissance*, Préface de Pierre Hadot, Vestigia 18 (Fribourg: Éditions Universitaires & Paris: Éditions du Cerf, 1996)

DOOLEY, W. E., *Alexander of Aphrodisias, On Aristotle Metaphysics 1*, Ancient Commentators on Aristotle (London: Duckworth, 1989)

DORANDI, T., 'Filodemo, Gli Stoici (*PHerc* 155 e 339)', *Cronache Ercolanesi* 12 (1982), 91-133

—— *Filodemo, Storia dei filosofi: La stoà da Zenone a Panezio (PHerc 1018)*, Edizione, traduzione e commento, Philosophia Antiqua 60 (Leiden: Brill, 1994)

DÖRING, K., *Exemplum Socratis: Studien zur Sokratesnachwirkung in der kynisch-stoischen Popularphilosophie der frühen Kaiserzeit und im frühen Christentum*, Hermes Einzelschriften 42 (Wiesbaden: Steiner, 1979)

DOUGAN, T. W., & R. M. HENRY, *M. Tulli Ciceronis Tusculanarum Disputationum Libri Quinque*, A Revised Text with Introduction and Commentary and a Collation of Numerous MSS, 2 vols (Cambridge: Cambridge University Press, 1905-34)

DOVER, K. J., 'Socrates in the *Clouds*', in G. Vlastos, ed., *The Philosophy of Socrates: A Collection of Critical Essays* (New York: Anchor, 1971), pp. 50-77

DUDLEY, D. R., *A History of Cynicism: From Diogenes to the 6th Century AD* (London: Methuen, 1937; repr. Bristol Classical Press, 1998)

DUHOT, J.-J., *Épictète et la sagesse stoïcienne* (Paris: Bayard Éditions, 1996)

EDELSTEIN, L., 'The Philosophical System of Posidonius', *American Journal of Philology* 57 (1936), 286-325

—— *The Meaning of Stoicism*, Martin Classical Lectures 21 (Cambridge, MA: Harvard University Press, 1966)

EDELSTEIN, L., & I. G. KIDD, *Posidonius, The Fragments*, Cambridge Classical Texts and Commentaries 13 (Cambridge: Cambridge University Press, 1972; 2nd edn 1989); see also Kidd

ENGBERG-PEDERSEN, T., *The Stoic Theory of Oikeiosis* (Aarhus: Aarhus University Press, 1990)

EPP, R. H., 'Stoicism Bibliography', *Southern Journal of Philosophy* 23 suppl. 'Spindel Conference: Recovering the Stoics' (1985), 125-82

ERASMUS, *Praise of Folly and Letter to Maarten van Dorp 1515*, Translated by Betty Radice with an Introduction and Notes by A. H. T. Levi (Harmondsworth: Penguin, 1993)

EVERSON, S., ed., *Epistemology*, Companions to Ancient Thought 1 (Cambridge: Cambridge University Press, 1990)

—— ed., *Psychology*, Companions to Ancient Thought 2 (Cambridge: Cambridge University Press, 1991)

FERGUSON, J., *Socrates: A Source Book* (London: Macmillan, 1970)

FIELD, G. C., *Plato and his Contemporaries: A Study in Fourth-Century Life and Thought* (London: Methuen, 1930)

FOUCAULT, M., *L'usage des plaisirs: Histoire de la sexualité 2* (Paris: Gallimard, 1984; repr. in 'Collection Tel' 1997); trans. as *The Use of Pleasure: The History of Sexuality 2*, trans. R. Hurley (Harmondsworth: Penguin, 1986)

—— *Le souci de soi: Histoire de la sexualité 3* (Paris: Gallimard, 1984; repr. in 'Collection Tel' 1997); trans. as *The Care of the Self: The History of Sexuality 3*, trans. R. Hurley (Harmondsworth: Penguin, 1988)

—— *Dits et écrits: 1954-1988*, Édition établie sous la direction de Daniel Defert et François Ewald, Bibliothèque des Sciences Humaines, 4 vols (Paris: Gallimard, 1994)

—— *The Essential Works of Michel Foucault 1954-1984*: vol. 1, *Ethics, Subjectivity, and Truth*, ed. P. Rabinow (London: Allen Lane The Penguin Press, 1997); vol. 2, *Aesthetics, Method, and Epistemology*, ed. J. D. Faubion (London: Allen Lane The Penguin Press, 1998); vol. 3, *Power*, ed. J. D. Faubion (London: Allen Lane The Penguin Press, 2001)

—— *L'herméneutique du sujet: Cours au Collège de France 1981-1982*, Édition établie sous la direction de François Ewald et Alessandro Fontana, Hautes Études (Paris: Gallimard & Seuil, 2001)

FREDE, M., 'The Sceptic's Beliefs', first publ. in *Neue Hefte für Philosophie* 15-16 (1979); repr. in M. Burnyeat & M. Frede, eds, *The Original Sceptics: A Controversy* (Indianapolis: Hackett, 1997), pp. 1-24

—— 'The Original Notion of Cause', in M. Schofield, M. Burnyeat, & J. Barnes, eds, *Doubt and Dogmatism: Studies in Hellenistic Epistemology* (Oxford: Clarendon Press, 1980); repr. in *Essays in Ancient Philosophy*, pp. 125-50

—— 'Stoics and Skeptics on Clear and Distinct Impressions', in M. Burnyeat, ed., *The Sceptical Tradition* (Berkeley: University of California Press, 1983); repr. in *Essays in Ancient Philosophy*, pp. 151-76

—— 'The Stoic Doctrine of the Affectations of the Soul', in M. Schofield & G. Striker, eds, *The Norms of Nature: Studies in Hellenistic Ethics* (Cambridge: Cambridge University Press, 1986), pp. 93-110

—— *Essays in Ancient Philosophy* (Oxford: Clarendon Press, 1987)

—— 'Euphrates of Tyre', in R. Sorabji, ed., *Aristotle and After*, BICS Supplement 68 (London: Institute of Classical Studies, 1997), pp. 1-11

GAUSS, H., *Plato's Conception of Philosophy* (London: Macmillan, 1937)

GEYTENBEEK, A. C. Van, *Musonius Rufus and Greek Diatribe*, trans. B. L. Hijmans, Wijsgerige Teksten en Studies 8 (Assen: Van Gorcum, 1963)

GIANNANTONI, G., *Socratis et Socraticorum Reliquiae*, 4 vols (Naples: Bibliopolis, 1990); an expanded edition of *Socraticorum Reliquiae* (Rome: Edizioni dell'Ateneo, 1983-85)

GIFFORD, E. H., *Eusebii Pamphili Evangelicae Praeparationis Libri XV*, 4 vols (Oxford: Clarendon Press, 1903)

GILDEMEISTER, J., & F. BÜCHELER, 'Pseudo-Plutarchos περὶ ἀσκήσεως', *Rheinisches Museum für Philologie* 27 (1872), 520-38

GILL, C., 'Did Chrysippus understand Medea?', *Phronesis* 28 (1983), 136-49

—— 'Ancient Psychotherapy', *Journal of the History of Ideas* 46 (1985), 307-25

GLUCKER, J., 'Socrates in the Academic Books and Other Ciceronian Works', in B. Inwood & J. Mansfeld, eds, *Assent and Argument: Studies in Cicero's Academic Books*, Philosophia Antiqua 76 (Leiden: Brill, 1997), pp. 58-88

GOLDSCHMIDT, V., *Le système stoïcien et l'idée de temps*, Bibliothèque d'Histoire de la Philosophie (Paris: Vrin, 1953; 4th edn 1979)

GÖRANSSON, T., *Albinus, Alcinous, Arius Didymus*, Studia Graeca et Latina Gothoburgensia 61 (Göteborg: Acta Universitatis Gothoburgensis, 1995)

GOULD, J. B., *The Philosophy of Chrysippus*, Philosophia Antiqua 17 (Leiden: Brill, 1970)

—— 'The Stoic Conception of Fate', *Journal of the History of Ideas* 35 (1974), 17-32

GOULET, R., *Cléomède, Théorie Élémentaire*, Texte présenté, traduit et commenté, Histoire des doctrines de l'Antiquité classique 3 (Paris: Vrin, 1980)

GOULET-CAZÉ, M.-O., *L'ascèse cynique: Un commentaire de Diogène Laërce VI 70-71*, Histoire des doctrines de l'Antiquité classique 10 (Paris: Vrin, 1986)

—— 'A Comprehensive Catalogue of Known Cynic Philosophers', in R. B. Branham & M.-O. Goulet-Cazé, eds, *The Cynics* (Berkeley: University of California Press, 1996), pp. 389-413; a revised version of 'Répertoire des philosophes cyniques connus', in *L'ascèse cynique* (Paris: Vrin, 1986), pp. 231-48

—— 'Who Was the First Dog?', in R. B. Branham & M.-O. Goulet-Cazé, eds, *The Cynics* (Berkeley: University of California Press, 1996), pp. 414-15

GOULET-CAZÉ, M.-O., & R. GOULET, eds, *Le Cynisme ancien et ses prolongements: Actes du Colloque international du CNRS* (Paris: Presses Universitaires de France, 1993); partially translated in R. B. Branham & M.-O. Goulet-Cazé, eds, *The Cynics* (Berkeley: University of California Press, 1996)

GOURINAT, J.-B., *Les stoïciens et l'âme* (Paris: Presses Universitaires de France, 1996)

—— 'Vivre la philosophie: Pierre Hadot, *Qu'est-ce que la philosophie antique?*', *Critique* no. 587, vol. 52 (1996), 227-46

—— *Premières leçons sur le Manuel d'Épictète* (Paris: Presses Universitaires de France, 1998)

—— *La dialectique des Stoïciens*, Histoire des doctrines de l'Antiquité classique 22 (Paris: Vrin, 2000)

GRANT, A., *The Ethics of Aristotle, Illustrated with Essays and Notes*, 2 vols (London: Longmans, Green, & Co., 3rd edn 1874)

GRAVER, M., *Cicero on the Emotions: Tusculan Disputations 3 and 4*, Translated and with Commentary (Chicago: University of Chicago Press, 2002)

GREENE, W. C., *Scholia Platonica* (Haverford, PA: American Philological Association, 1938)

GRIFFIN, M., 'Philosophy, Politics, and Politicians at Rome', in M. Griffin & J. Barnes, eds, *Philosophia Togata: Essays on Philosophy and Roman Society* (Oxford: Clarendon Press, 1989; repr. 1997), pp. 1-37

GRIFFIN, M., & J. BARNES, eds, *Philosophia Togata: Essays on Philosophy and Roman Society* (Oxford: Clarendon Press, 1989; repr. 1997)

GRIMAL, P., *Sénèque, sa vie, son oeuvre, avec un exposé de sa philosophie* (Paris: Presses Universitaires de France, 1948)

GROTE, G., *Plato, and the Other Companions of Sokrates*, 3 vols (London: Murray, 2nd edn 1867)

GULLEY, N., *The Philosophy of Socrates* (London: Macmillan, 1968)

GUTAS, D., 'Pre-Plotinian Philosophy in Arabic (Other than Platonism and Aristotelianism): A Review of the Sources', *ANRW* II 36.7 (1993), pp. 4939-73; repr. in his *Greek Philosophers in the Arabic Tradition* (Aldershot: Ashgate, 2000)

GUTHRIE, W. K. C., *A History of Greek Philosophy*; Volume I The Earlier Presocratics and the Pythagoreans; Volume II The Presocratic Tradition from Parmenides to Democritus; Volume III The Fifth-Century Enlightenment; Volume IV Plato, The Man and his Dialogues: Earlier Period; Volume V The Later Plato and the Academy; Volume VI Aristotle An Encounter, 6 vols (Cambridge: Cambridge University Press, 1962-81)

HACKFORTH, R., *The Composition of Plato's Apology* (Cambridge: Cambridge University Press, 1933)

—— 'Socrates', *Philosophy* 8 (1933); repr. in W. J. Prior, ed., *Socrates: Critical Assessments*, 4 vols (London: Routledge, 1996), vol. 1, pp. 1-13

HADOT, I., *Seneca und die griechisch-römische Tradition der Seelenleitung*, Quellen und Studien zur Geschichte der Philosophie 13 (Berlin: De Gruyter, 1969)

—— *Le problème du néoplatonisme alexandrin: Hiéroclès et Simplicius* (Paris: Études Augustiniennes, 1978)

—— 'The Spiritual Guide', in A. H. Armstrong, ed., *Classical Mediterranean Spirituality: Egyptian, Greek, Roman*, World Spirituality 15 (London: SCM, 1989), pp. 436-59

—— 'The Life and Work of Simplicius in Greek and Arabic Sources', in R. Sorabji, ed., *Aristotle Transformed: The Ancient Commentators and Their Influence* (London: Duckworth, 1990), pp. 275-303; a translation of 'La vie et l'oeuvre de Simplicius d'après des sources grecques et arabes', in I. Hadot, ed. *Simplicius, sa vie, son oeuvre, sa survie: Actes du colloque internationale de Paris (28 Sept.-1 Oct. 1985)*, Peripatoi 15 (Berlin: De Gruyter, 1987), pp. 3-39

—— *Simplicius, Commentaire sur le Manuel d'Épictète*, Introduction et édition critique du texte grec, Philosophia Antiqua 66 (Leiden: Brill, 1996)

HADOT, P., 'Une clé des *Pensées* de Marc Aurèle: les trois *topoi* philosophiques selon Épictète', *Les Études philosophiques* 1 (1978), 65-83

—— 'Les divisions des parties de la philosophie dans l'Antiquité', *Museum Helveticum* 36 (1979), 201-23; reprinted in *Études de philosophie ancienne*

—— *Exercices spirituels et philosophie antique* (Paris: Études Augustiniennes, 1981)

—— 'Philosophie, Discours Philosophique, et Divisions de la Philosophie chez les Stoïciens', *Revue Internationale de Philosophie* 45 (1991), 205-19

—— 'La figure du sage dans l'Antiquité gréco-latine', in G. Gadoffre, ed., *Les sagesses du monde* (Paris: Éditions Universitaires, 1991), pp. 9-26; reprinted in *Études de philosophie ancienne*

—— 'La philosophie antique: une éthique ou une pratique?', in P. Demont, ed., *Problèmes de morale antique* (Amiens: Université d'Amiens, 1993), pp. 7-37; reprinted in *Études de philosophie ancienne*

—— *Qu'est-ce que la philosophie antique?*, Folio Essais (Paris: Gallimard, 1995); translated as *What is Ancient Philosophy?*, trans. M. Chase (Cambridge, MA: The Belknap Press of Harvard University Press, 2002)

—— *Philosophy as a Way of Life: Spiritual Exercises from Socrates to Foucault*, Edited with an Introduction by Arnold I. Davidson, Translated by Michael Chase (Oxford: Blackwell, 1995); an expanded edition and translation of the 2nd edn of *Exercices spirituels et philosophie antique* (Paris: Études Augustiniennes, 1987)

—— *The Inner Citadel: The Meditations of Marcus Aurelius*, trans. M. Chase (Cambridge, MA: Harvard University Press, 1998); a translation of *La Citadelle intérieure* (Paris: Fayard, 1992)

—— *Études de philosophie ancienne* (Paris: Les Belles Lettres, 1998)

HAHM, D. E., *The Origins of Stoic Cosmology* (Columbus: Ohio State University Press, 1977)

—— 'The Ethical Doxography of Arius Didymus', *ANRW* II 36.4 (1990), pp. 2935-3055

—— 'Diogenes Laertius VII: On the Stoics', *ANRW* II 36.6 (1992), pp. 4076-182

HAMILTON, E., & H. CAIRNS, *The Collected Dialogues of Plato* (Princeton: Princeton University Press, 1961)

HANKINSON, R. J., 'Values, Objectivity, and Dialectic; The Sceptical Attack on Ethics: Its Methods, Aims, and Success', *Phronesis* 39 (1994), 45-68

—— *The Sceptics*, The Arguments of the Philosophers (London: Routledge, 1995)

—— 'Natural Criteria and the Transparency of Judgement: Antiochus, Philo, and Galen on Epistemological Justification', in B. Inwood & J. Mansfeld, eds, *Assent and Argument: Studies in Cicero's Academic Books*, Philosophia Antiqua 76 (Leiden: Brill, 1997), pp. 161-216

HEGEL, G. W. F., *Werke*, ed. E. Moldenhauer & K. M. Michel, 20 vols (Frankfurt: Suhrkamp, 1969-71)

—— *Lectures on the History of Philosophy*, trans. E. S. Haldane & F. H. Simson, 3 vols (Lincoln: University of Nebraska Press, [1892-96] 1995); a translation of *Vorlesungen über die Geschichte der Philosophie* (first published 1833-36), in *Werke*, vols 18-20

HERSHBELL, J., 'The Stoicism of Epictetus: Twentieth Century Perspectives', *ANRW* II 36.3 (1989), pp. 2148-63

HICKS, R. D., *Stoic and Epicurean* (New York: Russell & Russell, [1911] 1962)

HIJMANS, B. L., Ἄσκησις: *Notes on Epictetus' Educational System* (Assen: Van Gorcum, 1959)

—— 'A Note on φύσις in Epictetus', *Mnemosyne* [4th series] 20 (1967), 279-84

HOCK, R. F., 'Simon the Shoemaker as an Ideal Cynic', *Greek, Roman, and Byzantine Studies* 17 (1976), 41-53

HOROWITZ, M. C., 'The Stoic Synthesis of the Idea of Natural Law in Man: Four Themes', *Journal of the History of Ideas* 35 (1974), 3-16

IERODIAKONOU, K., 'The Stoic Division of Philosophy', *Phronesis* 38 (1993), 57-74

—— 'Alexander of Aphrodisias on Medicine as a Stochastic Art', in P. J. van der Eijk, H. F. J. Horstmanshoff, & P. H. Schrijvers, eds, *Ancient Medicine in its Socio-Cultural Context*, Clio Medica 27-28, 2 vols (Amsterdam: Rodopi, 1995), vol. 2, pp. 473-85

—— ed., *Topics in Stoic Philosophy* (Oxford: Clarendon Press, 1999)

IGNATIUS OF LOYOLA, *Sancti Ignatii de Loyola, Exercitia Spiritualia*, textum antiquissimorum nova editio, lexicon textus Hispani, opus inchoavit Iosephus Calveras, absolvit Candidus de Dalmases, Monumenta Historica Societatis Iesu 100 (Rome: Institutm Historicum Societatis Iesu, 1969)

—— *Personal Writings: Reminiscences, Spiritual Diary, Select Letters including the text of The Spiritual Exercises*, Translated with Introductions and Notes by Joseph A. Munitiz and Philip Endean (Harmondsworth: Penguin, 1996)

ILDEFONSE, F., *Les Stoïciens I: Zénon, Cléanthe, Chrysippe*, Figures du Savoir 25 (Paris: Les Belles Lettres, 2000)

INWOOD, B., 'Hierocles: Theory and Argument in the Second Century AD', *Oxford Studies in Ancient Philosophy* 2 (1984), 151-84

—— *Ethics and Human Action in Early Stoicism* (Oxford: Clarendon Press, 1985)

—— 'Goal and Target in Stoicism', *Journal of Philosophy* 83 (1986), 547-56

—— ed., *The Cambridge Companion to the Stoics* (Cambridge: Cambridge University Press, 2003)

INWOOD, B., & L. P. GERSON, *Hellenistic Philosophy: Introductory Readings* (Indianapolis: Hackett, 1988; 2nd edn 1997)

INWOOD, B., & J. MANSFELD, eds, *Assent and Argument: Studies in Cicero's Academic Books*, Proceedings of the Seventh Symposium Hellenisticum, Philosophia Antiqua 76 (Leiden: Brill, 1997)

IOPPOLO, A.-M., 'Presentation and Assent: A Physical and Cognitive Problem in Early Stoicism', *Classical Quarterly* 40 (1990), 433-49

IRWIN, T., *Plato's Moral Theory: The Early and Middle Dialogues* (Oxford: Clarendon Press, 1977)

—— *Plato, Gorgias*, Translated with Notes (Oxford: Clarendon Press, 1979)

—— *Plato's Ethics* (New York: Oxford University Press, 1995)

JACKSON, R., K. LYCOS, & H. TARRANT, *Olympiodorus, Commentary on Plato's Gorgias*, Translated with Full Notes, Introduction by Harold Tarrant, Philosophia Antiqua 78 (Leiden: Brill, 1998)

JAEGER, W., 'Aristotle's Use of Medicine as Model of Method in his Ethics', *Journal of Hellenic Studies* 77 (1957), 54-61

JAGU, A., *Épictète et Platon: Essai sur les relations du Stoïcisme et du Platonisme à propos de la Morale des Entretiens* (Paris: Vrin, 1946)

—— *Zénon de Cittium: Son Rôle dans l'établissement de la Morale stoïcienne* (Paris: Vrin, 1946)

JOHN OF SALISBURY, *Policraticus: Of the Frivolities of Courtiers and the Footprints of Philosophers*, trans. C. J. Nederman, Cambridge Texts in the History of Political Thought (Cambridge: Cambridge University Press, 1990)

JORDAN, W., *Ancient Concepts of Philosophy* (London: Routledge, 1990)

KAHN, C. H., *The Art and Thought of Heraclitus*, An Edition of the Fragments with Translation and Commentary (Cambridge: Cambridge University Press, 1979)

—— 'Discovering the Will: From Aristotle to Augustine', in J. M. Dillon and A. A. Long, eds, *The Question of "Eclecticism": Studies in Later Greek Philosophy* (Berkeley: University of California Press, 1988), pp. 234-59

—— 'Aeschines on Socratic Eros', in P. A. Vander Waerdt, ed., *The Socratic Movement* (Ithaca: Cornell University Press, 1994), pp. 87-106

—— *Plato and the Socratic Dialogue: The Philosophical Use of a Literary Form* (Cambridge: Cambridge University Press, 1996)

KANT, I., *Critique of Pure Reason*, trans. N. Kemp Smith (London: Macmillian, 1929; repr. 1990)

KENYON, F. G., *Books and Readers in Ancient Greece and Rome* (Oxford: Clarendon Press, 1932; 2nd edn 1951)

KERFERD, G. B., 'What Does the Wise Man Know?', in J. M. Rist, ed., *The Stoics* (Berkeley: University of California Press, 1978), pp. 125-36

—— *The Sophistic Movement* (Cambridge: Cambridge University Press, 1981)

KIDD, I. G., 'Stoic Intermediates and the End for Man', in A. A. Long, ed., *Problems in Stoicism* (London: Athlone, 1971; repr. 1996), pp. 150-72

—— *Posidonius, The Commentary*, Cambridge Classical Texts and Commentaries 14, 2 vols (Cambridge: Cambridge University Press, 1988); see also Edelstein & Kidd

—— *Posidonius, The Translation of the Fragments*, Cambridge Classical Texts and Commentaries 36 (Cambridge: Cambridge University Press, 1999); see also Edelstein & Kidd

KIERKEGAARD, S., *The Concept of Irony with Continual Reference to Socrates*, trans. H. V. Hong & E. H. Hong (Princeton: Princeton University Press, 1989)

KINDSTRAND, J. F., *Bion of Borysthenes*, A Collection of the Fragments with Introduction and Commentary, Studia Graeca Upsaliensia 11 (Uppsala: Acta Universitatis Upsaliensis, 1976)

—— 'Diogenes Laertius and the *Chreia* Tradition', *Elenchos* 7 'Diogene Laerzio Storico del Pensiero Antico' (1986), 217-43

KLOSKO, G., 'The Technical Conception of Virtue', *Journal of the History of Philosophy* 19 (1981), 95-102

KOFMAN, S., *Socrates: Fictions of a Philosopher*, trans. C. Porter (London: Athlone, 1998); a tranlsation of *Socrate(s)* (Paris: Éditions Galilée, 1989)

KRAYE, J., *Cambridge Translations of Renaissance Philosophical Texts 1: Moral Philosophy* (Cambridge: Cambridge University Press, 1997)

—— 'Ethnicorum omnium sanctissimus: Marcus Aurelius and his *Meditations* from Xylander to Diderot', in J. Kraye & M. W. F. Stone, eds, *Humanism and Early Modern Philosophy* (London: Routledge, 2000), pp. 107-34

KÜHN, C. G., *Claudii Galeni Opera Omnia*, 20 vols in 22 (Leipzig: Knobloch, 1821-33)

LACEY, A. R., 'Our Knowledge of Socrates', in G. Vlastos, ed., *The Philosophy of Socrates: A Collection of Critical Essays* (New York: Anchor, 1971), pp. 22-49

LAGRÉE, J., *Juste Lipse et la restauration du stoïcisme: Étude et traduction des traités stoïciens De la constance, Manuel de philosophie stoïcienne, Physique des stoïciens* (Paris: Vrin, 1994)

LAPIDGE, M., 'ἀρχαί and στοιχεῖα: A Problem in Stoic Cosmology', *Phronesis* 18 (1973), 240-78

—— 'Stoic Cosmology', in J. M. Rist, ed., *The Stoics* (Berkeley: University of California Press, 1978), pp. 161-85

LECLERCQ, J., 'Exercices spirituels', in *Dictionnaire de spiritualité*, vol. 4 (1960), cols 1902-08

LENZ, F. W., & C. A. BEHR, *P. Aelii Aristidis Opera Quae Exstant Omnia, Volumen Primum: Orationes I-XVI* (Leiden: Brill, 1976-80)

LEWIS, E., 'Diogenes Laertius and the Stoic Theory of Mixture', *Bulletin of the Institute of Classical Studies* 35 (1988), 84-90

—— 'The Stoics on Identity and Individuation', *Phronesis* 40 (1995), 89-108

LIPSIUS, J., *De Constantia Libri Duo, Qui alloquium praecipue continent in Publicis malis*, Tertia editio (Antwerp: Plantin, [1584] 1586)

—— *Manuductionis ad Stoicam Philosophiam Libri Tres: L. Annaeo Senecae, aliisque scriptoribus illustrandis* (Antwerp: Plaintin-Moretus, 1604)

—— *Physiologiae Stoicorum Libri Tres: L. Annaeo Senecae, aliisque scriptoribus illustrandis* (Antwerp: Plantin-Moretus, 1604)

—— *Two Bookes Of Constancie*, Englished by Sir John Stradling, Edited with an Introduction by Rudolf Kirk (New Brunswick: Rutgers University Press, 1939)

LONG, A. A., 'Carneades and the Stoic *telos*', *Phronesis* 12 (1967), 59-90

—— 'The Stoic Concept of Evil', *Philosophical Quarterly* 18 (1968), 329-43

—— 'Stoic Determinism and Alexander of Aphrodisias *De Fato* (i-xiv)', *Archiv für Geschichte der Philosophie* 52 (1970), 247-68

—— 'The Logical Basis of Stoic Ethics', *Proceedings of the Aristotelian Society* (1970-71), 85-104; repr. in *Stoic Studies*, pp. 134-55

—— ed., *Problems in Stoicism* (London: Athlone, 1971; repr. 1996)

—— 'Language and Thought in Stoicism', in A. A. Long, ed., *Problems in Stoicism* (London: Athlone, 1971; repr. 1996), pp. 75-113

—— 'Freedom and Determinism in the Stoic Theory of Human Action', in A. A. Long, ed., *Problems in Stoicism* (London: Athlone, 1971; repr. 1996), pp. 173-99

—— *Hellenistic Philosophy* (London: Duckworth, 1974; 2nd edn 1986)

—— 'Heraclitus and Stoicism', *Philosophia* 5 (1975), 133-56; repr. in *Stoic Studies*, pp. 35-57

—— 'Dialectic and the Stoic Sage', in J. M. Rist, ed., *The Stoics* (Berkeley: University of California Press, 1978), pp. 101-24; repr. in *Stoic Studies*, pp. 85-106

—— 'Soul and Body in Stoicism', *Phronesis* 27 (1982), 34-57; repr. in *Stoic Studies*, pp. 224-49

—— 'Epictetus, Marcus Aurelius', in T. J. Luce, ed., *Ancient Writers: Greece and Rome* (New York: Scribner's, 1982), pp. 985-1002

—— 'Socrates in Hellenistic Philosophy', *Classical Quarterly* 38 (1988), 150-71; repr. in *Stoic Studies*, pp. 1-33

—— 'Stoic Eudaimonism', *Proceedings of the Boston Colloquium in Ancient Philosophy* 4 (1988), 77-101; repr. in *Stoic Studies*, pp. 179-201

—— 'Representation and the Self in Stoicism', in S. Everson, ed., *Psychology*, Companions to Ancient Thought 2 (Cambridge: Cambridge University Press, 1991), pp. 102-20; repr. in *Stoic Studies*, pp. 264-85

—— 'Hierocles on *Oikeiōsis* and Self-Perception', in K. J. Boudouris, ed., *Hellenistic Philosophy* (Athens: International Center for Greek Philosophy and Culture, 1993), pp. 93-104; repr. in *Stoic Studies*, pp. 250-63

—— 'The Socratic Tradition: Diogenes, Crates, and Hellenistic Ethics', in R. B. Branham & M.-O. Goulet-Cazé, eds, *The Cynics: The Cynic Movement in Antiquity and its Legacy* (Berkeley: University of California Press, 1996), pp. 28-46

—— *Stoic Studies* (Cambridge: Cambridge University Press, 1996; repr. Berkeley: University of California Press, 2001)

—— *Epictetus: A Stoic and Socratic Guide to Life* (Oxford: Clarendon Press, 2002)

LONG, A. A., & D. N. SEDLEY, *The Hellenistic Philosophers*, Volume 1: Translations of the principal sources with philosophical commentary, Volume 2: Greek and Latin texts with notes and bibliography (Cambridge: Cambridge University Press, 1987)

LUTZ, C. E., 'Musonius Rufus: The Roman Socrates', *Yale Classical Studies* 10 (1947), 3-147

MACKENDRICK, P., *The Philosophical Books of Cicero* (London: Duckworth, 1989)

MANSFELD, J., '*Techne*: A New Fragment of Chrysippus', *Greek, Roman, and Byzantine Studies* 24 (1983), 57-65

—— 'Diogenes Laertius on Stoic Philosophy', *Elenchos* 7 'Diogene Laerzio Storico del Pensiero Antico' (1986), 295-382

—— *Prolegomena: Questions to be Settled Before the Study of an Author, or a Text*, Philosophia Antiqua 61 (Leiden: Brill, 1994)

MANSFELD, J., & D. T. RUNIA, *Aëtiana: The Method and Intellectual Context of a Doxographer. Volume One: The Sources*, Philosophia Antiqua 73 (Leiden: Brill, 1997)

MATTOCK, J. N., 'A Translation of the Arabic Epitome of Galen's Book Περὶ Ἠθῶν', in S. M. Stern, A. Hourani, & V. Brown, eds, *Islamic Philosophy and the Classical Tradition: Essays Presented by his Friends and Pupils to Richard Walzer on his Seventieth Birthday*, Oriental Studies 5 (Oxford: Cassirer & Columbia: University of South Carolina Press, 1972), pp. 235-60

MEJER, J., *Diogenes Laertius and his Hellenistic Background*, Hermes Einzelschriften 40 (Wiesbaden: Steiner, 1978)

MILLAR, F., 'Epictetus and the Imperial Court', *Journal of Roman Studies* 55 (1965), 141-48

MILLER, J., 'From Socrates to Foucault: The Problem of the Philosophical Life', *New Formations* 25 'Michel Foucault: J'Accuse' (1995), 48-56

MOMIGLIANO, A., *The Development of Greek Biography* (Cambridge, MA: Harvard University Press, 1971; expanded edn 1993)

MONTUORI, M., *Socrates: Physiology of a Myth*, London Studies in Classical Philology 6 (Amsterdam: Gieben, 1981)

—— *De Socrate Iuste Damnato: The Rise of the Socratic Problem in the Eighteenth Century*, London Studies in Classical Philology 7 (Amsterdam: Gieben, 1981)

—— *Socrates: An Approach*, Philosophica 2 (Amsterdam: Gieben, 1988)

—— *The Socratic Problem: The History – The Sources*, Philosophica 4 (Amsterdam: Gieben, 1992)

MORE, P. E., *Hellenistic Philosophies*, The Greek Tradition II (Princeton: Princeton University Press, 1923)

MOREAU, J.-P., ed., *Le stoïcisme au XVIe et au XVIIe siècle*, La retour des philosophies antiques à l'âge classique 1 (Paris: Albin Michel, 1999)

MORFORD, M., *Stoics and Neostoics: Rubens and the Circle of Lipsius* (Princeton: Princeton University Press, 1991)

—— *The Roman Philosophers: From the Time of Cato the Censor to the Death of Marcus Aurelius* (London: Routledge, 2002)

MORRISON, D., 'The Ancient Sceptic's Way of Life', *Metaphilosophy* 21 (1990), 204-22

—— 'On the Alleged Historical Reliability of Plato's *Apology*', *Archiv für Geschichte der Philosophie* 82 (2000), 235-65

MOWAT, J. L. G., 'A Lacuna in Arrian', *Journal of Philology* 7 (1877), 60-63

MUELLER, I., & J. GOULD, *Alexander of Aphrodisias, On Aristotle Prior Analytics 1.8-13*, Ancient Commentators on Aristotle (London: Duckworth, 1999)

NEHAMAS, A., 'Socratic Intellectualism', *Proceedings of the Boston Area Colloquium in Ancient Philosophy* 2 (1987); repr. in *Virtues of Authenticity*, pp. 27-58

—— 'What Did Socrates Teach and to Whom Did He Teach it?', *Review of Metaphysics* 46 (1992); repr. in *Virtues of Authenticity*, pp. 59-82

—— *The Art of Living: Socratic Reflections from Plato to Foucault* (Berkeley: University of California Press, 1998)

—— *Virtues of Authenticity: Essays on Plato and Socrates* (Princeton: Princeton University Press, 1999)

NEWMAN, R. J., '*Cotidie meditare*: Theory and Practice of the *meditatio* in Imperial Stoicism', *ANRW* II 36.3 (1989), pp. 1473-517

NIEHUES-PRÖBSTING, H., 'The Modern Reception of Cynicism: Diogenes and the Enlightenment', in R. B. Branham & M.-O. Goulet-Cazé, eds, *The Cynics: The Cynic Movement in Antiquity and its Legacy* (Berkeley: University of California Press, 1996), pp. 329-65

NIETZSCHE, F., *Nietzsche Werke: Kritische Gesamtausgabe*, Herausgegeben von Giorgio Colli und Mazzino Montinari (Berlin: De Gruyter, 1967-)

—— *Unfashionable Observations*, trans. R. T. Gray, The Complete Works of Friedrich Nietzsche 2 (Stanford: Stanford University Press, 1995)

—— *Unpublished Writings from the Period of Unfashionable Observations*, trans. R. T. Gray, The Complete Works of Friedrich Nietzsche 11 (Stanford: Stanford University Press, 1999)

NUSSBAUM, M. C., *The Fragility of Goodness: Luck and Ethics in Greek Tragedy and Philosophy* (Cambridge: Cambridge University Press, 1986)

—— *The Therapy of Desire: Theory and Practice in Hellenistic Ethics* (Princeton: Princeton University Press, 1994)

NUTTON, V., *Galen, On Prognosis*, Edition, Translation, and Commentary, Corpus Medicorum Graecorum V 8.1 (Berlin: Akademie, 1979)

O'BRIEN, M. J., *The Socratic Paradoxes and the Greek Mind* (Chapel Hill: University of North Carolina Press, 1967)

OLDFATHER, W. A., *Contributions Toward a Bibliography of Epictetus* (Urbana: University of Illinois, 1927)

—— *Contributions Toward a Bibliography of Epictetus: A Supplement*, edited by Marian Harman (Urbana: University of Illinois Press, 1952)

OLIVER, R. P., *Niccolo Perotti's Version of The Enchiridion of Epictetus*, Edited with an Introduction and a List of Perotti's Writings (Urbana: University of Illinois Press, 1954)

O'NEILL, W., *Proclus, Alcibiades I*, Translation and Commentary (The Hague: Martinus Nijhoff, 1965)

OSLER, M. J., ed., *Atoms, Pneuma, and Tranquillity: Epicurean and Stoic Themes in European Thought* (Cambridge: Cambridge University Press, 1991)

PALMER, R. G., *Seneca's De Remediis Fortuitorum and the Elizabethans* (Chicago: Institute of Elizabethan Studies, 1953)

PANIZZA, L. A., 'Stoic Psychotherapy in the Middle Ages and Renaissance: Petrarch's *De Remediis*', in M. J. Osler, ed., *Atoms, Pneuma, and Tranquillity: Epicurean and Stoic Themes in European Thought* (Cambridge: Cambridge University Press, 1991), pp. 39-65

PASQUINO, P., 'Le statut ontologique des incorporels dans l'ancien Stoicisme', in J. Brunschwig, ed., *Les Stoïciens et leur logique: Actes du Colloque de Chantilly 18-22 Septembre 1976*, Bibliothèque d'Histoire de la Philosophie (Paris: Vrin, 1978), pp. 375-86

PEMBROKE, S. G., 'Oikeiōsis', in A. A. Long, ed., *Problems in Stoicism* (London: Athlone, 1971; repr. 1996), pp. 114-49

PENNER, T., 'The Unity of Virtue', *Philosophical Review* 80 (1971); reprinted in G. Fine, ed., *Plato 2: Ethics, Politics, Religion, and the Soul*, Oxford Readings in Philosophy (Oxford: Oxford University Press, 1999), pp. 78-104

PETRARCH, F., *Francisci Petrarchae Florentini, Philosophi, Oratoris, & Poetae clarissimi, ... Opera quae extant omnia*, 4 vols (Basel: Henrichus Petri, 1554)

—— *Prose*, ed. G. Martellotti *et al.* (Milan: Riccardo Ricciardi, 1955)

—— *Remedies for Fortune Fair and Foul*, A Modern English Translation of *De remediis utriusque Fortune* with a Commentary by C. H. Rawski, 5 vols (Bloomington: Indiana University Press, 1991)

PIGEAUD, J., *La maladie de l'âme: Étude sur la relation de l'âme et du corps dans la tradition médico-philosophique antique*, Collection d'Études Anciennes (Paris: Les Belles Lettres, 1981)

POHLENZ, M., *Die Stoa: Geschichte einer geistigen Bewegung*, 2 vols (Göttingen: Vandenhoeck & Ruprecht, 1949; 3rd edn 1964)

POLITIAN, A., *Omnia Opera Angeli Politiani, et alia quaedam lectu digna, quorum nomina in sequenti indici uidere licet* (Venice: Aldus Manutius, 1498)

POMEROY, A. J., *Arius Didymus, Epitome of Stoic Ethics*, Society of Biblical Literature Texts and Translations 44 Graeco-Roman Series 14 (Atlanta: Society of Biblical Literature, 1999)

POWELL, J. G. F., ed., *Cicero the Philosopher* (Oxford: Clarendon Press, 1995)

PRIOR, W. J., ed., *Socrates: Critical Assessments*, 4 vols (London: Routledge, 1996)

RABBOW, P., *Seelenführung: Methodik der Exerzitien in der Antike* (Munich: Kösel Verlag, 1954)

REESOR, M. E., *The Nature of Man in Early Stoic Philosophy* (London: Duckworth, 1989)

REEVE, C. D. C., *Socrates in the Apology: An Essay on Plato's Apology of Socrates* (Indianapolis: Hackett, 1989)

REID, J. S., *M. Tulli Ciceronis Academica*, The Text Revised and Explained (London: Macmillan, 1885)

REYNOLDS, L. D., *The Medieval Tradition of Seneca's Letters* (Oxford: Oxford University Press, 1965)

RIST, J. M., *Stoic Philosophy* (Cambridge: Cambridge University Press, 1969)

—— ed., *The Stoics* (Berkeley: University of California Press, 1978)

—— 'Are You a Stoic? The Case of Marcus Aurelius', in B. F. Meyers & E. P. Sanders, eds, *Jewish and Christian Self-Definition 3* (London: SCM, 1982), pp. 23-45; repr. in his *Man, Soul and Body: Essays in Ancient Thought from Plato to Dionysius* (Aldershot: Ashgate, 1996)

—— 'Seneca and Stoic Orthodoxy', *ANRW* II 36.3 (1989), pp. 1993-2012; repr. in his *Man, Soul and Body: Essays in Ancient Thought from Plato to Dionysius* (Aldershot: Ashgate, 1996)

ROOCHNIK, D., 'Socrates' Use of the Techne-Analogy', *Journal of the History of Philosophy* 24 (1986); repr. in H. H. Benson, ed., *Essays on the Philosophy of Socrates* (New York: Oxford University Press, 1992), pp. 185-97

—— *Of Art and Wisdom: Plato's Understanding of Techne* (Pennsylvania: Pennsylvania State University Press, 1996)

ROSENTHAL, F., *The Classical Heritage in Islam*, trans. E. & J. Marmorstein (London: Routledge & Kegan Paul, 1975; repr. Routledge, 1992); a translation of *Das Fortleben der Antike im Islam* (Zürich: Artemis Verlag, 1965)

ROSS, W. D., *Aristotle's Metaphysics*, A Revised Text with Introduction and Commentary, 2 vols (Oxford: Clarendon Press, 1924)

—— 'The Problem of Socrates', *Proceedings of the Classical Association* (1933); repr. in W. J. Prior, ed., *Socrates: Critical Assessments*, 4 vols (London: Routledge, 1996), vol. 1., pp. 26-37

RUTHERFORD, R. B., *The Meditations of Marcus Aurelius: A Study* (Oxford: Clarendon Press, 1989)

SAMBURSKY, S., *Physics of the Stoics* (London: Routledge & Kegan Paul, 1959; repr. Princeton: Princeton University Press, 1987)

SANDBACH, F. H., 'Phantasia Kataleptike', in A. A. Long, ed., *Problems in Stoicism* (London: Athlone, 1971; repr. 1996), pp. 9-21

—— *The Stoics* (London: Chatto & Windus, 1975; repr. Bristol Classical Press, 1989)

—— *Aristotle and the Stoics*, Cambridge Philological Society suppl. vol. 10 (Cambridge: Cambridge Philological Society, 1985)

SANTAS, G. X., *Socrates: Philosophy in Plato's Early Dialogues*, The Arguments of the Philosophers (London: Routledge & Kegan Paul, 1979)

SCHLEIERMACHER, F. D. E., *Introductions to the Dialogues of Plato*, trans. W. Dobson (Cambridge: Deighton & London: Parker, 1836)

—— 'On the Worth of Socrates as a Philosopher', trans. C. Thirlwall; printed as an appendix to G. Wiggers, *A Life of Socrates* (London: Taylor and Watson, 1840), pp. 129-55

SCHOFIELD, M., 'Ariston of Chios and the Unity of Virtue', *Ancient Philosophy* 4 (1984), 83-96

SCHOFIELD, M., M. BURNYEAT, & J. BARNES, eds, *Doubt and Dogmatism: Studies in Hellenistic Epistemology*, Proceedings of the First Symposium Hellenisticum (Oxford: Clarendon Press, 1980)

SCHOFIELD, M., & G. STRIKER, eds, *The Norms of Nature: Studies in Hellenistic Ethics*, Proceedings of the Third Symposium Hellenisticum (Cambridge: Cambridge University Press, 1986)

SCHOPENHAUER, A., *The World as Will and Representation*, trans. E. F. J. Payne, 2 vols (New York: Dover, 1966)

SEDLEY, D., 'Philosophical Allegiance in the Greco-Roman World', in M. Griffin & J. Barnes, eds, *Philosophia Togata: Essays on Philosophy and Roman Society* (Oxford: Clarendon Press, 1989; repr. 1997), pp. 97-119

—— 'Chrysippus on Psychophysical Causality', in J. Brunschwig & M. C. Nussbaum, eds, *Passions and Perceptions: Studies in Hellenistic Philosophy of Mind* (Cambridge: Cambridge University Press, 1993), pp. 313-31

—— *Lucretius and the Transformation of Greek Wisdom* (Cambridge: Cambridge University Press, 1998)

SHARPLES, R. W., *Alexander of Aphrodisias on Fate*, Text, Translation, and Commentary (London: Duckworth, 1983)

—— *Alexander of Aphrodisias, Quaestiones 2.16-3.15*, Ancient Commentators on Aristotle (London: Duckworth, 1994)

SHOREY, P., 'Φύσις, μελέτη, ἐπιστήμη', *Transactions of the American Philological Association* 40 (1909), 185-201

SINGER, P. N., *Galen, Selected Works*, Translated with an Introduction and Notes (Oxford: Oxford University Press, 1997)

SLEEMAN, J. H., & G. POLLET, *Lexicon Plotinianum*, Ancient and Medieval Philosophy 2 (Louvain: Leuven University Press & Leiden: Brill, 1980)

SOLMSEN, F., 'Cleanthes or Posidonius? The Basis of Stoic Physics', in his *Kleine Schriften 1* (Hildesheim: Olms, 1968), pp. 436-60

SORABJI, R., *Matter, Space, and Motion: Theories in Antiquity and Their Sequel* (London: Duckworth, 1988)

—— ed., *Aristotle Transformed: The Ancient Commentators and Their Influence* (London: Duckworth, 1990)

—— ed., *Aristotle and After*, BICS Supplement 68 (London: Institute of Classical Studies, 1997)

—— 'Is Stoic Philosophy Helpful as Psychotherapy?', in R. Sorabji, ed., *Aristotle and After*, BICS Supplement 68 (London: Institute of Classical Studies, 1997), pp. 197- 209

—— *Emotion and Peace of Mind: From Stoic Agitation to Christian Temptation* (Oxford: Oxford University Press, 2000)

SPANNEUT, M., *Permanence du Stoïcisme: De Zénon à Malraux* (Gembloux: Duculot, 1973)

SPARSHOTT, F. E., 'Zeno on Art: Anatomy of a Definition', in J. M. Rist, ed., *The Stoics* (Berkeley: University of California Press, 1978), pp. 273-90

STADTER, P. A., *Arrian of Nicomedia* (Chapel Hill: University of North Carolina Press, 1980)

STANTON, G. R., 'The Cosmopolitan Ideas of Epictetus and Marcus Aurelius', *Phronesis* 13 (1968), 183-95

STARR, C. G., 'Epictetus and the Tyrant', *Classical Philology* 44 (1949), 20-29

STERNBACH, L., *Gnomologium Vaticanum e codice Vaticano Graeco 743*, Texte und Kommentare 2 (Berlin: De Gruyter, 1963)

STOCKDALE, J. B., 'Testing Epictetus's Doctrines in a Laboratory of Human Behaviour', *Bulletin of the Institute of Classical Studies* 50 (1995), 1-13

STRAATEN, M. van, *Panaetii Rhodii Fragmenta*, Philosophia Antiqua 5 (Leiden: Brill, 1952)

STRIKER, G., 'Κριτήριον τῆς ἀληθείας', *Nachrichten der Akademie der Wissenschaften zu Göttingen* 1 (1974); repr. in *Essays on Hellenistic Epistemology and Ethics*, pp. 22-76

—— 'Sceptical Strategies', in M. Schofield, M. Burnyeat, & J. Barnes, eds, *Doubt and Dogmatism: Studies in Hellenistic Epistemology* (Oxford: Clarendon Press, 1980); repr. in *Essays on Hellenistic Epistemology and Ethics*, pp. 92-115

—— 'The Role of *Oikeiōsis* in Stoic Ethics', *Oxford Studies in Ancient Philosophy* 1 (1983); repr. in *Essays on Hellenistic Epistemology and Ethics*, pp. 281-97

—— 'Antipater, or The Art of Living', in M. Schofield & G. Striker, eds, *The Norms of Nature: Studies in Hellenistic Ethics* (Cambridge: Cambridge University Press, 1986); repr. in *Essays on Hellenistic Epistemology and Ethics*, pp. 298-315

—— '*Ataraxia*: Happiness as Tranquillity', *The Monist* 73 (1990); repr. in *Essays on Hellenistic Epistemology and Ethics*, pp. 183-95

—— 'Following Nature: A Study in Stoic Ethics', *Oxford Studies in Ancient Philosophy* 9 (1991); repr. in *Essays on Hellenistic Epistemology and Ethics*, pp. 221-80

—— 'Plato's Socrates and the Stoics', in P. A. Vander Waerdt, ed., *The Socratic Movement* (Ithaca: Cornell University Press, 1994), pp. 241-51; also repr. in *Essays on Hellenistic Epistemology and Ethics*

—— *Essays on Hellenistic Epistemology and Ethics* (Cambridge: Cambridge University Press, 1996)

STRYCKER, E. DE, *Plato's Apology of Socrates: A Literary and Philosophical Study with a Running Commentary*, Edited and Completed from the Papers of the Late E. de Strycker by S. R. Slings, Mnemosyne Supplementum 137 (Leiden: Brill, 1994)

TARDIEU, M., 'Sabiens coraniques et "Sabiens" de Harran', *Journal asiatique* 274 (1986), 1-44

TAYLOR, A. E., *Varia Socratica: First Series*, St. Andrews University Publications 9 (Oxford: Parker, 1911)

—— *Socrates* (London: Peter Davies, 1932)

TODD, R. B., *Alexander of Aphrodisias on Stoic Physics*, A Study of the *De Mixtione* with Preliminary Essays, Text, Translation and Commentary, Philosophia Antiqua 28 (Leiden: Brill, 1976)

—— 'Monism and Immanence: The Foundations of Stoic Physics', in J. M. Rist, ed., *The Stoics* (Berkeley: University of California Press, 1978), pp. 137-60

—— 'The Stoics and their Cosmology in the First and Second Centuries AD', *ANRW* II 36.3 (1989), pp. 1365-78

TSEKOURAKIS, D., *Studies in the Terminology of Early Stoic Ethics*, Hermes Einzelschriften 32 (Wiesbaden: Steiner, 1974)

URMSON, J. O., *The Greek Philosophical Vocabulary* (London: Duckworth, 1990)

VANDER WAERDT, P. A., ed., *The Socratic Movement* (Ithaca: Cornell University Press, 1994)

—— 'Socrates in the Clouds', in P. A. Vander Waerdt, ed., *The Socratic Movement* (Ithaca: Cornell University Press, 1994), pp. 48-86

—— 'Zeno's *Republic* and the Origins of Natural Law', in P. A. Vander Waerdt, ed., *The Socratic Movement* (Ithaca: Cornell University Press, 1994), pp. 272-308

VERBEKE, G., *The Presence of Stoicism in Medieval Thought* (Washington: The Catholic University of America Press, 1983)

VERNANT, J.-P., *Myth and Thought among the Greeks* (London: Routledge & Kegan Paul, 1983); a translation of *Mythe et pensée chez les Grecs*, 2 vols (Paris: Maspero, 1965)

VLASTOS, G., 'The Paradox of Socrates', *Queen's Quarterly* (1958); repr. in revised form in G. Vlastos, ed., *The Philosophy of Socrates: A Collection of Critical Essays* (New York: Anchor, 1971), pp. 1-21

—— ed., *The Philosophy of Socrates: A Collection of Critical Essays* (New York: Anchor, 1971)

—— 'The Socratic Elenchus', *Oxford Studies in Ancient Philosophy* 1 (1983); repr. in G. Fine, ed., *Plato 1: Metaphysics and Epistemology*, Oxford Readings in Philosophy (Oxford: Oxford University Press, 1999), pp. 36-63

—— 'Socrates' Disavowal of Knowledge', *Philosophical Quarterly* 35 (1985); repr. in G. Fine, ed., *Plato 1: Metaphysics and Epistemology*, Oxford Readings in Philosophy (Oxford: Oxford University Press, 1999), pp. 64-92

—— 'Socrates', *Proceedings of the British Academy* 74 (1988); repr. in W. J. Prior, ed., *Socrates: Critical Assessments*, 4 vols (London: Routledge, 1996), vol. 1., pp. 136-55

—— *Socrates: Ironist and Moral Philosopher* (Cambridge: Cambridge University Press, 1991)

—— *Socratic Studies*, ed. M. Burnyeat (Cambridge: Cambridge University Press, 1994)

VOELKE, A.-J., *L'idée de volonté dans le stoïcisme*, Bibliothèque de Philosophie Contemporaine (Paris: Presses Universitaires de France, 1973)

—— *La philosophie comme thérapie de l'âme: Etudes de philosophie hellénistique*, Préface de Pierre Hadot, Vestigia 12 (Fribourg: Éditions Universitaires & Paris: Éditions du Cerf, 1993)

WACHSMUTH, C., & O. HENSE, *Ioannis Stobaei Anthologium*, 5 vols (Berlin: Weidmann, 1884-1912)

WALZER, R., 'New Light on Galen's Moral Philosophy (from a recently discovered Arabic source)', *Classical Quarterly* 43 (1949), 82-96

WALZER, R., & M. FREDE, *Galen, Three Treatises on the Nature of Science* (Indianapolis: Hackett, 1985)

WASZINK, J. H., *Timaeus a Calcidio Translatus Commentarioque Instructus*, Plato Latinus 4 (London: Warburg Institute & Leiden: Brill, 1962)

WATSON, G., *The Stoic Theory of Knowledge* (Belfast: Queen's University, 1966)

WENDLAND, P. *Hippolytus Werke Dritter Band: Refutatio Omnium Haeresium*, Die Griechischen Christlichen Schriftsteller (Leipzig: Hinrichs, 1916)

WESTERINK, L. G., *Proclus, Commentary on the First Alcibiades of Plato*, Critical Text and Indices (Amsterdam: North-Holland Publishing Company, 1954)

—— *Anonymous Prolegomena to Platonic Philosophy*, Introduction, Text, Translation and Indices (Amsterdam: North-Holland Publishing Company, 1962)

WHITE, N., 'The Role of Physics in Stoic Ethics', *Southern Journal of Philosophy* 23 Suppl. 'Spindel Conference: Recovering the Stoics' (1985), 57-74

WICKHAM LEGG, J., 'A Bibliography of the *Thoughts* of Marcus Aurelius Antoninus', *Transactions of the Bibliographical Society* 10 (1908-09, but publ. 1910), 15-81

WILLIAMS, B., *Ethics and the Limits of Philosophy* (London: Fontana, 1985)

—— 'Do Not Disturb', *London Review of Books* 16 no. 20 (20 October 1994), 25-26

—— 'Stoic Philosophy and the Emotions: Reply to Richard Sorabji', in R. Sorabji, ed., *Aristotle and After*, BICS Supplement 68 (London: Institute of Classical Studies, 1997), pp. 211-13

WITKE, E. C., 'Marcus Aurelius and Mandragora', *Classical Philology* 60 (1965), 23-24

WITT, R. E., 'The Plotinian Logos and its Stoic Basis', *Classical Quarterly* 25 (1931), 103-11

WRIGHT, M. R., *Cicero on Stoic Good and Evil: De Finibus Bonorum et Malorum Liber III and Paradoxa Stoicorum*, Edited with Introduction, Translation, & Commentary (Warminster: Aris & Phillips, 1991)

XENAKIS, J., 'Logical Topics in Epictetus', *Southern Journal of Philosophy* 6 (1968), 94-102

—— *Epictetus: Philosopher-Therapist* (The Hague: Martinus Nijhoff, 1969)

YOUNG, C. M., 'Plato and Computer Dating', *Oxford Studies in Ancient Philosophy* 12 (1994), 227-50

ZANKER, P., *The Mask of Socrates: The Image of the Intellectual in Antiquity*, trans. A. Shapiro, Sather Classical Lectures 59 (Berkeley: University of California Press, 1995)

ZANTA, L., *La renaissance du stoïcisme au XVIe siècle*, Bibliothèque Littéraire de la Renaissance (deuxième série) 5 (Paris: Champion, 1914)

ZELLER, E., *Socrates and the Socratic Schools*, trans. O. J. Reichel (London: Longmans, Green, and Co., 1868); translated from vol. II 1 of Zeller's *Die Philosophie der Griechen* (Tübingen: Fues, 1844-52)

—— *A History of Eclecticism*, trans. S. F. Alleyne (London: Longmans, Green, and Co., 1883); translated from vol. III 2 of Zeller's *Die Philosophie der Griechen* (Tübingen: Fues, 1844-52)

—— *The Stoics, Epicureans, and Sceptics*, trans. O. J. Reichel (London: Longmans, Green, and Co., 1892); translated from vol. III 1 of Zeller's *Die Philosophie der Griechen* (Tübingen: Fues, 1844-52)

Index Locorum

Many of the editions consulted are from the Oxford (OCT), Teubner (BT), Loeb (LCL), and Budé (CUF) series. Others can be found in *CAG*, *PG*, and *PL*. Full details of editions not in one of these collections can be found in the Bibliography under the editor's name. An invaluable work of reference has been L. Berkowitz & K. A. Squitier, *Thesaurus Lingae Graecae: Canon of Greek Authors and Works*, 3rd edn (New York: Oxford University Press, 1990), and the precise forms of Latin titles and the designation of works as genuine or spurious has, in general, followed their practice.

XENOPHON
Apologia Socratis, ed. Marchant (OCT)
  2: 177
  3: 20, 25, 54
  20: 38
Memorabilia, ed. Marchant (OCT)
  1.2.3: 92
  1.2.4: 36
  1.2.19: 49, 110
  1.2.51: 41
  1.2.54: 41
  1.3.1: 25
  2.4.3: 41

2.10.2: 41
3.1.4: 41
3.9.1-3: 49
3.9.5: 50, 51
3.9.10-11: 38
4.1.1: 26
4.2.22: 37
4.3.18: 25
4.4.1: 25
4.4.10: 20, 25, 26, 33, 50
4.6.6: 50
4.8.11: 62

General Index

Abelard, P. 174
adequate impressions 69, 94-6, 142, 156, 159-63, 173
Aeschines 24
Agrippa, modes of 89, 95
Albinus 131
Alciphron 18
Alexander of Aphrodisias 60, 71, 72-3, 126, 165, 172
Antipater 71-3
Antiphon 17
Antisthenes 9, 24, 59, 109
Apelles, the painter 102
Apollonius 18
appropriate actions 139-41
Arcesilaus 95
Aristippus 24
Aristo 76-7
Aristotle 2, 4, 7, 34-6, 43, 44, 50-53, 80-81, 126, 165, 172, 175
    as a source for Socrates 2, 34-5, 50-53
    his conception of an art 43
    his conception of philosophy 2, 35, 80-81
Arrian 29, 130, 132-3, 143, 178-9
art
    acquisitive 44
    analysis in Plato's *Gorgias* 39-42
    different types of 42-7, 70-75
    performative 44, 70, 74-5, 168
    productive 43, 70, 74
    stochastic 45, 70-74
    Stoic definition of 68-70, 75, 94
    theoretical 44
'art of living', the phrase 5-6, 55-7
assent 69, 94-6, 135, 141-2, 156-7, 159, 160-61, 162, 173
Athens, chairs of philosophy in 15
Aulus Gellius 155-7

biography 21-4
    definition of 1
    relationship with philosophy 21-31, 171-2
breath, Stoic conception of 124-5, 126, 151-2
Broad, C. D. 2

care of oneself, one's soul 36-9
Carneades 16, 95
Cato 61, 98
causes, internal and external 83, 134, 137-9
Chrysippus 2-3, 21, 59, 60, 64-8, 79, 83, 98-100, 126, 137-8, 143, 157, 165, 169, 172
    his cylinder analogy 83
Cicero, 16-17, 64-7, 74, 152, 174
Cleanthes 31, 144
Clement of Alexandria 112-15
Crates 22, 59, 62, 99
Crito 24
Critolaus 16
Cynics 1, 18, 26-8, 59, 61, 99-100
Cyrenaics 103

death, reflection upon 114-15, 153
Deleuze, G. 4, 169
Delphi, inscription at 38
Demonax 23
digestion of philosophical principles 121-2, 143, 154
Dio Chrysostom 9
Diogenes Laertius 4, 26-8, 172
Diogenes of Babylon 16
Diogenes the Cynic 26-8, 59, 61, 98, 99, 113-15
Domitian 18
'dyeing' one's soul 120, 154

CPSIA information can be obtained
at www.ICGtesting.com
Printed in the USA
LVHW082003130120
643463LV00006B/74/P